Cosmopolitan Spaces in Odesa
A Case Study of an Urban Context

Ukrainian Studies

Series Editor
Vitaly Chernetsky (University of Kansas)

Cosmopolitan Spaces in Odesa
A Case Study of an Urban Context

Edited by Mirja Lecke
and Efraim Sicher

BOSTON
2023

Published with Borderlines Foundation for Academic Studies (http://www.borderlinesfoundation.org/)

Library of Congress Cataloging-in-Publication Data

Names: Lecke, Mirja, 1972- editor, author. | Sicher, Efraim, editor, author.
Title: Cosmopolitan spaces in Odesa: a case study of an urban context/edited by Mirja Lecke and Efraim Sicher.
Description: Boston: Academic Studies Press, 2023. | Series: Ukrainian studies | Includes bibliographical references and index.
Identifiers: LCCN 2023015050 (print) | LCCN 2023015051 (ebook) | ISBN 9798887192567 (hardback) | ISBN 9798887192574 (adobe pdf) | ISBN 9798887192581 (epub)
Subjects: LCSH: Odesa (Ukraine)--History. | Odesa (Ukraine)--Ethnic relations. | Odesa (Ukraine)--Social life and customs. | Odesa (Ukraine)--Intellectual life. | City and town life--Ukraine--Odesa--History. | Jews--Ukraine--Odesa--History. | Sociology, Urban--Ukraine--Odesa--History.
Classification: LCC DK508.95.O33 C67 2023 (print) | LCC DK508.95.O33 (ebook) | DDC 305.8009477/2--dc23/eng/20230403
LC record available at https://lccn.loc.gov/2023015050
LC ebook record available at https://lccn.loc.gov/2023015051

Copyright © 2023 Academic Studies Press
All rights reserved.

Book design by PHi Business Solutions
Cover design by Ivan Grave.
On the cover: a drawing by Sandro Fazini (1915)

Published by Academic Studies Press
1577 Beacon Street
Brookline, MA 02446, USA

press@academicstudiespress.com
www.academicstudiespress.com

Contents

List of Illustrations   vi
Acknowledgments   vii

Introduction   1
Mirja Lecke and Efraim Sicher

1. Localism and Cosmopolitanism in Odesa: The Case of the Odesan Literary-Artistic Society, 1898–1914   21
   Guido Hausmann
2. The Ukrainian Odes(s)a of Vladimir Jabotinsky   37
   Yohanan Petrovsky-Shtern
3. Merchants, Clerks, and Intellectuals: The Social Underpinnings of the Emergence of Modern Jewish Culture in Late Nineteenth-Century Odesa   70
   Svetlana Natkovich
4. Elitism and Cosmopolitanism: The Jewish Intelligentsia in Odesa's School Debates of 1902   100
   Brian Horowitz
5. Ethnic Violence in a Cosmopolitan City: The October 1905 Pogrom in Odesa   118
   Robert Weinberg
6. The Cosmopolitan Soundscape of Odesa   139
   Anat Rubinstein
7. Gender, Poetry, and Song: Vera Inber and Isa Kremer in Odesa   165
   Mirja Lecke
8. The End of Cosmopolitan Time: Between Myth and Accommodation in Babel's *Odessa Stories*   193
   Efraim Sicher
9. Where the Steppe Meets the Sea: Odesa in the Ukrainian City Text   222
   Oleksandr Zabirko
10. The Ukrainization of Odes(s)a? On the Languages of Odesa and Their Use   252
    Abel Polese

11. Rereading Babel in Post-Maidan Odesa: Boris Khersonsky's Critical Cosmopolitanism   273
Amelia M. Glaser

Contributors   305
Bibliography   309
Index   333

List of Illustrations

Figure 1. *Pervonachal'nyia vremena Odessy*, 1894, black-and-white photograph. Source: Nicholas V. Iljine, ed., Odessa Memories (Seattle: University of Washington Press, 2003), 53. Exhibit at Odesa Historical Regional Studies Museum. Used with permission of University of Washington Press.   142

Figure 2. Pinkhas Minkowsky and the boys' choir in the Brody synagogue, Odesa, ca. 1910. Picture source: Archives of the YIVO Institute for Jewish Research, New York.   149

Figure 3. Sandro Fasini, "Isa Kremer," *Avto v oblakakh*, 1915. Photo credit: Mirja Lecke.   187

Figure 4. Aleksandr Roitburd, "View of Toledo in Bad Weather," from *Metaphysics of Myth*, oil on canvas, 150 × 200 cm), 2016. Reproduced with permission of the artist.   300

Figure 5. Aleksandr Roitburd, "Psychedelic Invasion of the Battleship *Potemkin* into Sergei Eisenstein's Tautological Hallucinations," still from black-and-white video, 1998, Museum of Modern Art, New York. Reproduced with permission of the artist.   301

Acknowledgments

The editors wish to thank Professor Yitzhak Hen, Iris Avivi, and all the staff at the Israel Institute for Advanced Studies, the Hebrew University of Jerusalem, for their guidance and encouragement, particularly during the Covid-19 crisis, as well as for the institute's generous support of this volume of essays, which originated in the research workshop held there in 2020—"Cosmopolitan Spaces in an Urban Context: A Case Study of Odessa, 1880–1925." The project started with Mirja Lecke's GIF young researcher grant, which brought her to Israel. Mirja was subsequently corresponding researcher in Efraim Sicher's ISF-funded project on Odesa cosmopolitanism (grant #438/17). We also wish to express our appreciation to Alessandra Anzani, Ekaterina Yanduganova, Daria Nemtsova, Kira Nemirovsky, Stuart Allen, and all the team at Academic Studies Press for their care and efficiency throughout the publication process. Ethelea (Leah) Katzenell assisted with the initial language editing, and Stefani Hoffman was thorough and meticulous in the compilation and editing of the manuscript. Finally, this book would not have seen the light of day without the patience and forbearance of the contributors through lengthy revisions and editing.

Introduction[1]

Mirja Lecke and Efraim Sicher

Cultural archaeology

Since its founding on the shores of the Black Sea by Catherine II in 1794 as the major port city of what the Russians called Novorossiia (New Russia), Odesa has been an object of fascination and nostalgia for visitors and scholars alike. However, Odesa has long become a place of non-encounter, that is to say, it has little in common with the Odesa myth that many travelers expect. Fanconi is no longer the bourgeois café where merchants and speculators used to hang out. De Ribas Street (Deribasovskaia in Russian) is not the smart shopping street it once was. The Odesa stairs, remembered from Sergei Eisenstein's movie *Battleship Potemkin* (USSR, Mosfilm, 1925), were blocked off from the port by an elevated main road on concrete pillars. The Brodsky synagogue, closed down in 1925, does not reverberate with the harmonious voices of Cantor Pinkhas Minkowsky and his boys' choir. Misha Yaponchik no longer roams the streets mugging well-dressed and bejeweled ladies in fur coats. The vibrant cosmopolitanism that thrived before World War I is no longer there.

Cosmopolitanism in Odesa, however one defines it, is difficult to recover. This is partly due to its morphing into the Odesa myth, which existed from the 1890s and subsequently developed according to various ideological narratives during the Soviet period and after the fall of communism. How cosmopolitan, indeed, was Odesa before the revolutions of 1917 and the civil war, and how unique was Odesa with its history of foreign mayors, architects, and political émigrés? Was the modernism of the 1910s merely an echo of the artistic and literary avant-garde in Moscow and St. Petersburg or did it develop its own artistic, musical, and literary talents and an aesthetics of its own? How much did Odesa's multiethnic make-up of Russians, Jews, Ukrainians, Greeks, Italians, Germans, French, Poles, and Turks, among others, provide a model of cosmopolitanism similar

---

1 Research for this chapter was funded by Efraim Sicher's grant #438/17 from the Israel Science Foundation.

to Trieste or Czernowitz (Chernivtsi) in the Habsburg Empire, or Saloniki (Thessaloniki) under the Ottomans?

In their work as scholars of culture and history, the contributors to this volume seek to reconstruct the spaces of cosmopolitan, multiethnic cultural life that existed before the Bolsheviks repressed it altogether, along with the bourgeoisie and the criminal underworld. The romance of prerevolutionary Odesa was conscripted to a counterculture that romanticized the gangsters and sang underworld songs accompanied by Leonid Utiosov's jazz band. The memory of prerevolutionary Odesa and its postmemory (passed on by later generations overseas) eclipsed much of the city's history and was largely based on self-perception and myth.

From the beginning, competing narratives circulated in the various language communities and cultural groups. Odesa is the cradle of modern Hebrew literature, which emerged in the nineteenth century as an outgrowth of the Haskalah, the secular Jewish enlightenment. The Jewish intellectuals who created modern Hebrew culture, the "Sages of Odesa" (*khakhmey odesa*), represented a closed elitist group of continually sparring intellectuals, but they nonetheless contributed to the wider heated debates about the revival of Jewish national culture (the *tekhiyah*). Their heritage was carried over into the canon of Hebrew literature, and one architectural vision of Mayor Meir Dizengoff's Tel Aviv was modeled on his native town of Odesa.[2] The Jewish national poet laureate Haim Nahman Bialik and the "Sages of Odesa" are, nonetheless, largely absent, or figure only incidentally, in the "Jewish" Odesa conjured up by Jarrod Tanny and other chroniclers of the city.[3] The myth that Odesa was a "Jewish city," as Brian Horowitz has shown,[4] is built on contradictions that conceal a complex history of the city and its perception by Jews and non-Jews. In the Russian, Yiddish, and Hebrew texts of Russian Jewish culture, and most famously in the Yiddish prose

---

2   See Joachim Schlör, "'On the third hand . . .': News from a Rediscovered Civilisation in Memories of Odessa," *Jewish Studies at the Central European University* 3 (2002–03): 159–74. On the Sages of Odesa, see "Rav tsa'ir" (Chaim Tczernowitz), *Mesekhet zikhronot: Partsufim veh'arakhot* [Memoirs: Portraits and Appraisals] (New York: Va'ad hayovel, 1945), 1–194; Dan Miron, "'Al khakhmei odesa / The Odessa Sages," in *Mekhvah leodesa* [Homage to Odesa], ed. Rahel Arbel (Tel Aviv: Beit Hatfutsot, 2002), 33–37.

3   For example, Jarrod Tanny, *City of Rogues and Schnorrers: Russia's Jews and the Myth of Old Odessa* (Bloomington: Indiana University Press, 2011); Roshanna P. Sylvester, *Tales of Old Odessa: Crime and Civility in a City of Thieves* (DeKalb, IL: North Illinois University Press 2005). See the portraits of leading Odesans in Charles King, *Odessa: Genius and Death in a City of Dreams* (New York: Norton, 2011).

4   Brian Horowitz, *The Russian-Jewish Tradition: Intellectuals, Historians, Revolutionaries* (Boston: Academic Studies Press, 2017), 38–52.

fiction of Sholem Aleichem and Mendele Moykher Sforim, Odesa was represented as a site of opportunity and moneymaking as well as modernity, but also a fool's paradise that lured unwary shtetl dwellers.

The place of Odesa in Ukrainian culture is no less mythicized. Although the Ukrainian peasants who came there from the surrounding steppes to sell their produce immortalized the city in folk songs as the site of a luxurious and idle life,[5] Odesa remained an important, yet marginal, city on the map of Ukrainian national consciousness. In imperial Russia, Ukrainians were generally denied cultural autonomy, but whereas in Kiev (Kyiv) or Kharkov (Kharkiv) Ukrainian nationalists could rely on strong support from cultural networks, in Odesa there were far fewer like-minded individuals. A number of important Ukrainian writers, from Lesia Ukraiinka in the fin-de-siècle period to the avant-gardist Iuryi Ianovs'kyi, lived for a while in the city and reflected on Odesa in their literary works. As a rule, however, Odesa was not a prominent space in Ukrainian culture.

By contrast, the Russian myth of "Old Odesa" drew on the exceptional status of this relatively new and modern multiethnic city, which was known as "Iuzhnaia Palmira" (Southern Palmyra)—to match St. Petersburg's epithet, "The Northern Palmyra" (named after the ancient trading city in Syria). Odesa offered a rival text to the Petersburg tradition in Russian literature that sometimes inverted the relationship of center and periphery in literary and artistic modernism.[6] Yet at the same time, Odesa's Russian poets in the 1910s revered Pushkin as an icon of a Russian national poet who, in the early 1820s, was exiled to Odesa and praised the city's European spirit. Cosmopolitan Odesa was a self-conscious mediator of Western and other foreign influences in Russian culture, while its European models of local government and urban architecture, introduced by the city's planners and administrators, some of whom were French or Italian émigrés, encouraged a more relaxed and relatively free political and cultural environment. Nevertheless, Odesa never became a truly liberal city, and in the early twentieth century it was notorious for having one of the most reactionary and antisemitic city councils in Russia.

From the outset, the city's Western outlook and lifestyle earned it the suspicion and resentment of the conservative "patriotic" Russian elite. Some blamed Odesa's multiethnicity for the perceived outranking of the Russian nation that threatened its assumed cultural superiority; for example, in a statistical report in 1863, Lieutenant-Colonel A. Schmidt wrote:

---

5   Doroteia Atlas, *Staraia Odessa, ee druz'ia i nedrugi* (Odesa: Tekhnik, 1911), 165–177.
6   Rebecca Stanton, *Isaac Babel and the Self-Invention of Odessan Modernism*, (Evanston, IL: Northwestern University Press, 2012), 4, 17.

> . . . русское население, т.е., великороссияне и украинцы, занимают здесь весьма невидные места [. . .] русские играют последнюю роль работников-тружеников. . . . Это ли русская столица, этим ли можно гордиться, и представительницу русского рабства называть столицею южной России?[7]

(The Russian populace, that is the Great Russians and the Ukrainians, occupy only unimportant positions here. . . .. the Russians perform the lowest tasks of workers and toilers. ... Is this really a Russian capital, is this something to be proud of, to call the representative of Russian slavery the capital of southern Russia?)

Conservative Russians resisted the liberalism and modernity, along with the multiethnic cosmopolitan culture of the early twentieth century; for example, they objected to the futurist artists and poets who performed their work in provocative shows on the eve of World War I. On the other hand, some leaders of ethnic and religious groups struggling for their rights saw cosmopolitanism as Russification in disguise. The tsarist administration, in turn, suspected the non-Russian population of sedition and disloyalty and at various times implemented vigorous Russification or issued discriminatory edicts.[8]

Although Odesa changed hands no less than nineteen times during the civil war, avant-garde Russian, Hebrew, and Ukrainian poets continued to be active and publish, and Odesa's bourgeois life of *cafés chantants* and theater performances endured despite the anarchy on the streets, the blockade, and famine. The Bolshevik reoccupation of Odesa in February 1920, however, put an end to the city's bourgeois lifestyle. The communists expropriated private property, repressed personal freedom, and enforced the proletarianization of cultural institutions. The Cheka (the Soviet secret police) rounded up bandits, synagogues were closed, and Zionist cells went underground. The printing press of Bialik's Hebrew publishing house Moriah was dismantled, and the *Evsektsiia*, the Jewish section of the Communist Party, waged war on any Jewish cultural activity that did not conform to communist ideology. Eduard Bagritsky and other poets in the "Zelenaia lampa" (The green lamp) and "Kollektiv poetov" (The poets' collective) continued the prerevolutionary traditions of Odesa modernism, while the internationalist group "Potoki oktiabria" (Streams of October) dedicated their multilingual poetry collections to the new era, although satirists such

---

7   Quoted in Atlas, *Staraia Odessa*, 138–39.
8   See Evrydiki Sifneos, *Imperial Odessa: Peoples, Spaces, Identities* (Leiden: Brill, 2017), 28–29.

as the early Ilia Ilf or Evgeny Petrov mocked some of the excesses of the New Economic Policy (NEP) in the mid-twenties.

Ivan Bunin and Semyon Yushkevich emigrated from Odesa, and in the mid-1920s most of the surviving Odesa writers moved to Moscow, where they made their name in Soviet literature and came to be known as the *Odesskaia shkola* (Odesa School). Viktor Shklovsky labeled it the "Southwest School" in 1933, after the title of Bagritsky's poetry collection,[9] acknowledging their combination of a Western literary heritage with a Levantine orientation; he was soon forced to retract the idea as an ideological error out of keeping with Stalinist monolithism, signaled by the inauguration of Socialist Realism. In the Thaw, rehabilitation of repressed writers and the publication of memoirs restored the "Odesa School," yet the term remained contentious.

After the destruction in the Holocaust of most of Odesa's Jewish community, the postmemory of Odesa cosmopolitanism remained a significant component in the ethnic identity of Soviet Jews and their descendants. For Russians, *Odessit* became a moniker for "Jew." Postwar and post-Soviet Russian cultural memory viewed Odesa largely as a source of a folk humor that was associated with "Jewish" anecdotes or "Odesa" types and became popular in the stand-up comedy of Mikhail Zhvanetsky and others.[10] Odesan music and humor thrived in Soviet popular culture. In the post-Soviet period, the work of Odesa writers from the 1920s and 1930s provided a foundation for a tertiary memory in Russia and émigré communities abroad. A hybridized cultural memory evolved that built on nostalgia for a vanished world.[11]

Odesa's cultural history became increasingly contested after Ukrainian independence in 1991. Stalin's elevation of Odesa to the status of a "hero city" after World War II later rankled with some post-Maidan Odesans because it perpetuated the Soviet incorporation of Odesa into the orbit of the Kremlin. Odesa was declared a Ukrainian city in 1926, but despite the official policy of *korenizatsiia*, the Soviet nativization campaign, Odesa remained a Russian-speaking city under Moscow's control. Indeed, local writers have debated whether Odesa's

---

9 Viktor Shklovsky, "Yugo-Zapad," *Literaturnaia gazeta*, January 5, 1933. See Rebecca Stanton, *Isaac Babel and the Self-Invention of Odessan Modernism* (Evanston: Northwestern University Press 2012).

10 See Alice Nakhimovsky, "Mikhail Zhvanetskii: The Last Russian-Jewish Joker," in *Forging Modern Jewish Identities: Public Faces and Private Struggles*, ed. Michael Berkowitz, Susan L. Tananbaum, and Sam W. Bloom (London: Vallentine Mitchell, 2003), 156–79.

11 See for example, Adrian Wanner, "'There Is No Such City': The Myth of Odessa in Post-Soviet Immigrant Literature," *Twentieth Century Literature* 65, no. 1–2 (2019): 121–44.

culture belongs to Russia or whether it has an independent cultural identity in its own right.[12] Tensions and ambiguities with regard to Russian and Ukrainian language usage in Odesa persisted in the early twenty-first century.[13] The cultural identity of Odesa was disputed, and there was further political appropriation of the Odesa myth at the time of Russia's annexation of Crimea and intervention in the Donbas in 2014, when it was conscripted as Russia's third literary capital (after Moscow and St. Petersburg), as we can see in the publication sponsored by the Moscow municipality of an anthology of Odesa Russian literature *Odessa – Moskva – Odessa* (2014). To give just one example of the Kremlin's struggle to reclaim Odesa from Ukraine: when, in accordance with the de-russification of Ukraine that followed the Russian invasion of the Ukraine on February 24, 2022, the city council decided in November 2022 to remove the statue of Catherine II symbolizing the colonization of "Novorossiia," the pro-Russian press bolstered the claim that Odesa could only be considered a Russian city by pointing to its place in Russian culture (not least the "Odesa School") and its "international" character.[14] The future of Odesa's relationship with Russia and Russian culture remains unresolved, and the port city is but one of several contested ideologically loaded and strategic spaces in the post-Soviet era. In fact, we write these lines as the Odesa Opera House and other public buildings are sandbagged against Russian bombardment, and its citizens seem ready to repel any incursion.

Below the palimpsest of narratives and counternarratives lies buried, in archives, newspapers, and literary texts, a forgotten history of intercultural activity and cosmopolitan spaces that deserves to be recovered and studied. Leaving aside the oft-repeated commonplaces about Odesa's commercial prosperity in the first half of the nineteenth century as a *porto-franco* and as a refuge for Greek and Italian nationalists, or the unavoidable evocation of sun and sea, we should remember that Odesa was one of the first cities in the Russian Empire to

---

12 See Amelia Glaser's chapter in this volume.
13 On the unresolved language conflicts in Odesa and in general in Ukraine, see Abel Polese and Anna Wylegala, "Odessa and Lvov or Odesa and Lviv: How Important Is a Letter? Reflections on the 'Other' in Two Ukrainian Cities," *Nationalities Papers* 36, no. 5 (2008): 787–814; Paul Robert Magocsi and Yohanan Petrovsky-Shtern, *Jews and Ukrainians: A Millennium of Coexistence*, 2nd rev. ed. (Toronto: University of Toronto Press, 2018), 137–47; Svetlana L'nyavskiy, "Odesa in Diachronic and Synchronic Studies of Urban Linguistic Landscapes of Ukraine Conducted Between 2015 and 2019," *East / West* 9, no. 2 (2022): 93–143. See also Abel Polese's chapter below.
14 Sergei Ivanov, "Ukrokhamy v Odesse – okkupanty, unichtozhaiushchie kul'turu," *Eurasia Daily*, November 11, 2022 https://eadaily.com/ru/news/2022/11/28/ukrohamy-v-odesse-okkupanty-unichtozhayushchie-kulturu

confront modernity: not just electricity, factories, streetcars, the early cinema, and aviation pioneers, but also the social problems of urbanization, pogroms, and class tensions.

Odesa cosmopolitanism: theories and practices

Cosmopolitanism is a contentious concept that, since the ancient Greeks first formulated it as world citizenship in opposition to citizenship solely of one's own *polis* (city), has catalyzed discussions of self-identification and dual loyalty. Implicitly, the term "cosmopolitanism" juxtaposes two spatial trajectories, a larger and a smaller one, and charges them with emotional valence regarding strangers. Should individuals belong and owe loyalty exclusively to their immediate surroundings and their political order? Or should individuals feel part of a larger whole, all of humanity, and prioritize this larger belonging over particular interests? The second choice would be cosmopolitan.[15]

Cosmopolitanism is a relational concept that changes in meaning with the spatial and temporal situation of its usage, expressing at times an ideal aim, at others a political and ethnic accusation or a nostalgic longing. The entangled notions of cosmopolitanism and nationalism, which Odesans hotly debated in the period around 1900, are rooted in Enlightenment philosophical debates about a just international order. Immanuel Kant's concept of cosmopolitanism is tied to the simultaneously emerging idea of the nation-state. Kant posited that nations were the only source of sovereignty, but because nations and states compete with each other and engage in international conflicts, Kant argued (drawing on Cicero and others), rationally thinking people, "world citizens," would perceive the overarching common good and work for peaceful coexistence, contributing to perfecting mankind, and ultimately transcending narrow understandings of national and territorial belonging.[16]

Postmodern and postcolonial criticism of Kant has laid bare his Eurocentrism and questioned the underlying universalist claim that the same meaning is

---

15 Janet Lyon, "Cosmopolitanism and Modernism," in *The Oxford Handbook of Global Modernisms*, ed. Mark Wollaeger and Matt Eatough (Oxford: Oxford University Press, 2012), 391; Martha C. Nussbaum, "Kant and Cosmopolitanism," in *The Cosmopolitanism Reader*, ed. Garrett Brown and David Held (Cambridge, Malden: Polity Press, 2010), 27–44.
16 Martha Nussbaum, "Kant and Cosmopolitanism," in Brown and Held, *The Cosmopolitanism Reader*, 27–44.

accessible to all.[17] Cosmopolitanism, additionally, has been criticized for covering up persisting global colonialism.[18] In our Odesan local context, moreover, Kant's implication that the cosmopolitan aligns with an Other from a faraway nation proves to be problematic, because the states of Central and Eastern Europe were empires and so was prerevolutionary Russia, an autocratic, multiethnic state that privileged Russian Orthodoxy as the state religion. This complicates the appearance of not only nations, but also nation-states. In addition, there were competing notions of what comprises a nation and citizenship—civic principles or cultural characteristics. Therefore, a re-evaluation is needed of cosmopolitanism as both a descriptive and normative concept. Self-identification on the grounds of nationality until well into the twentieth century remained only one of many options (along with religious affiliation, social/estate, ideological, gender, and local descent as categories); it was occasional and ambiguous. Additionally, the Russian Empire was not pluralistic, individuals were not equal, and evident hierarchies existed among Odesa's many ethnic groups, with Russians ranking higher than Greeks, Ukrainians, or Jews.[19] In studies of the global South, researchers have coined the term "translocality" for such multiethnic constellations in order to evade the Eurocentric connotations of cosmopolitanism.[20] But because Odesans have since the late nineteenth century often, although by no means consistently, let alone theoretically, referred to their personal experience as cosmopolitan, we decided to retain the term while concentrating on social practices in specific spaces and situations of ethnic, religious, and cultural contact. Following Henri Lefebvre,[21] we understand space as a socially constructed phenomenon that can be a lived environment as well as a symbolically represented entity (in a city map, for instance), or that can emerge and be transformed in aesthetic production.

---

17 See Daniel Chernilo, "Cosmopolitanism and the Question of Universalism," in *Routledge Handbook of Cosmopolitanism Studies*, ed. Gerard Delanty (London and New York: Routledge, 2012), 47–59. Jessica Bermann, *Modernist Fiction, Cosmopolitanism and the Politics of Community* (Cambridge: Cambridge University Press, 2001), 1–27.
18 Walter D. Mignolo, "The Many Faces of Cosmo-polis: Border Thinking and Critical Cosmopolitanism," in *Cosmopolitanism*, ed. Dipesh Chakrabarty, Homi K. Bhabha, Sheldon Pollock, and Carol A. Breckenridge (Durham, NC: Duke University Press, 2002), 157–89. See also Amelia Glaser's chapter below.
19 On local and regional patriotism, see Dmitry Shumsky, "An Odessan Nationality? Local Patriotism and Jewish Nationalism in the Case of Vladimir Jabotinsky," *Russian Review* 79, no. 1 (January 2020): 64–82.
20 Ulrike Freitag and Achim von Oppen, "Translocality: An Approach to Connection and Transfer in Area Studies," in *Translocality: The Study of Globalising Processes from a Southern Perspective*, ed. Ulrike Freitag and Achim von Oppen (Leiden: Brill, 2010), 3.
21 Henri Lefebvre, *The Production of Space* (Oxford and Cambridge, MA: Blackwell, 1991), 32.

In the growing metropolis of Odesa, modernity opened multiethnic spaces in mixed neighborhoods, at the port, on balconies, on the streets, in theaters, and in cafés, so that the exposure to ethnic, religious, and class differences formed an integral part of everyday experience. Mutual recognition or feelings of solidarity with strangers and members of other local groups thus did not necessarily denote mobile elites and a large spatial framework as implied in the Kantian understanding of cosmopolitanism. It could also be a matter of local patriotism, for instance. On the other hand, those calling for unity within their own particular group employed cosmopolitanism as a euphemism for treason. Sander Gilman has argued that the status of the Jews has always been a litmus test in these debates, which often reveal antisemitic attitudes in the criteria for inclusion or exclusion in citizenship rules and state formation.[22] "Cosmopolitans" became a derogatory term for those whom the regime labeled as internationally oriented "rootless" intellectuals (predominantly Jews) during Stalin's last years. This connotation of the term persisted throughout the rest of the Soviet period.

In addition to encompassing everyday contact among diverse Odesans, cosmopolitanism also existed in a way closer to the Kantian sense with its larger scale spatial implications and consciously elitist West European orientation. Especially in the fin de siècle, the bourgeoisie, as will become clear from our case studies, possessed a wide-ranging European identity, a sense of belonging to what was believed to be the civilized world, which for them set Odesa apart from tsarist Russia but also helped cultivate a certain openness among the emerging multiethnic elites. Cultural meanings could be negotiated and exchanged in spaces that provided what Janet Lyon calls cosmopolitanism's "liberatory set of ideals."[23] This is what the Hebrew-language writer Ben-David (Y. L. Dovidovitz) celebrated when he sat proudly at the public commemoration of the centenary of the taking of Hadzhibey by Russian forces in September 1789; of all the cities in the Russian Empire, he wrote, only in Odesa did the Jews enjoy freedom and "cosmopolitanism."[24] Precisely in this milieu of cross-cultural encounter, various nationalisms thrived and interacted, as we can observe, for instance, in the early writings of the Russian Jewish intellectual Kornei Chukovsky and of the Ukrainian novelist Ivan Nechui-Levyts'kyi, who each condemned cosmopolitanism as a default social practice of acculturation instead of Jewish or Ukrainian

---

22 Cathy S. Gelbin and Sander L. Gilman, *Cosmopolitanisms and the Jews* (Ann Arbor: University of Michigan Press, 2017).
23 Lyon, "Cosmopolitanism and Modernism," 394.
24 Ben-David, "Mikhtavim meodesa" [Letters from Odesa], *Hamelits*, October 9, 1889, 2. We are grateful to Jörg Schulte for this reference.

nation building. At the same time, the cosmopolitan openness towards foreign cultures created a fertile ground for innovations in literature, art, music, and science that impressed incoming visitors or migrants from abroad or from other parts of Russia as cosmopolitan and were disseminated by departing Odesans.

Importantly, in Odesa the ambiguity between national and broader imperial or cosmopolitan identities also pertained to language. Around the turn of the twentieth century, Russian was the dominant official language and functioned as a universally accepted medium for "civilized" intellectual exchange among Odesans, though any transnational neutrality was illusionary at best. Yet Odesan Russian, with its many Ukrainian and Yiddish elements, preserved a local identity that marked its significant difference from Russia proper, especially during the political reaction after 1905. The Russian language was at this time perceived by Ukrainian nationalists as a means of the Russian imperialist policy of Russification and marginalization of ethnic groups. That policy also affected ethnic groups and languages that were less visible in Odesa's multicultural history and demography, such as Moldovans or Turks.

Thus, cosmopolitanism or rather cosmopolitan spaces offer us a critical lens for reassessing Odesa's plural religious, ethnic, and political constellations around the turn of the twentieth century; when observed from an interdisciplinary perspective, Odesan cosmopolitanism is a complex phenomenon with its own *Begriffsgeschichte* in a multiethnic transnational society. In fact, cosmopolitanism is not only an apt critical tool for analyzing late imperial Russian and early Soviet ideas about multiethnic coexistence, but, as we see from Caroline Humphrey's and Vera Skvirskaja's published research, it also allows us to follow debates into the Soviet and post-Soviet period. This is because cosmopolitanism, or rather post-cosmopolitanism, still informs the troubled relationship between local Odesan self-presentations and loyalties, whether owed to the Ukrainian nation or Russian culture.[25]

Beyond "Jewish cosmopolitanism"

The local preconditions for Odesa's multiple religious, ethnic, and political life cannot be explained without taking into account Odesa Jewry. Jews in the premodern and modern period were attracted to port cities such as Odesa and

---

25 Caroline Humphrey and Vera Skvirskaja, "Introduction," in *Post-Cosmopolitan Cities: Explorations of Urban Coexistence*, ed. Caroline Humphrey and Vera Skvirskaia (New York: Berghahn Books, 2012), 7–8.

Trieste, where there were communities of strangers, bound more by commercial than religious and ethnic ties.[26] The question of whether the multiethnic context of Odesa is substantially different from the situation of the acculturated Russian-speaking Jews in other cities of the Russian Empire, or, for that matter, assimilated German-speaking Jews in the Habsburg Empire, cannot be a matter of simple comparison, as in Zipperstein's example of Odesa and Vilna, or Herlihy's example of Odesa and Trieste.[27] Odesa's Jews have also been compared to the "Port Jews" of the western Sephardim in the Mediterranean; yet, in the second half of the nineteenth century, they were not transient merchants but largely grain dealers, bankers, and middlemen, a privileged class, distanced from the elitist intellectuals who formed one of the first modern Jewish cultural centers in Eastern Europe.[28]

Cosmopolitan spaces arose in the unique conditions of cultural plurality and hybridity that obtained in Odesa, but this is also something that Jews brought to modern cities—for example, Warsaw or Czernowitz—peripheral cultural centers in multiethnic empires that played important roles in literary and artistic movements of the early twentieth century. The Haskalah had a major impact on secularized and modernized urban Jews in the Russian Empire, but the legal and social situation did not always match conditions in Germany or Austria, largely because the mass of Jews in the Pale of Settlement, the regions where Jews were allowed to reside legally in Russia, were isolated from the rest of society and lived traditional religious lives. In the late nineteenth century, at a time of pogroms and political reaction, nationalism and cosmopolitanism became accepted terms for describing a complex situation in which Jews were labeled as quintessential cosmopolitans and at the same time called upon to become a unified nation.[29]

---

26 See Francesca Trivellato, *The Familiarity of Strangers: The Sephardic Diaspora, Livorno, and Cross-Cultural Trade in the Early Modern Period* (New Haven: Yale University Press, 2009).
27 Steven Zipperstein, "Remapping Odessa," in *Imagining Russian Jewry: Memory, History, Identity* (Seattle: University of Washington Press, 1999), 63–86; John D. Klier, "A Port, Not a Shtetl: Reflections on the Distinctiveness of Odessa," *Jewish Culture and History* 4, no. 2 (2001): 173–78; Patricia Herlihy, "Port Jews of Odessa and Trieste: A Tale of Two Cities," *Jahrbuch des Simon-Dubnow-Instituts* 2 (2003): 183–98; see also David Cesarani, ed., *Port Jews: Jewish Communities in Cosmopolitan Maritime Trading Centres, 1550–1950* (Southampton: Frank Cass and the Parkes Centre, University of Southampton, 2001); Lois C. Dubin, "'Wings on their feet . . . and wings on their head': Reflections on the Study of Port Jews," *Jewish Culture and History* 7, nos. 1–2 (2004): 14–30.
28 See Steven Zipperstein, *The Jews of Odessa: A Cultural History, 1794–1881* (Stanford: Stanford University Press, 1985).
29 Michael L. Miller and Scott Ury, "Cosmopolitanism: The End of Jewishness?" *European Review of History* 17, no. 3 (2010): 337–59.

Whereas St. Petersburg opened a window to the West, Odesa strategically and culturally provided an opening to the Bosphorus and the eastern Mediterranean. We could equally zoom out into the larger perspective of Black Sea trading routes, which go back to ancient times, when Greek colonies could be found on the Black Sea's shores and Near East civilizations brought goods and cultures, as well as agrarian settlement. While the Black Sea region throughout the centuries was an arena of commercial and cultural exchange, it was also as a place of shifting populations. These groups mixed but also fought with each other and were often dominated by conquering or neighboring empires. As Neal Ascherson notes in his travelogue *Black Sea* (contemplating the region's history of violence, pogroms, and ethnic cleansing):

> Peoples who have lived in communion with other peoples, for a hundred or a thousand years, do not always like them—may, in fact, have always disliked them. As individuals, "the others" are not strangers, but neighbors, even friends. But my sense of Black Sea life, a sad one, is that latent mistrust between different cultures is immortal. Necessity, and sometimes fear binds such communities together. But within that binding—they remain a bundle of disparate groups—not a helpful model for the "multiethnic society" of our hopes and dreams.[30]

Odesa's history is certainly not characterized by innate interethnic hatred, but it was an outcrop of territorial and mercantile competition, and its story of growth and prosperity is tainted with authoritarianism and bloodshed.

In order to extricate ourselves from the limitations of talking about an exclusively "Jewish cosmopolitanism" or slipping into the easy cliché of Odesa as a "Jewish city," we must remove the disciplinary blinders of the various national historiographies and we must cross disciplinary boundaries into social and cultural history. Evrydiki Sifneos, in *Imperial Odessa*, helps us shift the focus to multiethnicity by looking at class and the economic histories of ethnic minorities—such as the Greeks, who settled in Odesa from the early nineteenth century and became Russified. Sifneos concludes that in modern cities "diverse ethnic groups coexisted and interacted primarily through commercial

---

30 Neal Ascherson, *Black Sea: The Birthplace of Civilisation and Barbarism*, new ed. (London: Vintage, 2007), 9; see also Charles King, *The Black Sea* (Oxford: Oxford University Press, 2005).

and maritime economic activities rather than cross-community socializing."[31] International trade encouraged entrepreneurs with kinship and ethnic networks of business acquaintances.

There are different cosmopolitan spaces here: the port, for example, must be factored into the socio-economic changes of the later nineteenth and early twentieth century. Sifneos and other scholars regard the port area as a "stage" of cosmopolitanism or alternatively as a site of a distinct cultural space where foreigners and residents came together for socializing, entertainment, and job opportunities.[32] Yet the harbor could also be a site of ethnic conflict imported from Constantinople, as in the fights between Armenian and Turkish dock workers in 1897. Sifneos contends that tensions between Greeks and Jews were partially transferred from Constantinople due to the two populations' heritage of tense coexistence with Ottoman Turks, whom the Jews saw as benign protectors and whom the Greeks saw as oppressors.[33] Sifneos demonstrates that the main cause of ethnic conflict in Odesa was economic. With the coming of the railroads, Greek merchants began to lose their preeminence to Jewish traders who could purchase grain and goods from middlemen in the towns and villages of the Pale of Settlement, instead of relying on Odesa's market fair.[34] The transition to middlemen and the railways changed the structure of the wheat trade, to the advantage of Jewish small venture capitalists in the Ukrainian interior, who could stock up on grain during a slack period for future sale.[35] The statistics show that by the end of the nineteenth century there was a sharp increase in Jewish traders in the grain market and a decrease in Greek traders; figures for factory ownership show a similar pattern. Although the animosity may have been motivated by religious dogma, the Greeks and later the Russians were provoked by the prospect of competition from Jews who dominated a number of manufacturing and trade sectors in Odesa.[36] Moreover, because of economic changes and the expansion of the Russian wheat market, Greek traders turned their attention to the Azov Sea or shifted their investments to real estate, which was enjoying a boom in Odesa from the 1870s, thanks to new, cheap construction and conversion of mansions into rented apartments.[37]

---

31 Sifneos, *Imperial Odessa*, 27. On the Greek community in Odesa, see also Patricia Herlihy, *Odessa Recollected: The Port and the People* (Boston: Academic Studies Press, 2018), 137–67.
32 Sifneos, *Imperial Odessa*, 33.
33 Ibid., 177.
34 Ibid., 117.
35 Ibid., 118–20.
36 Ibid., 176–77.
37 Ibid., 120–23.

Multiethnic interaction in Odesa occasionally erupted into urban riots. There had been violent clashes between the Greek and Jewish communities, including the 1871 pogrom. Rapid urbanization combined with an increase in the Jewish population (approaching a third of the city's inhabitants by the end of the century), many of whom were poor. With regard to the ethnic violence of 1871, 1881, and 1886, Sifneos highlights the participation of the unemployed, under-employed, and the unskilled, and, for the first time, marginal populations such as street urchins, orphans, and social outcasts. Newspaper coverage indicates that the attacks were driven not only by ethno-religious motivation but also significantly by class factors. Jewish property and homes were attacked and looted almost with impunity, but the homes of Greek merchants were also damaged, and windows of both Jews and Christians were smashed indiscriminately.[38] The violence, in Sifneos's assessment, vented the frustration of the unemployed and seasonal workers; the Jews served as scapegoats for the effects of modern capitalism.

The 1905 pogrom, by contrast, was fueled by right-wing and monarchist reactions to the promise of a constitution and emancipatory measures for minorities in the October Manifesto, as well as what Robert Weinberg calls the combustibility of the demographic and economic situation.[39] At the same time, the actions of some non-Jews to safeguard Jews from harm and the efforts of organized groups of workers to stop or prevent pogroms in Odesa require a nuanced view of ethnic relations in the context of the political changes wrought by the 1905 revolution.[40] Caroline Humphrey proposes that class was significant after 1905, rather than ethnic affinity, in the way these political changes affected interethnic relations. Members of different ethnicities in Odesa tended to affiliate with revolutionary or political movements across communities. Indeed, there were instances of revolutionary activists' collaboration or solidarity with Jews.[41]

Ethnic violence, however, should not be considered in opposition to cosmopolitanism; rather, diverse forms of sporadic and historically specific cosmopolitanism played out in the same space as interethnic violence. Humphrey notes: "Cosmopolitan networks and pogrom crowds created their own separate

---

38 Ibid., 181–82.
39 Robert Weinberg, "The Pogrom of 1905 in Odessa: A Case Study," in *Pogroms: Anti-Jewish Violence in Modern Russian History*, ed. John D. Klier and Shlomo Lambroza (Cambridge: Cambridge University Press, 1992), 248–89. See Robert Weinberg's chapter below.
40 Sifneos, *Imperial Odessa*, 188–89. See the documents in *Pogroms: A Documentary History of Anti-Jewish Violence*, ed. Gene Avrutin and Elissa Bemporad (Oxford: Oxford University Press, 2021).
41 Sifneos, *Imperial Odessa*, 193–94.

patterns of relations, which can be seen as topographies, defined by the overall connectivity of their different elements as assemblages."[42] These changed in different ways over time, crossing communal, professional, and social boundaries: "they interacted in different ways with the same physical features of the city."[43] Deribasovskaia Street, for example, which consistently had been a space of courteous social behavior, became a site of looting and rampage during the 1905 pogrom. Cosmopolitanism did not necessarily mean harmonic synergy between ethnic groups.[44]

Class and gender have too often been overlooked in studies of multiethnic Odesa, just as they have long been neglected in cosmopolitan thinking that privileges ethnicity and religion at the cost of differentiations of gender and social hierarchies. Yet it is evident that a woman from a minority group experiences cosmopolitan spaces elsewhere and at other times than her male contemporary. Intersectionality remains a blind spot and only a few in-depth studies have been dedicated to the interrelationship between ethnicity, class, and gender in Odesa.[45] Ethnic distribution in residential patterns in the 1897 census indicates that socio-economic boundaries rather than ethnic identities divided the outer areas of Petropavlovskii, Mikhailovskii, and Peresyp', which were populated by industrial workers and newcomers in substandard living conditions, from the inner suburbs, where middle- or upper-class merchants and administrative officials lived comfortably.[46] Despite its reputation as a Jewish "ghetto," Moldavanka was ethnically diverse and far from being completely lawless, but its unplanned growth broke up the city grid with crowded housing for new Jewish migrants from the Pale.[47] The 1897 census indicates a roughly equal residential distribution of Russian speakers and self-identifying Jews, Greeks, Poles, and Germans living mostly in the inner city, but present also outside it. The social stratification favored the lower middle-class *meshchane* (56.2 percent), while 27.9 percent were emancipated peasants; many of the lower classes moved from elsewhere in Russia in search of employment in the domestic sector or the port.[48] From this

---

42 Caroline Humphrey, "Odessa: Pogroms in a Cosmopolitan City," in Humphrey and Skvirskaja, *Post-Cosmopolitan Cities*, 18.
43 Ibid.
44 Ibid.," 55–56.
45 See Ilya Gerasimov, *Plebeian Modernity. Social Practices, Illegality, and the Urban Poor in Russia, 1906–1916* (Rochester, NY: University of Rochester Press. 2018); Roshanna P. Sylvester, *Tales of Old Odessa: Crime and Civility in a City of Thieves* (DeKalb, IL: North Illinois University Press, 2005).
46 Sifneos, *Imperial Odessa*, 45–47.
47 Ibid., 107–8. See Patricia Herlihy's analysis of the 1897 census results, *Odessa Recollected*, 117–35.
48 Sifneos, *Imperial Odessa*, 47–49.

we can conclude that the distribution of the population was influenced more by class than by ethnicity. Apart from wealth, the length of time that families had settled in Odesa predetermined their places of residence. Odesa was characterized by what Sifneos calls "residential porosity," a term she borrows from Walter Benjamin's description of the interpenetration of street and home in Naples. Porosity in Odesa's urban morphology facilitated interethnic contact and diversity as most residential buildings housed ethnically diverse inhabitants.[49]

When we speak of cosmopolitanism and cosmopolitan spaces, therefore, we should avoid generalizations that may be true for only some groups or individuals at certain times. Russians, Ukrainians, Greeks, and Jews from a less privileged background experienced ethnic coexistence in different places and aligned or delimitated themselves for different reasons. Generally, interethnic contact could take place in many forms and locations, sometimes in taboo social spheres such as those of prostitution or the criminal underworld. Ilya Gerasimov has shown that social networking in Odesa often went beyond normative groupings, although an ethno-religious awareness seems to have guided at least some criminals when homicidal violence was the only marker of difference: Jews killed only their own but robbed and blackmailed indiscriminately.[50] Moreover, gender roles were decisive for the development of cosmopolitan attitudes towards the broader multiethnic society.

Plan of the book

This book looks at Odesa as a test case of cosmopolitanism, questioning its meanings and its implications for cultural and ethnic diversity in a specific cityscape and local context with a special interest in how Odesa's Jews, Russians, and Ukrainians interacted in culture and daily co-existence. The essays focus on the late nineteenth and early twentieth century but pursue the legacy of cosmopolitanism and post-cosmopolitanism through to post-Maidan Ukraine. Guido Hausmann opens the discussion with an analysis of the Odesan Literary-Artistic Society (the Literaturka) during the years 1898–1914, tracing the different forms of interethnic contact and cultural cosmopolitanism that existed alongside a new interest in localism that was a result of Odesa's multiethnic

---

49 Ibid., 49.
50 Gerasimov, *Plebeian Modernity*, 15, 116–19.

elites' delimitation from Russian imperial nationalism.[51] Hausmann thus takes into consideration the concept of translocality and highlights the Literaturka's important role as a quasi-political arena and venue for cross-ethnic cultural self-exploration. Vladimir Jabotinsky, an active participant in the Literaturka, is a prime example of the intricate and paradoxical relationship between cosmopolitanism, understood as an orientation towards the Russian language and European high culture on the one hand, and Jewish nationalism on the other. Yohanan Petrovsky-Shtern examines the insufficiently studied Ukrainian context of Jabotinsky's Odesa years, showing how the Ukrainian language and Ukrainian national aspirations were formative in Jabotinsky's writing and thinking about Jews. In relating "Ukrainian Odesa" to Jabotinsky, Petrovsky-Shtern challenges our received wisdom about both the cosmopolitan character of the city and the exclusivity of the Russian-language environment of Odesa, asking us to recontextualize Jabotinsky's relationship with Kornei Chukovsky and both writers' thoughts about nationalism, Ukrainian and Jewish. Svetlana Natkovich follows with a nuanced analysis of the relationship between Odesa Jewish intellectuals and Odesa Jewish merchants and clerks. The diversity within the Jewish community did not prevent the different social groups from advancing their aims with each other's help, but their spatial conceptions about the national Jewish project differed significantly. Natkovich prefers to speak of multiple forms of identification that deconstruct homogenized Jewish group-formation along social lines and instead highlight different forms of cooperation or belonging to non-Jewish cultures. The terminology of multiple belongings and their intersection thus overcomes the limits of the term "cosmopolitanism" with regard to differentiations within groups.

Moving on to the early twentieth century, Brian Horowitz explores the approaches to and understandings of cosmopolitanism in the leadership of Odesa's enlightened Jewish intellectuals, as exemplified in the 1902 debates over education. The elitist approaches to education, a question at the center of the Jewish national revival, complicate any simple understanding of the relationship of cosmopolitanism to nationalism and dispel the notion of cosmopolitanism as a mass movement among Odesa Jews. Rather, cosmopolitanism reflected the Jews' individual self-conscious openness to non-Jewish elements, especially in public spaces. Horowitz shows that the twin concepts of democratization and cosmopolitanism were understood differently from what these terms signify to us today. The coexistence of ethnic minorities in Odesa was not, as we have

---

51 On localism, see Kristof Van Assche and Petruța Teampău, *Local Cosmopolitanism: Imagining and (Re-)Making Privileged Places* (Cham: Springer, 2015).

already noted, always harmonious. Robert Weinberg investigates, for example, the complex dynamics at work in the 1905 pogrom in Odesa. He shows that cosmopolitan values of tolerance and openness were no guarantee of peaceful and respectful relations among residents from different religious and ethnic backgrounds who shared urban spaces and that prejudice and violent hostility could prevail, once the 1905 constitution had generated a new political situation.

The multicultural soundscape of Odesa is the subject of Anat Rubinstein's survey of musical production and performance in the city space, as in cantorial liturgy and street song, in the early twentieth century. Cosmopolitan soundscapes, she asserts, accommodate the local and global, as well as negotiating national versus non-national factors. They bring together the musical traditions of different social and ethnic groups while establishing new local sounds in tune with modernity, but also aligned with national aspirations, as in the case of the Jewish cultural renascence. While cosmopolitanism meant something different to diverse ethnic groups and classes, the multicultural elements in Odesa music made an impact in Russia and beyond, and they still reverberate worldwide as an acoustic icon of the city. Mirja Lecke turns her attention to class and gender in a study of the singer Isa Kremer and the poet Vera Inber. Although their careers differed (one became an international Jewish opera star and the other a Soviet Russian writer), the unique combination of cosmopolitanism, Russian imperial culture, and nationalism in Odesa shaped their early artistic outlook and their empowerment as women. The contribution of women to cosmopolitanism in early twentieth-century Odesa's urban spaces, understood as self-conscious interethnic contact and orientation towards modern European culture, has been underestimated. This chapter shows, in the example of these two artists, how Odesa's own brand of pre-revolutionary cosmopolitanism could evolve into Soviet internationalism (Inber) or globalized nationalism (Kremer), facilitating the women's careers well beyond the city.

Efraim Sicher examines the case of Isaak Babel, perhaps the writer most associated with the Odesa myth, and suggests that Babel's adaptation of the myth in his Odesa stories after his move to Moscow represents a gradual accommodation with the new political reality that prevailed after the end of cosmopolitanism and the suppression of Jewish cultural institutions that had thrived before the communist takeover. The shift from a romanticization of the past in the early Odesa stories to a new, more restrained prose style and realist aesthetics coincides with the final demise of Jewish Odesa and Stalin's appropriation of the Russian poet Pushkin as a Soviet cultural icon. Here, nostalgia for a cosmopolitan past turns out to be a combination of self-invention and appropriation.

For his part, Oleksandr Zabirko investigates the place of Odesa on the Ukrainian cultural map and explains how Ukrainian writers presented Odesa in fact and in fiction against the backdrop of the dominant Russian claim to Odesa as a Russian city. Cosmopolitanism was criticized by Ukrainian nationalists as ultimately giving way to the Russian colonial drive, yet Lesia Ukraiinka for one was attracted to a cosmopolitan ethics of hospitality and welcomed a nonhostile foreignness. In the early years after the 1917 revolutions, and particularly during the Soviet nativization campaign, Odesa offered unique opportunities to Ukrainian poets, novelists, and scriptwriters who developed a civic national discourse that could accommodate Odesa's cosmopolitan past.

Abel Polese's anthropological empirical study of language use in the early twenty-first century sets the complex relations and status of Russian and Ukrainian in specific language use in Odesa within a nuanced application of a Kantian notion of cosmopolitanism that evades dichotomies and unfolds in complex social relations. Ukrainian-Russian competition for the city's cultural identity marks Odesa's post-Soviet history, and Polese's chapter describes the everyday effects of language policy in the first decade of the twenty-first century, before the situation was exacerbated in the lethal burning of the Trades Unions building in 2014. Amelia Glaser therefore demonstrates the ambiguities of Odesa's literary heritage, foremost the figure of Isaak Babel, in the poetry and social activism of Boris Khersonsky. His critique of cosmopolitanism as concealed pro-Russian ideology in post-Maidan Odesa provides both a retrospective and contemporary commentary on the uneasy relations between the Soviet past and the Ukrainian present, as well as the conflicts of memory between Russian, Ukrainian, and Jewish identities. Khersonsky provides an example of an attempt to reject the Soviet mixture of Russian imperialism and multinationalism promoted in the name of communist internationalism and to create a post-Soviet, Ukrainian vision of post-cosmopolitanism.

The conversation among the contributors prods and tests the different meanings of cosmopolitanism. It benefits from the contributors' varied methodologies and training, whether in East European history or Jewish studies, literature or cultural history, and applies the multidisciplinary approaches of history, comparative literature, textual criticism, gender studies, and sociology. Cosmopolitanism, however understood, emerges not as a nostalgia for a repressed and vanished past, but as a complex phenomenon from which we can learn about the management of diversity in a divided world where again imperial aggression draws on preexisting rival national and cultural claims to justify war and destruction.

In conclusion, a few words about the spelling of names. The names and spelling of certain persons and places sometimes differ in the various national historiographies and in international academic writing. While this reflects the heritage of Odesa's multiethnic cosmopolitanism, it also poses an editorial challenge. The Russian "Odessa" means something different than Hebrew and Yiddish "Odes" or "Ades." Nonetheless, for the sake of uniformity and consistency in the book, the spelling "Odesa" is used throughout. We use mainly the standard English versions of names of persons and places, indicating contemporary names of cities in brackets upon first mention. In contexts where a particular national perspective is crucial for the argument, however, we follow the usage of national terminology.

CHAPTER 1

Localism and Cosmopolitanism in Odesa: The Case of the Odesan Literary-Artistic Society, 1898–1914

Guido Hausmann

*In memory of Patricia Herlihy, an Odesa enthusiast,
colleague, and friend of many years.*

Background

Cosmopolitanism as a social practice of openness towards individuals and the wider world has played out very differently in space, time, and social contexts. In the urban environment of Odesa from the turn of the twentieth century until the outbreak of World War I, it manifested itself as a relational and process-oriented category. Cosmopolitanism seemed to be ubiquitous in Odesa at that time, but it is nevertheless hard to track down empirically. This chapter analyzes two parallel processes. One of them was manifest in new forms of cosmopolitanism, which seem to have coexisted with a different related phenomenon, namely, a new awareness of the local. This sensitivity among Odesans around 1900 can be called a new localism.[1] The amalgamation of these two interrelated phenomena led to the foundation of the Literary-Artistic Society (*Odesskoe literaturno-artisticheskoe khudozhestvennoe obshchestvo*) in 1897, which established a new

---

1   See the introduction above, 13–17.

space for cosmopolitan practices and new "forms of situated mutuality"[2] in a multiethnic imperial setting.

The term cosmopolitanism overlaps with the more recently coined term "translocality," which is less oriented towards European history and culture, the practices of urban elites, and global experiences, than the original term.[3] Reflecting the experience of the broader population, translocality has been used since the 1990s to explore the multiple effects of "interactions and connections between places, institutions, actors and concepts,"[4] and it has the advantage of carrying less cultural baggage. This chapter applies the concept of cosmopolitanism but takes into consideration the importance of the extensions of the concept into translocality as well and aims at a socially more representative balance sheet.

At the turn of the twentieth century, several examples of the significantly increased importance of the local in Odesa suggest the possibility of speaking of a new localism. For example, in 1894, lavish celebrations and various publications marked the city's centenary, showcasing its history to the public in detailed, sequential, and popular forms.[5] Although similar commemorative publications had appeared for earlier anniversaries, they were fewer in number and scope. The centenary publications celebrated Odesa's uniqueness in the Russian Empire, especially its status as an economic leader, its value as a seaport, an export hub of grain to the Mediterranean and, from there, to the whole world, not to mention its thriving social and cultural life, which was unique in the empire. These publications rarely highlighted signs of economic stagnation or political repression, instead featuring a feeling of homeliness and the cultural integration of the local population, which numbered about 403,000 persons in 1897 and approximately 630,000 by 1914. Odesa was the fourth largest city in the Russian Empire and was still characterized by strong immigration into the city from the surrounding region but also by rising emigration since the late nineteenth century.[6]

---

2   Ulrike Freitag and Achim von Oppen, "Translocality: An Approach to Connection and Transfer in Area Studies," in *Translocality: The Study of Globalising Processes from a Southern Perspective*, ed. Ulrike Freitag and Achim von Oppen (Leiden: Brill, 2010), 3.
3   Ibid., 1–21.
4   Ibid., 5.
5   Gorodskoe Obshchestvennoe Upravlenie, *Odessa, 1794–1894* (Odesa: n.p., 1895); Aleksandr I. Kirpichnikov and Aleksei I. Markevich, *Proshloe i nastoiashchee Odessy* (Odesa: n.p., 1894).
6   Patricia Herlihy, *Odessa: A History, 1794–1914* (Cambridge, MA: Harvard University Press, 1986), 233–34. For a detailed analysis of the 1897 census figures, see Patricia Herlihy, "The Ethnic Composition of the City of Odessa in the Nineteenth Century," *Harvard Ukrainian Studies* 1 (1977): 53–78—republished in Herlihy, *Odessa Recollected*, 117–36; Sifneos, *Imperial Odessa*, 42–49; more on the 1897 census in the two detailed volumes of Henning Bauer, Andreas Kappeler, and Brigitte Roth, eds., *Die Nationalitäten des Russischen Reiches in der Volkszählung von 1897*, 2 vols. (Stuttgart: Steiner Verlag, 1991).

Another example of localism is found in publications about "old Odesa" (*staraia Odessa*), among them one written by a descendant of the city's founder, Joseph de Ribas, in 1913.[7] They usually told the history of the city until the mid-nineteenth century following a chronological format, before its famous free port status was abolished and the reforms of Tsar Alexander II more thoroughly integrated Odesa into the empire. Such publications informed readers of Odesa's transformation and pointed to the loss of its earlier ethnic diversity. In addition, while referencing the founding years and the city's early development, including the founding generation's international background, they evoked Odesa's founding ethos, in contrast to growing nationalism and contemporary state neglect of the port and railway infrastructure.

The founding of new daily newspapers and various cultural associations at the end of the nineteenth century signaled the increased importance of the local and emphasized the growing social and cultural mobilization of both the emerging cultural elite and other expanding segments of the population. They gave Odesa a new image, especially within the Russian context, and had an internal, integrating effect. In 1884, a new newspaper, *Odesskie novosti* (Odesa news), was founded. The veteran newspaper, *Odesskii vestnik* (Odesa herald), ceased to appear in 1893–94. From 1896 onward, with a new team of publishers and editors, *Odesskie novosti* rapidly increased its circulation and recognition. Less well known, but of considerable importance to Odesa in the decade leading up to the 1905 Russian Revolution, was the newspaper *Yuzhnoe obozrenie* (Southern review) which from 1898 onward was politically more radical than the other major liberal newspapers *Odesskie novosti* and *Odesskii listok* (The Odesa sheet) and had gained a growing readership.[8]

The establishment of the Odesan Literary-Artistic Society at the end of 1897 belongs to this context of new public awareness of the city's changing position in imperial politics and the global economy. In Odesa, a number of societies were established for the promotion of culture, arts, and sciences over the course of the nineteenth century. These included such diverse organizations as the veteran Society for the Promotion of Agriculture of Southern Russia (founded 1828), the Society for History and Antiquities of New Russia (founded 1839), the University of Novorossiia (founded 1864), the Society for the Fine Arts (founded 1866), and new educational societies of various religious and ethnic

---

7   Aleksandr de Ribas, *Staraia Odessa: Istoricheskie ocherki i vospominaniia* (Odessa, 1913); Doroteia Atlas, *Staraia Odessa, ee druz'ia i nedrugi* (Odesa: Tekhnik, 1911).
8   Guido Hausmann, *Universität und städtische Gesellschaft in Odessa, 1865–1917* (Stuttgart: Steiner Verlag, 1998), 391–95, 407–10, 491–94.

groups, such as the Odesa branch of the Society for the Promotion of Enlightenment among the Jews in Russia (OPE, founded 1867).[9] Public figures in Odesa at the end of the nineteenth century, however, considered that the city would benefit from a new type of umbrella organization, uniting multiple cultural activities. Indeed, an opportunity to establish just such a society appeared with the ascension of Tsar Nikolai II to the throne in 1894, which created expectations of a more open political and cultural climate.

The new meaning given to the local at the end of the nineteenth century was closely related to the recent challenges facing Odesa from larger contexts, among which were its accelerated integration into the state structure and society of the late tsarist empire. With the institutional expansion during the previous decades, Odesa seemed to lose its uniqueness and special atmosphere. Odesans began to ask whether life was really still freer in Odesa than elsewhere in the tsarist empire, as it had been, for example, for Alexander Pushkin in the early nineteenth century and for the many Jews who had migrated at that time from northwestern shtetls to Odesa.[10] By 1897, about 32.5 percent of the population of Odesa was Yiddish speaking. Was Odesan life still very international at that time, or had many long-established merchant families left the city and settled elsewhere?[11] Did Odesa still possess greater ethnic and religious diversity than other Russian cities, or were the overall conditions converging? A part of the city's cultural and political elite perceived Odesa's greater integration into the late Russian Empire and its society as conducive to ethnic and religious homogenization, a process they saw as a loss of the city's cultural and social identity.

---

9   For a detailed analysis of the society, see Alexis Hofmeister, *Selbstorganisation und Bürgerlichkeit. Jüdisches Vereinswesen in Odessa um 1900* (Göttingen: Vandenhoeck & Ruprecht, 2007), 125–74. For more general information on associations in the tsarist empire, see Joseph Bradley, *Voluntary Associations in Tsarist Russia: Science, Patriotism, and Civil Society* (Cambridge, MA: Harvard University Press, 2009); Guido Hausmann, ed., *Gesellschaft als lokale Veranstaltung. Selbstverwaltung, Assoziierung und Geselligkeit in den Städten des ausgehenden Zarenreiches* (Göttingen: Vandenhoeck & Ruprecht, 2002). "An Innovative Agent of an Alternative Jewish Politics: The Odessa Branch of the Society for the Promotion of Enlightenment among the Jews of Russia," in Brian Horowitz, *Russian Idea, Jewish Presence: Essays on Russian-Jewish Intellectual Life* (Boston: Academic Studies Press, 2013), 72–85. See also chapter 4 below by Brian Horowitz.

10 On Jewish migration and life in Odesa to the end of the nineteenth century, see Zipperstein, *The Jews of Odessa*; Oleg Gubar, *Ocherki rannei istorii evreev Odessy* (Odessa: BMB, 2013); a broader context may be found in Yohanan Petrovsky-Shtern, *The Golden Age Shtetl: A New History of Jewish Life in East Europe* (Princeton: Princeton University Press, 2015).

11 Herlihy, *Odessa: A History, 1794–1914*; Guido Hausmann, "Die wohlhabenden Odessaer Kaufleute und Unternehmer: Zur Herausbildung bürgerlicher Identitäten im ausgehenden Zarenreich," *Jahrbücher für Geschichte Osteuropas* 48 (2000): 41–65; for a slightly different view, see Sifneos, *Imperial Odessa*, 124–30.

Among the new challenges facing the Odesa administrative and economic elites was finding a rightful place in the globalizing economy amidst increasingly unfavorable political circumstances. The seaport and grain exports (especially wheat) were the heart of the city's economy, but the necessary ongoing development of the port facilities was not carried out. From the late nineteenth century, the construction of a separate grain port was yet another unrealized urban scheme.[12] The government policy in place since the mid-nineteenth century of privileging and promoting the city (the free port, etc.) was replaced by the equal regional promotion of all the Black Sea ports, such as Nikolaev (Mykolaiv), Kherson, and Rostov-on-Don. Odesa and Russia in general were less and less able to compete in the world grain market with other grain exporting nations such as the US, Argentina, Canada, and Australia, especially with regard to the quality and the price of the exported grain.[13] The necessary passage through the Dardanelles Strait meant constant dependence on political contingencies, with the permanent threat of closure by the Ottoman Empire.

Finally, Odesa faced another major challenge in the new social and political mobilization that was spreading in the city and empire, taking on more specific forms than elsewhere in Europe. New political ideologies proliferated in legal and, even more so, in illegal ways, first within intellectual circles and then disseminated everywhere. The circulation of these political ideologies was virtually unstoppable in a city such as Odesa with its high immigration rate and major international seaport. These ideologies included, above all, socialist ideas, as well as nationalist ones, nourished by the economic crises, new social inequality, and physical violence, manifested, for example, in the outbreak of pogroms (1881, 1905), which led to social cohesion on a new socialist and nationalist basis.[14] Russian nationalists defending the autocratic state spoke of a rivalry between Russians and Jews for dominance in Odesa. By contrast, contemporary critical circles increasingly regarded society and the state as antagonistic forces. They placed the autocratic state in opposition to the liberal, cosmopolitan society, which represented, in their view, a specific Odesa tradition.[15] In this context,

---

12 Pavel S. Chekhovich and A. M. Dragana, *Novaia khlebnaia gavan' v Odesse* (Kiev [Kyiv]: n.p., 1906); *Opisanie Odesskago porta* (St. Petersburg, n.p., 1913).
13 Steven C. Topik and Allen Wells, "Warenketten in einer globalen Wirtschaft," in *1870–1945: Weltmärkte und Weltkriege*, ed. Emily S. Rosenberg (München: C. H. Beck, 2012), 687–728. See chapter 3 by Svetlana Natkovich in this volume.
14 On the workers' movement in Odesa, see Robert E. Weinberg, *The Revolution of 1905 in Odessa: Blood on the Steps* (Bloomington, IN: Indiana University Press, 1993) and his contribution to this volume (chapter 5).
15 On the liberal movement in Odesa before 1905, see Hausmann, *Universität*, 462–94.

Odesan intellectuals and the cultural elite saw themselves as a profoundly marginal group in a city dominated by commerce, especially the grain trade, and economic considerations. How should they face these new challenges? What new cultural spaces might be developed? Could their cosmopolitan heritage, from the time of the city's founding, be reactivated and transformed to respond adequately to the new challenges?

The Odesa Literary-Artistic Society: A historical analysis

The Odesa Literary-Artistic Society, founded in 1897 and opened in 1898, was the most important new cultural society in Odesa from that period. It is, however, rarely mentioned in the historical studies of Odesa, although it deserves its own monographic study. From 1894 at the latest, there were attempts to establish a new "Odesa Circle for the Arts," and in May 1897, its establishment was finally confirmed by the Ministry of the Interior, enabling the forty-three founding members to plan cultural activities.[16] It was to become the new umbrella organization that would absorb all the separately existing informal circles and legal societies by providing new opportunities for public discussion and interaction. Its chairman, Pavel Semyonovich Chekhovich, remarked at the opening on January 24, 1898:

> Наш город – умственный и художественный центр юга России – до настоящего времени не имел подобного учреждения. У нас процветают разные общества, поставившие себе задачу культивировать одну или несколько отраслей или мелких специальностей. Многие общества и даже отдельные лица достигли уже громадных и благотворных результатов, но все они действуют отдельно и очень много прекрасных идей и симпатичных стремлений не получило желательного осуществления, только благодаря тому, что не было объединяющей среды, некому было провести их в жизнь, так как единицы и группы лиц стояли отдельно.
>
> (Our city is the intellectual and artistic center of the south of Russia and, thus far, it has not had an institution of this kind. We have several flourishing societies dedicated to various

---

16 *Ustav Odesskago literaturno-artisticheskago Obshchestva* (Odessa: n.p., 1897), 3; Rossiiskii Gosudarstvennyi Arkhiv fond 1284, opis 187, delo 79–1903 g ll. 42–55.

branches of the arts and culture. Many associations and separate individuals have attained remarkable beneficial accomplishments, but they all operate separately and, therefore, many brilliant ideas and welcome endeavors could not be realized only for lack of an adequate shared milieu, for there was nobody to bring them into existence, since the individuals or groups of people stood on their own.)[17]

The society became a socializing place for the critically thinking intellectuals and artists and thus a new venue for the educated public alongside the other well-established cultural societies of Odesa. The statutes of the society stated its objectives in section 1:

> а) объединение и сближение литераторов и артистов всех отраслей изящных искусств, б) доставление начинающим литераторам, артистам и художникам возможности совершенствоваться, в) содействие целям взаимопомощи путем выдачи ссуд или пособий своим членам и безвозвратных пособий нуждающимся литераторам и артистам.
>
> (a. to bring together writers and artists from all branches of the fine arts; b. to provide opportunities for young writers and artists to develop; and c) to offer loans or stipends to the society's members and grants to needy writers and artists.)

Plans were made for public lectures, concerts (including competitions), a reading room, publications, and also opportunities for mere socializing at card games.[18] Membership lists with full names were attached to the annual reports or published separately. It is obvious that Odesa's merchant class did not participate in this association.

A few surviving statements indicate that this society also received assessments different from the one stated by the chairman, Pavel Semenovich Chekhovich. The young radical journalist, Aleksandr S. Izgoev (Aron Solomonovich Lande, 1872–1935), who became famous ten years later for his participation in the publication of *Vekhi*, had come to Odesa in 1896 from Paris and St. Petersburg and

---

17 *Otchet pravleniia Odesskago literaturno-khudozhestvennoogo Obshchestva za 1898 g.* (Odesa: n.p., 1899), 5
18 Ibid.

was one of the most active journalists of the newspaper *Yuzhnoe obozrenie* in the following years.[19] In March 1897, in fact, and in the same newspaper, Izgoev called for a new central cultural society in Odesa, one which would have a function similar to that performed by the Free Economic Society in St. Petersburg.

The Free Economic Society was an intellectual center of critically thinking intellectuals in St. Petersburg at that time, especially of the so-called "legal Marxists" around Petr B. Struve.[20] Izgoev was in contact with them and wanted a similar venue in Odesa. His comparison of the two cities was a sign of the model role of the imperial capital to which Odesan intellectuals now increasingly turned for orientation.

The Literary-Artistic Society, which first met in the house of the Greek merchant and former mayor, Grigorii G. Marazli, developed rapidly. By 1898, it already had 638 members and by 1902, 1167 members. Chekhovich was elected as chairman because, as a professor, he conferred external respectability and political reliability upon the society. Other board members included the well-known Moscow journalist, Vlas M. Doroshevich, who spent some time in Odesa to avoid the censorship in the capital; the painter, Petr A. Nilus; the sculptor, Boris V. Edwards; after 1903, the influential editor of *Odesskie Novosti*, Israel Moiseevich Heifetz, joined the society's board.

The society's activity included the formation of various organizational sections (literature, painting, music, etc.) and the organization of events of a more general scope. For example, the first literary evening sponsored by the society was dedicated to the poet, Nikolai A. Nekrasov, on the twentieth anniversary of his death. Other such soirées followed about prominent Russian writers such as Alexander Pushkin and Leo Tolstoy, the literary critic, Vissarion G. Belinskii, and Central and Western European writers such as Gerhard Hauptmann and Émile Zola. Last but not least, in 1903 there was a jubilee celebration in honor of the founder of modern Ukrainian literature, Ivan Kotliarevs'kyi, and prominent local representatives of the Ukrainian cause, such as Serhii Shelukhyn, came to speak at the society in February 1904 about the Ukrainian national poet Taras G. Shevchenko. In general, the society displayed an interest in writers engaged in social criticism, whether from Russia or Europe, including representatives of the repressed Ukrainian literature. In contrast, Jewish writing was not a topic of discussion until 1904.

---

19 About Izgoev, see Karl Schlögel, *Petersburg: Das Laboratorium der Moderne, 1909–1921* (Munich: Hanser, 2002).
20 Richard Pipes, *Struve: Liberal on the Left, 1870–1905* (Cambridge, MA: Harvard University Press, 1980).

In those years, this society was also a very important cultural venue for liberal Jews such as the young journalist Vladimir Jabotinsky, who before the Kishinev pogroms had wanted to become a Russian writer. Jabotinsky attended these literary evenings with enthusiasm; moreover, in March 1903 he gave a talk on the changes in Russian journalism and about the demise of the "thick journals" (traditional Russian literary magazines during the period of the Russian Empire). In his novel *Piatero* (*The Five*), he referred to the literary section of the society (the Literaturka) as "an oasis of the free word."[21] The politicization of the society, which served as a pre-1905 substitute for political parties, increased significantly in 1903–1904. This initially led to the temporary closure of the *Literaturka* in 1903 and, finally, to the closure of the entire society in 1904.[22]

An outstanding example that illustrates Odesa's cultural climate is the reception of the Dreyfus affair, after the trial and conviction of a Jewish artillery officer shook France in September 1894, which kept it in turmoil until 1899, even until his rehabilitation in 1906.[23] The Odesa coverage of the affair, of antisemitism and civic courage in France, catapulted the fledgling local newspaper *Odesskie novosti* to public attention, making it the largest local newspaper and one of the most widely circulated Russian newspapers outside the capitals. The newspaper's progressive European orientation was indeed outstanding, even in comparison to the press coverage of the affair in St. Petersburg, a fact proudly emphasized in a 1909 jubilee article.[24]

Indeed, *Odesskie novosti* covered the trial in detail during the first half of 1899 by means of articles written by its own correspondent and those translated from the French ("Vesti iz Frantsii") and from international press releases. The historian Oleksii I. Markevych (Aleksei Markevich, 1847–1903), a popular professor at the local University of Novorossiia and a well-known Ukrainophile, presented

---

21 Vladimir Jabotinsky, *Piatero* (Jerusalem: Biblioteka Aliya, 1990), 23; Jabotinsky, *Story of My Life* (Detroit: Wayne University Press, 2016); see Brian Horowitz, *Vladimir Jabotinsky's Russian Years: 1900–1925* (Bloomington: Indiana University Press, 2020), 14–15, 27.

22 *Yuzhnoe obozrenie*, April 23, 1903, 4; *Otchet pravleniia Odesskogo literaturno-khudozhestvennogo Obshchestva za 1903 g.* (Odesa: n.p., 1904), 14–18; Rossiiskii Gosudarstvennyi Arkhiv: fond 1284, opis' 187, delo 331–1904 g.ll. 1–1 ob; see also on the association, Konstantin Azadovskii, "Aleksandr Bisk i Odesskaia 'Literaturka,'" *Diaspora* [Paris and St. Petersburg] 1 (2001): 95–115.

23 Hans Rogger, "The Beilis Case: Anti-Semitism and Politics in the Reign of Nicholas II," in *Hostages of Modernization: Studies on Modern Antisemitism, 1870–1933/39*, vol. 2, *Austria, Hungary, Poland, Russia*, ed. Herbert A. Strauss (Berlin: De Gruyter, 1993), 1257–73. See Guido Hausmann, "Paradise Anticipated: The Jews of Odesa in the 19th and 20th Centuries—An Introduction," in "Schwerpunkt: Das jüdische Odessa," ed. Dan Diner and Guido Hausmann, special issue, *Simon Dubnow Institute Yearbook* 2 (2003): 172–76.

24 *Odesskie novosti*, December 1, 1909, 3. Its circulation numbers were: 1895—eight thousand copies; 1906—twenty thousand; 1914—twenty-five thousand.

the literary oeuvre of Dreyfus's advocate, Emile Zola, at the Odesan Literary-Artistic Society in 1898, the year in which the writer was slanderously accused for his famous intervention ("J'accuse!"). The society's lecture hall was full and later, in his personal memoirs, Doroshevich highly esteemed this lecture.[25] Markevych talked about Zola as "пожалуй, самый выдающийся беллетрист в настоящее время, после графа Льва Толстого" (probably the best fiction writer of our time, after Count Lev Tolstoy), but he remained cautious about making political statements, probably for fear of political prosecution:

> Я уклонюсь от оценки самого факта этого вмешательства Золя, так как положительное суждение о нем представляется мне . . . преждевременным; . . . Ибо считаю важным не факт виновности или невиновности Дрейфуса, а столь резко выяснившееся в этом деле отсутствие чувства правосудия у руководящих классов Франции: но так как это было давно известно и не относительно одной Франции . . .

> (I refrain from evaluating the very fact of Zola's intervention because a positive opinion seems premature; . . . I find not the guilt or innocence of Dreyfus important, but rather the acutely evident absence in this affair of a sense of justice and fairness among the governing classes of France, although this fact has long been known, not just with regard to France.)[26]

The reception of the Dreyfus affair in Odesa indicates a remarkable similarity: Zola was prominently discussed in the Literary-Artistic Society, and the newspapers devoted attention to the Dreyfus affair, followed by a more general attention to Jewish politics, both in Western Europe and in Russia. The journalist Izgoev discussed the topics of antisemitism, Jewish acculturation, and Zionism among Russia's Jews in a series of articles entitled "Letters on Zionism" in the liberal-left newspaper *Yuzhnoe obozrenie*. He called the idea of a Jewish state "utopian" and rejected Zionism, stating:

---

25 Aleksei I. Markevich, "O literaturnoi deiatel'nosti Emilia Zola," in *Otchet pravleniia* (Odesa, n.p., 1899), 9; on Markevich, see Hausmann, *Universität*, 538–39; on Doroshevich, see Louise McReynolds, "V. M. Doroshevich: The Newspaper Journalist and the Development of Public Opinion in Civil Society," in *Between Tsar and People: Educated Society and the Quest for Public Identity in Late Imperial Russia*, ed. Edith W. Clowes, Samuel D. Kassow, and James L. West (Princeton: Princeton University Press, 1991), 233–47.
26 Aleksei I. Markevich, "E. Zola kak belletrist," *Yuzhno-russkii al'manakh* 5, no. 2 (1899): 1.

> Есть среди русского еврейства одна часть, для которой сионизм представляет интерес совершенно платонический, не больше, чем борьба национальностей в Австрии или борьба рас в Америке. Это, именно, та часть интеллигенции, которая умственно и нравственно окончательно слилась с Россией, для которой нет и не может быть другой родины, кроме России, другого будущего, чем то, которое считает русский народ.

> (For a segment of Russian Jewry, Zionism is merely of platonic interest, like the struggle between the nationalities in Austria or the races in America. And this is precisely that segment of the intelligentsia that has finally integrated intellectually and morally with Russia and can have no other native land or future than the future of the Russian people.)[27]

Izgoev recognized only slight differences between European intellectuals and the local populations in Europe and in Russia:

> Разве Золя и Пикарда не преследуют за то, что они пытались спасти Францию от позора, разоблачить бандитов и мошенников? Народ тысячелетиями жил во тьме и невежестве, нельзя же требовать от него, чтобы он сразу поднялся на высшую ступень справедливости и понимания.

> (Don't they persecute Zola and Picquart because they tried to save France from shame and to unmask gangsters and scoundrels? For millennia the common people were living in darkness and ignorance; you really can't expect them to rise immediately to the highest level of justice and understanding.)[28]

He admitted the existence of some differences between the roles of Russian and Russian Jewish intellectuals:

> Но у еврея интеллигента к этому осадку должен присоединиться еще другой, специальный еврейский, оставшийся в итоге от всех оскорблений и обид, наносимых ему только как еврею.

---

27 Izgoev, "Pis'ma o tsionisme," *Yuzhnoe obozrenie*, July 11, 1899.
28 Ibid.

(But a Jewish intellectual of this type in addition to the bitter taste that any intellectual has to bear, has to put up with another, special one as a result of all the insults and humiliations that he must endure only because he is a Jew.)[29]

The detailed account of the Dreyfus affair in Odesan newspapers and at the Odesan Literary-Artistic Society attests both to the interest in it and to the manner of its reception. Around 1900, the topic was raised publicly, although in an indirect manner, suggesting that a growing segment of the city's elites regarded themselves and Odesa as part of a common European cultural and political space. That public space expanded to include political issues over the following years, later leading to the closure of the society in 1904.

Like other local cultural and political associations, the Odesan Literary-Artistic Society was not allowed to reopen until 1909. A new statute strictly regulated its activities, permitting it to function only as a club, allowed to organize concerts, theater performances, exhibitions, and other non-political cultural events. As the literary evenings had been the primary engine of politicization before 1905, they were forbidden at first and reinstated only a few years later, in 1912. Section 2 of the society's statutes summarized the objectives as:

> доставлять своим членам и их семействам возможность проводить свободное от занятий время с удобством, приятностью и пользой на почве лит.-арт. интересов, а также сближение литераторов, артистов, художников. . . .
>
> (to allow its members and their families to spend their free time in a pleasant and useful manner on the basis of their literary-artistic interests and to bring writers and artists together.)[30]

Section 9 explicitly excluded politics and matters of the state from the program of the Literary and Artistic Club.[31] Thus, during the years after 1909, public political discussions remained forbidden at the club, despite repeated requests to amend those statutes that limited its attractiveness.[32] At the end of 1912, the club's board proposed the reinstatement of public discussions, following lectures

---

29 Ibid.
30 *Ustav Odesskago literaturno-artisticheskago Kluba* (Odesa: n.p., 1909), 5.
31 Ibid., 5.
32 *Otchet pravleniia Odesskago literaturno-artisticheskago Kluba za 1914-i god* (Odesa: n.p., 1915), 4.

on literary topics, "as the most important and only suitable way to revitalize the club." However, attempts to again make the club a "society" (*obshchestvo*) and to restore its previous status and relevance as a hub of discussions about matters of common interest were unsuccessful. At the same time, the club strived for a broad social reach, rejecting high fees as they would have further limited the club's public resonance.[33] An additional limiting factor was the relative lack of space, as it was necessary first to acquire a more appropriate property for the club's activities, which required considerable financial resources.

The refashioning of the association into a club led to significant changes. Although the new organizational form was clearly distinguishable from its predecessor, it nevertheless attracted growing public interest once again in Odesa. The Literary and Artistic Club's membership increased to 348 members in 1914 and rose to 738 in 1917. However, it no longer fulfilled the same function as its predecessor. Political and public cultural life in the city became markedly differentiated, stripping the club of its former political functions.[34]

The history of other cultural societies in Odesa, such as the ethnic ones, shows clear parallels. By the end of October 1905, a local Prosvita Society (a Ukrainian educational society) emerged in Odesa, which had spread from eastern Galicia to the other Ukrainian settlements during the late nineteenth century.[35] The Russian authorities considered Prosvita to be a hotbed for the political mobilization of Ukrainians for the 1905 Russian Revolution and ordered its closure in November 1906. Not until 1910 was a Society of All Slavs in the City of Odesa founded, in which well-known local Ukrainians became active. This society was followed, somewhat later, by the opening of the Ukrainian Club, which was seen primarily as a purely social environment, but not as a place for the dissemination of education and enlightenment.[36]

The editor of *Odesskii listok*, Sergei F. Shtern (1886–1947), added some skeptical remarks when he wrote in a letter to the newspaper editors that the Literary and Artistic Club mainly gathered "the middle-class or average intelligentsia, primarily Jewish intelligentsia" and that: "the really moving themes have yet to come."[37] However, in 1912 and 1913, the club did, in fact, highlight certain

---

33 "V literaturno-artisticheskom Klube," *Odesskie novosti*, January 1, 1913, 3.
34 See Hausmann, *Universität*, 486.
35 "Obshchestvo 'Prosvita' v Odesse," *Kievskaia starina* (November-December, 1905): 105–16. See chapter 5 in this volume by Yohanan Petrovsky-Shtern.
36 *Ustav ukrainskago Kluba, Statut Odesskago ukrainskago Kluba* (Odesa: n.p., 1910); Rossiiskii Gosudarstvennyi Istoricheskii Arkhiv, fond 1284, opis 1871, delo 245 – 1909 g., ll. 1–6 ob, 62–62 ob.
37 Sergei F. Shtern, "Gde intelligentsiia (pis'mo v redaktsiiu)," *Odesskii listok*, March 4, 1912, 3.

special cultural themes that might be interpreted also as political ones. On March 5, 1912, the well-known Zionist Jewish scholar Yosef Klausner (1874–1958) lectured on "Young Jewish poetry in the works of Haim Nahman Bialik, Shaul Tchernichovsky, and Semyon Grigorevich Frug," including readings of poems by Bialik and Frug—possibly the first evening that the Literary and Artistic Club dedicated explicitly to Jewish literature.[38] On January 31, 1913, at the new theater, the club held an evening on Haim Nahman Bialik, which received an enthusiastic response.[39] Bialik (1873–1934) was the most outstanding and popular representative of contemporary Hebrew and Yiddish poetry, who lived in Odesa from 1900 to 1922; he subsequently left for Warsaw and Berlin and then went on to Tel Aviv in 1924.[40] From February 2, 1913 *Odesskie novosti* reported quite extensively on the Bialik evening, celebrating the twentieth anniversary of Bialik's literary activity and reporting the massive applause by the audience. At that event, three speakers, including Klausner, presented various aspects of the life and works of Bialik and read some of his poetry. The enthusiastic audience also welcomed the fact that Bialik was sent a congratulatory telegram. The newspaper review concluded, however, with an expression of regret—that the current laws did not permit a public discussion of the three scholarly presentations.[41]

At the same time as the club focused again on contemporary Hebrew literature, two figures from Odesa and the Russian right, the rector of the University of Novorossiia, Sergei V. Levashov, and Bishop Anatolii, were elected to the State Duma in St. Petersburg. Hopes for the election of the prominent Jewish liberal lawyer, Genrikh Borisovich Sliozberg (1863–1937), were dashed, apparently because certain groups of Odesan Zionists did not vote for him.[42] These elections were marked by the attempted intimidation of the liberal opposition, especially the Jewish electorate in Odesa.

The Club's programming reflected a shift in the cultural orientation of many Odesan Jews towards Zionism between 1905 and 1914. If liberal circles in Odesa had hoped, however, that this renewed local and Russian political escalation would lead to a strong mobilization of Odesan society, receiving attention comparable to that which had accompanied the Dreyfus affair in France, they were disappointed. At the very least, a sentence in the club's annual report of

---

38 *Otchet pravleniia Odesskago literaturno-artisticheskago Kluba za 1915-i god* (Odesa: n.p., 1916), 7.
39 *Odesskie novosti*, January 31, 1913, 3.
40 David Aberbach, *Bialik* (New York: Grove Press, 1988).
41 "Vecher o Kh. N. Bialike (lit.-art. Klub)," *Odesskie novosti*, February 2, 1913, 3.
42 *Odesskii listok*, October 28, 1912, 3; *Novoe Vremia*, August 17, 1912, 5.

1914 indicated clearly that, although it gained public recognition, it had not yet fully regained its earlier importance:

> Давно в нашем клубе не царило подобного оживления: казалось, что наступил момент, когда прежнее равнодушие общества окончательно исчезло, и клуб наш вновь сделается средоточием местной интеллигенции.

> (We haven't had such animation in our club for a long time. It seemed that the moment has finally arrived when the earlier societal indifference has finally disappeared, and our club was again becoming the heart of the local intelligentsia.)[43]

Conclusion

By the turn of the century, the Odesa Literary-Artistic Society, founded only recently in 1897, was serving an important function in Odesa as a cultural umbrella association. It was also an expression of the reawakening of local society, restoring vital energy and suggesting the prospect of a renewed future to the city, a place rife with rich local traditions. It restructured the Odesan cultural space, giving it a new home and quickly assumed a central role within pre-1904 cultural life in Odesa. The society guided the orientation of intellectual life and determined the marginality and centrality of the cultural actors. Less concerned with preserving the uniqueness of Odesa's traditional identity, it dealt more with integrating Odesan culture and politics into the prevailing Russian context, akin to the changing orientation of the city's political life. In addition, by 1900, the society demonstrated other possibilities and new cultural orientations, primarily in West-European literatures and arts. The different orientations towards Russian and West European cultures and politics could, at times, clash. Nonetheless, in Odesa, the awareness of both the Jews and the non-Jews regarding the Dreyfus affair showed how important this openness to West European culture was to them all.

Last, but not least, the society exemplified the emancipation of cultural life from state control and state-related institutions. The nineteenth century was a

---

43 *Otchet pravleniia Odesskogo literaturno-artisticheskago Kluba za 1914 i god* (Odesa: n.p., 1915), 4. See Roshanna P. Sylvester, *Tales of Old Odessa: Crime and Civility in a City of Thieves* (DeKalb, IL: Northern Illinois University Press, 2005).

time when Russia's universities and their professors dominated cultural societies and periodicals. With the advent of the twentieth century, those links were broken, and culture came into its own rightful space amid Odesa's local society within the larger Russian context. This society was an important venue for open cultural exchange, beyond ethnic and national barriers; meanwhile, it also served as a place where ethnic and/or political identifications could be reinforced. As in other social spaces in the city, it temporarily brought non-dominant groups, such as Ukrainians and Jews, closer.

By 1909, acculturated Odesan Jews no longer considered the renewed society, now called a club, as suitable because it opened its doors to additional Jewish cultural orientations, including Zionism. It was now a venue where politics played a less important role than before, as other new spaces came into existence where political discourse could develop, even locally, despite all the restrictions. Nevertheless, one might ask: To what extent should the history of the Odesa Literary-Artistic Society/Club be considered as two renditions of the same organization or perhaps as two separate entities that clearly differed in their legal standing, activities, and self-images? By the time of its reestablishment in 1909, the role of the renamed society—the Odesa Literary-Artistic Club—changed significantly; it existed in the shadow of the former society (1897–1904). However, it was in this new phase that it became less elitist than before 1905 and regained some of its previous importance. Its role from 1909–1917 might be seen as serving to counterbalance the unconditionally loyalist and Russian nationalist Odesan administration (the governor, mayor [*gradonachal'nik*], municipal officers and city duma) and that of the university. The history of the Odesa Literary-Artistic Society/Club attests to the fact that cosmopolitanism is, essentially, a relational category. In this respect, the society/club safeguarded the cosmopolitan heritage of the city and served as a rallying point for new cultural and spatial orientations and venues, such as the Jewish settlement in Palestine. It tried to realize alternatives to present conditions and to promote promising futures for Odesa. It reflected and practiced "multiethnic cosmopolitanism" in times of rising nationalisms in Odesa and more generally in Russia and Europe.[44] Before the outbreak of World War I, the society/club once again became a place where non-dominant ethnic or cultural groups could meet socially and interact intellectually.

---

44 See introduction above, 7–8.

CHAPTER 2

The Ukrainian Odes(s)a of Vladimir Jabotinsky

Yohanan Petrovsky-Shtern

Introduction

Vladimir Jabotinsky was in love with Odesa. Deep affection for his native city permeates his essays, journalism, memoirs, short stories, and novels. The scholar of Zionism Dmitry Shumsky calls Jabotinsky's affection "local patriotism" and the source of his distinct nationalism.[1] We also know that Jabotinsky supported Ukrainian revivalism. Jabotinsky preached a Ukrainian-Jewish political alliance in his oral presentations and programmatic articles from 1905 through 1913, even though Russian Zionists considered these sympathies scandalous, unworthy of a real Jewish nationalist.[2] Both Odesa and Ukraine are the obvious

---

1 Dmitry Shumsky, "An Odessan Nationality? Local Patriotism and Jewish Nationalism in the Case of Vladimir Jabotinsky," *Russian Review* 79, no. 1 (2020): 65–66, 68, 69, 80.
2 On Jabotinsky and the Ukrainian question in the context of East European Jewish Diaspora nationalism, see Olga Andriewsky, "'Medved' iz berlogi': Vladimir Jabotinsky and the Ukrainian question, 1904–1914," *Harvard Ukrainian Studies* 14 (3–4) (1990): 249–67; Israel Kleiner, *From Nationalism to Universalism: Vladimir (Ze'ev) Jabotinsky and the Ukrainian Question* (Edmonton: CIUS, 2000); Colin Shindler, "Jabotinsky and Ukrainian Nationalism: A Reinterpretation," *East European Jewish Affairs* 31, no. 2 (2001): 122–31; Ivan Dziuba, "Z orlynoiu pechalliu na choli . . .," in *Vladimir (Zeev) Zhabotyns'kyi i ukrains'ke pytannia. Vseliuds'kist' u shatakh natsionalizmu*, by Izrail Kleiner (Edmonton: Kanads'kyi Instytut Ukrains'kykh Studii, 1995), 7–26; Serhii Kal'ian, "Natsional'na polityka V. Zhabotyns'koho u kontektsi odes'koho periodu ioho diial'nosti," in *Odessa i evreiskaia tsivilizatsiia: k 100-letiiu so dnia rozhdeniia Saula Borovogo*, ed. Mikhail Rashkovetskii et al. (Odesa: Negotsiant, 2004), 167–73; I. Mel'nychuk, "Natsional'ni pohliady V. Zhabotyns'koho," in *Evrei v Ukraini: istoriia i suchasnist'* (Zhytomyr: ZhDU, 2009), 224–28; Oleksandr Muzychko, "Vladimir Zhabotinskii i Dmitrii Dontsov: nekotorye parralleli k istorii ukrainskogo i evreiskogo natsional'nykh dvizhenii v pervoi polovine XX veka," in *Piataia Mezhdunarodnaia konferentsiia "Odessa i evreiskaia tsivilizatsiia,"* ed. Mikhail Rashkovetskii et al. (Odesa: Negotsiant, 2007), 42–49.

East European contexts that shaped Jabotinsky's life and works. The idea of a "Ukrainian Odesa" in relation to Jabotinsky, however, challenges our received wisdom of both the cosmopolitan character of the city and the exclusivity of the Russian-language environment of Odesa. This idea suggests that we should recontextualize Jabotinsky's nationalism and revisit the dominant characterization of Odesa as cosmopolitan and Russian-speaking.

The absence of a *Ukrainian* Odesa in the studies of that city's urban history is hardly surprising. The fame of Odesa-born Russian Jewish writers eclipsed the city's reputation as one of the major centers of Ukrainian cultural life in the Russian Empire, on a par with Kyiv and Kharkiv. Odesans spoke a Russian-based *koine* with borrowings from Italian, Yiddish, Polish, Armenian, and Greek, which obscured the fact that Odesa had a significant Ukrainian-speaking population.[3] With rare exceptions, this Russo-centric scholarly approach to Odesa has almost entirely omitted its Ukrainian substratum, which, as we shall see, Jabotinsky admired.[4]

Looking at the years Jabotinsky spent in Odesa, from the 1880s through 1915 and his literary reminiscences about that time, I argue that a Ukrainian cultural constituency transforms our understanding of Odesa's distinct cosmopolitanism and of Jabotinsky's diaspora nationalism. Of course, there are various ways to conceptualize political cosmopolitanism yet there exists a consensus regarding cultural cosmopolitanism, the core of Jabotinsky's program. A cultural cosmopolite would acknowledge the rights of the ethno-national minorities and would simultaneously reject his or her own identification with a particular culture as nationalist. Jabotinsky's cosmopolitanism was utterly different. He saw Odesa as an urban environment where individuals and groups strongly identified themselves ethnically and culturally, nurtured their ethno-nationalism, communicated in ethnic versions of the Odesa Slavic language and associated themselves with the broader Mediterranean world. We shall discover how Jabotinsky associated himself with both Jews and Ukrainians, spoke Russian with a soft Odesan accent—which apparently made the language sound cosmopolitan—and treated the imperial Russian culture as a threat to both Jews and Ukrainians. Jabotinsky's "Ukrainian Odesa" helps explain that cosmopolitanism was the other side of his nationalism and the opposite of what he called assimilation.

---

3   On the metaphorically understood Odesa *koine*, see Yevhen Stepanov, *Rosiis'ke movlennia Odesy* (Odesa: Astroprynt, 2004), 74–91.
4   See, for example, Guido Hausmann, *Universität und städtische Gesellschaft in Odessa, 1865— 1917: Soziale und nationale Selbstorganisation an der Peripherie des Zarenreiches* (Stuttgart: Franz Steiner, 1998), 421–31.

Jabotinsky's "Ukrainian Odessa" also challenges the scholarly perception of Jewish and Ukrainian cultural groups in Odesa as two separate entities. I will show that Jabotinsky's interest in things Ukrainian is of Odesan origin and that the Ukrainian question functions as a foil for Jabotinsky's discussion of Jewish self-determination, an aspect that has been missed by those who study Jabotinsky the Zionist as well as those who focus on his Ukrainian affinities.[5]

Discovering Ukraine

Before turning to Jabotinsky's writings on Ukrainian matters, one must ask what Jabotinsky knew about Ukraine and what his sources of knowledge were. An avid and voracious reader, Jabotinsky knew at least half a dozen poems by the Ukrainian national bard Taras Shevchenko by heart, and he not only quoted them at length but also referred to them in his Odesa-period essays, when the Russian regime bent over backwards suppressing the commemoration and celebration of Shevchenko. During the same period, Jabotinsky alluded to the persecution of Ukrainian language and culture in the Russian Empire, referring to the Ems Edict and the Valuev decree of the tsarist government, which stifled the Ukrainian cultural revival in the 1860s–1870s.[6] In Odesa, Jabotinsky became very familiar with Ukrainian ethnography: he could map Ukrainian ethnic territories culturally and linguistically.[7] Most likely, he read publications on these issues as early as 1901–1905, and could make an intelligent judgment on Ukrainian urban assimilation and nationalist strivings in the Russian and Austro-Hungarian Empires.

We do not know whether Jabotinsky had access to *Літературно-науковий вістник* (Literary and scholarly herald), which the paramount Lviv-based Ukrainian writer and poet Ivan Franko established and edited from 1899 onward. Yet we do know that Jabotinsky closely followed the Ukrainian sociocultural revival in Galicia, then the easternmost province of the Habsburg Empire. He read what he called the "Ukrainian press," which was most likely the Ukrainian daily *Громадська думка* (Public opinion; after 1909 renamed *Рада* [Council]) or *Українська хата* (Ukrainian hut), a monthly journal issued from

---

5   See, however, Shumsky, "An Odessan Nationality," 66; Shumsky, *Beyond the Nation-State: The Zionist Political Imagination from Pinsker to Ben-Gurion* (New Haven: Yale University Press, 2018), 127.
6   See, for example, Vladimir Jabotinsky, "O iazykakh i prochem," *Fel'etony* (St. Petersburg: Gerol'd, 1913), 226–27.
7   See Jabotinsky, "Urok iubileia Shevchenko," *Fel'etony*, 131–41.

1909 through 1914.[8] He may also have read the daily *Діло* (Cause; 1880–1939) and the monthly *Ukrainische Rundschau* (Ukrainian Review; 1905–1914). Jabotinsky's writing appeared in the *Украинский вестник* (Ukrainian Herald) from the very beginning of this St. Petersburg-based short-lived periodical (only fourteen issues appeared in 1906), which represented the interests of the first Ukrainian club in the First Russian Duma. For that purpose, Jabotinsky must have been in contact with Maksym Slavyns'kyi, its editor, with whom he ran for the Second Russian Duma in the same electoral district in 1906.[9] Jabotinsky also published in *Украинская жизнь* (Ukrainian life, 1912–1917), a Moscow-based monthly that featured the most important Ukrainian thinkers and literati of the 1910s and was edited by Symon Petliura. Jabotinsky therefore knew Petliura, at least from 1912, as a journalist and a man of letters. In addition, Jabotinsky carefully read Mykhailo Hrushevs'kyi, the founding father of Ukrainian national historiography, with whom he polemicized as early as 1906.[10]

Furthermore, Jabotinsky easily discerned Ukrainian or at least elements of it in Odesa Russian first, due to his sensitive linguistic ear, and second, because of the significant presence of Ukrainian speakers in late nineteenth-century Odesa. Of the 403,815 Odesa residents in 1897, 49 percent indicated their spoken language as Russian (197,232), 31 percent as "Jewish," that is, Yiddish (124,511), 9.4 percent as "Malorossiiskii," that is, Ukrainian (37,945), 4.3 percent as Polish (17,395), 2.5 percent as German (10,248), and 1.3 percent as Greek (5,047).[11] Ukrainians formed the third most important ethno-linguistic group in Odesa, although we do not know how many ethnic Ukrainians indicated Russian as their spoken language. Most Ukrainians came from the rural areas of Kherson and Taurida provinces, constituting the lowest social niche in the city. Katerina Korneichukova, of Ukrainian peasant stock, an abandoned woman with two children settled in Odesa as a laundress. Her social status helped preserve her Ukrainian language, although any social mobility for her children—and for thousands of other Odesa Ukrainians—meant the rejection of Ukrainian and the adoption of Russian. Korneichukova was the mother of the literary critic and

---

8 Jabotinsky, "Pis'ma o natsional'nostiakh i oblastiakh. Evreistvo i ego nastroeniia," *Russkaia mysl'* 32, no. 1 (1911): 113.

9 For an important discussion of Jabotinsky's relations with Slavyns'kyi, particularly in connection to the demise of the Ukrainian People's Republic, see Kleiner, *From Nationalism to Universalism*, 106–09, 116–20.

10 See Jabotinsky, "O iazykakh i prochem," in his *Fel'etony*, 226; Zhabotinskii, "Tochka nad i," *Ukrainskii vestnik* 7 (July 2, 1906): 399.

11 N. A. Troinitskii, ed., *Pervaia Vseobshchaia perepis' naseleniia Rossiiskoi imperii 1897 g.*, 89 vols. (Odessa: Izdanie Tsentral'nogo statisticheskogo komiteta ministerstva vnutrennikh del, 1904), 47:36–37, 152–53.

writer Kornei Chukovsky (pen name of Nikolai Korneichukov, 1882–1969), an illegitimate son of a Jewish student who became Jabotinsky's close friend, school fellow, and his future protégé.

Jabotinsky discovered things Ukrainian precisely when the leadership of the Odesa Ukrainian community reorganized after the widespread arrests of the late 1870s. From the mid-1890s through 1905, the national-liberal activists in the Ukrainian community grew from twenty-five to 532 persons, forming in the wake of the 1905 Russian revolution the first, most numerous, and influential Prosvita (Enlightenment) Society in Ukraine under Russian imperial control, which imitated its Galician namesake in Lviv under Austrian rule.[12] Two individuals were at the head of Odesa's Ukrainians associated with the ethno-cultural work of the Prosvita. Leonid Smolens'kyi (1844–1905), a historian and high school teacher, was one of the first Ukrainian activists in Odesa under Alexander II. Although Smolens'kyi worked at the Richelieu Lyceum long before Jabotinsky came to study there, Smolens'kyi gave lectures at the Ukrainian society and taught at the Junkers' school and other Odesa private schools, where he gained an impressively large audience. Before he became paralyzed in 1900 and died in 1905, Smolens'kyi was a highly visible public figure in town, known as a "god to whom everybody bowed," "rabbi-teacher," and "the most consistent Ukrainophile."[13]

Smolens'kyi was close with Mykhailo Komarov (1844–1913), the founder of Ukrainian *Shevchenkoznavstvo* (Taras Shevchenko studies) and a prolific literary critic particularly interested in Jewish literary endeavors in Yiddish, Russian, and Ukrainian.[14] In his private library, Komarov had Ukrainian and Russian translations of plays by Sholem Asch, Yakov Gordin, Avrum Reizen, and Sholem Aleichem.[15] He also had three of the five books of Hryts'ko Kernerenko (pseudonym of Grigorii Kerner, 1863—ca. 1941), the first Jew to write poetry and

---

12 S. G. Chmyr, "Odes'ka hromada v ukrains'komu natsional'nomu rusi (kinets' XIX – pochatok XX st.)," *Pivdenna Ukraina XX stolittia: Zapysky naukovo-doslidnyts'koi laboratorii istorii Pivdennoi Ukrainy ZDU* 1, no. 4 (1998): 107–14.

13 O. E. Muzychko, "Rid Smolens'kykh v istoriohrafichnomu protsesi seredyny XIX – pershoi tretyny XX st.," *Zapysky istorychnoho fakul'tetu*, vyp. 20 (Odesa: Odes'kyi natsional'nyi universytet, 2009), 271.

14 About Komarov, see G. Shvyd'ko, *Mykhailo Komarov i Katerynoslavshchyna* (Dnipropetrovsk: Natsional'nyi hirnychyi universytet, 2011) and Komarov's bibliography in Nadia Myronets' review of the above-mentioned publication in *Ukrains'kyi arkheohrafichnyi shchorichnyk* 16/17 (19/20) (2012): 659–66.

15 See N. A. Brodets'ka and N. O. Yatsun, *Biblioteka M. F. Komarova: kataloh kolektsii Odes'koi natsional'noi naukovoi biblioteky imeni M. Gor'koho* (Odesa: Brovkin, 2014), 61, 65, 75, 92, 84, 92, 126–127.

prose in the Ukrainian language, and to whom Komarov devoted a review.[16] Jabotinsky knew Komarov as a notary public, who at least once signed his bill of sale, and most likely as a Ukrainian activist and member of the Literary-Artistic Society (Literaturka), of which Jabotinsky was also a member.[17]

An unusually liberal and tolerant atmosphere prevailed in the Odesa nationalist group of Ukrainian activists. Furthermore, the leadership and members of the Prosvita comprised Odesans of Russian, Jewish, and Polish descent, while its most influential members, such as one of its major sponsors Yevhen Chykalenko (1861–1929) strongly supported the Ukrainian-Jewish dialogue. The leaders of the group were confident that they were following in the footsteps of Mykhailo Drahomanov (1841–1895), a key figure in Ukrainian sociopolitical thought, who, despite his strong anti-Jewish bias, invited Jews to publish their contributions in his journal, *Вольное слово* (Free word).[18]

Jabotinsky's teachers of Ukrainian descent, under whom he studied at the Second Gymnasium and the Richelieu Lyceum, were probably close to if not members of the Ukrainian cultural groups.[19] For example, the classicist, poet, and composer Petro Nishchyns'kyi taught Greek at the Second Gymnasium when Jabotinsky attended the school and most likely the latter learned his Greek in Nishchyns'kyi's class. He recalled that "with the exception of inconsistent knowledge of Latin and Greek (which I value until this day), everything that I learned during my childhood, I did not learn at school."[20] Under the penname Petro Baida, Nishchyns'kyi translated Homer and Sophocles into Ukrainian and helped Komarov with his *Slovar' rossiis'ko-ukrainskii* (Ukrainian-Russian dictionary, published pseudonymously in Lviv, 1893–98).[21] He could have shared with his students his translations from Greek into Ukrainian.

Nikolai Korneichukov, the future Kornei Chukovsky, had several Ukrainian activists among his immediate friends. Chukovsky knew Komarov personally, and he was close to classmate Vladimir Sigarevich, whose brother Dmitrii

---

16 About Grigorii Kerner and his contacts with Ukrainian literati, see Yohanan Petrovsky-Shtern, *The Anti-Imperial Choice: the Making of the Ukrainian Jew* (New Haven: Yale University Press, 2009), 24–61.
17 See Evgeniia Ivanova, *Chukovskii i Zhabotinskii* (Moscow and Jerusalem: Mosty kultury/Gesharim, 2005), 33, 40, 51.
18 Ben-Ami [Mark Rabinovich], "Moi snosheniia s M. Dragomanovym i rabota v Vol'nom slove," *Evreiskaia starina* 3–4 (1915): 347–66.
19 See Lilia Bilousova, "Natsional'ni tovarystva v Odesi v XIX – na pochatku XX st." *Ukrains'kyi istorychnyi zhurnal* 2 (2017): 46–63.
20 See Jabotinsky, *Povest' moikh dnei* (Jerusalem: Biblioteka Aliya, 1989), 16.
21 T. Zarubenko, "Pereklad 'Odissei' v interpretatsii Petra Baidy," *Mova i kultura* 17, no. 5 (2014): 11–12.

became one of the most active founders of the Prosvita in 1905.[22] They all could have met at the Thursday parties of the cosmopolitan Literaturka that brought together most of the Odesa literati of various ethnicities to listen to debates or reports, all in Russian.[23] At the same time, Chukovsky (and probably Jabotinsky himself) heard a presentation by Maksym Slavyns'kyi (1868–1945) on the hot issue of nationalism. Slavyns'kyi is remembered as a Ukrainian nationalist and the editor of important literary periodicals, as a minister in the cabinet of the Ukrainian People's Republic, its representative in exile in Prague, and co-author of the famous Ukrainian poetess Lesia Ukraiinka (1871–1913), with whom he translated Heinrich Heine into Ukrainian. Arrested by Soviet troops in Prague as a "bourgeois nationalist" and starved to death in a Kyiv prison in 1945, Slavyns'kyi was a very different individual when he spoke in Odesa in the early twentieth century, preaching the opposite of what he later defended and died for.

On October 7, 1904, Slavyns'kyi gave a talk at the Literaturka entitled "Психические элементы национальности" (Psychological elements of nationality). The text of his speech did not survive, but we can accurately reconstruct his main points through Chukovsky's refutation of it. Half a century before Jacques Derrida and almost a century before Rogers Brubaker, Slavyns'kyi proclaimed nationality a fiction that cannot be defined by race, language, or religion. Slavyns'kyi claimed that as nationality is an aberration of the mind with no objective parameters, nationalism, therefore, has no reason to exist. Thus, Slavyns'kyi celebrated the universal man, a man of the world, a cosmopolitan. Himself a man of the world, Chukovsky was scandalized by this naïve and idealistic vision. He maintained that Slavyns'kyi ignored the deepest meaning of the great writers who articulated above all the truth of the people, their national truth. To prove his point, Chukovsky portrayed Odesan Jews as cleaving to Russian culture, which they perceived quite superficially through the lens of class. These Jews, who filled the libraries, literary clubs, and lecture halls, were unable to grasp the Russian national idea in Dostoevsky and Tolstoy, yet they entirely detached themselves from Jewish artistic creativity. They were as equally removed from

---

22 On the rise of the Prosvita Society in the wake of the first Russian Revolution, see Oleksandr Boldyrev, *Odes'ka Hromada: Istorychnyi narys pro ukrains'ke national'ne vidrodzhennia v Odesi u 70-ti rr. XIX – pochat. XX st.* (Odesa: Maiak, 1994) and a source guide in the exhibition catalog, O. G. Archykova et al., *Dzherela pam'iati: kataloh vystavky do 90-richchia Ukrains'koho tovarystva "Prosvita" v Odesi (1905–1909)* (Odesa: n.p., 1995). See also Hausmann, *Universität und städtische Gesellschaft in Odessa*, 426–27.

23 Jabotinsky, *Povest'*, 33.

Russian as from Jewish national ideas, because they dismissed the national and strove for the universal.[24]

Chukovsky's arguments follow almost verbatim what Jabotinsky had written a year earlier in his essay "Тоска о патриотизме" (Longing for patriotism), in which he bemoaned the loyalty of the Jewish intelligentsia to the "master" Russian culture, reproaching his brethren for their condescending attitude toward their own Jewish culture. He pointed out the dire necessity for the Jews to become patriots of their own people—that is, nationalist leaders.[25] Chukovsky's critique of Slavyns'kyi also prefigures major themes that Jabotinsky subsequently developed in his journalism, such as the futility of Jewish assimilation into Russian culture and the urge to contribute to one's own people.[26] Both Jabotinsky and Chukovsky supported a kind of cosmopolitanism that would treat seriously any ethno-national issue. They underscored the significance of national ideas reflected in great works of literature. Paradoxically, they discussed and articulated some of these points while arguing against cosmopolitans of both Jewish and Ukrainian descent.

Chukovsky articulated Jabotinsky's key ideas on nationalism but also exposed Jabotinsky to things Ukrainian long before their debates at the Literaturka. The two friends knew each another from early childhood. Their ego-documents portrayed a multi-ethnic environment in which both were growing up in Odesa. Precisely because Odesa boasted cosmopolitan, that is, ethnically tolerant educational institutions, Chukovsky and Jabotinsky found themselves in one and the same Bekhtereva kindergarten, when Chukovsky turned five and Jabotinsky seven.[27] One was the fatherless and illegitimate son of a Ukrainian mother and the other, also fatherless, yet a legitimate orphan of a Jewish mother.

For several years both studied together at the Second Odesa Gymnasium, which Chukovsky remembered with warm humor and sharp social critique in his autobiographical short novel Гимназия (Lyceum, 1938), better known in its later version as Серебряный герб (Silver coat of arms, 1961). In this novel, Jabotinsky appears as the short, curly haired, and swift Munia Blokhin, a good friend and classmate of the narrator. In the novel, but even more so in real life in

---

24 Kornei Chukovskii, "Sluchainye zametki," *Evreiskaia zhizn'* 11 (1904): 177–182; reprinted in Ivanova, *Chukovskii i Zhabotinskii*, 85–93.
25 See Jabotinsky, "Toska o patriotizme," *Yuzhnye zapiski* 17 (May 16, 1903); reprinted in *Chukovskii i Zhabotinskii*, 54–58.
26 See Jabotinsky, "O 'evreiakh i russkoi literature'"; "Strannoe iavlenie"; and "Na lozhnom puti," *Fel'etony*, 61–70; 242–247; and 248–263.
27 Chukovskii, *Sobranie sochnenii v piatnadtsati tomakh*, vol. 13, *Dnevnik (1936–1969)* (Moscow: Terra-Knizhnyi klub, 2006), 461.

1890s Odesa, Vladimir Jabotinsky was a welcome guest at Chukovsky's home. Jabotinsky's address book lists Chukovsky's address as no. 14 Novorybnaia Street. Police surveillance testifies that they often got together, walking through the streets of Odesa, dropping in on publishing houses. Jabotinsky also served as best man at Chukovsky's wedding ceremony and acted as his ad hoc attorney in an informal arbitration between friends.[28] When Jabotinsky was out of touch, Chukovsky complained in his diary, referring to his friend by one of his most well-known pen-names, "Альталены нету" (Altalena is not around).[29] While the relationship between the two friends has been discussed, most scholars, including Evgeniia Ivanova, have missed a curious aspect relevant to our discussion, the aspect of Ukrainian culture.[30]

According to family legacy, Chukovsky spoke fluent Ukrainian, his mother tongue. He knew by heart almost all of the "Енеїда" (Eneida) by Ivan Kotliarevs'kyi and "Кобзар" (Kobzar) by Taras Shevchenko and was well-read in Ukrainian classics, including Panteleimon Kulish. Chukovsky retained his knowledge of Ukrainian throughout his life, and half a century after leaving Odesa, he could still converse in that language.[31] The literary critic Miron Petrovsky, Chukovsky's literary secretary in the late 1950s and early 1960s and author of the first monographic study on Chukovsky, related that Chukovsky would recite Shevchenko's verse from memory, including "У тієї Катерини" (By that Kateryna), "Неофіти" (Neophytes), and "Марія" (Mary). Petrovsky explained that Chukovsky knew these poems "in the language of the original from his childhood, from his mother."[32]

---

28 See Natal'ia Panasenko, *Zhabotinskii v Odesse: literaturno-kraevedcheskii spravochnik* (Odessa: Astroprint, 2018), 32, 40, 46, 60, 65.
29 See Chukovsky, "Dnevnik (1901–1921)," *Sobranie sochinenii*, 9:109.
30 Contrary to Chukovsky's family memories, Evgenia Ivanova denies that the Ukrainian language was Chukovsky's native tongue, arguing that his mother was illiterate, and ignores the power of oral cultural traditions (Ivanova, *Chukovskii i Zhabotinskii*, 105–203).
31 See the 2016 conversation of Dmitrii Chukovsky, Kornei Chukovsky's grandson with Andrei Korolev and Elena Poliakovskaia, journalists at Radio Free Europe/Radio Liberty, May 4, 2021, https://www.svoboda.org/a/27560521.html, accessed December 4, 2022.
32 Chukovsky, "Shevchenko," edited and with a preface by Miron Petrovsky, *Raduga* 3 (1989): 121. See also Miron Petrovsky, *Kniga o Kornee Chukovskom* (Moscow: Sovetskii pisatel', 1966). On Miron Petrovsky, see Samuil Lur'e, "Ne plakat', ne smeiat'sia," afterword to *Knigi nashego detstva*, by Miron Petrovsky (St. Petersburg: Ivan Limbakh, 2006), 416–21; Stepan Zakharkin and Andrei Puchkov, eds., and Yulia Veretennikova, compiler, *Miron Petrovsky. Biobibliografiia* (Kiev [Kyiv]: Izdatel'skii dom A+C, 2007); Ol'ga Kanunnikova, "Khudozhnik i okrestnosti," *Novyi mir* no. 4 (2002): 175–79; Vadim Skuratovskii, "Vernost' sebe," *Toronto Slavic Quarterly* no. 40 (2012): 227–31.

This language shapes Chukovsky's literary image of Odesa, which speaks in his autobiographical novel with a strong Ukrainian accent. The owner of a clandestine casino uses the Ukrainian word *shukaet*, instead of the Russian *ishchet*, in his inquiry to the narrator. The history teacher calls a corrupt school director a *khabarnyk*, the Ukrainian word for *grifter*. A janitor in his Polish classmate's house speaks only Ukrainian. He witnesses physical violence in the family but refuses to call the police, saying "Батько лупцуе дытыну, щоб була розумнийше" (The father slaps his child so he will be smarter).[33] The narrator himself cracks Ukrainian words as if they were sunflower seeds, using *brekhnia* (lie) and *zhmenia* (handful), carefully glossing their meaning in parentheses. Chukovsky depicts Odesans who pepper their Russian speech with Ukrainian words and idioms, and even the narrator's slouched figure provokes street boys to nickname him *handrybatyi*, Ukrainian for hunchback.

Chukovsky introduces the figure of his mother under her Russified name Katerina Osipovna; like the central character in Taras Shevchenko's poem "Kateryna," she was also an abandoned Ukrainian woman. Chukovsky uses Shevchenko's word for a village beauty to portray his mother's features: *chernobrovaia*, Ukrainian for black-browed. She speaks "по-южному, певуче и мягко, наполовину по-украински, наполовину по-русски" (with a southern accent, mellowly and softly, half in Ukrainian, half in Russian). Among the dozens of Ukrainian words she uses, she calls a petty thief a *ledashcho* (Ukrainian for lazy-bones), because he does not really know how to steal. Chukovsky's elder sister Marusia corrects her every now and then, and she becomes so ashamed of her "прекрасной украинской речи" (beautiful Ukrainian tongue) that she prefers to keep silent in public. Unlike his purist sister, Chukovsky admired his mother's Ukrainian: "Но мне почему-то нравилось, когда вместо 'шея' она говорила 'шыя', вместо 'умойся' 'умыйся,' вместо 'грязный' 'замурзанный,' вместо 'воробей' 'горобец' (For some reason, I loved that instead of *sheia*, she pronounced the word neck as *shyia*, instead of *umoisia umyisia* (wash yourself), instead of *griaznyi zamurzanyi* (dirty), instead of *vorobei horobets'* (sparrow)."[34] These Ukrainian references strengthen the image of Chukovsky's blue-collar home, portrayed as the epitome of warmth and justice that sharply contrasts with the brutal world of class stratification, corruption, and chauvinism of Chukovsky's *gimnaziia*, the school from which he had been expelled.

While Shevchenko seems an obvious choice for a modern-day reader familiar with Shevchenko's canonization in post-1917 Ukraine, it was by no means

---

33 Chukovsky, *Serebrianyi gerb* (Moscow: Detskaia literatura, 1961), 89.
34 Chukovsky, *Serebrianyi gerb*, 37.

obvious late in the nineteenth and early in the twentieth century, particularly for Jabotinsky. Perhaps Jabotinsky's choice was prompted not only by his Ukrainian-minded teachers at the Richelieu Lyceum and his acquaintance with Chukovsky's Ukrainian household and literary preferences. In the early 1910s, Russian bureaucrats bent themselves backwards to shuffle the commemoration of the fiftieth anniversary of Shevchenko's death and the centennial of his birth. That suppression of Shevchenko's memory transformed the Ukrainian nineteenth-century poet and artist into a quintessential bard of the colonized and suppressed Ukrainian culture, its paradigmatic national symbol. An avid reader of the Russian and Ukrainian press, Jabotinsky could not have missed that symbolic moment when the empire used censorship and violence to suppress the voice of its most significant Slavic ethno-national minority.

For Jabotinsky, Chukovsky's home represented the quintessence of Ukrainian language and folklore. Busy with laundry or ironing, Katerina Osipovna would sing Ukrainian folk songs. Chukovsky increased the Ukrainian aspects, already prominent in his story, even more in the second version of his novel—something that literary scholars entirely overlooked. The 1938 version ends with the narrator acknowledging that he does not want to return to the school from which he had been expelled. At the end of the 1961 version, however, the narrator has his first essays finally published—in real life this happened because of Jabotinsky's intervention on Chukovsky's behalf—and begins earning enough money to allow his mother finally to quit her hard manual labor as a laundress. She turned to her favorite task—embroidering Ukrainian towels and shirts. Using the plural of *rushnyk*, Ukrainian for the Russian *polotentse* (towel), Chukovsky adds that his mother was a master in this art and that she freely invented "все новые сочетания линий и красок" (ever new combinations of lines and colors).[35]

Thanks to the Chukovskys, Vladimir Jabotinsky encountered the Ukrainian language, heard Shevchenko's poetry, and became familiar with Ukrainian folklore.[36] This discovery of a genuine island of Ukrainian culture, albeit suppressed, in the heart of the cosmopolitan city had long-lasting ramifications. In 1911, Jabotinsky and Chukovsky both wrote essays on Shevchenko commemorating the fiftieth anniversary of the Ukrainian poet's death in the midst of the draconian measures the Russian regime undertook to suppress any public

---

35 Ibid., 159.
36 Kleiner overlooked this aspect of Jabotinsky's early contacts with things Ukrainian in *From Nationalism to Universalism*.

commemorations of Shevchenko.[37] Each took a very different angle, chose a different genre, focused on different aspects of the Ukrainian poet's work, but both arrived at almost the same conclusion. Chukovsky wrote a lengthy piece of literary criticism, perhaps the first analysis of Shevchenko's poetics based on the frequency of certain keywords, major motifs, the structure and the function of images, and the reflection of the artistic universe in the language—all of which prefigured the methodological discoveries of the formalists, structuralists, and semioticians. No one has made this observation about Chukovsky's methodological innovations because Chukovsky wrote, as always, in his intensely emotional journalistic style rather than in dry scholarly prose.

For Chukovsky, Shevchenko the poet was the mouthpiece of Ukrainian folklore and the Ukrainian popular worldview. He finds almost nothing in Shevchenko's poetry about his long life in St. Petersburg or his urban experience. Chukovsky declares that Shevchenko speaks on behalf of the entire Ukrainian people and that his poetry is a folk song. Shevchenko feels empathy toward all who are oppressed and humiliated, starting with widows and orphans. His tenderness for the humiliated and oppressed is quasi-religious, bordering on prayer. Suffering turns people into saints. Shevchenko elevates a pregnant and abandoned woman to the level of a Christian martyr whom he comes to worship. This important Christological motif parallels the motif of rage—unbridled, irrational, and unstoppable. Chukovsky depicts Shevchenko as a poet who switches from pietistic love of an abandoned woman such as Kateryna to the bloodthirsty vengeance of a man such as Yarema, the central image of his long poem "Haidamaky." Shevchenko reconciles his opposite motifs through what Chukovsky identifies as Christian all-forgiveness. Here Shevchenko's prayer and curse are mitigated by his sermon of peace and mercy. Chukovsky concludes by saying that Shevchenko, for all his rebellion against God, is a deeply religious poet who is simultaneously "жрец и жертва своего народа" (a priest and the sacrifice of his people).[38] Thus, Chukovsky sets out to meticulously analyze Shevchenko's functional motifs and the semantics of his epithets and ends up presenting Shevchenko as a sui generis Ukrainian messiah.

In contrast to Chukovsky, Jabotinsky used Shevchenko as a springboard for a discussion of the Ukrainian ethnic minority and its place in the oppressive Russian Empire. He uses Shevchenko to make his own political statements

---

37 First published, Jabotinsky, "Urok iubilieia Shevchenki," *Odesskie novosti*, February 27, 1911; Jabotinsky Institute, F-1911/908/RU; Kornei Chukovskii, "Shevchenko," *Russkaia mysl'* 4 (1911): 86–101; 5 (1911): 99–110.
38 Chukovskii, *Sobranie sochinenii*, 9:426–451.

and give direction to Jewish diaspora nationalism. For Jabotinsky, Shevchenko is a "яркий симптом национально-культурной жизнеспособности украинства" (vivid symptom of the national-cultural vitality of what is Ukrainian). He quotes Shevchenko, of course, but only to differentiate Russian from Ukrainian and prove that Shevchenko was well aware of that unbridgeable divide. Jabotinsky moves from a discussion on Shevchenko to a discussion on Ukraine and Ukrainians. He focuses on the thirty-million-strong Ukrainian sea washing the Russian-speaking cities of the Ukrainian lands. He is interested in the rights of Ukrainians as an ethno-national minority, in the self-determination of Ukrainians, neglected for too long, and in Shevchenko's language as that of the Ukrainian national minority.[39] Shevchenko as a poet interested him very little. Instead, Jabotinsky evokes Shevchenko as proof of his own Zionist-centered anti-assimilationist program. To understand Shevchenko, Jabotinsky argues, is to understand that "нет и может быть единой культуры в стране, где живет сто и больше народов" (the country of more than a hundred peoples cannot have a unified culture).[40]

While Chukovsky writes as a literary scholar and Jabotinsky as a political journalist, they concur in their conclusions. Both declare that Shevchenko's greatness is that he is a national bard, not only a folkloric poet. Both underscore the importance of his verse in Ukrainian and both acknowledge that Shevchenko is bleak when he changes language and writes in Russian. Jabotinsky observes that "'общерусский' язык чуждался украинского поэта, и не склеилось у него ничего путного на этом языке" (the Russian language shunned the Ukrainian poet, and he produced nothing good in this language).[41] Chukovsky says practically the same thing: when Shevchenko wrote in Russian, his words turned dry and "вдохновение отлетало от него" (inspiration left him). As if concluding in Jabotinsky's voice, Chukovsky writes, "Гениальность есть явление национальное, и на эсперанто еще не творил ни один великий поэт" (Genius is a national phenomenon: no great poet has yet written in Esperanto).[42]

Curiously, Jabotinsky and Chukovsky share a European comparative framework: Jabotinsky discusses the Romanesco verse of Giuseppe Belli, Chukovsky the Scottish verse of Robert Burns. These poets sounded genuine in their own language or dialect, but lost their appeal by switching to the national language,

---

39 See Jabotinsky's views on the right of a national minority to autonomy, if not to self-determination, for example, in his speech in Whitechapel on April 27, 1936, in A330/41 ("Jabotinsky. Revisionists. Jewish Army. Jewish Dominion"), ll. 1–2.
40 Jabotinsky, *Fel'etony*, 241.
41 Ibid., 233.
42 Chukovsky, *Sobranie sochinenii*, 9: 451.

Italian and English respectively. These striking parallels between Jabotinsky and Chukovsky compelled Miron Petrovsky to suggest that "они писали эти свои статьи за одним столом" (they wrote their articles at the same desk).[43] And, one should add, sharing the same programmatic vision of the centrality of Ukrainian for Shevchenko and Shevchenko for a Ukrainian national revival.

The vindication of Ukraine

Jabotinsky penned his essay on Shevchenko while constantly on the move across the Russian Empire, lecturing and urging Jews to switch to the Hebrew language in schooling. Hebrew represented Jabotinsky's symbol of faith, his anti-assimilationist credo, and his program of forging a modern Jewish self.[44] At the same time, Jabotinsky was championing Ukrainian language and culture among his fellow Zionists. He expected that nationalist-minded Jews in East Europe would recognize that Ukrainians, like the Jews, were also a stateless minority marginalized and assimilated culturally into the Russian Empire. In his autobiography, Jabotinsky writes: "В сфере местной политики я требовал союза между меньшинствами, переговоров с украинцами и литовцами; . . . у меня было много друзей в среде украинской общественности . . . но остальные сионистские деятели относились к этим моим затеям с ленивой и нескрываемой насмешкой" (In the realm of local politics, I stood for the union of ethnic minorities and for negotiations with Lithuanians and Ukrainians; . . . I had many friends among Ukrainian public figures, but the other Zionists treated my initiatives with lazy and poorly concealed mockery).[45]

Jabotinsky conceptualized any national minority language as a tool for forging a people into a nation and as a trigger pushing the stateless nation toward statehood. Jabotinsky maintained that the path toward national liberation began by teaching a national minority language. For his brethren, this language had to be Hebrew, which connected Jews to their ancestors' land, not diaspora Yiddish.

---

43 Miron Petrovsky, "Kornei Chukovskii i Vladimir Zhabotinskii," presentation at the international conference "Jewish Culture, History, and Traditions," Odesa, November 29-December 3, 1994.

44 See Shlomo Haramati, "Halashon haivrit bamishnato shel Zeev Jabotinsky" [The Hebrew language in Zeev Jabotinsky's theory], *Leshonenu la'am* 32, nos. 3–5 [313–315] (1981): 67–152; Zoia Kopelman, "Zhabotinskii i ivrit," in *Zhabotinskii i Rossiia: sbornik trudov Mezhdunarodnoi konferentsii "Russian Jabotinsky: Jabotinsky and Russia"* (Stanford: Department of Slavic Languages and Literatures, Stanford University, 2013), 207–36.

45 Jabotinsky, *Povest'*, 97.

Jabotinsky wrote in his autobiography that in dozens of cities and towns he advocated for the adoption of Hebrew in Jewish schools: "древнееврейский язык – единственный язык обучения во всякой еврейской национальной школе в России" (the Hebrew language is the only language to be taught in Jewish national [minority] schools in Russia).[46] Teaching Hebrew was the only way to perpetuate ethno-national identity. Therefore, he defended Hebrew *and* Ukrainian, and he did so in his impeccable Russian, of which he was a master but not a devotee.

Jabotinsky defended Ukrainian language use against Russification with the same fervor with which he defended the use of Hebrew, focusing on both Ukrainian and Jewish enforced assimilation to imperial Russian culture and on the significance of their corresponding national languages.[47] Urging Jews to stand firm against Polonization and Russification, he drew a parallel in his public presentations and journalistic publications with the problems the Ukrainian movement faced. In his essay "Со стороны" (From the outside, 1910), Jabotinsky pondered the manipulation of Galician Ukrainians by the Poles and by the Russians. The former imposed Polish-language schooling and introduced inadequate deputy representation. The latter sponsored a pidgin-Russian-language newspaper published in Austrian Lemberg (Lviv) and deceived Galician Ukrainians with false mottos of pan-Slavic solidarity.[48]

In his essay "Отпор" (The act of resistance, 1913), Jabotinsky argued against the Russification trend among his fellow Jews and reminded them of the sad fact that Ukrainian intellectuals considered the Jews the main Russifiers of urban Ukraine.[49] Jabotinsky had a point, as the intelligentsia of ethno-national minorities in any imperial environment chose to acculturate into the imperial mainstream. Such acculturation promised protection, facilitated upward mobility, and gave a sense of security. Late in the nineteenth century, the Jewish and Ukrainian elites followed the same trend. Those individuals who did not were in the minority. Members of that minority among Ukrainians were ready to forgive their under-urbanized and semi-educated brethren who sought Russian acculturation; yet they could not forgive the urbanized, self-aware, and much better educated Jews who Russified themselves, deprecated their own ethnic

---

46 Ibid., 93–95.
47 On Jabotinsky's identification with the complaint of the Ukrainians against the Russifying role of the assimilated Jewish intelligentsia in Ukrainian cities, see Jabotinsky, "Pis'ma o natsional'nostiakh i oblastiakh," 113.
48 Jabotinsky, "So storony," *Odesskie novosti*, October 29, 1910.
49 Jabotinsky, "Otpor," *Razsvet* no. 11 (March 15, 1913); no. 12 (March 22, 1913); no. 14–15 (April 4, 1913).

roots, and neglected national values. In this regard, Jabotinsky was ready to take the Ukrainian side precisely because he, as well as Ukrainians, condemned the Russia-oriented assimilation trend among Jewish intelligentsia. Hence he argued in his oral interventions and published articles that not the diasporic Yiddish that ninety-seven percent of all Jews in the Russian Empire spoke but rather Hebrew was the only genuine national language of the Jews.[50] At almost the same time, he addressed the question of the Ukrainian language in schooling, often using the same line of argument, justifying the right of Ukrainians as the demographically second largest group in the empire to teach new generations in Ukrainian.[51]

Jabotinsky's audiences admired him as a superb speaker, yet his passionate political sermons fell on arid soil. Russian Zionist leaders shrugged their shoulders in response to Jabotinsky's exhortations regarding Ukrainians and their distinct language, whereas the prominent Jewish tycoons turned their backs on his requests for financial support of the Hebrew educational programs in Palestine. One of them was the Hebrew University, which now sounds like a normal Israeli university, for we have lost the groundbreaking significance of the word "Hebrew" and of the arduous battles over the suitable language of instruction for the young generations of students arriving in British Mandate Palestine.

In fact, Jabotinsky was fighting in the Russian Empire the same struggle that the visionary linguist Eliezer ben Yehuda (Eliezer Yitzhak Perlman, 1858–1922), the founding father of the modern Hebrew language, was fighting in Ottoman Palestine.[52] For Jabotinsky, it was obvious that Jews should speak Hebrew, which he had promoted from his earliest activities in the Zionist political arena. One can imagine Jabotinsky's dismay when, after receiving two hundred thousand francs from Bendersky, Kyiv's nouveau riche Jewish merchant, he found no support for the Hebrew University from the wealthy Kyiv capitalist Brodsky or from Vladimir Guenzburg of the famous St. Petersburg family of financial tycoons. When the funds were finally raised, however, and the discussion turned to the

---

50 See, for example, the report on Jabotinsky's presentation in *Odesskie novosti*, March 8 (21), 1911, and Jabotinsky, "Priezzhii," *Odesskie novosti*, December 23, 1911 (January 5, 1912), 3–4; quoted in Panasenko, *Zhabotinskii v Odesse*, 90, 100.
51 See, in particular, Jabotinsky, "Fal'sifikatsiia shkoly," *Fel'etony*, 206–17.
52 On the battles over the Hebrew language in Ottoman Palestine, see Eliezer Ben-Yehuda, *A Dream Come True*, trans. T. Muraoka, ed. George Mandel (Boulder: Westview Press, 1993); Galila Whitmarsh, *Eliezer Ben Yehuda and the Revival of Modern Hebrew: Language and Identity* (Saarbrücken: Lambert Academic Publishing, 2009); Arieh Saposnik, *Becoming Hebrew: The Creation of a Jewish National Culture in Ottoman Palestine* (New York: Oxford University Press, 2008); Ron Kuzar, *Hebrew and Zionism: A Discourse* (Berlin: De Gruyter, 2001).

pedagogical process at the new university, Jabotinsky went as far as to request that the authors of the first primers for future Hebrew University students use punctuation (most likely, he meant the *nikud* system of vowel pointing) to facilitate the entry of unprepared students into science courses.[53]

Jabotinsky's most important essays were structured on parallels between Jewish and Ukrainian issues and appeared from 1910 through 1913, the period which he considered the acme of his journalistic career.[54] At that time, Jabotinsky entered into a fierce polemical debate with Petr Struve (1870–1944), the doyen of the Russian liberals, who proved to be blatantly chauvinist in his treatment of Ukraine and Ukrainians.[55] A Russian democrat, an opponent of the regime, and a champion of Russian free journalism, Struve suggested that the Ukrainian people and Ukrainian language should dwell in their rural niche, but once they moved to the cities, they needed to acculturate into the all-equalizing civilization, which was without doubt Russian.[56]

Jabotinsky responded with several articles contra Struve, not only because he was a supporter of the Ukrainian cause, but also because he opposed the general and universal and championed the particular and specific. Enlightened universalism had enabled him to attend the Richelieu Lyceum and become a celebrity among Russian journalists, but he abhorred that imperial universalism for its scorn of minority cultures. In the case of his polemical exchange with Struve, his political philosophy translated into the key question of the *Sprachenfrage*, the question of the spoken language of a minority culture. There were various ways to conceptualize it, yet for Jabotinsky this minority language was only about dissolving in the imperial or promoting the ethno-national. Struve generously accepted what he called the Little Russian language (Ukrainian) and the Little Russian peoplehood (the Ukrainians) with the other peoples and languages of minor ethnicities into Russian civilization and its great Russian language. He was confident that the language of the Russian nation would elevate the minor ethnicities and make them part of the greater whole. The Ukrainian language was no more than a dialect for Struve, as for many other Russian liberals, and

---

53 "Correspondence on Palestinian Hebrew University and Research Institute" (April–May, 1914), 1 (Central Zionist Archives, Z3/1609).
54 Jabotinsky, *Povest'*, 92.
55 On Jabotinsky and Struve, see Andriewsky, "Medved' iz berlogi," 260–67; Brian J. Horowitz, *Vladimir Jabotinsky's Russian Years, 1900–1925* (Bloomington: Indiana University Press, 2020), 101–9; Kleiner, *Zhabotyns'kyi i ukrains'ke pytannia*, 92–136.
56 See P. B. Struve, "Obshcherusskaia kul'tura i ukrainskii partikuliarizm. Otvet Ukraintsu," *Russkaia mysl'* 1 (1912): 65–86.

the Ukrainian people just a subgroup within the big family of Slavs in which Russians were the leading civilized force.

In this debate, Jabotinsky adduced one example after another, apparently reinforcing Struve's viewpoint. He spoke of the ancient Greeks who used a pan-Hellenistic *koine*, although they spoke multiple local dialects; the Germans, who cherished their local parlances such as Plattdeutsch but accepted the all-German version of the language; and, finally, the Italians, whom Jabotinsky knew first hand and who used all sorts of dialects, including Sicilian, Neapolitan, and Venetian. No doubt, Giovanni Grasso, Giuseppe Belli, Carlo Goldoni, the literary giants of Italy wrote in their dialects, not in standardized Italian. Apparently, those from different geographic regions managed successfully to balance their attachment to the local parlances and their loyalty to the national tongue. They never resisted the imposed national language, accepting it as the language of education, jurisprudence, and politics.

Placing Struve's approach in the larger European sociolinguistic context, Jabotinsky then proceeded to explain why, in the case of Ukrainian, all those examples were irrelevant. All these cases worked perfectly well, he said, because the dwellers of Piedmont and the residents of Sicily, despite their sharp linguistic differences, still considered themselves part of the same Italian nation. With this logic, Jabotinsky maintains, one might observe that the ancient Greeks in Sparta or Ithaca and those in Corinth knew that they were Greeks, members of a larger peoplehood and parts of one distinct community. Do "Little Russians" (Ukrainians), however, wonders Jabotinsky, really consider themselves "частью единой общерусской нации" (a part of a unified Russian nation)?

Jabotinsky is clearly familiar here with some fundamental philosophical theories of nationalism. We know that Jabotinsky was very well read in different fields of the humanities. He was captivated by the relationship between a national minority and the state and was well versed in the literature on that subject, which he read in the original languages, including English, German, Italian, and French. Jabotinsky sympathized with Johann Caspar Bluntschli, a Swiss lawyer who advanced the formula that "every nation should become an autonomous province," referring to legal and cultural independence (*Unabhängigkeit*) of any ethno-national group in the world. Subsequently understood as "liberal nationalism," that formula fit well in Jabotinsky's vision of cosmopolitan endorsement of a plethora of ethno-national strivings. He studied the German economic historian Julius Neumann, who demonstrated the semantic complexities of the notions of "people" and "nation." Jabotinsky was familiar with the writings of Karl Renner (under the pen name Springer) in which he defended ethno-national autonomy. He also knew well Ernest Renan's famous essay, "What is a

Nation?" and followed Renan's conceptualization of a nation based on collective "moral consciousness."[57] However, Jabotinsky's familiarity with these and other scholars should not detract attention from one thinker omitted in the studies of Jabotinsky: Johann Gottfried Herder (1744–1803).

While the study of Jabotinsky in relation to Herder and nineteenth-century Herderians remains a scholarly desideratum, it is illuminating to trace direct parallels between Herder's and Jabotinsky's approaches to the national question. It goes without saying that Herder's ideas were appropriated by dozens of nationalist thinkers in the nineteenth century and Jabotinsky could borrow from Herder through multiple intermediaries, including those in Eastern Europe.[58] Both Herder and Jabotinsky represented stateless nations. Both were critics of the radical rationalism of enlightened thought. For both, the nation was a state of mind, the result of collective self-cognition that leads to a collective volition. One finds additional parallels in their treatment of what Herder called national groupings and what Jabotinsky placed in the framework of stateless nations—Czechs, Hungarians, Ukrainians, as well as Italians before Vittorio Emmanuel. Herder was convinced of the intrinsic value of such groupings, and Jabotinsky's essays on the Ukrainian question and stateless ethnic groups were built on his deeply ingrained belief in the absolute value of ethnonational singularities.

Jabotinsky seems to have adapted Herderian principles to intra-ethnic and minority-state conflicts. Herder argues against any coercing of minor groupings into a greater nation. Jabotinsky calls this coercion "assimilation" and presents it as a major threat to minority cultures, Jews and Ukrainians alike. Herder talks about the *Volksseele* and the *Geist des Volkes*, the spirit of the people that defines the uniqueness of an ethno-national group (the notion of the *Volksgeist* was coined later by Hegel, who drew heavily upon Herder).[59] For Herder, this spirit or soul is best manifested in the literature of a people, in its folk songs.

---

57 See the only extant chapter of Jabotinsky's lost dissertation, "Samoupravlenie natsional'nogo men'shinstva" (Self-rule of a minority), defended in Yaroslavl in 1913 (Jabotinsky Institute, f. 901/1913).

58 See Peter Drews, *Herder und die Slaven: Materialien zur Wirkungsgeschichte bis zur Mitte des 19. Jahrhunderts* (Munich: Sagner, 1990); Alexander Maxwell, "Herder, Kollár, and the Origins of Slavic Ethnography," *Traditiones* 40 (2) (2011): 79–95; Dušan Ljuboja, "Herder's Ideas and the Pan-Slavism: A Conceptual-Historical Approach," *Pro&Contra* 2, no. 2 (2018): 67–85.

59 See Dirk Hoerder, "Migration and Cultural Interaction across the Centuries: German History in a European Perspective," *German Politics and Society* 26, no. 2 [87] (2008): 5–6. See also Ofri Ilany, *In Search of the Hebrew People: Bible and Nation in the German Enlightenment* (Bloomington: Indiana University Press, 2018), 97.

He combined the "songs" of different peoples in his famous poetic anthology *Volkslieder* (Folk songs, 1778–1779) to convey the beauty of their *Volksseele*, national soul. Jabotinsky looks for what Herder calls the *Volksdichtung*, folk poetry, and finds it in Shevchenko, underscoring the poet's role as the spirit of Ukrainian peoplehood, its immediate cultural embodiment. Jabotinsky elevates Shevchenko to the status of a *Nationaldichter*, a national poet embodying the essence of folklore (as Chukovsky proved), whom Jabotinsky views as the most vivid manifestation of the Ukrainian national spirit, developing and applying a Herderian principle to a Slavic people. For Jabotinsky, this was particularly significant, as he first heard Shevchenko's lyrics performed as folk songs by Katerina Korneichukova, Chukovsky's mother.

Using Herder's enlightened principles that Herder himself did not necessarily apply consistently, Jabotinsky flatly rejected any attempt at forcing an ethno-national "soul" into the assimilationist process, declaring that forced assimilation of minor ethnicities into Russian language and culture was immoral and coercive. He could not envision any kind of cosmopolitanism without a strong ethno-national allegiance. For him, the one who despised one's own tradition could not be a cosmopolitan. Paradoxically, assimilation or Russification for Jabotinsky was a hindrance toward a true cosmopolitanism. When Struve condescendingly admitted that Jews, Georgians, and Lithuanians (but not Ukrainians) should develop their own cultures, Jabotinsky reacted with sharp sarcasm: oh, thank you very much; now all those minor entities (he used the colloquial metaphor "small fry") were free from the duty of Russification. Freedom for Jabotinsky was coterminous with ethnic minority cultural growth. Any attempt to curb this growth, he believed, was imperialist coercion, even if articulated by a liberal such as Struve. In answer to Struve, Jabotinsky argued that "one cannot tempt the soul" of the Ukrainians. By contrast, Ukrainians should be given every chance to create in this language, meaning Ukrainian, their own "всестороннюю и полноценную культуру" (comprehensive and rich culture), which should be taught "от детского сада до университета" (from kindergarten to university).[60] Here, too, Jabotinsky seems to be guided by Herderian admiration for the particular.

Struve was convinced a priori that Ukrainians and Russians were one nation and one culture, with some minor deviations, whereas Jabotinsky, following Herder's empiric approach, suggested checking to find out whether Ukrainians ("Little Russians" in Struve's words) really wanted to become "Great Russians."

---

60 Jabotinsky, "Struve i ukrainskii vopros," *Odesskie novosti*, March 2, 1912 (Jabotinsky Institute, f. 923/1912).

Here, Jabotinsky reveals his direct reliance on Herderian tradition. He underscores the national consciousness of a population as a key nation-making mechanism. Only this consciousness can differentiate a national minority dialect from a state-imposed language. One can analyze linguistic similarities ad libitum, but from Jabotinsky's perspective it is national consciousness that defines a people as part of the Russian people or a separate Ukrainian nation. Here, Jabotinsky is practically quoting Friedrich Carl von Savigny's concept of the *Volksbewusstsein* (consciousness of a people), which emerges directly from Herder's ideas of self-knowledge as one of the functions of the spirit of a people.[61]

Based on his reliance on the Herderian approach to minorities, Jabotinsky insisted on one principal difference between Jewish relations with Poles and the Jewish attitude toward Ukrainians. This bifurcation of his political and cultural alliances seems strange: Poles suffered from imposed imperial Russification in the Kingdom of Poland (under the Russian Empire). They had to kowtow to Vienna's agendas in Galicia, at that time under the Austrian Empire. They were also a stateless nation that rebelled several times against their imperial oppressors. They, of course, deserved sympathy, yet Jabotinsky sympathizes with the Ukrainian cause and not with the Polish one. Why? From the Poles, he demanded that which he found among the different nationalities in Odesa: "добрососедское сожительство" (friendly coexistence) based exclusively on mutual respect and the principle of equality. The Polish national parties were denying that equality to the Jews, whom they saw as legitimate citizens only if they became Poles of Mosaic persuasion, in other words, if they assimilated.

The relationship between Ukrainians and Jews was different. Jabotinsky argued that the Ukrainian nationalist parties did acknowledge the Jewish right to a Jewish national culture. Like us Zionists, he maintained, Ukrainians were protesting Jewish Russification, and they were not trying to assimilate Jews. Furthermore, Ukrainians celebrated any Jewish national endeavor; hence the leaders of the Ukrainian *irredenta* did not treat Jews as Poles did. Ukrainians, emphasized Jabotinsky, "по крайней мере, теперь смотрят на нас, как на равноценный народ" (at least now, they consider us an equally worthy people) and have been building their relations with the Jews "по крайней мере, теперьна почве добрососедского сожительства" (at least now, on the basis of friendly coexistence). In demanding that a nation respect the dignity of its national minorities, Jabotinsky further developed Bluntschli and repeated the same principle on which Herder established his imaginary *Nationalitätenstaat*,

---

61 See *Fel'etony*, 224.

multi-ethnic state: "или все народности имеют равное право на свою культуру, и национальное чувство каждой из них священно и неприкосновенно, или такого же права вовсе нет, и национальные чувства поляков столь же мало священны, как и чувства евреев" (either all peoples have equal rights for their own culture and their national feelings are sacred—or such rights do not exist at all and the national feelings of the Poles are as little sacred as the feelings of the Jews).[62] Hence, the Jews should establish political alliances with Ukrainian nationalist parties and disassociate themselves from Polish nationalists. Jabotinsky's response to subsequent events in Ukraine was the unfolding of that program.

Jabotinsky's passionate defense of the Ukrainian cause did not go unnoticed. Yevhen Chykalenko (1861–1929), one of the most significant sponsors of the Ukrainian cultural revival, left two important diary entries in this respect. On January 12, 1911, he wrote that V. E. Jabotinsky, a renowned Zionist journalist, came from Odesa to Kyiv seeking to come to agreement with the leaders of the Ukrainian press. Although we do not have Jabotinsky's speech at the Ukrainian Club, Chykalenko succinctly explains Jabotinsky's arguments. Ukrainians and Zionist Jews have common goals and common enemies. Both have to fight the Russifiers and the Polonizers. Both consider national minority education a key point of their agenda. Jabotinsky confirmed that he would compel major Jewish press venues in Yiddish and Hebrew to pay more attention to the Ukrainian movement and stop acting like agents of Russification. Three months later, on March 20, 1911, Chykalenko again mentioned Jabotinsky, promoting the publication of his articles in *Рада* (Council) and praising Jabotinsky's stand in defense of the Ukrainian language in schools against Struve.[63]

During the first fifteen years of his career as a journalist, the writer whom Chykalenko admired for his attention to Ukrainian issues was focused on the particular versus the general and on ethno-national versus imperial in almost all his essays, beginning with his first short sketches sent from Italy to Odesa. A specific gesture of an unusual custom or the accent of a linguistic alien would trigger his admiration. Likewise, within the Russian Empire, Jews and Ukrainians fascinated him not only because he was sympathetic to both but because they were so different. He cherished their particularities, fiercely defended their

---

62 Jabotinsky, "Otpor." On Herder and the multi-ethnic state, see Dominic Eggel, Andre Liebich, and Deborah Mancini-Griffoli, "Was Herder a Nationalist?" *The Review of Politics* 69, no. 1 (2007): 48–78.

63 Yevhen Chykalenko, *Shchodennyk, 1907–1917* (Kyiv: Tempora, 2011), 146, 170.

right of difference, and argued against those who sought to assimilate this difference through a cultural or political program into a general, faceless whole. Paradoxically, the more he admired the particularities of various stateless minorities, the more universalistic his program became and the more it was reminiscent of his multi-ethnic Odesa.

The image of Ukraine

Looking back at the Odesa of his youth in the 1930s as a celebrity Russian journalist and Revisionist Zionist leader, Jabotinsky portrayed seven peoples who contributed "кто свой гений, кто свой пот, чтобы создать эту жемчужину вселенной" (either their spirit or their sweat to this pearl of the universe), producing "до матерей родившееся дитя Лиги наций" (the premature baby of the League of Nations).[64] Perhaps his unwavering love for this "pearl of the universe" had something to do with the fact that all the languages of cosmopolitan Odesa were spoken with an accent that made the cultural profile of Odesa unique. The language of Odesans was cosmopolitan with an ethnic minority accent, a peculiar amalgam of the cosmopolitan and the national.

Odesa was not a linguistic mixture, but a cultural entity in and of itself. Among the nationalities instrumental in creating what Jabotinsky called the Odesan Tower of Babel were the Ukrainians. In Jabotinsky's words:

> . . . а Украина дала нам матросов на дубки, и каменщиков, и главное ту соль земную, тех столпов отчизны, тех истинных зодчих Одессы и всего юга, чьих эпигонов, даже в наши дни, волжанин Горький пришел искать и нашел настоящего полновесного человека . . . Очень длинная вышла фраза, но я имею в виду босяков.

> (. . . Ukraine gave us sailors for the ships, and masons, and, above all, that salt of the earth, those pillars of the fatherland, the true builders of Odessa and all of the south, for whose epigones, even in our day, Volga-region-born Gorky came to search—and

---

64 Jabotinsky, "Moia stolitsa," in his *Causeries. Pravda ob ostrove Tristan da Run'ia*, 2nd ed. (Paris: Tipografiia d'Art Voltaire, 1931), 76–77, 79.

found—what he considered the real men. . . . this sentence ended up very long, but what I'm referring to are the vagabonds.)[65]

A significant feature of Odesa's Ukrainians is their language. Yes, agrees Jabotinsky, Ukrainian is of Slavic origin, yet he rejects a common misunderstanding that it was just Russian, or corrupted Russian. He emphatically adds, "во-первых, не испорченный; во-вторых, не русский" (First, it is not spoiled and second, it is not Russian).[66] Twenty years after his defense of Ukrainian and after a failed Ukrainian statehood, Jabotinsky was fighting the same battle for the defeated people to whom the international community denied the status of a separate nation.

Scholars who have pointed out Jabotinsky's empathy toward the Odesan idiolect have missed that it was the Ukrainian part that made it so dear to him. As he insists in his "Трактат по филологии" (Treatise on philology), grammatically correct and morphologically pure Russian was for him a "cold," austere language that he termed *kazennyi*, a Russian word meaning "official," "false," and "non-genuine." Unlike Russian, the autochthonous Odesa language was the unkempt talk of plebeians, with whom he identified. It was a "warm" language, and the examples Jabotinsky provides are all from Ukrainian. He makes this point unequivocally by using the term *khokhlatskii* (a Russian derogatory word for Ukrainian) in a *positive* sense: "Хохлацкое придыхательное «г» это очаровательно; когда я слышу слово 'он говорит' с хохлацким 'г' с ударением посередке и с мягким знаком на конце, я чувствую себя растроганным" (the Ukrainian fricative sound "g" is charming; when I hear the word *on govorit* (he speaks) with the Ukrainian "g," with the emphasis on the middle syllable and a soft sound at the end (*hovóryt'*—Y. P. S), I am touched).[67]

Jabotinsky continued pondering Odesa's Ukrainian aspects in his prose writing as well as his journalism before and long after he left the Russian Empire. Ukrainian expressions appear in many of Jabotinsky's literary essays, primarily those linked to Odesa or its inhabitants. For example, in his "Акация" (Acacia), he uses "from whence" (*otkogda*, a literal translation of Ukrainian *vidkoly*) and says that a tree had a maddening smell, "как скаженная" (Ukrainian *skazhena*, literally "as crazed"). In "Белка" (Squirrel), he uses the Ukrainian word for watermelon (*kavun*). In "Описание Швейцарии" (Description of Switzerland),

---

65 Ibid., 78.
66 Ibid., 80.
67 Jabotinsky, "Traktat po filologii," *Odesskie novosti*, July 23, 1912 (Jabotinsky Institute, F-935/1912).

he uses the Ukrainian for "climb" (*piorla* from Ukrainian: *perty*).[68] Not only did he come to admire this Ukrainian phraseology suggesting that a "courageous" writer should use it in the future, but he also taught it! Jabotinsky related how in the early 1910s, three Odesan moms from middle-class families dispatched him with their children to the sea shore. Jabotinsky trained them to do all sorts of things their mothers considered forbidden. One of the key elements of Jabotinsky's pedagogy was language: "Я добиваюсь, чтоб язык их стал красочнее, лексический запас обогатился, фразеология стала гибче и звучнее" (I am striving to make their language more picturesque, their vocabulary richer, and their phraseology more flexible and resonant). What is this special language that transformed his wards into real men? Of course, it was the language filled with Ukrainian expressions and idioms (such as *khloptsy* for boys, *spoimaesh* for catching, *smet'ie*, literally, rubbish for pals).[69]

What he tried out in his sketches, Jabotinsky continued in his novels. During one of his prewar trips to Palestine, Jabotinsky visited one of the agricultural settlements, where he met a certain Avinoam, an Arabic-speaking Jewish teenager who became his guide and took him on a tour of an Arab village school. Avinoam was agile, strong, and fearless. It turns out that he was from the Russian Empire, where he learned how to defend himself verbally and physically. He learned this from the "locals," Russian-speaking boys who bullied Avinoam. Only someone who belongs to a genuine people knows how to curse in one's own language and hit back, insisted one of these locals as he beat Avinoam, who was unable at the time to defend himself.[70] Jabotinsky transposes Avinoam's situation into his novel *Самсон Назорей* (Samson the Nazarene), where Samson's buddies prove incapable of defending themselves in wrestling against the Philistines. It is more important for us here, however, that in his short sketch about Avinoam, Jabotinsky calls the resident villagers "locals" (*tuzemtsy*)—a word he uses at least seventy-five times in his novel *Samson the Nazarene* when discussing one of the large tribal groups participating in the inter-ethnic conflict. As Jabotinsky claims that his narrative is independent of both the Biblical corpus and archaeological discoveries, I will now read it as a parable, in which Ukrainians and Odesans emerge in a very counter-intuitive ancient biblical context.[71]

---

68 Jabotinsky, *Sochineniia v deviati tomakh* (Minsk: Met, 2007), 1:501, 504, 507, 546.
69 Altalena [Vladimir Jabotinsky], "Traktat po pedagogike," *Odesskie novosti*, July 8, 1912 (Jabotinsky Institute F-912/1912).
70 Jabotinsky, *Sochineniia*, 1:561–65.
71 Among other interpretations of the novel, see Svetlana Natkovich, "*Samson*, the Hebrew Novel: The History of the Writing and Reception of Jabotinsky's Novel and the Consolidation

The first of Jabotinsky's major players is the tribe of Dan, to which Samson belongs, from the town of Tsora and its environs. Samson's tribe apparently stands for the Jewish diaspora, although the action takes place in the Land of Israel in the era of the Book of Judges. As the sickly diasporic Jews in the fin-de-siècle Zionist thought, the people of Tsora are physically weak, poor, and envious of their more affluent and better organized brethren from other tribes. They work hard on their arid land. Describing their dwellings and customs, Jabotinsky wittily juxtaposes what he takes from the Midrash and the Bible about ancient settlements in the Land of Israel with what he knows personally about the wretched small towns of the Pale of Settlement. In a word, Tsora is a shtetl, and its inhabitants, the Danites, are pre-Zionist East European Jews before their self-discovery as a national entity. Jabotinsky turns the biblical Tsor (Tyre), masculine in Russian, into the feminine Tsora, most likely to stress its concurrence with the Yiddish word *tsores*, misery.

The second obvious realm in *Samson* is the biblical Timna, the kingdom of joy and gaiety, which Jabotinsky transforms into the philistine Timnata with the help of the suffix -*ta*, which can be either Aramaic or Slavic or both. Timnata is strikingly reminiscent of the Slavic word *temnota*, darkness. Precisely this darkness, however, attracts Samson, who says that "Там я бодрствую"—I am awake there, in Tsora, but in Timnata, "я вижу сны" (I see my dreams). At night, Timnata provides Samson with what he loves most—excessive libations and gluttony, available women and exotic eroticism, music and dances, riddle-solving and sports competitions, impersonations and off-color jokes, endless caresses and wild sex, dressing up, gambling, and cheating. Everything that his short-lived father-in-law called the sense of love and death as a game. "Игорный дом Филистия" (Philistia is a casino), wrote Jabotinsky, "входи, кому любо" (anybody could enter).[72]

The cosmopolitan and welcoming Timnata is the opposite of the nationalist Tsora; yet it also exemplifies a type of urban culture that Jabotinsky rejects. Timnata turns everything into a game, sometimes light-hearted, sometimes dangerous. Here Samson treats his oaths as a Nazir as a joke, his loyalty to his tribe as a laughing matter, and everything becomes a toy, with which to play. Timnata turns its dwellers and guests into actors and gamblers. Samson calls all of Philistia "государство красивых пиявок" (a country of beautiful leeches).

---

of the Norms of Realism in Hebrew Literature," *Jewish Quarterly Review* 110, no.4 (2020): 733–755.

72 Jabotinsky, *Piatero. Samson Nazorei. Romany* (Odessa: Optimum, 2010), 288.

Work here was not even considered infamous. Everyone was a gambler: "Бедных было много, особенно разоряла их игра: обедневшие кормились подачками вельмож, или опять игрой в кости, или уходили в Египет, или кидались на меч: мысль о труде руками не могла им придти в голову, как мысль о ходьбе на руках вместо ног" (There were many poor people; gambling particularly ruined them: the poor ate a pittance from the tables of the nobility or returned to a game of dice, or else left for Egypt, or threw themselves against a sword. The thought of physical labor could not enter their heads, because for them, it was tantamount to walking on their hands).[73] Timnata wooed Samson and enchanted him with its irresistible gaming attitude toward life.[74] And all this happens under the cover of the darkness of night in Timnata (*temnota*).

The three-syllable Timnata distinctly resembles the three-syllable Odesa, which Jabotinsky loved as Samson loves Timnata: a town of joy, playfulness, and gaiety.[75] However, Timnata is *Jabotinsky's* Odesa, not necessarily the real one. In his novel Пятеро (*The Five*), Odesa is also about the interplay of eroticism and merriment, hoax and fun, playing and performing. Like Samson, Sergei Milgrom, one of "the five," plays games of chance and gambles with his own life and that of his family, close friends, and acquaintances. Marusia, the central female character in *The Five*, plays the role of the lover of a Russian captain; the narrator plays her loyal page, and her sister, Lika Milgrom, performs the role of a married high-society lady spying on her husband, an undercover secret police agent, for the socialist underground. Jabotinsky also called Samson "великий игрок перед Господом, и притом одаренный исключительной фантазией" (a great *gambler* before God, also granted with an exceptional imagination [my emphasis]).[76]

All these performances, in the Timnata of *Samson* and in the Odesa of *The Five*, end badly. One of Odesa's most talented performers, Lika is the double of Elinoar/Dalila from Timnata. Both are consumed by jealousy, both fanatically bent on self-destruction in the pursuit of their goals, both ready to play the dirtiest tricks, both are treacherous and viciously merciless. Of course, both change their names: Elinoar becomes Dalila, which among other things means "diluted" in Hebrew. Lika turns into Madeleine de la Pervenche (*Madlen Lapervansh*)—in French a *pervenche* also means a person working for the police. The two female

---

[73] Jabotinsky, *Samson Nazorei*, 311.
[74] In this connection, see Uri Haitner, "Hamiskhak batfisato hakalkalit vehakhevratit shel zhabotinsky" [Play in Jabotinsky's social and economic thinking], *Haumah* 160 (2005): 35–39.
[75] See Jabotinsky, *Sobranie sochinenii*, 1:576–77.
[76] Jabotinsky, *Samson Nazorei*, 181.

characters unite Odesa and Timnata by bringing eroticism, charm, and games of chance to their self-defeating extreme. Perhaps, both the characters of Lika Milgrom and Dalila date back to Jabotinsky's early poem on Charlotte Corday, who killed the person with whom she lived to compensate for her ordinary life as a place-holder, as did both Lika Milgrom and Dalila.

In addition to the wretched inhabitants of the shtetl-esque Tsora, and the bourgeois dwellers of the Odesa-esque Timnata, there is a third group constantly present in the novel: the "locals" (*tuzemtsy*). They had been free people in the past, but now they were enslaved. They were beaten, treated as slaves, and their daughters became concubines of Judaic tribes and Philistines. They did not have their own towns but lived instead on the outskirts of Jewish or Philistine towns and villages. They often rebelled against their oppressors, the Philistines, although their rebellions were brutally suppressed. They appeared at every public event, though they remained in the background. Rebellious and unruly, they were physically strong rural workers, socially and culturally lower than the other dwellers of the land of Canaan. Elinoar suffers, among other things, because unlike her sister, whom Samson adores, she originates from the "locals." If Timnata is the corrupt Russian port of Odesa and the tribe of Dan represents the shtetl Jews, then the locals, whom Jabotinsky always treats with empathy, are the Ukrainians, rebellious and oppressed.

The locals seem transposed directly from Bol'shaia Lepetikha to the Middle East. In the novel, they are culturally and politically very close to the tribe of Dan, the Jews. The conquerors—the Philistines—mock the tribe of Dan because they live in the same type of huts as the locals, dress like them, and speak like them. The tribe of Dan learns from the locals how to plow the land. Both the Dan tribe and the locals oppose Philistia. Humiliated and enslaved, the locals identify with the Danites during sports competitions, angering their masters, the Philistines.

The 1906 short-lived political alliance of Ukrainians and Jews in Galicia, which Jabotinsky welcomed on a number of occasions, is represented in the eventually failed political alliance between Samson and the locals. Even before Samson starts planning a joint rebellion and entices his brethren to coopt the locals, Jabotinsky mentions that Samson is supported by the locals in many different ways. They come to Samson in his capacity as a judge: they admire, accept, and respect his decisions. Samson is omnipresent, omniscient, and omnipotent because all locals are his messengers on errands for him. They never betray him and are ready to be flogged and tortured for his sake. They hide him when he is running from the Philistinian soldiers; they love and adore him to the extent that they make idols for themselves with seven horns, imitating Samson's seven braids.[77] To emphasize their extraordinary role in the life of Samson, Jabotinsky makes one of the locals a loyal servant of Manoi, Samson's father, and avenger of the honor of Samson's mother. The same local provides shelter to the blinded Samson when he is taken into Philistinian bondage. Perhaps Jabotinsky was representing his own assiduous attempts to reconcile Ukrainians and Jews in Samson's friendly relations with and support of the locals. With the same ardor and the same result, as we have seen, Jabotinsky tried to convince his Zionist colleagues of the urgent necessity of enlisting the help of the oppressed locals, the Ukrainians.

Jabotinsky takes this anti-imperialist battle into some of his short stories and novels, where Ukraine appears in disguise, although it is not unrecognizable. Not only *Samson*, but also *The Five* are the most obvious examples. Most scholars have ignored their Ukrainian aspects, not only because of unsatisfactory English translations, but also because of the established perception of Jabotinsky's fictional works.[78] If it is taken for a given that he was an ardent Zionist and vociferous critic of Jewish assimilation, his novel about Odesa's Russian Jewish bourgeoisie, if anything, must be a treatise connecting the Russian and the Jewish, a drama of things Russian Jewish, and a tragedy of those seeking to merge the Jewish and the Russian. Although this is one of the main themes of the novel, Jabotinsky's portrayal of fin-de-siècle Odesa is much more complex and captivating. After all, the narrator confesses at the beginning of the novel that linguistics is his hobbyhorse.[79] It is not surprising, therefore, that Jabotinsky reconstructs the urban idiolect of Odesa's cosmopolitanism in the novel, although his observations are not as straightforward as his obvious intent to portray the futility of Russian-Jewish assimilation.

It is Odesa's Ukrainian linguistic substratum with its pronunciation, vocabulary, and phraseology (more than the Yiddish one) that helps Jabotinsky humanize or de-humanize his characters. The exceptionally talented Sergei Milgrom, a bon vivant, musician, jack-of-all-trades, the embodiment of laughter and joy, turns by the end of the novel into a jaded cynic. He blackmails and extorts

---

77 The locals' idolizing of Samson was taken from Hebrew translations of the novel; see Piotr Kriksunov, "Tainy Samsona Nazoreia: Razmyshleniia nad perevodom *Samsona Nazoreia* Zhabotinskogo," in *Zhabotinskii i Rossiia: sbornik trudov Mezhdunarodnoi konferentsii "Russian Jabotinsky: Jabotinsky and Russia"* (Stanford: Department of Slavic Languages and Literatures, Stanford University, 2013), 194–95.

78 Translations from Jabotinsky's novel *The Five* are my own; for a different English version, see *The Five: A Novel of Jewish Life in Turn-of-the-Century Odessa*, trans. Michael R. Katz (Ithaca, NY: Cornell University Press, 2005).

79 See Altalena [Vladimir Jabotinsky], *Piatero* (New York: Rausen Broth & Jabotinsky Foundation Inc., 1947), 12.

money from family friends, corrupts a married woman and her daughter, and becomes their gigolo. At the beginning of the story, however, Jabotinsky presents him in a different light, through his specific mode of expression peppered with Ukrainian idioms. He uses the words *bosiavka* (a contaminated Ukrainian metaphor for barefoot poor and a shrimp), *kavuny* (Ukrainian for watermelons), *tudy* (Ukrainian: there), *storchat* (Ukrainian: for sticking out). Sergei closely observes the card players, *k khloptsam prismatrivaius'* (Ukrainian for watching the fellas). He himself is very agile, *kudy lovchee* (Ukrainian for far more nimble), ready to leave his parents in peace so that they can rest, *nekhai otdokhnut* (let them have a rest).[80] All these words—*khloptsy, kudy, nekhai*—are Ukrainian. They make Sergei's speech much more earthy, warm, and humane than the lofty and bombastic talk of other characters. To depict Sergei's downfall, his story is told by an assimilated, baptized Jewish lawyer, who speaks straight, distilled Russian, with no trace of an accent.

The story of the janitor Khoma (Ukrainian for Foma) replicates Sergei Milgrom's linguistic transformation, yet the character moves up, not down. From Kherson province and a first-generation urban dweller, this black-bearded *muzhik* speaks predominantly Ukrainian. Whatever he is doing or planning to do—opening the gates, checking the chimney—he explains in his pure Ukrainian with a minor Russian accent (*odchynial fortku, pobachyt' chy truba ne dymyt'*). When he tries to change to Russian to sound more convincing, even then he uses Ukrainian exhortations rather than Russian rebukes (*dlia zdorov'ia shkoda*).[81] Yet the moment the tsarist police engage Khoma to help suppress socialist demonstrations along with dozens of other Odesa janitors, he feels himself an important cog in the bureaucratic wheel and switches to Russian. He observes that the postman is delivering suspicious mail to the narrator's house and asks with a sense of reproach, if not political accusation: "Заграничные газеты получаете?" (You are getting foreign newspapers, aren't you?). For Jabotinsky, the switch from Ukrainian to Russian is not only a sign of moving up and collaborating with the regime, but also of abandoning one's Ukrainian identity. Khoma's next step is using physical violence against peacefully protesting students and perhaps joining the Black Hundreds. Jabotinsky implies this direction merely by giving a new turn to Khoma's mode of expression, using Ukrainian linguistic nuances as one of the key markers of a person's social path.

---

80 Jabotinsky, *Piatero*, 12, 14, 15, 74, 75.
81 Ibid., 47–48.

In order to portray the ordinary people of Odesa with warmth and empathy, Jabotinsky has them speak Ukrainian. The housemaid Gapa finds herself listening to a lecture on Zionism, after which the landlady asks her, "So, Gapa, did you like it?" The housemaid answers in Ukrainian, which makes her reply seem folkish, honest, naïve beyond measure yet utterly precise: "що ж, барыня, треба йихати до Палестыны!" (Oof, madam, we ought to move to Palestine!).[82] In Petersburg, the good-for-nothing Marko meets a prostitute named Valentina Kukuruza, from Odesa. He gives her shelter, becomes her protector, and helps her abandon sex work. The semi-literate Valentina has something Marko entirely lacks, common sense. Jabotinsky enriches her speech with Ukrainian colloquialisms such as *pahanyi* (Ukrainian for bad), *nikudy* (Ukrainian for nowhere), *tuiu luzhu* (the first word is Ukrainian for that).[83] She swears, using the Ukrainian emphatic word (*bohato*, literally rich) that she will be very rude, trying to make Marko abandon his crazy idea of volunteering for the Russo-Japanese front.

Ultimately, Ukrainian language envelops Marusia, the most sympathetic character in the novel, whom Jabotinsky emphatically named after Marusia, Kornei Chukovsky's sister. She is the only one who marries within the Jewish flock. Before she dies a tragic death, Jabotinsky introduces the voice of her son, who speaks pure Ukrainian, and to make his speech more amusing and poignant, the child uses feminine verb endings: "Бачь, мамо, я пришла!" (look, mom, I have come); "Бачь, мамо я видчыныла!" (look, Mom, I have opened), as if the child hears his mother, but never a male, speaking Ukrainian.[84]

Of course, these Ukrainian linguo-stylistic aspects of Jabotinsky's prose do not contradict the reading of *Samson* as a clash between the Zionist Jews and the British in Mandate Palestine and the conceptualization of *The Five* as a quintessential Silver Age novel about the disintegration of the Russian Jewish bourgeoisie.[85] It will be a very different task subsequently to integrate the Ukrainian elements of Jabotinsky within a broader sociopolitical conceptualization of his literary output.

---

82 Ibid., 45.
83 Ibid., 111.
84 Ibid., 165, 167, 172.
85 For the alternative geopolitical contexts of Jabotinsky's *Samson*, see Rafael Tsirkin-Sadan, "Imperiya, leumiyut, vayakhasei mizrakh uma'arav baroman 'shimshon' meet vladimir (zeev) zhabotinsky" [Empire, nationalism, and East-West relations in Vladimir (Zeev) Jabotinsky's novel *Samson*], *Teoriya uvikoret: bamah yisraelit* 48 (2017): 81–104; Elina Vasil'ieva, "Prostranstvo v romane Zhabotinskogo 'Samson Nazorei,'" *Filologicheskie chteniia* (2002): 59–68; see also Patricia Herlihy, *Odessa Recollected: The Port and the People* (Boston: Academic Studies Press, 2018), 91.

Conclusion

While the genesis and function of "Ukrainian discourse" in Jabotinsky's writings requires further research, several preliminary conclusions are in order. Whatever the network of Jabotinsky's later contacts with Ukraine and Ukrainians, his first encounters with Ukrainian culture, works of Ukrainian literature ranging from Taras Shevchenko to Mykhailo Hrushevs'kyi, and activists in the Ukrainian revivalist movement date back to his Odesa years. As Jabotinsky's Ukrainian discourse is of Odesan origin, we may, therefore, speak of the Ukrainian Odes(s)a of Jabotinsky.

Jabotinsky turned to the discussion of Ukrainian language, ethnography, history, and culture in order to broaden his understanding of the Russified, marginalized, and humiliated Jewish minority in the Russian Empire. His writings about the Ukrainian question were groundbreaking for two reasons: first, because very few if any leading Jewish journalists were concerned with the predicament of the Ukrainians, and second, because Jabotinsky consistently used Ukrainians as a foil for Jews, Ukrainian language for Hebrew, the Ukrainian national revival for Jewish Diaspora nationalism. He established the parallelism of Ukrainian and Jewish destinies in the imperial framework on a solid philosophical basis. He seems to have drawn from a set of ideas, concepts, and methodology advanced by Johann Gottfried Herder and multiple Herderian followers of the late nineteenth century.

By stepping outside his self-imposed framework of stalwart Jewish nationalism and identifying with the Ukrainian cause, Jabotinsky transformed the meaning of cosmopolitanism, which Chukovsky associated with "застой культурного творчества" (the stagnation of cultural creativity) and Jabotinsky with the basic duties of a Russian subject, which he called a "лояльный космополитизм" (loyal cosmopolitanism).[86] Both Chukovsky and Jabotinsky rejected cosmopolitanism, the former for the sake of literary creativity, the latter for the sake of nationalist praxis. Yet, in a way, both used precisely the Odesa all-transcending cosmopolitan orientation, which eventually drew Chukovsky toward literature as a means of educating children and teenagers, and Jabotinsky toward his vision of nationalism as a means of emancipating ethnic minorities.

Although Jabotinsky left his beloved Odesa in the mid-1910s, Ukrainian references, like Odesa itself, did not disappear from his writings. Ukrainian themes

---

86 Chukovskii, "Dva slova o kosmopolitizme i natsionalizme. Iz pis'ma k odnomu antisionistu," *Iuzhnye zapiski*, no. 17 (May 16, 1903): 701–703; reprinted in *Chukovskii i Zhabotinskii*; Jabotinsky, *Fel'etony*, 66.

were diffused yet palpable in at least two of his novels, and Ukrainian ethnolinguistic references helped Jabotinsky shape and ethnically mark his images. Although *Samson* was based on the book of Judges and *The Five* on Jabotinsky's Odesa experiences, both novels reflect diasporic conflicts rather than the Land of Israel. The closer Samson, as a Jewish national leader, stood to the locals, the Ukrainians, the greater were his chances of winning. Likewise, the farther Jabotinsky's characters in *The Five* drifted from their Jewish roots, the sparser the Ukrainian elements in their speech. As in *Samson*, in *The Five*, too, the Ukrainian references humanize and, quite paradoxically, Judaize some of the characters. In one of his essays, Jabotinsky confessed what had long become common knowledge: "Как пламенный патриот своего родного города, я всюду ищу что-нибудь, напоминающее Одессу" (As an ardent patriot of my native city, I look everywhere for something that reminds me of Odesa).[87] As surprising as it may seem, some of the things that reminded Jabotinsky of Odesa were the Ukrainian language and culture. We have only just begun to understand what the fin-de-siècle port city of Odesa was all about.

---

87 Jabotinsky, "Egal'," *Sochineniia v deviati tomakh*, 2:83.

CHAPTER 3

Merchants, Clerks, and Intellectuals: The Social Underpinnings of the Emergence of Modern Jewish Culture in Late Nineteenth-Century Odesa

---

Svetlana Natkovich

Introduction

In 1894, Mendele Moykher Sforim (Sholem Yankev Abramovich, 1835–1917) published a long story in Hebrew entitled "Biymei hara'ash" (In days of tumult), which satirically portrayed a Palestinophilic or proto-Zionist milieu in late nineteenth-century Odesa. In one of the episodes in this story, Mendele depicts an encounter between two destitute provincial Jews—who dream of emigrating to the Land of Israel—with a petty Jewish Odesan wheeler-dealer. The impoverished friends, Mendele's eponymous narrator and a clueless Torah teacher (*melamed*) named Leib, are mistakenly identified by the local grain broker as provincial grain merchants. Flattered by this misconception and unwilling to reveal their true objectives, the two friends convince the broker that they might do business with him and, under that false pretext, use his services to lead them to the offices of the Odesa Committee of Hibbat Tsion (The Lovers of Zion), the whereabouts of which they do not know. "You are smart, reb Khaikel,"—thinks Mendele the Book Peddler of the broker—"and you want to know every secret of your colleague, but Mendele is smarter than you, he will make you his slave and, like a beast of burden, you will carry his troubles and loads."[1]

Although all the participants in this episode—Mendele and Leib, as representatives of the proto-Zionist forces in Odesa, and Khaikel the broker, as a representative of Odesa's business world—are portrayed as marginal, failing, and deluded characters, I propose interpreting the satiric encounter between them as emblematic of a broader interaction between Jewish intellectuals and the Jewish commercial world in Odesa. Each group perceived the other as a facilitator of its own vision for the future of the Jewish community. But willingly or unwillingly, certain factions in the Odesan business world not only sponsored the activities of Jewish intellectuals materially but also provided a conceptual infrastructure for the development of a modern national imagination.

When we speak about cosmopolitanism, we often presuppose the internal cohesiveness of the community that participates in cultural interactions. In this chapter, I shall try to shed light on the internal fragmentation among different groups of Jewish commercial and intellectual elites in the city and to pinpoint the dynamics of their relationships—from isolation and disinterest to various modes of cooperation. Rather than speaking of identities as a fixture, I would like to present my actors in situational terms, as existing in an intersection of various fields of belonging and skipping between various positions. Nira Yuval-Davis claims that "although discourses of race, gender, class, etc. have their own ontological bases which cannot be reduced down to each other, there is no separate concrete meaning of any facet of these social categories, as they are mutually constitutive in any concrete historical moment."[2] Although the creators of Jewish literary and political culture in Odesa shared their gender (male) and ethnic identities, their different social backgrounds often made them steer toward different cultural positions. The core of this chapter deals with intra-Jewish relationships, but it also sheds light on the different forms of interrelation with the surrounding cultures—local Odesan, Russian imperial, and broader international ones. The terminology of multiple belongings and their intersection is more effective in this case than operating with the term "cosmopolitanism." That term presupposes opposition with non-cosmopolitanisms—whether in the form of national ideology and culture or other formations of cohesive groupness. Here I will speak about multiple forms of identification that deconstruct Jewish group-formation along social lines and present different forms of cooperation or belonging to non-Jewish cultures. Working in the framework

---

1 Mendele Moykher Sforim, "Biymei hara'ash," *Pardes* 2 (1894): 38–39.
2 Nira Yuval-Davis, *The Politics of Belonging: Intersectional Contestations* (London: Sage, 2011), 7.

of Pierre Bourdieu's cultural production paradigm, I concentrate on different positions that various actors of Jewish social and cultural fields in Odesa occupied across time and the external circumstances and dispositions that brought them to specific places in these fields.[3] While some of these actors were oriented toward Russian or European cultures, the convergence of two specific groups starting with the late 1880s enabled the creation of an Odesan Jewish national subculture that introduced the opposition "cosmopolitan" versus "national" in a Jewish context and whose influence on the development of modern Jewish nationalism extended far beyond the borders of Odesa. My approach enables me to discuss various forms of belonging as questions of contingency and social circumstances rather than stable notions.

This chapter deals with educated and literate leading figures in Odesan Jewish society—not because I consider that the lower and illiterate classes did not participate in the creation of Odesan Jewish culture but because an understanding of the latter type of participation demands a different methodological approach.[4] Steven Zipperstein was among the first to speak about Jewish modernity in Odesa through the "nexus of economics and acculturation."[5] He presented, however, three main types of actors in Jewish modernization there—businessmen, salesclerks, and intellectuals [maskilim]—as distinct groups, each with its own narrative about modernization, institutions, and sensitivities. Proceeding from Zipperstein, I would like to single out various groups within the Odesan intellectual and commercial elites, outlining the connections between the social backgrounds, ideologies, aesthetics, and dispositions of each one with regard to the others.

In the first three parts of this chapter, I will delineate various groups among Odesa's Jewish elites and suggest a sociohistorical explanation of their complex interrelationships. The fourth part will characterize "the habits of the Odesan mind" associated with Odesan forms of commerce and their possible influences on Odesan literary idioms and ideological initiatives developed in the city. One of my central objectives is to discuss the difference between the members of the Jewish commercial elites in Odesa who cooperated with the Jewish intellectuals and those who chose to ignore them. After profiling the rich or affluent

---

3   Pierre Bourdieu, *The Field of Cultural Production*, ed. Randal Johnson (Cambridge: Polity Press, 1993), 61–67.
4   On the methodological aspects of research on subaltern populations, see Ilya Gerasimov, *Plebeian Modernity* (Rochester, NY: University of Rochester Press, 2018), 4–12, 18–54.
5   Steven Zipperstein, *Imagining Russian Jewry: Memory, History, Identity* (Seattle: University of Washington Press, 1999), 67; Zipperstein, *The Jews of Odessa: A Cultural History, 1794–1881* (Stanford: Stanford University Press, 1985).

supporters of Jewish intellectual initiatives in the city, I will return to Mendele's story "In Days of Tumult"; I will interpret the comical connection it presented between the commercial sphere and the Palestinophilic imagination as Mendele's commentary on the influence of Odesan forms of commerce on the new poetic and political language of Odesa's cultural elites.

Four circles of Jewish elites in Odesa and their mutual disposition (1860s–1890s)

Zipperstein has discussed the relationship between the Jewish commercial elites in Odesa and its maskilic newcomers in terms of the center and margins of Odesan society, presupposing a relationship inside a circular domain, rather than in binary opposition.[6] I would like to complicate this picture and to schematize the Jewish social milieu of Odesa as a series of concentric circles. In the center of this construction stand powerful large-scale grain merchants, whose trade was at the hub of the socioeconomic and political life of the city. The large majority of these merchants, such as the Rafalovich or Ephrussi families, rose to prominence in the 1830s and amassed substantial capital towards the end of the century. In their most prosperous periods, their annual commercial turnover often exceeded tens of millions of rubles.[7] Surrounding them, in the second circle, was a cadre of smaller business owners, many of whom attained prominence only towards the last third of the nineteenth century. Representatives of this group often grew in stature as senior assistants in the larger businesses or started as merchants of the second guild but, over time, established their own commercial institutions and became independent and successful players in the business world of Odesa. Around them, in the third circle, were representatives of the peripheral professions, who provided services to the merchants—such as lawyers, accountants, notaries, managers, clerks, and doctors. And the maskilim, as in Zipperstein's schema, were on the margins of this system, in the outer circle, working as teachers, journalists, and petty officials in philanthropic organizations, constantly dependent on those located in the three inner rings. They perceived themselves as 'elites' when, in fact, they were among the weakest groups in Odesan Jewish society. In Mendele's *Fishke der krumer* (Fishke the lame, 1888), a *maskilic* author, seeking funds for his book, is explicitly compared

---

6   Zipperstein, *Imagining Russian Jewry*, 79.
7   Vladimir Morozan, "Krupneishie torgovo-bankirskie doma Odessy XIX veka," *Ekonomicheskaia istoria. Ezhegodnik* 9 (2007): 164–69, 177–81.

to a beggar who goes from door to door of the rich Odesans to collect his pennies and is considerably more successful than an aspiring author.[8] The antidote of the maskilim in the 1860s and 1870s against the poison of powerlessness was to perceive other groups as being essentially flawed, lacking both Jewish culture and true European education.

Moshe Leib Lilienblum (1843–1910) described his encounter with the new generation of Jewish businessmen in Odesa in his seminal 1876 autobiography *Khatot ne'urim* (The sins of youth):

> I was hoping to find bread and relief [in Odesa], but there was no bread and no relief! . . . I begged for relief in a city without any Jewish literature, . . . in a place where isolation and loneliness reign unchallenged: the *hasid* continues his fanatical ways, the merchant accumulates his capital, and thousands of charlatans live immoral lives, lives without any national sentiment, life without any moral unity between two people—in this city you won't find relief for a person like me, so where then can I look for relief?[9]

Lilienblum began his attempts to sustain himself in Odesa in the offices of the local branch of the Society for the Promotion of Enlightenment among the Jews of Russia (OPE) and of the maskilic rabbi, Simeon Leon (Arie) Schwabacher (1820–1888). While OPE paid him a lump sum of twenty-five rubles, from Schwabacher he received only futile advice.[10] In order to make their living in Odesa, Lilienblum and other maskilim had to rely on the informal network of their peers and acquaintances to find lodging, lessons, positions, and funding opportunities.[11] Indeed, Odesa's prosperous Jewish merchants were contributing to philanthropic causes, but they simply chose to donate to other ones.

The most prosperous Odesan Jews chose to contribute to general, rather than specifically Jewish, causes. The Ephrussi family financed the erection of a monument in 1869 honoring the deceased Governor-General Mikhail Vorontsov

---

8 Mendele, *Fishke der Krumer* (Odesa: n.p., 1888), 133–35. For an English translation see "Fishke the Lame," in *Tales of Mendele the Book Peddler*, ed. Dan Miron and Ken Friedman and trans. Ted Gorelick and Hillel Halkin (New York: Schocken Books, 1996), 3–298.
9 Moshe Leib Lilienblum, "Khatot ne'urim" [Sins of youth], in *Ktavim otobiografiyim* [Autobiographical writings], 3 vols. (Jerusalem: Mossad Bialik, 1970), 2:30–31.
10 Ibid., 10–11.
11 Besides Lilienblum's autobiography, another account of maskilic life in Odesa of the 1860s is Abraham Uri Kovner (Kornev), *Bez iarlyka (Vne kolei)* (St. Petersburg: n.p., 1872).

(1782–1856) and founded and maintained one of Odesa's municipal schools (in 1868 and 1879).[12] They made smaller donations to the Odesa municipal orphanage (1871) and contributions to the Odesan poor (1888).[13] The Rafalovich and Ephrussi families also contributed scholarships for students at the local university;[14] in addition, from 1875 on, the Rafalovich family granted scholarships to wards of the Odesa orphanage in commemoration of the family's deceased patriarch.[15] The Kogan family sponsored the building of a subsidized housing complex for poor Odesans (1873), famously called Когановские учережения (the Kogan institutions).[16] Indeed, some of these families— Rafalovich (in 1861 and 1865), Ephrussi (in 1874 and 1882), and Ashkenazi (in 1890, 1893, 1895, and 1900)[17]—continuously contributed new wings and buildings to the Jewish hospital, which, however, did not discriminate between its patients on the basis of ethnicity or religion, and was clearly recognized by the general, gentile Odesan establishment.

Among the richest Odesan Jews, only Abraham Brodsky and, to a lesser degree, Luisa Ashkenazi, systematically contributed to specifically Jewish causes: in 1867, Brodsky founded the Odesa branch of OPE[18] and, one year later, established the Jewish Orphanage of Odesa, which he and his heirs supported for many years. In 1883, Brodsky extended his philanthropy to the general population as well, funding a municipal shelter for the poor.[19] Luisa Ashkenazi was active, together with the wives and widows of other, less prominent Jewish Odesan merchants, in the establishment of the Society for the Support of Jewish Parturient Women.[20]

Without diminishing the humanitarian aspects of the donations by Odesa's most wealthy Jewish residents, and in order to understand their charitable strategies, it is important to emphasize the substantial role of philanthropy as

---

12 Lilia Belousova, "Integratsiia Evreev v Rossiiskoe soslovnoe obschestvo: Pochetnye grazhdane goroda Odessy Evreiskogo proiskhozhdeniia," *Moria* 5 (2006): 17.
13 Ibid.
14 *Kratkii otchet imperatorskogo Novorossiiskogo universiteta* (Odesa: n.p., 1882), 21.
15 Belousova, "Integratsiia evreev," 23. See Morozan, "Krupneishie torgovo-bankirskie doma Odessy, 166.
16 Oleg Gubar', "Valikhovskii priiut i Koganovskie ucherezhdeniia," *Almanakh Deribasovskaia-Rishel'evskaia* 24 (2006): 6–13.
17 Mikhail Polishchuk, *Evrei Odessy i Novorossii: Sotsial'no-politicheskaia istoria evreev Odessy i drugikh gorodov Novorossii 1881–1904* (Moscow: Mosty kultury, 2002), 187–88.
18 Brian Horowitz, *Jewish Philanthropy and Enlightenment in Late-Tsarist Russia* (Seattle: University of Washington Press, 2011), 42–43.
19 Evrydiki Sifneos, *Imperial Odessa: People, Spaces, Identities* (Leiden: Brill, 2018), 155.
20 Polishchuk, *Evrei Odessy i Novorossii*, 190.

a status symbol in various geographical and historical contexts.[21] Its impact was especially significant in the Russian Empire, where social organizations relied extensively on personal connections. One cannot overestimate the importance of seeing one's name on the lists of the board members of charitable organizations, next to the names of the most powerful and respected people in Odesa and the empire.

Moreover, there was an ideological dimension to the large-scale Jewish contributions to general relief efforts. By contributing to ethnically or religiously nonpartisan institutions, rich Jews were essentially proclaiming that they viewed the Jewish population as an integral part of the general Russian public. Evrydiki Sifneos recognized similar dynamics among Greek tycoons, claiming that "Odessa's wealthy . . . entrepreneurs practiced what was in effect social integration across national and ethno-religious affiliations."[22] As a result of this policy, however, there was a neglect of Jewish cultural initiatives that exceeded the rigid framework of the OPE program, which concentrated on promoting Russian imperial education, predominately in the form of scholarships and textbooks in Russian and Hebrew. One of the most salient examples of this negligence was the refusal of the St. Petersburg OPE Committee to fund the publication of the collected works of the first Yiddish-language novelist Yisroel Aksenfeld (1787–1866), under the pretext that developing Yiddish literature was not part of OPE's program.[23] Unable to raise the necessary funds, Aksenfeld's friends postponed the publication until his manuscripts perished during the Odesa pogrom in 1871.[24] Perhaps the Jewish poor might have obtained relief from the general charitable programs that existed in Odesa, in addition to being extensively supported by the traditional Jewish charitable societies;[25] however, Jewish writers and intellectuals in the 1860s and 1870s often found themselves with scarce communal or institutional support.

Summarizing the approach taken in the 1860s and '70s by those rich Odesan Jews who belonged to both the highest economic strata and the second circle of

---

21 Thomas Adam, *Buying Respectability: Philanthropy and Urban Society in Transnational Perspective, 1840s to 1930s* (Bloomington: Indiana University Press, 2009), 89–125.
22 Sifneos, *Imperial Odessa*, 109, 171.
23 Judah Leon Rozenthal, *Toldot khevrat marbei haskalah beyisrael beerets rusiyah meshnat 1863 'ad shnat 1885* [History of the OPE in the land of Russia from 1863 to 1885]. (St. Petersburg: Ts. H., 1885), 6.
24 Israel Zinberg, *A History of Jewish Literature*, trans. Bernard Martin (New York: Ktav Publishing, 1978), 11:158.
25 On those in Odesa, see Polishchuk, *Evrei Odessy i Novorossii*, 146–53.

Odesa's commercial elite (consisting of more traditionally oriented merchants), Lilienblum wrote:

> ... people in the new city [Odesa], as compassionate as they are, are used to spending their money generously: on the ladies at the parties, on the theater, on expensive and inexpensive jewelry, on the *tzadiks*, on the dignified and undignified poor, on the synagogue beadles ["gabaim"], and on emissaries from Jerusalem—they do not humiliate writers as well, buying their books and paying their *shekels* for them, or more, according to what one can afford.[26]

In Lilienblum's inventory of the non-essential expenses of Jewish Odesan businessmen, he placed the support of Jewish writers at the end of the list, after their amorous, cultural, and charitable expenditures. This indicated Lilienblum's perception of the priorities and cultural horizon of those rich Odesan Jews. Although some of them were ready to buy one or several copies of Hebrew or Yiddish books, their philanthropy for Jewish cultural causes rarely extended beyond that. That situation changed, however, towards the late 1880s, with the emergence of a new business leadership in the Odesan Jewish community, which not only started contributing to Jewish political and cultural causes but also began to participate in cultural initiatives at the levels of planning and execution.

Four groups of Odesan Jewish intelligentsia and their patrons

The predominant narrative on the everyday experience of the circles of Odesan Jewish writers and intellectuals, the "Sages of Odesa," is their detachment from the everyday life in the city. Perhaps the origins of this narrative can be found in the accounts of their contemporaries and junior peers, such as Ya'akov Fichmann (1881–1958) and Yitskhak Dov Berkowitz (1885–1967).[27] This narrative was disseminated later in research that emphasized the isolation and

---

26 Lilienblum, "Khatot ne'urim," 2:39.
27 Ya'akov Fichmann, *Rukhot menaganot: sofrei polin* [The tune of the winds: Writers from Poland] (Jerusalem: Mossad Bialik, 1952), 2; Fichman, *Amat habinyan: sofrei Odesa* [The foundation of the building: Odesa writers] (Jerusalem: Mossad Bialik, 1951). Yitskhak Dov Berkowitz, *Harishonim kevnei adam* [The first generations seen personally] (Tel Aviv: Dvir, 1958), 2:285.

self-containment of the intellectual circles of those "Sages of Odesa."[28] Other sources, however, most importantly the autobiography of a central member of that circle, Simon Dubnow (1860–1941), shows to what extent the intellectual activities of these writers and thinkers, at least from the 1890s, were accompanied and supported by the substantial network of Odesa's economic elite and professional intelligentsia.

Contrary to the general tendency to see the nationally mobilized Jewish intelligentsia in Odesa as part of the same circle, Dubnow differentiated between two interconnected, but separate, intellectual groups. The first group was the Palestinophilic circle led by Ahad Ha'am (Asher Ginsberg, 1856–1927), with Elhanan Leib Lewinsky (1857–1910), Haim Nahman Bialik (1873–1934), and Yehoshua Hana Rawnitzki (1859–1944), among its prominent members.[29] The second group was less politically focused and included Mendele; Dubnow himself; Russian Jewish writer, Ben-Ami (Mark Rabinovich, 1854–1932); lawyer, journalist and community activist, Mikhail (Menashe) Morgulis (1837–1912); and Rawnitzki, who was a member of both circles.[30] In the memoir by Sholem Aleichem's son-in-law, Yitskhak Dov Berkowitz, members of these two groups were presented as one, integrated circle of the "Sages of Odesa."[31] However, Berkowitz recognized an additional, third group of Jewish authors in Odesa, lacking a solid ideological or aesthetic common denominator. This group included the rising star of Yiddish literature in the 1860s, Yitskhok Yoel Linetskii (1839–1915), who, in the shadow of Mendele, failed to maintain his literary status beyond the 1870s; a converted journalist and theater entrepreneur, Joseph Judah Lerner (1849–1907); a minor Hebrew language poet, teacher of Hebrew at an Odesa yeshiva and champion of biblical Hebrew, Elimelekh Weksler (1842–1919); and a Hebrew and Yiddish poet and businessman, Paltiel Zamoshchin (1851–1909).[32] According to Berkowitz, the sentiment that united this group was a collective grudge they felt towards Mendele regarding his moral and poetic stature and towards the aesthetic trends he had introduced into Hebrew and

---

28 Zipperstein, *Imagining Russian Jewry*, 73; Dan Miron, *Bodedim bemo'adam: ledyokanah shel harepublikah hasifrutit ha'ivrit betekhilat hameah ha'esrim* [When loners come together] (Tel Aviv: Am oved, 1987), 350.
29 For the composition of Ahad Ha'am's circle, see Steven Zipperstein, *Elusive Prophet: Ahad Ha'am and the Origins of Zionism* (Berkeley: University of California Press, 1993).
30 Simon Dubnow, *Kniga zhizni: Materialy dlia istorii moego vremeni: Vospominaniia i razmyshleniia* (St. Petersburg: Peterburgskoe vostokovedenie, 1998), 154–58.
31 Berkowitz, *Harishonim kevnei adam*, 296.
32 See *Khag yovel: Di iubilei faierung im 17-ten november 1890 in Odesa dem folkes shraiber yitskhok yoel linetskii* [The jubilee celebration of the people's writer Yitskhok Yoel Linetskii on November 17, 1890, in Odesa] (Odessa: n.p., 1890).

Yiddish literature. Although, with the exception of Lerner,[33] none of this group left political writings, it is plausible to hypothesize that they resented the harnessing of Jewish languages to national projects, striving to preserve maskilic affinity between the communal and imperial. Together with Lerner's writings, another evidence of this hypothesis is Weksler's opposition to modernization of Hebrew, which could be seen as a protest against its nationalization.

The fourth group that may be distinguished among the Jewish intelligentsia in Odesa at that time was the most dispersed and elusive—lacking a program, a fixed structure, regular habits, or its own institutions. Its existence is indicated in the biographies and autobiographies of its members' children and grandchildren, who became prominent figures in Russian art, literature, academia, and politics not directly associated with Odesa. Among the scions of these Odesan families were the painter Leonid Pasternak (1862–1945); his wife, the pianist Rozalia Kaufmann (1867–1939); their Moscow-born son, the Nobel-prize-winning poet, Boris Pasternak (1890–1960); their niece, classical philologist, Olga Freidenberg (1890–1955); and Olga's father, inventor, journalist and writer, Mikhail Freidenberg (1858–1920).

In this context, another representative clan was the Gessen family. Its two first generations in Odesa, beginning at the start of the nineteenth century, were second-guild grain merchants; their children and grandchildren born after the 1860s included an influential theoretician of law and future member of the Duma, Vladimir Gessen (1868–1920); lawyer and liberal Russian politician, Iosif Gessen (1865–1943); a historian of Russian Jewry, Yulii Gessen (1871–1939); and other prominent Russian authors and scholars in the generations that followed. The Pasternak-Freidenberg clan, as well as the Gessens and many other acculturated Odesa Jews, were born into families of social upstarts and were first or second generation native Russian speakers. As Leonid Pasternak wrote in his autobiography, the utmost desire of his parents, innkeepers from an impoverished background, was to make their children prosperous people: "вывести своих детей в люди"[34] (to make human beings out of their children), that is, to improve their status. Pasternak explained that this meant giving their offspring an adequate education that would enable them to become lawyers or physicians. Therefore, the young Leonid was systematically discouraged from his interest in drawing and painting but, nevertheless, had opportunities to develop his talent in the elitist gymnasium to which his parents sent him.

---

33 For the loyalist political writings of Lerner see the two issues of the journal he published in 1876–77 under the title *Zapiski grazhdanina* [Notes of a citizen].
34 Leonid Pasternak, *Zapisi raznykh let* (Moscow: Sovetskii khudozhnik, 1975), 15.

Although Pasternak's parents' idea of prosperity presupposed mainly accumulation of financial capital, he attained stability and status through earning cultural capital in Russian society.

The father of Leonid Pasternak's future wife, Rozalia, like the Gessen family's patriarchs, belonged to a higher stratum of Jewish nouveaux riches, as one of Odesa's earliest producers of carbonated water. For him, success meant not only achieving economic stability but also imperial cultural belonging and a respectable social status. From the age of five, Rozalia had been trained as a pianist and, from the age of eight, she began to perform in concerts, first in the southern provincial centers and then in St. Petersburg and Western Europe.[35] The best friend of Leonid Pasternak and, later, his brother-in-law, Mikhail Freidenberg, was an autodidact, who had been active from his youth in the Russian theatrical scene and in journalism.[36] Although he referred to Jewish themes in his writings,[37] his main orientation was towards Russian culture. These people socialized in the mixed circles of the journalistic-artistic milieu of Odesa, mainly among writers at the Одесский Листок newspaper, where both Leonid Pasternak and Mikhail Freidenberg worked.[38] Nonetheless, their most intimate connections, despite the high degree of their acculturation and sense of belonging to Russian culture, were formed among acculturated Russian Jews like themselves.[39]

As the present investigation focuses on the relationships between Odesa's Jewish commercial and intellectual elites, groups three and four are less relevant for further discussion. The members of group four were either self-sufficient professionals or supported by their affluent families; focused on their personal development, they rarely participated in the communal cultural enterprise—either as contributors or as supplicants.[40] Culturally, they and their children associated themselves with Russian language and Russian social and political milieu in its liberal iteration, separating ethnic, cultural, and political belongings.

---

35 Ibid., 96; Ernst Zaltsberg, "In the Shadows: Rosalia Pasternak, 1867–1939," *East European Jewish Affairs* 28 (1998): 30.
36 Evgenii Pasternak, "Vstuplenie," in *Boris Pasternak, pozhiznennaia priviazannost': Perepiska s O. M. Freidenberg* (Moscow: Art-Fleks, 2000), 5.
37 Mikhail Freidenberg, *Nakhodchivyi redaktor i evreiskii vopros* (Odessa: n.p., 1885).
38 Leonid Pasternak met his future wife at a party held by journalist Semion Titovich Vinogradskii, who worked at the *Odesskii listok* newspaper (L. Pasternak, *Zapisi raznykh let*, 31). For more on *Odesskii listok* journalists, see Anna Bilyk, "Teatral'no-kriticheskaia elita Odesskogo listka," *Almanakh Deribasovskaia-Rishel'evskaia* 30 (2007): 230–38.
39 I am grateful to Mirja Lecke for this insight.
40 On the Gessen family's activities in the Jewish community, see Iosif Gessen, *V dvukh vekakh: Zhiznennyi otchet* (Berlin: Speer & Schmidt, 1937), 18; Polishchuk, *Evrei Odessy i Novorossii*, 190.

Likewise, the members of the third group, consolidated around the figure of Linetskii, relied on their families or their professional skills for sustenance. As Berkowitz attests, the always bitter Linetskii was sustained by his son—a successful Odesan architect.[41] Weksler taught in an Odesa yeshiva and was probably also later supported by his son, Alexandre Besredka, a prominent microbiologist at the Pasteur Institute in Paris.[42] Lerner and Zamoshchin were small-scale entrepreneurs in their own right.[43] Perhaps the members of this group would have been glad to find sponsors among the commercial aces of Odesa, but they lacked the charisma, program, and tact needed to attract sympathetic supporters.[44] Although they acted primarily within the boundaries of Jewish languages (with the exception of Lerner who also wrote in Russian), they disassociated their cultural activity, understood in communal terms, from their political identification with the Russian Empire.

Unlike the two latter groups, when we analyze the membership lists of the circles that met at the homes of Ahad Ha'am and Mendele-Dubnow, or the activists of the Odesa Palestinophilic Committee and the Odesa branch of the Society for the Promotion of Culture among the Jews of Russia (OPE), together with authors and intellectuals, we find a recurring group of prominent businessmen and white-collar professionals, who supported, advised, sponsored or raised funds for multiple activities of these groups. These figures undermine the thesis regarding the total isolation of the "Sages of Odesa" from the business world in Odesa and, thus, may be seen as a link between the "Sages'" insulated living rooms and the Odesan port, warehouses, streets, and commercial offices. Despite the political and cultural differences between these two groups, their activists and sponsors understood ethnic belonging also in political terms and expressed it both culturally and politically. One of the major differences between the camps of Ahad Ha'am and Mendele-Dubnow was in the way they associated between the political and cultural. Dubnow conceived a national culture that could equally exist in the local vernacular, Yiddish or Hebrew, while Ahad Ha'am and his followers considered that only Hebrew was the true national language of the Jews.

---

41 Berkowitz, *Harishonim kevnei adam*, 298.
42 Getzel Kressel, *Leksikon hasifrut ha'ivrit badorot haakhronim* [Lexicon of Hebrew literature in recent generations], 2 vols. (Merhavia: Sifriyat poalim, 1965), 1:684.
43 For more on Lerner, see Saul Borovoi, "*A fargesener nihilist (Yehudah Yosef Lerner)*" [A forgotten nihilist: Yehudah Yosef Lerner], *Filologishe shriftn* 3 (1929): 473–84; see on Zamoshchin, Kressel, *Leksikon hasifrut ha'ivrit*, 1:756.
44 On Linetskii's blackmailing tactics in his dealings with Sholem Aleichem, see Berkowitz, *Harishonim kevnei adam*, 296–98.

From Dubnow's informative autobiography, we learn that frequent participants in the Mendele-Dubnow circle included the head of the OPE in Odesa, a flour-mill magnate, engineer and first-guild merchant, Grigorii Emmanuilovich Weinstein (1861–1929); the notary Berman Gurovich; the son of an Odesan exchange broker, Yakov Saker;[45] the doctors Himmelfarb, Bertenson, Finkelstein, Gold, and Michelson; and attorneys Granov and Blumenfeld.[46] If we check the protocols of the Odesa Society for Aid to Jewish Farmers and Artisans in Syria and Palestine[47]—which was the official name of the Odesa committee—among its active members who belonged to Odesa's commercial and professional milieu, we find several members of the previous group, such as Grigori Weinstein and Dr. Himmelfarb but also first-guild merchants, Samuel Matusovich Barbash (1845–1921) and Abraham Grinberg (1841–1906); a high-ranking employee in Barbash's bank, Moisei Kleiman; as well as second-guild merchants Solomon Puritz, Moisei Fisherovich, and Getsl Tovbin.[48] Unlike Weinstein, who, by the beginning of the twentieth century, had distanced himself from the Palestinophilic activities, all Jewish merchants supporting the Odesa committee were more traditionally observant than supporters of OPE. A majority of them were members of the traditional Great Synagogue (Bet hamidrash hagadol) congregation,[49] and along with participation in modernized Palestinophilic activities, they generously contributed to traditional Jewish charities. Thus, Solomon Puritz, a follower of the Hasidic rebbe, was a board member of multiple Jewish charitable institutions, such as the Jewish hospital, school, yeshivot, as well as the Committee for the Distribution of Coal to Poor Jews.[50]

Any preliminary explanation of the reasons for Odesan Jewish merchants' support of the intellectuals' cultural and political activities must first take into account the crisis that emerged in the established Jewish plutocratic leadership

---

45 On his father, see *Spisok torgovykh domov i kupechestva Odessy, 1892–1894* (Odessa: n.p., 1892), 88.
46 Dubnow, *Kniga zhizni*, 171, 186, 199, 228–29.
47 "God deiatel'nosti Odesskogo Obshchestva Vspomoshchestvovania Evreiam v Palestine," in *Sion: Evreisko-Palestinskii Sbornik* (St. Petersburg: n.p., 1892), 209–272; Yossi Goldstein, *Anu hayinu harishonim: toldot hibat tsion, 1881–1918* [We were the first: history of Hibbat Tsion movement] (Jerusalem: Mossad Bialik, 2015), 310.
48 For the names of these people who appear in the list of Odesa merchants, see *Spisok torgovykh domov*, 83, 98, 95.
49 For the profiles of the members of the *Bet hamidrash hagadol* [Great synagogue], see Aron Perelman, "Vospominaniia," *Almanakh Evreiskaia Starina* 4, no. 63 (2009), http://berkovich-zametki.com/2009/Starina/Nomer4/APerelman4.php.
50 Polishchuk, *Evrei Odessy i Novorossii*, 142.

in the Russian Empire after the pogroms of the early 1880s.[51] Until 1881, the Jewish commercial elite established itself as the unequivocal leadership of the Jewish community in Russia, functioning as a mediator between the problems and needs of Russian Jews and the corridors of power. Their main methods of influence were the submission of petitions and unofficial or semi-official behind-the-scenes lobbying.[52] These methods, however, failed to prevent or halt the pogroms and the ensuing reactionary wave of anti-Jewish legislation. The leadership vacuum during the 1880s allowed the intellectuals to rise to prominence and to promote their own vision for the reformation of Jewish life and the cultivation of new modes of Jewish politics. Odesa became the hub of the national "Palestinocentric" mode. The local intellectual circles attracted the rich, who wanted to participate in the formation of a new Jewish polity. Unlike the pre-1880 relationships between the wealthy plutocrats and the maskilim, based on hierarchic relationships between benefactors and supplicants,[53] this new model of cooperation between the commercial and intellectual elites was built on partnership and involvement in a common cause. The new cohort of wealthy Odesans, motivated by a sense of communal responsibility, willingly participated as partners in the process of planning the Jewish communal future. Odesa's Jewish nationally inclined intellectual circles, in turn, contributed their reputations within the Jewish community, confidence in their ideological direction, eloquence, and the ability to formulate and express their programs clearly and persuasively, with passion, dignity and charisma; they had the ability to communicate with the masses, while disseminating the most updated European intellectual and ideological trends. A new type of partnership was formed, but, as I will show below, the upheavals of the 1880s were not the only turning point in the history of cooperation between wealthy Jews and Jewish intellectuals in Odesa. The preceding economic crisis of the 1850s and 1860s enabled the rise of a new formation of Jewish entrepreneurs with stronger connections to the Pale. In the following section I will discuss the reasons according to which some groups of Jewish businessmen supported Jewish cultural and political initiatives

---

51 Jonathan Frankel, *Prophecy and Politics: Socialism, Nationalism, and Russian Jews, 1862–1917* (Cambridge: Cambridge University Press, 1981), 74–90; Eli Lederhendler, *The Road to Modern Jewish Politics: Political Tradition and Political Reconstruction in the Jewish Community of Tsarist Russia* (New York: Oxford University Press, 1989), 155.

52 Benjamin Nathans, *Beyond the Pale: The Jewish Encounter with Late Imperial Russia* (Berkeley: University of California Press, 2002), 38–59.

53 On the maskilim's relationships with the commercial elites, see Svetlana Natkovich, "'What is Permitted to Jupiter is not Permitted to an Ox': *Maskilim* as a Class Phenomenon," *Jewish Social Studies* 27, no. 3 (Fall 2022): 158–88.

of the intellectuals, while others remained indifferent to them, investing more in broader imperial projects.

The emergence of a new generation of the Jewish commercial elite in Odesa in the late 1880s

As we have seen, the richest Jews of Odesa—Ephrussi, Rafalovich, Halpern, Kogan, Ashkenazi, and other families of the first circle—were for the most part reluctant to support Jewish cultural initiatives and contributed mainly to causes that were not specifically Jewish, with rare exceptions such as the Jewish hospital. Evrydiki Sifneos offers a hypothesis concerning the factors that influenced the differing charitable practices and social involvement of distinct groups of Jewish tycoons. She claims that the imperial practice of granting the titles "Honorary Citizen" and "Hereditary Honorary Citizen" to the most successful merchants isolated the most energetic and powerful strata of business magnates from the rest of the merchant community. "Incorporating the entrepreneurial elite (by means of the status of honorary citizenship) into the echelons of the cities' aristocracy and bureaucratic and military notables created a serious impediment to the formation of the bourgeois class."[54] This logic may be extended to questions of national belonging because the privileges accompanying hereditary honorary citizenship freed the honorees and their offspring from certain limitations associated with the restrictive anti-Jewish laws and, thus, also somewhat reduced Jewish communal solidarity. This status of honorary citizenship granted exemption from corporal punishment and capitation tax; the right to choose and to be chosen to serve in various positions in the municipal government; to be respectfully addressed by the use of an honorific, such as ваше благородие (your nobleness)[55]; and, in accordance with the 1859 right of the first-guild merchants to settle freely across the Russian Empire, awarded its honorees *de facto* equal privileges of nobility.

In checking the lists of Jewish honorary citizens of Odesa, however, we cannot find any strict delineation according to the principle of cultural belonging. Indeed, among the seven earliest personal Jewish "Honorary Citizens" in Odesa, registered in 1841, were the patriarchs of the richest families, such as Hayim Ephrussi ("Hereditary Honorary Citizen" from 1864), Abraham Rafalovich ("Hereditary Honorary Citizen" from 1857), Moisei Halpern, Hirsh Karasin,

---

54 Sifneos, *Imperial Odessa*, 128.
55 Belousova, "Integratsiia evreev," 9, 14.

and others.[56] Nevertheless, in the later period, among the personal and hereditary honorary citizens, we find not only Jewish merchants but also representatives of the Jewish intelligentsia. As early as 1858, a teacher in Odesa's Jewish school and father of the future founder of the Hibbat Tsion movement, Simkha Pinsker, was granted the personal status "Honorary Citizen,"[57] and the founder of Russia's first Hebrew and Yiddish newspapers, Alexander Tsederbaum, was granted the status "Hereditary Honorary Citizen" in 1884.[58] Moreover, the later head of the Odesan branch of the OPE and member of the Odesa Palestinophilic Committee, Grigorii Weinstein, was an "Hereditary Honorary Citizen" too,[59] as was the OPE activist, Dr. Gold.[60]

Apparently, there is no direct correspondence between the status of "Honorary Citizen" or "Hereditary Honorary Citizen" and communal and national affiliations. This status is meaningful, however, in elucidating the difference between those Jewish merchants who ignored and those who supported Jewish cultural initiatives in Odesa. An additional significant factor is the tectonic shift occurring in the trade and social life in Odesa during the 1850s and 1860s that produced a tidal wave of new patterns of merchant activity and a new class of Jewish merchants in the city.

If we consider those Jewish merchants who were granted honorary citizenship before the Crimean War (1853–1856), indeed, we can recognize a pattern of supra-national solidarity and sociocultural orientations, either to the highest elites in Russian society or to the major European centers. The upheavals caused by the Crimean War and the Great Reforms produced a new kind of Jewish commercial elite, however, that developed an orientation towards Jewish national causes and was less defined by privileges granted by the Russian Empire. Lilia Belousova (from the Odesa State Regional Archive) argued that, after the abolition of serfdom in 1861, combined with the deterioration in the status of the nobility, the award of honorary citizenship lost its previous appeal of privilege and exclusivity.[61] The new Jewish players in Odesa's commercial world, therefore, were looking for novel avenues to define their status and communal belonging.

There is a scholarly consensus regarding the dramatic transformations in Odesa's status in the international cereal trade over the period of the Crimean

---

56 Ibid., 13.
57 Ibid., 16.
58 Ibid., 20.
59 Nadezhda Beliavskaia, *"Vaynshteyn Grigorii Emmanuilovich," Odesskii Biograficheskii Spravochnik*, accessed June 1, 2020, http://odessa-memory.info/index.php?id=457.
60 Belousova, "Integratsiia Evreev," 21.
61 Ibid., 14–15.

War and its aftermath.[62] When Odesa's trade became paralyzed during the war, innovative transportation and production technologies emerged that brought new actors to the scene, such as grain producers from the United States and Argentina. The Russian grain, exported through Odesa, could hardly compete in quality and price in this dynamic market.[63] In addition, in 1857, the Russian government changed its priorities and stripped Odesa of its preferred status as a *porto franco*.[64] For Odesa's grain merchants, the only way to compete and stay in business was to start dropping their prices, thus reducing their profit margins. As Patricia Herlihy showed, at the inception of Odesa's grain trade, which was dominated by Greek commercial firms, the most common marketing strategy was the transportation of grain to the port by the producers and then its direct sale to foreign purchasers by the merchants.[65] The merchant's most valuable asset was a developed network of agents throughout the main centers of European cereals commerce. The change in the market during the 1850s–1860s brought about the emergence of new business models. Unlike the Greek firms and a few Jewish tycoons that had dominated in the 1830s and 1840s, the new cohort of Jewish merchants was able to buy grain directly from the producers, modernize the chain of transportation, reduce their profit margin, and keep their businesses active, despite the stiff competition.[66] Thus, the growing domination of a new generation of Jewish merchants in Odesan trade and the deterioration of the economic status of Odesa in the Russian Empire were precipitated by a common cause: the profound changes in the dynamics of the international grain trade and the diminishing role of Russia as the supplier of the world's bread.

Table 1. Percentage of Greek and Jewish merchant firms in the Odesa cereals trade[67]

Years	Greek Merchants	Jewish Merchants
1834–1839	44.3%	12.2%
1856–1864	30.1%	38.6%
1883–1891	10%	56.3%
1906–1914	9.8%	66.4%

---

62 Herlihy, *Odessa: A History*; Morozan, *Delovaia zhizn' na iuge Rossii v XIX-nachale XX veka* (St. Petersburg: Dmitri Bulanin, 2014).
63 Wolfgang Sartor, "Khlebnye eksportery Chernomorsko-Azovskogo regiona," in *Gretske pridpriemnyctvo i torhivlia u pivnychnomu prychornomorii XVIII-XIX st.*, ed. G. V. Boriak (Kiev [Kyiv]: Institut Istorii Ukrainy, 2012), 164.
64 Herlihy, *Odessa: A History*, 213.
65 Ibid., 84.
66 Zipperstein, *The Jews of Odessa*, 71–72.
67 Data from Sartor, "Khlebnye eksportery," 168–75.

Table 2. Export of cereals through Odesa port and percentage of total Russian cereals exports[68]

Year	Weight of cereal exported from Odesa port. (per million *chetvert'* = ca. 192 kgs)	Percentage of Odesa cereal trade in total Russian cereals exports.
1835	6.6	49.2%
1845	9.4	56.9%
1853	21.7	38%
1865	22.5	33.9%
1875	40.9	22.6%
1885	75.6	22%
1895	122.1	29.7%
1904	98.9	17.2%
1910	73.6	8.7%

Concomitant with these processes was the decline of profit margins. In the 1860s, the average profit of the dealer was still 5–10 kopecks per *pud* of grain sold but in the following decades, that profit had decreased to only 1/4 kopeck per *pud*.[69] Those people able to compete successfully in this situation had to be extremely mobile and adaptable. These viable merchants successfully prioritized utilization of a network of local agents within Russia who could buy the grain cheaply and transport it efficiently over connections with foreign agents.

When we analyze the distribution of the various branches of different Odesan firms, a clear pattern emerges. The biggest Jewish firms active in Odesa before the Crimean War, such as Ephrussi and Rafalovich, already had established branches in Paris, Vienna, and Berlin; the large, local family firms founded in Odesa after the war, for example, Brodsky and Ashkenazi, had their branches in Kiev (Kyiv), Kishinev (Chişinău), and Nikolaev (Mykolaiv). However, Samuel Barbash, who started his firm in 1866 in Tulchyn,[70] amassed his capital during the Russo-Turkish War (1877–1878), settled in Odesa in the early 1880s, and in 1885 still held the status of a second-guild merchant.[71] He established branches of his business across the Pale, in Tulchin, Kishinev, Vinnitsa (Vinnytsia),

---

68 Ibid., 161–64.
69 Taisia Kitanina, *Khlebnaia torgovlia Rossii v 1875–1914* (Leningrad: Nauka, 1978), 82.
70 Regarding his Tulchin connection, see Moshe Kleinmann, ed., "Barbash, Shmuel," in *Entsiklopediyah letsiyonut* [Encyclopedia of Zionism] (Tel Aviv: Chechik Press, 1947), 1:76.
71 For Barbash's merchant certificate, see *Derzhavnyi arkhiv Odes'koi Oblasti* (DAOO), f. 175, opys 1, sprava 3; accessed June 2, 2020, http://www.desgensinteressants.org/samuel-matusovitch-barbash/index.html.

Gaysin (Haisyn), Fastov (Fastiv), Beltsy (Bălți), Rybnitsa (Rîbnița), and elsewhere.[72] Indeed, he had a branch in Königsberg (Kaliningrad) and commercial connections across Europe, but, according to his company's statement in the 1905 registry of Russia's commercial institutions, "... its main essence—is its connections with the [Russian] provincial area, knowledge of it, service of its commercial needs, and linking it to the big centers."[73]

Although Barbash began his career as a simple grain merchant, in the 1880s, he steered his business towards banking activities. Nonetheless, unlike the previous generation of grain merchants turned bankers, such as the Ephrussis and Rafalovichs, his business acumen remained anchored in provincial Russia and not in the imperial centers or elsewhere around the globe. All the while, his cultural affiliation and sense of belonging were linked to the centers of the Jewish population in the Pale. Like Barbash, Grigorii Weinstein's family established itself in Odesa only in the second half of the 1860s, quickly becoming a major player in the flour mill sector. Weinstein's uncle Ber had already obtained the status of "Hereditary Honorary Citizen" in 1869.[74] By the 1880s, however, when young Grigorii studied at St. Petersburg's Technological Institute, even this status could not protect him from persecution and the feeling of being an outcast. Weinstein's company also had various branches across the empire but, unlike Barbash's firm, they were not located in the Pale but rather in imperial centers—in Kherson, Nikolaev, St. Petersburg, Tiflis (Tbilisi), and Riga, as well as in Constantinople (Istanbul).[75] Despite the ideological differences, Weinstein and Barbash cooperated on many common projects initiated by members of the Odesan Jewish intellectual elites, such as Dubnow, Ahad Ha'am, Mendele, Bialik, and others.[76]

For an intermediary conclusion, to understand the cultural and philanthropic policies of the Jewish merchant elites in nineteenth-century Odesa, two separate distinctions should be made: first, between those who came to prominence before the transformations caused by the Crimean War and the Great Reforms and those who came thereafter. The second distinction arises among the Jewish postwar elites during the 1880s and thereafter, who rose to positions of leadership in the community—between, on the one hand, supporters of a Jewish

---

72 V. V. Shevchenko, "Organizatsia funktsiiuvannia bankyrs'kykh ustanov pivdennoi Urkainy (XIX – pochatok XX st.)," *Problemy istorii Ukrainy XIX-pochatku XX st.* 16 (2008): 192.
73 Vasilii Dmitriev-Mamonov, ed., *Ukazatel' deistvuiushchikh v imperii aktsionernykh predpriiatii i torgovykh domov* (St. Petersburg: E. Vern, 1905), 362–63.
74 Belousova, "Integratsiia Evreev," 17.
75 Morozan, *Delovaia zhizn' na iuge Rossii*, 190.
76 Dubnow, *Kniga zhizni*, 228.

national policy oriented towards Russian culture, and, on the other hand, those who assisted in the establishment of the Palestinophilic movement.

The elites that amassed their capital before the Crimean War were shaped by dynamic business practices oriented towards foreign partners and had privileges granted by the Russian state, equalizing them *de facto* with the Russian nobility. Under those conditions, their cultural belonging was anchored in the imperial elites, regardless of the readiness of those Russian elites to accept rich Jews in their midst. When the trade climate changed and the latent hostility of the regime towards Jews became clearly formulated, however, those Jewish merchant families were ready to move their activities to other European capitals, aligning themselves with the Jewish global business world, rather than with Russian Jewry. This is the only group among Odesa's Jewish elites that might be considered culturally and politically cosmopolitan. But rather than a question of ideology, their cosmopolitanism was a result of their economic positions and strategies. Unlike them, having more modest incomes, the wealthy Jews who became prominent in Odesa during the last third of the nineteenth century were more oriented towards the Jewish community in the Pale, both commercially and culturally.

From the late 1880s onwards, factors of education and business orientation represent an element that serves to distinguish between the elite Jewish merchants leaning towards Palestinophilic causes and those supporting Russian Jewish cultural projects. Characteristically, those who supported the OPE tended to have higher levels of formal education and more intensive business dealings with the imperial elites. In contrast, more traditional religious backgrounds and closer business connections within the local Jewish community (in the Pale and Odesa) were more typical of the affluent members of the Odesa Committee of the Hibbat Tsion Movement.

Of course, these characteristics provide only general guidelines, whereas personal will and circumstances were often more decisive factors in choices of ideological affiliations. These might vary from person to person, even within the same demographic group or family, or at different points in individual lives. Nevertheless, these characteristics may provide some indication regarding the predominant ideological trends and attachments associated with members of certain Jewish social groups.

With regard to members of the free professions, in contrast to businessmen, it is more difficult to pinpoint a clear connection between personal biographies and ideologies. Some doctors, lawyers, and high-level clerks were ardent participants in both Jewish national groups, while others supported various streams of socialism or Russian liberalism. Perhaps the different dynamics during the intelligentsia's processes of acculturation and reformulation of social belonging partially account for this divergence. Whereas, for many businessmen, acculturation was an outcome of practical experience and adaptation, with ideological underpinnings secondary to praxis, the intelligentsia with all its subgroups relied more on ideology when choosing or fashioning socioeconomic circles of affiliation. Consequently, as a group, they showed greater mobility and flexibility in their ideological attachments. In their case, ideological choices played more significant roles than life's circumstances.

The phenomenon of various Jewish businessmen supporting national, cultural, and political initiatives was characteristic not only of Odesa. Other substantial donors to Jewish national Palestinocentric and Russian culture-oriented causes included the Guenzburgs in St. Petersburg, the Moscow-based Wissotsky family, the Vilna-based Goldbergs, and others. What made Odesan merchants different was the unique nature of Odesan trade and their special mental habits accompanying it, which impacted their perceptions and methods of processing reality. These mental habits and business practices, I suggest, were among factors that enabled Jewish intellectuals to imagine the political return of Jews to the land of Israel as a feasible endeavor.

The "mental habits" of Odesan traders and the emergence of the Palestinophilic imagination

The tectonic change in Odesan commercial patterns following the Crimean War took place not only in the domain of ethnic rivalry but also in the models of commercial exchange.[77] Whereas, at the inception of Odesa's grain trade, the most common marketing strategy was the direct sale from the producers to the foreign purchasers, with only brief mediation by a grain broker—then, from the mid-nineteenth century on, futures trading became prevalent in Odesa.[78] Futures commerce presupposes the existence of contracts between merchants and producers for future crops, the profit from which is generated by the difference between the agreed price and the actual price of each commodity on the specific day of the consummation of the relevant contract (the accounting day).

---

77 For a detailed description of the models of commercial exchange in Odesa, see Svetlana Natkovich, "Odessa as 'Point de Capital': Economics, History, and Time in Odessa Fiction," *Slavic Review* 75, no. 4 (2016): 847–71.
78 Sergei Moshenskii, *Rynok tsennykh bumag Rossiiskoi imperii* (Moscow: Ekonomika, 2014), 348; see Morozan, *Delovaia zhizn' na iuge Rossii*, 232.

From the moment of its ratification, such a futures contract becomes a commodity in itself, one that may be bought, sold, or speculated (as promissory notes), regardless of the actual conditions of the production and demand for the original commodity.

The introduction of futures trading into the Odesa grain markets happened just as the Jewish merchants were prevailing over Greek companies as the dominant commercial forces in the city. Although both these processes were precipitated by their own, not necessarily linked, reasons, the dynamics of futures commerce and the resulting patterns of subjectivity, especially in the Russian context, became associated with the profile of Jewish Odesan businessmen and, later, with Odesan mental habits and worldview in general. In an earlier article, I proposed viewing this specific pattern of grain commerce that had gradually developed in Odesa throughout the nineteenth century as one of the formative factors of the "Odesan mental habits" and unique cultural traits.[79]

The emergence of credit economies in the West during the eighteenth and nineteenth centuries necessitated the formation of new models of cognitive, temporal, aesthetic and psychological perceptions.[80] The appearance of novel financial instruments, such as credit and futures contracts, problematized the concept of what is 'real.' As literary scholar Anna Kornbluh noted:

> Credit instruments and the development of credit markets fomented a state of trade in which, as an 1840 House of Commons report held, "It is impossible to decide what part (of the trade) arises out of real *bona fide* transactions, such as actual bargain and sale, or what part is *fictitious, and mere accommodation paper*—that is, where one bill is drawn up to take another running, in order to raise fictitious capital." In the initial stride of this 'running,' credit instruments operate by deferring the completion of a sale. It is impossible to decide in the present tense whether that sale will be completed; only the future may finalize the sale. Any creditized transaction remains in a state of perpetual suspense respecting its *bona fides* until such moment in the future when its authenticity will have been confirmed.[81]

---

79 Natkovich, "Odessa as 'Point de Capital.'"
80 Mary Poovey, *Genres of the Credit Economy* (Chicago: University of Chicago Press, 2008); Anna Kornbluh, *Realizing Capital* (New York: Fordham University Press, 2014).
81 Kornbluh, *Realizing Capital*, 5.

One of the central features of the profound social upheaval associated with the introduction of novel instruments of commerce was the emergence of new modalities of causality and temporal perception. Literary scholar Joshua Clover emphasized the disruption of cause-and-effect relationships under the conditions of futures trading.[82] The operation of financial markets presupposes the retroactive actualization of value. The effect (i.e., the final price of a certain commodity set for an agreed date of consummation of contract, the "accounting day") is perceived as determining "the cause" (i.e., the ensuing chain of speculative stock transactions). Clover defined the new perception and meaning of time behind the method of futures trading produced under conditions of contemporary finance as a result of the constant tension between the anticipation of future outcomes and the retroactive reformulation of concepts and premises articulated in the past. In this ontology, the present appears as the most illusory and unstable moment, squeezed between the factual certainty of the past and the value-designating promise of the future.

Odesa was not the only place in the Russian Empire where a futures commerce was practiced, but its uniqueness lay in the combination of direct contact with grain (as an actual product of production, export and consumption) and its manipulation as an abstract object of exchange. The market conditions forced Odesan businessmen to develop expertise in several fields of specialization, often kept separate in other markets. According to Patricia Herlihy, the advantage of the Jewish merchants in Odesa's grain market was precisely their ability to "talk with both the local producers and the foreign purchasers, [to be able to] link, as it were, two worlds."[83]

As I have claimed previously,[84] although grain was and is the most basic product of consumption relative to other commercial products, the grain trade presupposed much more complicated schemes of transition from product to commodity to profit. Due to historical reasons, the final prices of Russian grain, unlike other exchange-traded commodities, were set not within the framework of a conjuncture of Russian markets, nor between the producers, agents, exporters, and purchasers during the course of their direct interactions, but rather between all these factors and rates, mainly set by the London and Berlin exchanges.[85] This complicated commercial scheme created numerous gaps between the variables

---

82 Joshua Clover, "Retcon: Value and Temporality in Poetics," *Representations* 126, no. 1 (2014): 9–30.
83 Herlihy, *Odessa: A History*, 85, 212.
84 Natkovich, "Odessa as 'Point de Capital,'" 854.
85 For more on the dependency of Russian markets on foreign associations, see Kitanina, *Khlebnaia torgovlia Rossii*, 101–02.

in the chain of the grain transactions. These gaps were filled by various forms of narratives or fictions—based on statistical analyses, meteorological data, and other information, ranging from news reports to personal, political, and financial gossip. Only the data received from London or Berlin on "accounting day" retroactively stabilized the chain of unattested calculations and factual transactions, endowing them with meaning and value.

Odesa was the place of intersection between local trade and the global economy, between the abstract time of capitalist commerce and the concrete time of agricultural production. There the ultimate value of things was repeatedly revealed, designated, and destabilized until the finalization of the next run of transactions. Although existential indeterminacy was the most characteristic condition of the Odesan business world, its merchants conceived their own function as that of mediators between production and consumption, the factual (real) and the unattested (fictitious), as the only stable point in the global system of political economics. This perception was formulated, in a nutshell, by Jabotinsky in his novel *Пятеро* (The Five), set in Odesa's business circles. One of the protagonists of this novel, a quintessential Jewish Odesan merchant, Abram Moiseevich, tends to represent world history as a derivative of the Odesan grain trade, as a cause defined by its ultimate effect—the price of the grain set at the Odesa exchange. "The old man could recount in entertaining and enjoyable terms," writes Jabotinsky, "the history of the Sevastopol campaign, Abraham Lincoln's death, the Paris Commune, Skobelev, Zhelyabov's trial, Boulanger and various affairs pertaining to the Black Sea grain trade."[86]

In my previous research, I suggested that one of the factors that played an important role in coining Odesa's literary idiom in Russian literature was the readiness of its authors to refer to Odesa's commercial climate not only as an object for description, but also as a poetic principle that structures the perception of space and time, as well as a figurative language.[87] Jewish representatives of this literary tradition came of age at the beginning of the twentieth century, coming from families belonging predominantly to the third circle of Jewish clerks, accountants, and small-scale businessmen. Although they remained connected to the framework of middle-class Jewish Odesan discourse, their upbringing was anchored in Russian culture.

In contrast, the Odesa School of Hebrew literature and Jewish nationalist-political thought that developed in the city earlier within the circles of the nationally oriented "Sages of Odesa" strove to define fixed, clearly formulated

---

86 Vladimir Jabotinsky, *The Five*, trans. Michael Katz (Ithaca: Cornell University Press, 2006), 30.
87 Natkovich, "Odessa as 'Point de Capital,'" 857.

notions of the Jewish past and present.[88] Whereas the aesthetic imperative of this tradition called for the most truthful representation of what is real in the experience of the nation, Odesan literature in Russian (which appeared more than a decade later) celebrated the gap between the factual and the unattested. Uprooted Jewish intellectuals among the "Sages of Odesa," such as Lilienblum, Dubnow, Ahad Ha'am, Bialik, and others, were living in the city that celebrated and profited from the commercial potential of the mutually agreed transmutation of the real and the fictitious. However, precisely on this unsteady ground, they tried to discern, imagine, and grasp the values of stability and immutability.

The ideas of modern Jewish nationalism in both its Palestinocentric and autonomist versions were formulated by the "Sages of Odesa." Raised and educated in the Pale, they arrived in Odesa with predetermined worldviews and they had personally experienced the rupture in the Jewish tradition, disruptions in their narratives of the self and in the perception of the flow of time. Nonetheless, they rebelled against these ruptures by means of the creation of a new kind of continuity—that of enduring national spirit and peoplehood. Their marginality against the backdrop of a multinational and cosmopolitan city brought them even closer together. Paradoxically, in order to formulate and animate this national spirit, they needed both the conditions existing in Odesa and awareness of the rebellion against the very values and worldview that Odesa represented. Odesa provided the financial infrastructure that enabled them to make their living and to promote their projects, but no less importantly, it exemplified the potential for realizing the most daring and fantastic projects and rearranging reality into new kinds of fiction that might be put into circulation to produce a new run of profits. The "Sages of Odesa" despised the local nouveaux riches, whom they considered detached from Jewish experience and the Jewish people; however, they imitated the latter's novel thought patterns—their ability to think beyond the constraints of existing conditions and to imagine alternative realities. Odesa's port was not only an outlet for the export of Russian grain but also a place from which passenger ships embarked for Palestine. The transportation of people and commodities across national borders and political realities looked equally feasible from the Odesa shoreline: it just required thinking out of the box, serious planning, and shrewd organization.

In his recollection of the beginning of his activities in the Hibbat Tsion movement, Lilienblum specifically associated the early stages of his conceptualization of Palestinocentric Jewish nationalism with his location in Odesa:

---

88 On Odesan literature in Hebrew, see Dan Miron, "'Al khakhmei Odesa," in *Mekhvah leodesa / Homage to Odessa*, ed. Rahel Arbel (Tel Aviv: Beit Hatfutsot, 2002), 33–37.

> From the place of my habitation, built on the Black Sea shore, twice a week ships embark to the Near East, which pass through the shores of Jaffa and Haifa; this was the way from our country to the Holy Land and the majority of travelers [there] made their passage through this city. I lived in this city and was one of the first among our writers to raise the question of the settlement in the land of Israel in times of pogroms; I was forcefully drawn to become a partner in the project of the settlement even before this city became a center of Hibbat Tsion. The majority of travelers had to pass through this city and in so doing visited me to speak about the settlement.[89]

Although Lilienblum spoke mainly on social occasions and his encounters with travelers in Odesa, his recurring emphasis on the association between his residence in the city and the Palestinophilic movement suggests a deeper affinity between the locus and the ethos. Not unlike the place of Odesa merchants, his location at the intersection of the transportation routes between the Pale and the Mediterranean basin enabled him to function as an agent of exchange and accumulation of ideas rather than of commodities; his mind was a site where various fictions—dreams, fantasies, and yearnings—were converted into concreate plans of actions in the real world: planning the travel, soliciting funds, looking for companions, arranging their stay in the land of Israel, formulating ideological underpinnings of the project, and more. In this sense, despite the contempt Lilienblum felt toward Jewish members of Odesa's business world, his role was homological to that of the Odesa merchants that enabled the flow of commodities between the private, communal, imperial, and global.

Despite distancing themselves, on the rhetorical level, from the Odesa business world, the object of the intellectuals' open disdain was mostly the failing small-scale wheeler-dealers. For instance, in Bialik's short story "Hasokher" (The merchant) such a businessman is represented as vulgar, ignorant, pitiful, and lacking any self-awareness.[90] When speaking about their more successful sponsors and supporters in Odesa, maskilim were much more ambivalent. In his autobiography, Dubnow gave an ironic portrayal of Samuil Barbash, a successful merchant who relentlessly supported the "Sages of Odesa," ridiculing his unpolished manners and language fraught with Yiddishisms.[91] However, in

---

89 Lilienblum, "Hatsa'adim harishonim" [First steps], in *Ktavim otobiografiyim*, 3:10.
90 Haim Nahman Bialik, "Hasokher," in *Sipurim* [Stories] (Tel-Aviv: Dvir, 1953), 281–296.
91 Dubnow, *Kniga zhizni*, 228.

Dubnow's recollection, these traits were presented as parts of Barbash's colorful personality, not as an evidence of an essential flaw in his character. Adopting an idealistic conception of culture as incompatible with mercantile considerations, intellectuals tried to downplay the economic aspects of their activities, which nevertheless did not reduce their dependence on the merchants' support.

Despite their actual marginality, the "Sages of Odesa" were able to produce a new narrative that appealed to both the broad masses of Jews in the Pale and to a certain class of businessmen and white-collar professionals in Odesa. Amid irreversible changes in Jewish traditional way of life that undermined a stable perception of reality, they suggested narratives of continuity that could be grasped in traditional, messianic terms, as well as within the modern vocabulary of ethnic nationalism.

But unlike proto-Zionist intellectuals belonging to the circle of Ahad Ha'am and unlike his friend Dubnow, Mendele refused to distinguish between economic and cultural spheres or to perceive stable and continuous notions of national culture and identity as a given truth. Contrary to Dubnow and Ahad Ha'am, who suggested narratives of national continuity and revival, Mendele explored the cracks of incongruity between the ideological narratives and reality.[92] I suggest that Mendele's unique literary and epistemic approach lies between Dubnow's and Ahad Ha'am's systemized classicism and Odesa's later Russian-language modernism.

Mendele's simultaneous ability critically to observe Odesa's commercial culture from the viewpoint of the nationally aligned intelligentsia and to perceive the detached intelligentsia from the viewpoint of Odesa's commercial culture is exemplified in the story "In Days of Tumult" with which I began this discussion. In this story, two friends—Leib and Mendele—escaping the pogroms and destitution in the Pale, arrive in Odesa (called *Shikhur* in this story), with a vague dream of emigrating to Palestine and becoming farmer-pioneers. Apart from their knowledge of the Hebrew language and rabbinic studies, they have no professional skills nor any assets that might help them to succeed in the 'Promised Land.' Equipped only with letters of recommendation from their local activists in the shtetl, they try to find their way to the Palestinophilic circles of the city. Their ultimate hope is to visit the Karliner—a character modeled on Leon Pinsker and Ahad Ha'am—the head of the local Hibbat Tsion committee, whom

---

[92] For an analysis of Mendele's work that dismantles nationalist readings, see Amir Banbaji, *Mendele vehasipur haleumi* [Mendele and the national narrative] (Or Yehudah: Kinneret Zmora Beitan Dvir, 2009). For Dubnow's criticism of Mendele's ways of thinking, see Dubnow, *Kniga zhizni*, 158, 176.

they believe has the power to grant them an estate in the Land of Israel. During their wanderings in the streets of Odesa in the search for Karliner's address, they encounter laborers storing wheat—the main item in the Odesan grain trade.

> Reb Leib stood still, grabbed a fistful of wheat and looked at it carefully, like a person who takes a sample to evaluate its cost. At that very moment, a Jew suddenly jumped out and asked reb Leib: "Are you looking for wheat? Would you like to buy some wheat? I know a place where you can buy it cheaply; I am a broker."
>
> Reb Leib shook his head, and wrinkled his nose, as if saying no. Indeed, reb Leib hadn't the slightest intention of buying wheat. Then, why did he grab it? Because he was thinking of himself as a 'man of the land'; therefore, grain was among his interests. Hence, when he encountered the pile of wheat on his way to a desired estate [in the Land of Israel], he looked at it, so that when the time would come, he'd be able to say: "Wheat I understand, thank God! I've seen a lot of wheat in my life, and I don't need other people's explanations on that matter."[93]

This episode juxtaposes the delusions of two Palestinophiles with those of the impoverished broker, who dreams of finding an ideal, provincial client with whose help he would be able to restore his commercial fortune; here, the wheat functions as a key to multiple doors, each connecting its holder to a different kind of reality.

The same action, that of Leib holding the grains of wheat, signifies two contradictory paths, each of which reflects a dream of some of the Jews who came to Odesa. The first dream is to become an important merchant, an inseparable part of the big world of global commerce; the other is to emigrate to Palestine and to become an agricultural laborer and a pioneer. In this instance, the wheat appears as a dense, polysemic sign, representing simultaneously the most basic product in human consumption, a commodity upon which Odesa's glory was built, and the potential symbol of Jewish national revival. Unlike other locations, in the context of Odesa streets, the concrete act of merely holding some wheat activates multiple meanings. Mendele uses this multiplicity for its comic effect, to

---

93 Mendele, *"Biymei hara'ash,"* 38.

produce mutual misunderstanding; nevertheless, I suggest reading this situation as a cultural commentary.

This scene and its comic effect would have been impossible without the semantic potential of the act of taking hold of wheat as a super-signifier of modern Jewish existence in Odesa. Moreover, this occurrence may also be perceived as a zero degree in the system of coordinates of the Odesan Jewish imagination, generating passion and enabling the fantasy of alternative routes through history. This framework provides the merchants' fertile ground for concocting business schemes and the ideologues for calculating programs for Jewish modernity.

Mendele presents both the aspiring proto-Zionist pioneer and the aspiring businessman as miserable paupers struggling to make a living, but he goes even further in his critical evaluation of the role of the Odesa grain trade for the Palestinophilic ideology. He turns the broker into the guide, "the beast of burden," who brings the two friends to their target. Indeed, in some sense, the Odesan merchants did carry the intellectuals, the "Sages of Odesa," not only by financing the latter's programs but also by supplying them with a pattern of thinking and the ability to imagine plans beyond the constraints of the currently possible, until the ultimate realization of those alternative realities.

Hanan Hever and Amir Banbaji, in their analysis of the economic tropes in Hebrew literature, present two ways of interpreting Mendele's grotesque depictions of the shtetl Jews. While the majority of Zionist critics regarded these depictions as aimed at ridiculing the Jews' failure to become effective actors in the capitalist economy, Hever and Banbaji saw Mendele's criticism as condemning the dehumanizing aspects of capitalism itself.[94] My reading of "In Days of Tumult" simultaneously undermines and aligns with this interpretation. On the one hand, I have shown the admiration with which Mendele presents Odesan capitalism as a powerful economic force that generates initiative and imagination. On the other hand, I have pointed to the gap that Mendele emphasizes between the reality of Jewish impoverishment and the castles in the air provided by modern economic and national narratives instead of viable solutions to Jewish problems. At the end of the story, Mendele understands the futility of both national and capitalist dreams and leaves Odesa to go back to the shtetl, which, in his opinion, is the main site of the real work for the sake of the Jews. While Odesa's Palestinophiles hoped to reform the unproductive Jew and to integrate him into the vision of national revival, Mendele showed the incongruities between dreams and actual Jewish realities.

---

94 Amir Banbaji and Hannan Hever, "Mavo" [Introduction], in *Sifrut vema'amad* [Literature and class], ed. Amir Banbaji and Hannan Hever (Jerusalem: Van Leer Institute, 2014), 42.

Odesa Jewish merchants and intellectuals alike strived to frame modernity and to find a place for themselves and their people within it. In their search for the most active and advantageous position in modernity, the representatives of both groups moved through various fields of economic and cultural production, creating numerous alliances and abandoning others. Whether they admitted it or not, the world of Odesa' Jewish wheelers-dealers was inseparable from the creative and political imagination of its intellectuals, leaving its imprint on some of the ways in which Jewish modernity is experienced and perceived.

CHAPTER 4

Elitism and Cosmopolitanism: The Jewish Intelligentsia in Odesa's School Debates of 1902

Brian Horowitz

Introduction

The Jewish intelligentsia and leadership in tsarist Russia at the time of the 1905 Revolution—a period of "democratization" and "mass politics"—actually operated according to an elitist pattern of activity more similar to earlier models of Jewish leadership in Russia than we might think. Leadership by the Jewish intelligentsia was not so different in terms of elitism from other forms of leadership, such as the *shtadlanut*, characterized by the informal requests of a local wealthy Jew, Haskalah (the Jewish Enlightenment), or the Hasidic movement, with its focus on the rebbe's total control. Similarly, Jewish cosmopolitanism in Russia, the idea of Jewish unity with other ethnic groups (in some cases conceived as unification with the Russian intelligentsia), had a specific quality. Whereas today "cosmopolitanism" is often understood as commitment to a society in which national borders as well as internal ethnic and religious differences have less significance than universal values, for Odesan Jews it was rather a specific kind of individual self-consciousness. In late nineteenth-century Russia, Jewish cosmopolitanism meant one's own openness to people of other nationalities, to integration into non-Jewish society, and to a rejection of Jewish exclusivity. Phrased differently, I consider that cosmopolitanism among Russia's Jews of the nineteenth century had primarily a personal dimension; it reflected back on the individual mentally and psychologically as a synthesis of Russian and

Jewish elements; the Jews themselves did not perceive it in terms of a pluralistic society made up of different kinds of individuals. To clarify the distinction, I shall allude to Vladimir Jabotinsky's view of cosmopolitanism and nationalism. Jabotinsky maintained that cosmopolitanism in Russia meant living as a Jew passively, in contrast to Zionism in which the individual asserted national identity first and foremost. As an example of cosmopolitanism, he describes himself and his schoolmates in late nineteenth-century Russia as fully aware that they were Jews but attaching no meaning to it.[1] They viewed themselves as cosmopolitans because they read European and Russian literature, attended a non-religious school, and they studied with non-Jews. Their emphasis was on the Jew's subjective attitude rather than on society as a whole.

This chapter tests the assertion that two "truths" of nineteenth-century Russian Jewish consciousness—democratization and cosmopolitanism—were understood differently in Russia circa 1905 than today. In order to do so, I turn to Odesa and to the debates over education that took place in 1902. At the time, members of the Jewish intelligentsia engaged in a polemic about what constitutes an intellectual and how Jewish intellectuals should be educated. In my view, Odesa offers the optimal case study because it was the first city in the Russian Empire where, at least within the Jewish community, the intelligentsia succeeded in adopting an active role. They displaced the leadership of the wealthy Jewish elite and began to negotiate with the local government on behalf of Russian Jews around 1860.[2] It would be difficult to find a Jewish community in Russia that was more democratic and cosmopolitan. It was not so much unique regarding Jewish cosmopolitanism except that Odesa was unique in itself—a large Jewish population consisting of many modern secularized Jews in a large urban space. It is hard to think of another example in the Russian empire; perhaps Warsaw in Congress Poland. However, as I will show, even in movements and groups that seemed democratic and cosmopolitan, the leadership remained elitist and embodied notions of cosmopolitanism that differ from current Western notions.

This issue is important because during the period that we associate with the post-Haskalah Russian Jewish intelligentsia (1860–1917), we often take for granted that Jews rejected elitism, embracing democratic ideas and cosmopolitan integration. We find, however, that the Jewish intelligentsia was as elitist as

---

1   Vladimir Jabotinsky, *Story of My Life*, ed. Brian Horowitz and Leonid Katsis (Detroit: Wayne State University, 2016), 43.
2   See John Klier, *Imperial Russia's Jewish Question, 1855–1881* (Cambridge: Cambridge University Press, 1995).

its predecessors, the *shtadlanim,* and they perceived cosmopolitanism more as the *maskilim* did than we might have supposed. Maskilim conceived of cosmopolitanism as a way of thinking that spurred the goals of integration and unity with the majority population. I intend to show, however, continuities between the earlier maskilim and the Russian Jewish intelligentsia, such as a penchant for top-down solutions and an attraction to the idea of a Russian-Jewish synthesis. After giving an abbreviated history of the intelligentsia in the Jewish leadership of Odesa, I shall then turn to the 1902 debates on education.

A history of Odesa's Jewish intelligentsia

Odesa's Jewish leadership was divided between its economic elite—the Brodskys, Poliakovs, and other oligarchs—and the liberal Jewish intelligentsia. The latter group included writers and editors such as Osip Rabinovich and Leon Pinsker in the 1860s and Ilya Orshansky and Mikhail Morgulis in the 1870s and later. In the 1880s, a new generation of Jewish intellectuals arrived on the scene, nationalists such as Moshe Leib Lilienblum, Ahad Ha'am, Rav Tsair (Chaim Tczernowitz), and, later, Menachem Ussishkin.

In the rich and varied history of Jews in Odesa, I would like to concentrate on one episode that reflects the Jewish community's ideological divisions and the conflicts between the "Russifiers" (a term used at the time) and those who leaned toward Jewish nationalism. I am referring to the "extraordinary sessions" of the Odesa branch of the Society for the Promotion of Enlightenment among the Jews of Russia (OPE), which took place over several weeks, starting on May 17, 1902. The arguments, charges, insults, and criticisms also point to the Haskalah, as characterized by two different and opposing trajectories, one leading to Jewish separatism, the other to integration into the surrounding society.

Although the debate was ostensibly about the curriculum in Jewish schools subsidized by the OPE, it was really an argument between two very different groups of intellectuals who battled one another over existential questions (who am I, what do I stand for, how will I affect the world?). Among these issues, one could point to Zionism and nationalism but also liberalism, progress, acculturation, and, perhaps above all, Jewish identity in Russia, and the value of an elite culture as opposed to practical education.

The supplicants called themselves "the Nationalization Committee" and included Ahad Ha'am, Simon Dubnow, Meir Dizengoff, Yehoshua Rawnitzki, and Ben-Ami (Mark [Mordechai] Rabinovich). Simply put, they wanted greater commitment to Jewish learning and the study of modern Hebrew.

Their opponents, the official leadership of the Odesa branch of OPE—Yakov Saker, S. Vainshtein and Mikhail Morgulis—were mocked as "ассимиляторы" (assimilationists), although that label is inaccurate. This group of established leaders favored Russification and immersion in secular subjects that could help Jews gain employment in a difficult economic environment. They did not favor the disappearance of the Jews as such and therefore should have been called integrationists. Admittedly, the term assimilationists delivered a polemical charge.

From the start, the two groups actually had a great deal in common. First, neither was religious, unlike the vast majority of Jews in the Pale of Settlement. They were both educated in secular subjects and spoke Russian well, but they were also knowledgeable on Jewish subjects. Second, both groups were devoted to serving the Jewish people. In this sense, they absorbed, consciously or not, the values of the Russian intelligentsia. Third, they were both elitist and recognized that their position in Jewish society was unusual and limited to a small number of highly talented individuals who combined Western-Russian and Jewish knowledge together. Fourth, they employed a top-down approach to political leadership; problems were formulated and solutions devised at the top and imposed from above.

They battled one another as only members of the Russian Jewish intelligentsia could, over minor differences rather than essentials. In their similarities and differences, they reflected transformations that had occurred in the city, such as vociferous discussion and participation about how the Jewish community should be organized. Odesa's Jewish community, I contend, was similarly divided between those who supported integration (the majority) and a smaller, rarified group that enthusiastically embraced Jewish nationalism.

The 1902 debates

As mentioned, the debates took place at the Odesa branch of the OPE. The organization was established by Evzel Gintsburg, Russia's wealthiest Jew, in St. Petersburg, in 1863.[3] Its goal was to spread secular knowledge among the Jews and enable them to integrate into Russian society. Almost immediately a branch opened in Odesa (1867). Unlike the Petersburg branch, the intelligentsia

---

3   On the Society for the Promotion of Enlightenment among the Jews of Russia, see Brian Horowitz, *Jewish Philanthropy and Enlightenment in Late-Tsarist Russia* (Seattle: University of Washington Press, 2009).

gained control rather than the plutocrats.⁴ The tsarist authorities permitted only these two cities to have OPE branches until the mid-1880s, but because of government resistance to its many initiatives, the OPE was relatively inactive during the 1870s and 1880s. In the late 1880s, the OPE revived in Odesa, and in the 1890s, it became active in expanding access of poor Jews to educational institutions in the city.

The timing of the educational debates in 1902 reflects a moment of crystallization in Odesa and spotlights two opposing Jewish intelligentsias in the city: the so-called "nationalists" and the "integrationists" (known as "assimilationists"). The opening speech was given by Mikhail Morgulis, a well-known Odesan lawyer, writer, and civic activist, and the head of the assimilationists. Morgulis claimed that although he did not disagree in principle with the nationalists, he adhered to a different concept of a modern Jewish school. An elementary school, Morgulis argued, should not imitate the traditional religious schools, the *kheder* or yeshiva. Students who attended a school instead of a kheder did so precisely in order to acquire secular knowledge lacking in the kheder. Even in the kheder, Morgulis asserted, parents were requesting that Russian be taught—according to a 1901 study on Odesa's kheders.⁵ In addition, Morgulis saw no reason to increase the number of hours of Hebrew, because "в заключение комитет полагает, что даже допущенное увеличение числа уроков еврейского языка до 12 часов в неделю не достигло бы цели, преследуемой 'Запиской.'" (In conclusion, the committee maintains that even the proposed increase in the number of lessons of Hebrew to twelve hours a week would not achieve the goal pursued by the "Note.")⁶

Morgulis continued his attack on Hebrew, arguing that Hebrew should not serve as a tool for transmitting content. Nor should Hebrew become the object of instruction: "Но не дико ли считать язык основным орудием знания? Суть должна заключаться не в филологическом материале, а в том, что именно написано на данном языке. Лучшие еврейские ученые писали по-арабски, и о духе еврейской национальности можно найти много написанного на разных европейских языках." (Isn't it bizarre to consider language the basic tool of knowledge? The essence should consist not of the philological material, but what precisely is written in that language. The best Jewish scholars wrote in

---

4 Ibid., 47–50.
5 *Spravochnaia kniga po voprosam obrazovaniia evreev: posobie dlia uchitelei i uchitel'nits evreiskikh shkol i deiatelei po narodnomu obrazovaniiu* (St. Petersburg: n.p., 1901), 27–46.
6 Mikhail Morgulis, "Mnenie komiteta odesskogo otdeleniia Obshchestva rasprostraneniia prosveshcheniia o evreiskoi narodnoi shkole," *Ezhenedel'naia Khronika Voskhoda*, April 19, 1902, 6.

Arabic, and one can find a great deal about the spirit of Jewish nationality written also in various European languages.)[7]

Along with these criticisms, Odesa's governing board believed that offering too many Jewish subjects would frighten away parents from OPE schools.

> Комитет полагает, что школа должна стремиться дать своему питомцу общее образование, в программу которого входит познание самого себя и как члена великой человеческой семьи, и как члена известного общественного и исторического организма; с этой точки зрения, еврейские предметы должны найти себе место в ряду общих предметов, а не впереди их.
>
> (The board maintains that a school should strive to give its students a general education which would inculcate an understanding of oneself both as a member of the grand human family and a member of a specific social and historical organism. From this point of view, Jewish subjects have their place along with general subjects, but should not come before them.)[8]

Although the above phrase, "member of the human family and a member of a specific social and historical organism," is a common definition of cosmopolitanism, the nationalists decried it. Ahad Ha'am, the first speaker for the nationalists, opposed Morgulis' idea. Although cosmopolitanism sounded attractive, he said, Jewish children were educated in ways that alienated them from their own culture:

> Условия нашей несчастной жизни таковы, что еврейский ребенок вырастает в атмосфере чуждой духа его собственной нации; он окружен со всех сторон совершенно иной жизнью, которая не только не благоприятствует как у детей других народов, бессознательному развитию национального склада ума и способа чувствования, но, напротив, мешает этому развитию на каждом шагу. То же самое происходит в школе.

---

7 Ibid.
8 Ibid., 5.

(The conditions of our unfortunate life are such that the Jewish child grows up in an atmosphere that is alien to the spirit of his own nation. He is surrounded on all sides by an entirely different life which, unlike the situation with children of other nations, does not facilitate the unconscious development of a nationally oriented mind-set and way of feeling . . ., but, on the contrary, interferes with this development at every step. The same occurs in school.)[9]

A proper education, in Ahad Ha'am's view, would produce a holistic person who combined universal and Jewish elements. This person would be equal to children of other ethnicities but would have a particularistic Jewish dimension, knowledge, skills, and character. A proper education would prepare children for life's challenges rather than make them deficient.

> Именно с точки зрения борьбы за существование необходимо давать еврейским детям внутреннюю нравственную опору в их будущей тяжелой жизни. Необходимо, чтобы они знали и любили то еврейство, за которое им впоследствии придется всю жизнь бороться и страдать.

(Precisely from the perspective of the struggle for existence, Jewish children should be given an inner moral anchor [to give strength] for their future difficult life. They ought to know and love that Jewishness for whose sake they will have to struggle and suffer their entire life.)[10]

After Ahad Ha'am had finished speaking, Dubnow offered a similar message about the dangers of cultural alienation or Russification:

> Еще более неестественною следует признать школу, воспитывающую своих питомцев в духе другой национальности. Отчужденные от родной среды и лишь искусственно ассимилированные с чужой средой, влиявшей на их воспитание, питомцы таких школ страдают нравственною

---

9 "Rech' Akhad-Gaama na soveshchaniiakh OPE v Odesse, 15 maia 1902 g.," *Nedel'naia khronika voskhoda*, June 21, 1902, 488.
10 Ibid.

раздвоенностью, и они образуют впоследствии тот национально-безличный элемент общества, к-ый повсюду оказывается беспочвенным и шатким.

(Admittedly, a school that educates children in the spirit of a different nationality is extremely unnatural. Alienated from one's own environment and artificially assimilated to a foreign environment that influences one's education, the students of such schools suffer from a moral dualism and, as a consequence, make up a nationally alienated element in society, which ends up deracinated and unstable.)[11]

The nationalists and others were openly critical of the board's emphasis on practical skills. Nonetheless, the board members, Saker and Morgulis, insisted that the OPE's purpose was to provide practical skills for the job market. These skills would allow young Jews to remain Jews and resist the temptation to convert to gain a livelihood. Perhaps not surprisingly, the board won the vote, thwarting the nationalists, who had tried to consolidate their position by telling supporters to retain party discipline at the election meeting, avoiding catcalls and other disruptive behavior. Despite that strategy and the popularity of Ahad Ha'am and Bialik, they lost. The integrationist orientation still dominated many areas of Odesa's Jewish life.

Analysis of the debates

Although these debates are not surprising—Ahad Ha'am and Morgulis had been at odds since the emergence of the Bnei Moshe group (1889)—the curriculum which the nationalists proposed was ambitious and ambiguous. What was their actual goal? Although it had long been the dream of some maskilim to build schools that taught Jewish subjects in a modern way (akin to Jewish rabbinical seminaries in Western Europe, such as Breslau [Wrocław]), this ideal never gained traction in Russia for a variety of reasons. For one, if parents refrained from sending their children to religious schools, it was because they hoped to give their children a secular education, including instruction in the Russian language and other practical subjects. In some cases, the schools might include

---

11 Simon Dubnow, "O natsional'nom vospitanii," *Nedel'naia khronika voskhoda*, January 1, 1902, 11.

Latin and Greek, which helped students pass the difficult university entrance examination. Other concerns, however, mattered, too; in Russia, there were few jobs or paying occupations for Jews educated in modern Jewish Studies. Writing for Jewish newspapers in Russia was an exception but hardly lucrative or even reliable, owing to censorship.[12]

In addition, the dual rabbinate set-up in Russia reduced the need to approach Jewish Studies in a modern way. In Western Europe, each community had a single rabbi who was expected to know secular and religious subjects and to be able to teach Judaism in a modern way, but in Russia, each community had two rabbis. The "state rabbi" (*kazennyi ravin*, or *rav meta'am*) was a tsarist official charged with keeping records—birth, death, marriage, while the "spiritual rabbi" (*dukhovnyi ravin*) was the community's actual spiritual leader. The presence of two rabbis meant it was not urgent to provide a religious Jewish and secular non-religious course of study nor to cultivate an individual who combined rabbinical training and modern education.

These points were voiced in an article by Pinkhus Marek about the Odesa debates. Marek, an educator and activist from Moscow, wrote:

> В противоположность авторам национализации, народ не только не признает за школой способности «иудаизировать» воспитание, но, наоборот, всячески отрицает за нею право вторгаться в национально еврейскую область: эта область принадлежит *только* хедеру. И, если от школы требуется только знание, то к хедеру предъявляется еще одно требование, которое само по себе не есть знание, но превращает последнее в нечто свое, родное, именно, в то, что инициаторы одесского спора называют национальным, а народ – религиозно-национальным воспитанием.

> (In contrast to the authors of nationalization, the people not only do not acknowledge the school as capable of "judaizing" education, but, on the contrary, by all means negate the right [of schools] to interfere with the sphere of Jewish national culture: that sphere belongs *solely* to the kheder. And, if one expects only knowledge from the school, then another demand is directed at the kheder, a demand that is not merely knowledge

---

12 Dmitry Eliashevich, *Pravitel'stvennaia politika i evreiskaia pechat' v Rossii, 1797–1917* (St. Petersburg and Jerusalem: Mosty kul'tury/Gesharim, 1999).

but transforms it into something of one's own, precisely what the initiators of the Odesa debate call national but which the people label a religious national education.)[13]

Another voice in the local press, Saul Gruzenberg, the editor and owner of *Budushchnost'* (The future), a Jewish newspaper in the Russian language, sided wholeheartedly with the nationalists. Gruzenberg mocked the OPE committee leaders as men who

> с поразительною откровенностью отвергли все, что дорого еврейскому сердцу. Еврейский язык был объявлен отжившим свой век мертвым филологическим материалом, для еврейских детей не только ненужным, но крайне обременительным, даже вредным вследствие его головоломности. Не нужна в школе и еврейская история, ибо ребенку нужно дать знакомство с ожидающей его действительной жизнью, а не с тем, что происходило 2000 лет тому назад. Не объяснено только одно: зачем еврейским детям вообще оставаться евреями. Еврейство только обуза, и ссылками на американских практиков нетрудно доказать что человек должен идти в уровень с веком, быть свободным от всяких предрассудков и не стеснять свою карьеру какими-то ветхозаветными идеями

(with amazing nerve, repudiated everything that is dear to a Jewish heart. Hebrew was declared a dead philological subject that had outlived its natural lifespan, not only unnecessary for Jewish children but also extremely burdensome, even harmful, due to its complexity. Jewish history, too, is unnecessary in schools, which should familiarize children with present reality, not 2,000-year-old history. Only one thing is not explained: why Jewish children should remain Jews at all. Judaism is only a burden, and it's easy to prove with references to American pedagogues that one should keep up with the times, be free of all prejudice, and not hamper one's career with some kind of "Old Testament" ideas.)[14]

---

13 Pinkhus Marek, "Natsionalizatsiia vospitaniia i evreiskie uchebnye zavedeniia," *Evreiskaia Shkola* 3 (1904): 6.
14 Saul Gruzenberg, "Po povodu odesskogo sobraniia obshchestva prosveshcheniia," *Budushchnost'*, June 21, 1902, 488.

Critics and readers, similarly to the Odesa Jewish intellectuals, were divided. They took sides depending on where they stood on the questions of Jewish acculturation into Russian culture versus advancing a Jewish national culture. To understand this split, we should examine the players and their ideas more carefully.

The ideas

The debates in the Society for the Promotion of Enlightenment show that Jewish intellectuals in Odesa were divided. One group promoted a vision of the Jew as a modern person just "like everyone else." Their message reflected changes in public life that permitted Jews to integrate into Russian or Ukrainian society through religious reform and behavioral modification—speaking and writing in Russian and dressing and acting like others. Another group, however, envisioned the development of a unique modern Jewish and national culture. Its goal was not integration into a foreign world but the cultivation of a particularistic Jewish culture, pursued through modern means, in the arts, literature, poetry, music, and philosophy. As one might guess, both orientations had their origins in the Haskalah, especially the Haskalah in Odesa, where the earliest impetus for economic integration was balanced with struggles for new Jewish identities.[15]

Throughout the nineteenth century, Odesa served as a beacon of economic prosperity and modernity, where Jews could reinvent themselves as individuals. Therefore, it was a place that (in sociological terms) was the antithesis of Lithuanian towns—Vilna (Vilnius) or Kovno (Kaunas), for example—where religious hierarchies reigned unchallenged and economic activity was sluggish. In such places, Jewish life was identified in collective categories—collective taxation, observance of religious events, and family life; this world did not emphasize individualism.

In the maskilic literary tradition, individualism was associated with Odesa. The life of the protagonist was cast as a liberation story, divided between past and present. The author/hero was born and spent his (it is almost always a male) childhood and early adulthood in Lithuania or Volhynia, where he knew only suffering and disappointment. Leaving his hometown (either by force or

---

15 Olga Litvak, *Haskalah: The Romantic Movement in Judaism* (New Brunswick: Rutgers University Press, 2012), 26.

voluntarily), he reached Odesa: liberation. This is certainly the plot of Moshe Leib Lilienblum's "Khatot ne'urim" (The sins of youth) and other works.[16]

Lilienblum's memoir tells us that Odesa's Jewish life resembled Jewish life in Western Europe but was also *sui generis* because it combined individualism with elements of Jewish collectivism. A Jew in Odesa did not feel like a member of a tiny minority, as in Western Europe, but, rather, like part of a larger population, as in Lithuania. The Jew in Odesa lived differently, however, without fear of religious authorities, in a city whose employers prized talent, education, and ambition.

The history of the Russian Jewish intelligentsia as the leader of the Jewish community is based largely on the role of education in the consciousness of Odesa's Jewish population, which considered education the primary engine of economic and social progress. Intellectuals represented the fruit of education and served as a model for how education could transform a Jew and permit him/her access to non-Jewish society and (at least potentially) a lucrative job. The rise of modern Jewish schools in Odesa in the 1880s is associated with Mikhail Morgulis, who almost single-handedly revitalized the OPE branch in Odesa by turning its focus to elementary education.[17] In the next decade, the branch's activities continued in this direction with additional subsidies for schools, for school lunches, books, and, especially, vocational training.[18] In addition, branch officials consulted with kheder teachers (*melamedim*) and gave subsidies to kheders that included secular subjects. Although the resources available could not satisfy all the needs of the Jewish poor, Odesa of the 1890s witnessed an earnest attempt at the practical realization of mass education.

The efforts to expand secular education were not without critics. Some claimed that a weakened Jewish identity might contribute to a breakdown in the Jewish collective and ultimately lead to mass assimilation. What could stop assimilation? National-oriented Jews in Odesa had an answer: creating and sustaining a modern national Jewish culture. It is noteworthy that Morgulis' form of school expansion relied on money from wealthy individuals, industrialists in

---

16 Lilienblum, *Khatot ne'urim, o, vidui hagadol shel ekhad hasofrim ha'ivrim* [Sins of youth, or the great confession of one of the Hebrew writers] (Vienna: Buchdruckerei von Georg Brög, 1876).
17 Horowitz, *Jewish Philanthropy*, 47–50. See the society's annual report for 1884 in V. D-ov. "Iubilei 'Prosveshcheniia'; O dvadtsatiletnei deiatel'nosti Odesskogo otdeleniia Obshchestva rasprostraneniia prosveshcheniia mezhdu evreiami Rossii (1867–1892)," *Voskhod* 7 (July 1893): part 2, 12.
18 *Otchet o deiatel'nosti komiteta odesskogo otdeleniia Obshchestva dlia rasprostraneniia prosveshcheniia mezhdu evreiami v Rossii v 1901 g.* (Odesa: Obshchestvo dlia rasprostraneniia prosveshcheniia, 1902), 1–5.

the city, and his efforts were largely philanthropic. Furthermore, his approach was undemocratic, entirely top-down. Decisions were made by the organizers on behalf of the students and their families. In this way, the older generation retained the elitist aspect of the original maskilim.

Some aspects of maskilic culture, however, took root. By the century's end, a veritable renaissance of Jewish culture was underway. The development of modern Hebrew in Odesa was a central preoccupation of the nationalists, who employed Hebrew as the linguistic vehicle for such literary journals as *Hashiloakh* (The messenger) and *Hapardes* (The orange grove). Haim Nahman Bialik, Ahad Ha'am, and Yehoshua Rawnitzki, for example, spoke in the spirit of Jewish nationalism and literary modernism rather than that of Jewish enlightenment.[19] Given that cultural production in modern Hebrew was elitist, when the nationalists began to devote themselves to producing an ideal curriculum, they created one that matched their interests. The qualities that Ahad Ha'am, Dubnow, Dizengoff, and Ben-Ami wanted to cultivate in others were precisely those they prized in themselves: knowledge of world culture, accompanied by strong expertise in modern Hebrew and Judaica. An undoubtedly elitist aspect reflects the levels of erudition that they hoped students could attain.

Zionism is an important subtext in the school debates. In particular, one hears echoes from the Bnei Moshe group of the late 1880s and the struggles of the Democratic Faction against Theodor Herzl around 1900. In particular, some individuals, for example Ahad Ha'am, played a major role in the school debates and discussions over Zionism. For those familiar with Ahad Ha'am's arguments there is no reason to rehearse them here, but it is worth noting that his vision entailed the formation of an elite within Hibbat Tsion devoted to his ideas. In his account, Steven Zipperstein, Ahad Ha'am's biographer, emphasizes his subject's political tactics, his secrecy, and devious conduct: "What was to be made accessible to the public had to differ from what the elite knew to be true."[20] Zipperstein also underscores the formation of an elite. In contrast to Ahad Ha'am's critique of the Hibbat Tsion movement in such articles as "Lo ze haderekh" (Not this way) and "Emet meerets yisrael," (Truth from Eretz Yisrael), membership in Bnei Moshe was limited to an exclusive group of individuals chosen by Bnei Moshe's leaders. As envisioned, each Bnei Moshe member would have qualities transmitted through the education that the nationalists proposed in 1902.

---

19 On Hebrew in Odesa, see Avner Holtzman, *Hayim Nahman Bialik: Poet of Hebrew* (New Haven: Yale University Press, 2017).

20 Steven Zipperstein, *Elusive Prophet: Ahad Ha'am and the Origins of Zionism* (Berkeley: University of California Press, 1993), 39.

They would be well educated in religious and secular subjects; they would have outstanding physical and mental qualities; they would be humble; they would even accept anonymity.[21] The focus was on cultural renewal and personal realization, which were understood partly in opposition to Hibbat Tsion as it was conceived as practical settlement on the land.[22] In this way, one could clearly see that Ahad Ha'am emphasized an anti-cosmopolitan consciousness, while accepting at the same time the reigning concepts of individual consciousness and collectivist action.

Other subtexts connect Odesa in 1902 to the Zionist movement generally and the nationalists' struggles against Theodor Herzl and his political Zionism. Undoubtedly, Ahad Ha'am inspired members of Zionism's Democratic Faction (Bernstein-Cohen, Bialik, Joseph Klausner, Avram Idelson, and others) who challenged Herzl at the Congress in 1901 (December 26–30). It was the "cultural question" that animated the fraction. As David Vital describes it:

> The surface issue in dispute had been the placing of the debate on "culture" on the agenda of the Congress; the underlying issue was the place of culture on the agenda of the movement. Herzl was reluctant to back the promoters of yet another debate on the subject for fear, as has been said, of an irreparable quarrel with the orthodox. The members of the Democratic Party were encouraged to persist in the effort to force a decision by the conviction that what divided them from Herzl was a fundamental disagreement on the nature and content of Zionism itself, which they conceived in broader terms than those which they ascribed to Herzl. They judged his views to be simplistic in his reliance on diplomacy as a method and in his confidence in the future Jewish state as the prime engine of national revolution and revival. They had no time or taste for compromise with orthodoxy, resented Herzl's tendency to seek it, and discounted his belief in the "power of the rabbis" over the Jewish masses.[23]

According to Vital, the cultural question also included a direct political challenge to Herzl's leadership. The term "Democratic Faction" was a sloppy translation from the German; better put, it would be the "Democratic Party," as the

---

21 Ibid., 41.
22 On Hibbat Tsion, see Goldshtein, *Anu hayinu harishonim*.
23 David Vital, *Zionism: The Formative Years* (Oxford: Clarendon Press, 1982), 193.

members sought power in the Zionist movement as a recognizable group with its own ideas—people who disagreed with the political emphasis of the movement and pressed for change. They emphasized the importance of cultural creation, non-religious Jewish education, and the development of the individual. One may connect the dots of the Democratic Faction's demands to the educational program formulated by the nationalists in Odesa at nearly the same time.

The link between these Russian Zionists and Ahad Ha'am is obvious when one examines the role of the Faction members at the 1902 Second Conference of Russian Zionists in Minsk. The members suggested creating a unique elite society of "young bachelors," which would devote two years of their lives entirely to Zionist activity.[24] Ahad Ha'am spoke at the conference, arguing that "neither through politics nor economics could the Land of Israel solve the Jewish problem; [it could be done] only spiritually."[25] He added that the spiritual problem was the most important in Zionism, and he offered two proposals: "To establish a world union to promote national cultural activity that would be independent of the Zionist movement but would participate in it," and "to give equal attention to the two tendencies in education, the religious and modern, and to create two committees, one—a religious committee and the second—a modern one."[26] It is fascinating to contemplate whether the long-time existence of the dual rabbinate modeled Ahad Ha'am's willingness to have two educational organizations. In any case, the emphasis on modern education as a solution to the Jewish problem and Zionism clearly weighed on him.

The role of cosmopolitanism

I maintain, in addition, that the Odesa Jewish intelligentsia's usage and understanding of the term "cosmopolitanism," unlike today's view, did not signify a completed phenomenon in which Jews and non-Jews lived together in harmony. Rather, cosmopolitanism reflected a notion regarding the Jews' self-conscious openness to non-Jewish elements, especially in public spaces. The concept refers to Judah Leib Gordon's proposition when he wrote of the ideal of the Haskalah: "A man on the street and a Jew in one's tents."[27] In other words, act in accordance

---

24 Yosef Klausner, *Opozitsiyah lehertzl* [Opposition to Herzl] (Jerusalem: Hotsaat Akhi'ever, 1960), 197.
25 Ibid., 196.
26 Ibid.
27 Michael Stanislawski, *For Whom Do I Toil? Judah Leib Gordon and the Crisis of Russian Jewry* (New York: Oxford University Press, 1988), 52.

with non-Jews in public spaces but retain one's Jewish conventions at home. In this interpretation, the focus is less on the external result and more on self-reflection: "Am I open to the outside world, its books, language, way of life, at least in public?"

Although some interpret Gordon's phrase as two selves for two different contexts, Michael Stanislawski considers that the phrase "was a call not for the bifurcation of Jewish identity, but for its integration; it advocated being both a full-fledged man—a free, modern, enlightened Russian-speaking Mensch—and a Jew at home in the creative spirit of the Hebrew language." This central point, that the modern Jew blended two orientations within himself, is key to understanding Jewish thought in Russia. Although the meaning of "secular" and "Jewish" changed, the idea of a synthesis remained especially strong among Jewish thinkers for a century. Clearly, this unity was shared by Jews in Western Europe, too, and, in fact, the model of emancipated Jews clearly influenced Gordon's conception. Although I do not disagree with Stanislawski, my emphasis is on the Jew's psychology, the person who focused on the adoption of that synthesis.

An example of cosmopolitanism in this sense is found in the writings of Mikhail Morgulis, who claimed that Judaism was ideal because it combined universalistic and particularistic elements. In his essay "Сущность еврейства" (The essence of Jewry, 1893), he writes:

> Общность и всесторонность найденного иудаизмом принципа заключается именно в том, что раз для человека найдено подобие, отличающееся недосягаемыми для него совершенство, он должен стремиться к усовершенствованию, должен стремиться бесконечно, чтобы каждый раз стать ближе и ближе к своему идеалу. Далее, идеал этот заключает в себе все светлые стороны: добра, разума, красоты, справедливости, любви и пр. Человек, стало быть, обязан стремиться к развитию в себе всех этих светлых сторон недосягаемого идеала.

> (The commonality and breadth of the principle discovered by Judaism inheres exactly in the following: since people have discovered an image that is characterized by ideals that are beyond their reach, they must strive for perfection, ceaselessly strive in order to come closer to this ideal. Further, this ideal consists of all that is hopeful: kindness, reason, beauty, justice, love, and so on. People, it turned out, are obligated to strive for the

development within themselves of all these hopeful aspects of the unattainable ideal.)[28]

In 1902, Morgulis answered the nationalists directly, arguing in favor of cosmopolitanism but emphasizing the inner attitude or psychological position. He explained that assimilation should be welcomed, as you can learn a great deal from non-Jews that can be appropriated for one's own culture. Whereas negative assimilation consisted of a total negation of one's identity, positive assimilation was a laudable goal. Assimilation represented "integration only in external forms with the dominant environment, but in spirit, in its strivings toward the creation of its own culture, [integration] meant love for the past and its historical monuments, sympathy for the people, and the illumination of various spheres of Jewish knowledge."[29] He was confident that the future of Russian Jewry lay in a synthesis of Jewish and Russian qualities and the integration of the Jews into Russian imperial culture.

Despite his ideological differences with Morgulis, Dubnow had a similar attitude, seeing cosmopolitanism as a kind of synthesis whose primary purpose was to transform and improve the Jew. This comes through in Dubnow's manifesto of the *Folkspartei* (People's Party, 1906), in which he demanded full civil rights under state law but also rights to an autonomous sphere of Jewish culture.[30] An examination of Dubnow's writings shows his broad commitment to cosmopolitanism, or learning from the non-Jewish world, in order to strengthen his own nationalism. The kind of cosmopolitanism that Dubnow and many other nationalists imagined was not (as we understand it) life in a world of differing people, ethnicities, and religion; rather, it was an openness of the Jew to the outside without sacrificing the Jewish core. In fact, cosmopolitanism was supposed to enrich that core.

Conclusion

This study shows that the two groups clearly resemble one another more than they diverge from each other. In their elitism and concept of cosmopolitanism, they represent two branches of a single tree, the Haskalah. Although the future belonged to the assimilators—most Russian Jews under Soviet rule assimilated,

---

28 Mikhail Morgulis, "Sushchnost' iudaizma," *Voskhod* 1 (January 1891): 75–76.
29 Mikhail Morgulis, "Nationalizatsiia i assimiliatsiia," *Voskhod* 5 (May 1902): 110–11.
30 See *Evreiskaia narodnaia partiia* (St. Petersburg, 1907).

chose general education, and rejected Jewish separatism (voluntarily or not)—that form of assimilation had little in common with what the board of the OPE in Odesa desired. At the same time, one can ask whether the nationalists got their way in Odesa, or even in Israel. In any case, in their elitism and notions of cosmopolitanism in education and elsewhere, both groups show the limits, positive and negative, of the intelligentsia as leaders of the Jewish community. For over half a century, Odesa was the center of the Russian Jewish intelligentsia (the city became identified with it), but those Jewish intellectuals are often misunderstood. Anyone who idealizes democracy, the masses, and American-style cosmopolitanism will miss the essential truth that Odesa's Jewish intellectuals reflected elitist principles and preferred leadership top-down, rather than bottom-up.

CHAPTER 5

Ethnic Violence in a Cosmopolitan City: The October 1905 Pogrom in Odesa

Robert Weinberg

Introduction

Cosmopolitanism connotes tolerance of others: inclusiveness, multiculturalism, acceptance of the values and ideas of others, open-mindedness, sophistication, and worldliness. It is a mindset as well as a way of life that tends to be the preserve of the privileged, educated stratum of society and plays out in many spaces throughout the urban environment. Moreover, a city's cosmopolitan populace shares urban spaces with other residents who do not subscribe to the same cultural values and who occasionally engage in behaviors that are distinctly non-cosmopolitan. As the anthropologist Caroline Humphrey has noted, cosmopolitanism does not preclude harboring prejudices that all too frequently give rise to ethnic (or more precisely inter-faith) violence. Indeed, such assaults disrupt the cosmopolitan features of a city, serving as its "reverse" and "perforating" its social fabric.[1] The history of Odesa demonstrates that ethnic prejudice and hostility co-existed with cosmopolitan values, which were no guarantee of peaceful and respectful relations among residents. The twentieth century, sadly, is full of examples of educated and seemingly cultured individuals sharing the venomous hatred of Jews that led to deadly expressions of antisemitism. In other

---

1 Caroline Humphrey, "Odessa: Pogroms in a Cosmopolitan City," *Ab Imperio*, no. 4 (2010): 17, 54.

words, the persistence of anti-Jewish prejudices, even in a bastion of urbane cosmopolitanism like Odesa, should not surprise us.

As a port city, Odesa was the quintessential cosmopolitan center: residents hailed from all over the empire and Europe, rubbing shoulders with people from diverse cultures and backgrounds in a city that was little older than a century. Many languages were spoken, and the flourishing heart of the city had all the attributes of a modern metropolis such as sewers, electric streetlights, trams, and other up-to-date amenities. By the turn of the twentieth century, Odesa was an economic juggernaut as it became the country's most important port and was home to banks, brokerage houses, food processing plants such as sugar refineries, and other manufacturing enterprises.

The city boasted a rich cultural and educational life with a first-rate university, theaters, opera house, and cinemas. A thriving cultural and educated privileged elite endowed the city with its well-deserved reputation as Russia's "little Paris" and "El Dorado." Much of the city's cosmopolitanism stemmed from its history as a port city that attracted Germans, Greeks, French, Armenians, and Poles over the course of the nineteenth century. Russians and Jews, who comprised around 80 percent of the city's population, occupied prominent positions in realms of culture, education, and business. The multiethnic mix was balanced by the preponderance of Russian and Yiddish speakers who had moved to the city from other areas of the Russian Empire and contributed, in part, to the city's cosmopolitan atmosphere. In 1897, speakers of Russian numbered nearly 51 percent of the population, while just under 6 percent of Odesans claimed Ukrainian as their mother tongue or nationality. Those Jews who declared Yiddish as their first language were 32.5 percent of the population. Odesa, then, was more multiethnic than St. Petersburg and Moscow, where Russians, based on native language, comprised 87 and 95 percent of those two city's inhabitants, respectively.[2] Most Odesans, however, had attenuated roots in the city, and few could trace their family's presence in Odesa back beyond one or two generations, if that. Many inhabitants of the empire's fourth largest city were strangers to urban life and to each other; in the early twentieth century, some ten thousand persons arrived each year, contributing to the city's rapid population growth.[3] In the early 1880s, a little more than two hundred thousand people lived in the

---

2   Patricia Herlihy, *Odessa: A History 1794–1914* (Cambridge, MA: Harvard University Press, 1986), 242 and 251. The number of Jews based on nationality (i.e., religion) was slightly higher as some Jews claimed Russian as their native tongue.
3   Tsentral'nyi gosudarstvennyi istoricheskii arkhiv, fond 23, opis' 20, delo 1, list 174.

city; by 1905, the number had reached nearly half a million.[4] But not all Odesans were cosmopolitan in demeanor, education, lifestyle, and attitudes. According to the 1897 census, slightly over 40 percent of the populace could not read.[5] The cosmopolitanism of the city was diluted by the presence of many Odesans who did not share the attitudes, values, and lifestyles of the city's privileged elite. In other words, Odesa was culturally and socially complex and variegated, and the worlds of the cosmopolitan and non-cosmopolitan inhabitants frequently bled into each other throughout the city. The cosmopolitan spaces of Odesa, however, did not prevent pogroms. As in the case of earlier pogrom waves, the pogroms that occurred during Russia's first revolution of the twentieth century took place in the context of a political crisis and widespread social unrest. The pogroms of 1905 were considerably more violent, deadly, and destructive than those that occurred in the wake of Tsar Alexander II's assassination in 1881, but they did not reach the levels of bloodshed seen in 1918–1920, when the collapse of state authority and the contending armies of the civil war resulted in the largest loss of Jewish life prior to World War II. In terms of death and destruction, the pogroms of 1905 were a way station between those of 1881 and 1918–1920, when marauding soldiers engaged in wanton, unrestrained violence against Jews. In 1881–82, rioters targeted primarily property and shouted "Beat the Kikes," but in 1905 pogroms turned deadly as gentiles threatened to kill, butcher, and slaughter Jews.[6] Some historians consider that the pogroms graduated to ethnic cleansing and genocide by the time of the civil war.[7]

Nearly seven hundred pogroms broke out after Tsar Nikolai II issued the October Manifesto, which granted civil liberties, promised the establishment of an elected legislative assembly, and heralded the initial steps of political modernization in Russia. Throughout the Pale of Settlement and even in towns and cities outside the Pale where Jews resided, pogromists destroyed thousands of homes and stores owned by Jews, wounded thousands, and murdered in cold blood approximately one thousand persons. Property damage totaled some

---

4   Herlihy, *Odessa*, 242.
5   Ibid.
6   See Giovanni Savino, "A Reactionary Utopia: Russian Black Hundreds from Autocracy to Fascism," in *Entangled Far Rights: A Russian-European Intellectual Romance in the Twentieth Century*, ed. Marlene Laruelle (Pittsburgh: University of Pittsburgh Press, 2018), 40; Albert Kaganovich, *The Long Life and Swift Death of Jewish Rechitsa: A Community in Belarus, 1625–2000* (Madison: University of Madison Press, 2013), 73. See also Vald Knekherg, "Mohyliv-Podilskyy, Ukraine," accessed December 6, 2022, https://kehilalinks.jewishgen.org/mohyliv_podilskyy/1905_pogrom_narrative.html.
7   Elissa Bemporad, *Legacy of Blood: Jews, Pogroms, and Ritual Murder in the Land of the Soviets* (New York: Oxford University Press, 2019).

sixty-two million rubles.[8] Abraham Ascher notes that 690 pogroms occurred after the announcement of the October Manifesto, resulting in 876 persons dead and between seven thousand and eight thousand persons wounded.[9] The deadliest and costliest pogrom occurred in the Black Sea port city of Odesa, where thousands of Jews suffered at the hands of pogromists who rioted unchecked for several days before government forces restored law and order. Police in Odesa claimed that at least four hundred Jews and one hundred gentiles were killed and approximately three hundred, mostly Jews, suffered injuries; some 1,632 houses, apartments, and stores belonging to Jews incurred damage.[10]

In this chapter, I focus on the events in Odesa that led to a four-day rampage by non-Jews against the Jewish residents of the city. I draw upon my book published some thirty years ago and repeat my argument that the pogrom was the culmination of trends that had been unfolding in the city; in particular, I noted that the combination of intra-class tensions with ethno-religious prejudices laid the groundwork for the pogrom.[11] Like nationhood and national identity, ethnic violence is not a primordial or essentialist phenomenon; the politicization of ethnicity is very much situational, contingent upon a confluence of multiple factors and circumstances. I shall examine the long-term factors and short-term catalysts that account for the outbreak of ethnic violence and explain why labor unrest in Odesa deteriorated into ethnic bloodletting; indeed, for most of the year, Jewish and non-Jewish workers did not clash. For example, the general strike that occurred in June and coincided with the arrival of the battleship *Potemkin*, whose crew had mutinied, culminated in the shooting of hundreds of Odesans by government troops on the Primorsky Stairs (an incident later made famous by Sergei Eisenstein's 1925 film *Battleship Potemkin*), but that labor unrest was free of ethnic strife. Several months later, however, when another

---

8   Abraham Ascher, *The Revolution of 1905: Russia in Disarray* (Stanford: Stanford University Press, 1988).
9   Ibid., 255.
10   These figures are estimates at best, particularly in terms of the number wounded, which was higher than the police reported. See Robert Weinberg, *The Revolution of 1905 in Odessa: Blood on the Steps* (Bloomington: Indiana University Press, 1993), 164.
11   Unless otherwise indicated, the following discussion is based on my *The Revolution of 1905 in Odessa: Blood on the Steps* (Bloomington: Indiana University Press, 1993) and the following articles by Gerald Surh: "Ekaterinoslav City in 1905: Workers, Jews, and Violence," *International and Labor Working-Class History* no. 64 (2003): 139–166; "Russia's 1905 Era Pogroms Reexamined," *Canadian-American Slavic Studies*, no. 44 (2010): 253–95; "The Jews of Ekaterinoslav in 1905 as Seen from Town Hall: Ethnic Relations on an Imperial Frontier," *Ab Imperio*, no. 4 (2003): 217–238; and "The Role of Civil and Military Commanders during the 1905 Pogroms in Odessa and Kiev," *Jewish Social Studies* 15, no. 3 (Spring/Summer 2009): 39–55.

general strike paralyzed the city, many gentile workers turned their sights on Jews. Although not all pogromists were workers, an overwhelming number of them were Russian dockworkers, day laborers, and unskilled factory workers. They were presumably the least cosmopolitan of residents of Odesa and did not have to jettison their cosmopolitan "skin" when they attacked Jews. Patricia Herlihy notes that Russians and Ukrainians tended to be employed in "occupations that conferred relatively low status in the social hierarchy."[12]

Moreover, as Evrydiki Sifneos comments on earlier incidents of anti-Jewish violence, "The riots and looting that occurred during ethnic clashes in Odessa in 1871, in 1881, and 1886 were basically carried out by the lowest strata of the population, the unemployed, the partly employed and the unskilled."[13] What accounts for the deterioration of relations between Jews and non-Jews, and what does the violence reveal about the political landscape that characterized Odesa in 1905? Why did ethnic co-existence, which tended to be peaceful and free of strife for years, turn into bloodletting? In short, why was the cosmopolitan atmosphere of the city "perforated" in the words of Caroline Humphrey?

I shall offer some insight into how the revolutionary juncture of 1905, which pitted pro-autocratic, reactionary forces against the anti-monarchical forces of reform and revolution by the time Tsar Nikolai II issued the October Manifesto, led to a devastating pogrom. The pogrom was the culmination of trends that had been unfolding in the city. Examination of the pogrom in Odesa illuminates how anti-Jewish violence resulted from the social and political turmoil and instability that characterized late imperial Russia in the early years of the twentieth century. Anti-Jewish violence in 1905 stemmed in part from long-standing prejudices against Jews, but it required a confluence of particular social, political, and economic factors to spark physical attacks on Jews. The erosion of autocratic authority and widespread labor unrest in the city transformed antisemitism into violent behavior. Once antisemitism turned violent, local authorities had difficulty restoring law and order. Historian Ilya Gerasimov is certainly correct when he notes that ideology does not account for the behavior of all pogromists.[14] Not all the people who trashed Jewish homes, looted Jewish stores, and harmed Jews physically were motivated by opposition to the October Manifesto. Yet,

---

12 Herlihy, *Odessa: A History*, 249.
13 Evrydiki Sifneos, *Imperial Odessa: Peoples, Spaces, Identities* (Leiden and Boston: Brill, 2018), 181.
14 Ilya Gerasimov, "Review of *Anti-Jewish Violence: Rethinking the Pogrom in East European History*," *Ab Imperio*, no. 3 (2012): 396–412.

explanations that do not take into account the prevailing political climate fall short of elucidating the causes of the pogrom.

Several questions are critical to understanding the outbreak and dynamics of the pogrom. First, what was the role of the state? What responsibility, if any, did governmental representatives in St. Petersburg and Odesa have for the outbreak of the violence? Second, how important is it to distinguish between long-term and short-term factors, between longstanding tensions between Jews and gentiles and the catalysts that impelled non-Jews to attack Jewish Odesans. Third, which people or groups of people were predisposed or inclined to participate in the violence against Jews and why? Did socio-economic circumstances of individual pogromists play a role in the outbreak of pogroms? Finally, why did the cosmopolitanism of Odesa fail to prevent the outbreak of ethnic violence?

Role of the state

Two aspects of the question about the role of the state merit attention. First, a question that has persisted ever since observers and historians began writing about the pogroms of the early 1880s: did officials help organize pogroms? A general consensus has emerged since the late 1980s that the central government in St. Petersburg did not conspire to instigate pogroms or even encourage the violence. It is undeniable, however, that Tsar Nikolai II and many of his ministers sympathized with the attacks on Jews and provided funds for extremist monarchist groups. The same assessment holds for the earlier unrest of 1881–82.

Local officials—the police and the military—in the vast majority of cases did not initiate or instigate the violence. Doing so would have been career suicide as their job was to maintain law and order, particularly during times of acute social and political unrest. There is no denying, however, that the police and soldiers did little to interfere with the pogromists' fury; sometimes they waited two or three days before setting out to restore the peace. In many instances, police and soldiers participated in beating Jews, looting Jewish homes and businesses, even directing rioters to buildings where Jews lived. In sum, the eruption of anti-Jewish violence throughout the empire was an unplanned occurrence, but its duration of three, or even four, days in some cases such as Odesa raises questions about government complicity. Or perhaps it was simply a case of sheer incompetence and lack of preparation?

The second aspect of the question concerns what I term the health of the state. Was the state's authority and power so weak as to encourage pogromists to act with little fear of official intervention? Did the straitened circumstances of the autocracy permit the outbreak of ethnic violence? Succinctly put, the attacks on Jews and their property that took place in the wake of political concessions granted by Tsar Nikolai II in October 1905 marked the culmination of events that had been eroding autocratic power and authority since the beginning of the year. The absence of a strong, confident state power created a vacuum in which extremists of all stripes had virtual free reign until government forces reasserted themselves. The three major waves of pogroms occurred in 1881–1882, 1905–1906, and 1919–1920, when the power and authority of the central government was either called into question or had collapsed, leaving a power vacuum filled by warring armies.

Short-term catalysts: The crisis of the autocracy

Examination of the pogrom in Odesa helps to illuminate the link between political revolution and the outbreak of pogroms, particularly the link between anti-Jewish violence and the social and political turmoil and instability that characterized late imperial Russia in the early years of the twentieth century. To be sure, the anti-Jewish unrest in 1905 stemmed in part from deep-rooted anti-Jewish animus, but antisemitic sentiments had to combine with certain social, political, and economic factors to spark violence. Ethnic conflict was rooted in a constellation of events, and its outbreak derived from a specific crisis besetting the autocracy in 1905. This crisis impelled Russian inhabitants of the city to attack Jews in October 1905.[15]

In 1905, the regime of Nikolai II found itself challenged by a series of events largely of its own making. The decision in 1904 to provoke Japan into a war that ended in disastrous and embarrassing losses for Russia and the shooting of unarmed men, women, and children who had marched to the Winter Palace seeking a peaceful redress of grievances on January 9, 1905 (known as Bloody Sunday) sparked months of turmoil all over the empire. Workers, students, professionals, national minorities, revolutionaries, and liberals alike organized to demand political reform. The tsarist government responded to these calls for the granting of a constitution, civil rights, and political liberties with halfhearted overtures that radicalized the opposition forces and chipped away at the authority and power of the autocracy. Before October, the government's concessions were too timid and too late to satisfy much of Russian society. By mid-October,

---

15 Given the ethnic make-up of Odesa, it is reasonable to conclude that the categories "non-Jews" and "gentiles" refer primarily to Russians (with a smattering of Ukrainians).

a general strike paralyzed the country, prompting the tsar begrudgingly to grant civil and political rights and promise the formation of a popularly elected legislative assembly. The issuance of the October Manifesto on October 17 set the stage for the pogroms that broke out as the opposing forces—either advocating reform, if not revolution, or supporting reaction—took to the streets to celebrate or decry the erosion of autocratic power.

Events in Odesa in 1905 hewed closely to the pattern that characterized developments on an empire-wide basis: workers demanded the right to organize in defense of their interests; strikes engulfed the city on and off for most of the year; and educated Odesans agitated for reforms that would undermine the foundations of the autocracy. Politics in Odesa became increasingly polarized during 1905 as anti- and pro-government forces coalesced and mobilized. In addition to the organized revolutionary parties that had been active for several years in Odesa, radical student groups also emerged as significant political forces, along with extremist patriotic activists and nascent organizations that appealed to those Odesans who resented the offensive against the tsar and his government. The stage was set for a confrontation between the forces of revolution and reaction, and the pogrom occurred amidst the political rift that divided Odesa.

The legacy of ethnic relations and the fragility of cosmopolitanism

The ethnic composition of Odesa helps to explain why the country-wide crisis turned violent there and pitted Russians against Jews; it thus offers an opportunity to explore the effect of interethnic relations on events during Russia's first brush with political revolution. The political unrest of 1905 has to be seen in part through the lens of long-standing ethnic relations and the collapse of cosmopolitan values that characterized social relations in the city.

The large number of Jews living in the city and their visible presence in the commercial and industrial life of the city contributed to resentment against Odesa's Jewish community. In the mid-nineteenth century, Greek merchants found their control of the grain trade challenged by the emergence of Jewish competitors. This situation contributed to the outbreak of pogroms in 1859 and 1871 in which Greek residents attacked Jews and their property.[16] The decline of Greeks' importance in the local economy and the rise of Russian-owned

---

16 Weinberg, *The Revolution of 1905 in Odessa*, 16–17; Herlihy, *Odessa*, 299–303.

businesses by the last two decades of the century led to heightened tensions between Jews and Russians. In the 1880s, firms owned by Jews controlled 70 percent of the export trade in grain, rising to over 90 percent by 1910. In addition, Jews and Russians not only lived in the same residential areas but also shared working space in some cases. For instance, Jews and Russians competed for work at the docks as stevedores and day laborers but tended to be occupationally segregated in manufacturing enterprises, whether workshops or small factories.[17]

Already predisposed to dislike Jews due to well-entrenched antisemitism in late imperial Russian society, Russians, Ukrainians, and other gentiles in Odesa utilized the Jews' economic role in the city to accuse them of exploiting non-Jews. This popular belief that Jewish capitalists exploited Russians had less basis in reality, however, than was commonly assumed. The preponderance of the wealth in Odesa, not to mention political influence and power, remained in the hand of non-Jews, who controlled half of all large commercial enterprises and brokerage firms and most of the factories.[18]

In fact, most Jews eked out meager livings as shopkeepers, second-hand dealers, salesclerks, petty traders, domestic servants, day laborers, and workshop employees. In 1905, nearly eighty thousand Jews requested financial assistance from the Jewish community in order to buy matzah during Passover, a telling sign that well over half of the Jews in Odesa experienced difficulties making ends meet.[19]

Despite the disparity between popular perception and the reality of Jewish wealth and power, Jews found it difficult to dispel this attitude, a situation that held especially true during the recession that gripped the country after 1900. Russia entered a deep crisis, and Odesa's economy suffered a setback due to a decrease in the demand for manufactured goods, the drop in the supply of grain available for export, and the drying up of credit. Conditions continued to deteriorate as the year 1905 approached, due to the outbreak of war between Russia and Japan in 1904.[20]

During the first half of 1905, tensions between Jews and Russians ran particularly high. Fomented in part by the sentiment that Jews were not contributing to the war effort against Japan, these resentments nearly reached a breaking point in the spring, when rumors of an imminent pogrom circulated among the Jewish

---

17 Weinberg, *The Revolution of 1905 in Odessa*, chapters 1 and 2.
18 Ibid., 17–19.
19 Ibid., 19.
20 Ibid., 21–22.

community during Russian Orthodox Holy Week in April. In the past, Jews had not taken precautions, but in 1905, they mobilized. In the aftermath of the 1903 Kishinev pogrom, Jews began to organize in anticipation for future outbreaks of anti-Jewish violence: they procured weapons, formed armed brigades that were ready to act at a moment's notice, and coordinated efforts with revolutionaries. Just before Orthodox Easter, the National Committee of Jewish Self-Defense distributed a series of leaflets threatening non-Jews with armed retaliation in the event of a pogrom. The committee urged all Jews to join self-defense brigades and prepare to counter any attack on Jewish lives and property with guns, while it encouraged Jewish women to prepare solutions of sulfuric acid to throw at pogromists. City governor Dmitri Neidgart, afraid of the potential for public disorders, took the unusual step of publicizing the preparedness of the Jewish community to resist a pogrom with force. No disturbances occurred, but fears of a pogrom emerged once again in June in the aftermath of a general strike and the disorders occasioned by the arrival of the battleship *Potemkin*, whose crew had mutinied.

On June 13, Cossack troops shot several workers from factories that had been on strike since the beginning of May. Workers retaliated on June 14 by initiating a general strike and attacking police with guns and rocks. The arrival of the *Potemkin* during the night of June 14 diverted the workers' attention. On June 15, instead of confronting their employers, thousands of Odesans jammed the port district in order to view the battleship and rally behind the mutinous sailors. By late afternoon, some members of the crowd began to ransack warehouses housing wine and vodka and set fire to the harbor's wooden buildings. Although available sources do not enable a precise determination of the composition of the rioters, arrest records reveal that non-Jewish vagrants, dockworkers, and day laborers comprised the overwhelming majority. The military cordoned off the harbor and opened fire on the trapped crowd. By the next morning hundreds had died, victims of either the soldiers' bullets or the fire that ravaged the harbor.

During these disorders, rumors of an impending pogrom once again surfaced, as the Jewish community feared it might become the target of Russian workers' wrath. Indeed, right-wing agitators attempted to incite Russian workers against the Jews. Several days after the massacre, a leaflet blaming Jews for the bloodshed at the port appeared on the streets. The leaflet accused Jewish students and self-defense squads of fomenting the unrest and inciting unwitting Russians to set fire to the docks.

In Odesa, the populace and city authorities tended to associate civil unrest and political opposition with Jews, a word synonymous with revolutionaries.

While many reports of Jewish revolutionary activity were exaggerations or even fabrications, Jews were behind some of the social and political ferment enveloping Odesa. The emergence of sustained labor unrest for most of 1905 and accusations by right-wing agitators that Jews were responsible for the political crisis gripping the country led to heightened tensions between Jews and Russians. During the summer months, the police arrested a group of Jewish revolutionaries for making and stockpiling bombs, urging Jews to arm themselves, to struggle for civil and political freedom, and overthrow the autocracy. Radical Jewish students organized rallies at the university and directed student strikes and public demonstrations. Jewish youths, students, and workers filled the ranks of the crowds that attended rallies at the university in September and October. Jews actively participated in the work stoppages, demonstrations, and street disorders that overwhelmed Odesa by the time the general strike in mid-October brought the country to a standstill. Moreover, Jewish youths joined forces with the revolutionary parties to organize self-defense units designed to protect the Jewish community. Such preparation saved Jewish lives and protected Jewish property, but it also reinforced the perception of Jews as revolutionaries and the instigators of trouble.

These events confirmed many high-ranking police and other officials' belief that Jews were a seditious element. Government officials in Odesa had a history of blaming Jews for fomenting trouble in the city. This situation signaled to antisemites that the authorities in Odesa sympathized with anti-Jewish agitation. Combined with economic resentments and frustrations as well as religious prejudices, the belief that Jews were revolutionaries helped create an explosive situation. To those residents of Odesa alarmed by the opposition to the tsar and government, Jews were convenient targets for retaliation.

Politics in Odesa polarized during 1905 as both anti- and pro-government forces coalesced and mobilized. Militant monarchist organizations and patriotic student groups emerged and appealed to Odesans who supported the autocracy. In addition to the organized revolutionary parties that had been active for several years in Odesa, radical student groups also emerged as a significant political force. The stage was set for a confrontation between the forces of revolution and reaction, and the pogrom occurred in the context of this unrest that propelled antisemitism, normally dormant and passive, into a paroxysm of bloodletting.

In short, supporters of the tsar viewed Jews as responsible for the unrest that nearly toppled the autocracy, and they gave vent to their anger at this development by turning on Jewish workers. The pogroms were the expression of the crisis besetting the Romanov dynasty as the tsarist government tried to stem the tide of revolution and its supporters mobilized to defend the autocracy.

The anti-Jewish violence grew out of the confrontation between those seeking to topple the government and those wanting to prevent any erosion of autocratic power. And Jews were associated with revolution as well as economic exploitation.

Why did a pogrom erupt in October, however, and not in June when, as we have learned, a general strike devolved into the mass shooting of Jews and non-Jews alike who gathered in the port to celebrate the mutiny on the battleship *Potemkin*? In both cases, Odesans supported anti-government forces, and many of the same Russian workers who rioted in June turned against Jews in October. In both cases, fervent defenders of the autocracy tried to foment a counter-insurgency, but only in mid-October did anti-Jewish violence break out. In my opinion, we need to consider the catalyst that led to the explosion of violence, namely the issuance of the October Manifesto, which demonstrated the desperate efforts of the autocracy to pacify the populace. In addition, in June, government troops did not distinguish between Jewish and non-Jewish rioters caught in the crossfire at the harbor. In October, on the other hand, they aimed their guns only at Jews.

The October pogrom[21]

The killing by soldiers of several students supporting striking workers on October 16 sparked public disturbances and confrontations between government forces and radical students, revolutionaries, and workers who had walked off the job in protest. The storm broke on October 18. News of the October Manifesto had reached Odesa officials on the previous evening, and by the next morning, thousands of people thronged the streets to celebrate. As one university student exclaimed, "A joyous crowd appeared in the streets; people greeted each other as if it were a holiday."[22] Many non-Jews joined Jews in enthusiastically celebrating the granting of civil rights and political liberties.

Soon after the demonstrations began, several individuals began to unfurl red flags and banners with anti-government slogans. Others shouted phrases such as "Down with the Autocracy" and "Long Live Freedom." Apartment dwellers draped red carpets and shawls from their balconies and windows, while groups

---

21 Unless otherwise noted, information about the pogrom is based on ibid., chapter 7.
22 *Materialy k istorii russkoi kontr-revoliutsii*, tom 1, *Pogromy po offitsial'nym dokumentam* (St. Petersburg: Tipografiia tovarishchestva "obshchestvennaia pol'za," 1908), 97.

of demonstrators forced passersby to doff their caps or bow before the flags. In the city council building, demonstrators ripped down the portrait of the tsar, substituted a red flag for the imperial colors, and collected money for weapons. City Governor Dmitrii Neidgart also reported that one group of demonstrators tied portraits of the tsar to the tails of dogs and then released them to roam the city. The mood of the demonstrators grew confrontational as the day wore on. Groups of demonstrators—primarily Jewish youths, according to official accounts—viciously attacked and disarmed policemen. By mid-afternoon, Neidgart had received reports that two policemen had been killed or wounded and twenty-two disarmed and that many others had abandoned their posts in order to avoid possible injury. He ordered the police back to their stations and permitted only patrols in groups.

The clashes were not limited to attacks on policemen by angry demonstrators. Toward the end of the day, tensions between those Odesans who heralded the manifesto and those who disapproved of the concessions granted by the tsar had reached a breaking point. Outraged by the sight of desecrated portraits of the tsar, supporters of the monarchy gave vent to their anger and frustration not by attacking Russians celebrating in the streets but by turning on the Jewish community exclusively, which they considered as the source of problems besetting the country. Clashes occurred as groups of armed demonstrators, chiefly Jewish students and workers, fought with bands of gentile vigilantes. These instances of violence, which marked the beginning of the pogrom, underscored the deep-seated ethnic animosities in Odesa.

Armed confrontations broke out in the afternoon and early evening of October 18. The clashes apparently started when a group of Jews carrying red flags in celebration of the October Manifesto demanded that a group of Russian workers doff their caps to the flags. Harsh words were exchanged, scuffles ensued, and both groups scattered, only to reassemble in nearby streets and resume their fighting. The clashes soon turned into a pogrom, as Russians indiscriminately attacked Jews and began to vandalize and loot Jewish homes, apartments, and stores.

Self-defense brigades that emerged in June redoubled their efforts with the blessing of the Coalition Council, an organization of radicals at the university who sought to bring down the autocracy. Members from the various revolutionary parties active in Odesa such as the Bund, Po'ale-Zion, Bolsheviks, and Mensheviks established self-defense units. So did radical students who entreated the thousands of workers and students—Jewish and Russian—who attended rallies at the university to protect the lives and property of Jews. Self-defense activists could also have been neighbors who gathered in the courtyards of apartment buildings and decided to seek out a brigade at the university to join. A special committee centered at the university collected money to buy weapons, although the sources do not describe how it obtained guns, ammunition, and grenades. In some instances, those seeking to fight pogromists pillaged gun stores.[23]

The pogrom began in full force the next day, October 19. In mid-morning hundreds of Russian children, women, and men gathered in various parts of the city and organized marches to display their loyalty to the tsar. Patriotic, rightwing political organizations, comprised primarily of Russians known as the Black Hundreds, embraced a virulent form of Russian nationalism and helped mobilize inhabitants of the city by organizing public displays of support for the autocracy. Day laborers, especially those employed at the port, comprised a major element of the crowd that assembled at the harbor. Factory and construction workers, shopkeepers, salesclerks, workshop employees, and vagrants soon joined the rallies, where organizers distributed flags, icons, and portraits of the tsar. The marchers also passed around bottles of vodka. Some plainclothes policemen reportedly handed out not only vodka but also money and guns. Onlookers and passersby joined the processions as the demonstrators from all parts of Odesa made their way to the center of the city. Singing the national anthem and religious hymns, they stopped at the city council building and raised the imperial colors to replace the red flag that students had raised the previous day. They then headed toward the city's main Orthodox cathedral, stopping *en route* at the residence of Baron Aleksandr Kaulbars, commander of the Odesa Military District. Kaulbars, fearing confrontation between the patriotic marchers and revolutionaries, asked them to disperse. Some heeded his request, but most members of the procession continued their march. Neidgart, on the other hand, greeted the patriots enthusiastically and urged them to hold a prayer service at the cathedral.

After the service, the procession continued to march through the streets of central Odesa. Suddenly, shots rang out, and a young boy carrying an icon lay dead. Most accounts of the incident assert that the shots came from surrounding buildings. No one knows for certain who was responsible for the shots, but evidence indicates that revolutionaries or members of Jewish and student self-defense brigades fired upon the pro-tsarist processioners and reportedly threw homemade bombs. The crowd panicked and ran through the streets as more shots were fired from rooftops, balconies, and apartment windows.

---

23 *Odesskii pogrom i samooborona* (Paris: Izdanie zapadnago tsentral'nago komiteta Po'ale-Tsion, 1906), 49–54 and Weinberg, *The Revolution of 1905 in Odessa*, 88–89 and 164–188.

The shootings triggered a chain reaction. Convinced that the Jews were responsible for the shootings, members of the patriotic demonstration began shouting "Beat the Kikes" and "Death to the Kikes," and went on a rampage, attacking Jews with wild abandon and destroying Jewish apartments, homes, and stores. The course of events was similar in other parts of the city; members of student and Jewish self-defense brigades fired on Russians who were holding smaller patriotic processions and provoked similar pogromist responses. By mid-afternoon a full-fledged pogrom had developed, and it raged until October 22. The list of atrocities perpetrated against the Jews is too long to recount here but suffice it to say that pogromists brutally and indiscriminately beat, mutilated, and murdered defenseless Jewish men, women, and children. They hurled Jews out of windows, raped women of all ages, and slaughtered infants in front of their parents.

The violence and destruction were in large measure made possible by the failure of the authorities to adopt any countermeasures. In fact, policemen reportedly compiled lists of Jewish-owned stores and Jews' apartments to facilitate attacks. Other evidence indicated that policemen were instructed not to interfere with pogromists. Indeed, some testimony gathered by the government inquiry pointed toward police involvement in the planning and organization of the patriotic counterdemonstrations and pogrom. According to one military officer, as early as October 15 and 16, policemen were proposing to use force against Jews as punishment for their purported role in instigating the current wave of strikes and disorders. As one policeman reportedly stated: "Захотели они свободы, – вот мы их уложим две-три тысячи, тогда они будут знать, что такое свобода" (They wanted freedom, let's stack up two or three thousand. Then they'll know what freedom is.)[24] A group of day laborers on the morning of October 18 told this same officer that they had just received instructions at a police station to attack Jews that evening. An army captain stated that a policeman had told him that his superiors had given their permission for three days of beating because Jews had destroyed the portrait of the tsar in the municipal duma.

Low-ranking policemen and soldiers did not interfere with the pogromists, and in some instances some participated in the looting and killing. At times, policemen, seeking to avenge the attacks of October 16 and 18 on their colleagues and on themselves by self-defense brigades once the pogrom broke out, went so far as to provide protection for pogromists by firing on members of the

---

24 Ibid., 100.

Jewish self-defense units. Some policemen discharged their weapons into the air and told the rioters that the shots had come from apartments inhabited by Jews, leaving the latter vulnerable to vicious beatings and murder. Eyewitnesses reported seeing policemen directing pogromists to Jewish-owned stores or Jews' apartments while preventing the rioters from damaging the property of non-Jews. In addition, policemen and pogromist agitators went from door to door and spread rumors that Jews were slaughtering Russian families, urging Russian residents to repel the Jews with force. For their part, soldiers, concluding from the actions of the police that higher authorities sanctioned the pogrom, stood idly by while pogromists looted stores and murdered unarmed Jews. Given the poor training and supervision of the military and municipal police forces throughout the empire, it is little wonder that soldiers and policemen got caught up in the moment and willingly joined the pogromist mobs. Conceivably, they believed they should participate in the bloodletting, notwithstanding their oath to maintain law and order.

Unfortunately, no evidence indicates which police officials were responsible for these directives. Nor does any evidence link Neidgart to the planning and approval of pogrom agitation or the pogrom itself. Considering his efforts prior to October to avert unrest through patient negotiation with workers and employers, it would have been out of character for him to have approved, let alone, planned a major public disturbance. Neidgart would have balked at sanctioning any kind of public protest for fear of events getting out of hand. To be sure, he knew about the patriotic procession as it took shape and even welcomed it, but this does not warrant the conclusion drawn by many observers that Neidgart had advance knowledge of the pogrom. In fact, Neidgart so feared an eruption of violence on October 19 that he requested Kaulbars to withdraw permission for a funeral procession planned for that day by revolutionaries and radical students to commemorate the students killed on October 16. Moreover, the quickness with which the authorities acted on October 18 to suppress street disorders suggests that Neidgart and Kaulbars hoped to avert a major conflagration.

Not surprisingly, some officials took vigorous measures from the start to suppress attacks on Jews and their property. For the most part, however, local authorities were helpless to stop the violence, although as we have seen, the city governor and military commander turned a blind eye to the breakdown of public order for several days. This inaction signaled to the mobs that they had a green light to beat Jews. Police also had to contend with armed revolutionaries, which made it all the more difficult to maintain law and order and undoubtedly prompted many of them to lash out at those trying to injure, if not kill them.

Yet, questions remain. Why did the police and military fail to act quickly on October 19 and 20? Why did Neidgart not prevent individual policemen from looting and pillaging? How can we explain his delay in officially requesting the assistance of the military and his callous refusal to heed the pleas of pogrom victims and of a rabbi and a bank director who begged him to intercede? Neidgart may simply have had no choice in the matter. Individual policemen already had begun to abandon their posts before he issued his directive of October 18. Furthermore, they refused to return to their posts on October 22, despite the city governor's order to do so. Neidgart may have realized that he could not depend on the severely underpaid, poorly trained, and disgruntled police force to maintain order in Odesa and that he could no longer control the men under his command.

Neidgart's sense of helplessness notwithstanding, his behavior was certainly not blameless: his sympathies undoubtedly lay with the pogromists. In the midst of the unrest, Neidgart reportedly told a delegation of Jewish leaders that they had themselves to blame for the violence, which was retribution for the Jews' responsibility for the civil disorders. Thus, although Neidgart did not plan the pogrom, he sympathized with the actions of the mobs and may have viewed attacks on Jews as an effective method of squelching the revolution.

Kaulbars also shared the burden of responsibility for not acting more promptly to restore order. The Odesa district military commander not only ignored reports that his troops were participating in the pogrom, but he even remarked to an assembly of policemen on October 21, "все мы в душе сочувствуем этому погрому." (We all sympathize in our hearts with this pogrom.)[25] He also insisted that he had no authority to assume control of the city until Neidgart requested assistance in writing. Such a request did not arrive until October 20. Kaulbars tempered his remarks, however, by acknowledging that neither his personal sympathies nor those of the police and military relieved these groups of the responsibility to maintain law and order and protect Jews. This conflict between personal values and official duty helps account for the failure of the city governor and military commander to act more decisively.

The pogrom, apparently, assumed the characteristics of a secular ritual whereby some pogromists hoped to celebrate and reinforce their identity as Orthodox Christians devoted to tsar and motherland. From their perspective, the challenges confronting the autocracy threatened to unravel the religious bonds that tied them to the tsar. The destruction of portraits of Nikolai II, a

---

25 *Materialy k istorii russkoi kontr-revoliutsii*, clxv.

symbolic offense akin to the destruction of an icon, elicited feelings of resentment and anger and helped mobilize the forces of reaction eager to stand up to the provocative behavior of those rejecting the values that undergirded the autocracy. The pogromists can be viewed as striving to strengthen the foundation of tsarist rule by physically attacking the regime's existential enemy, the Jew, in the hope of destroying all perceived threats to autocratic institutions and values. Like the pogrom wave that targeted Jews as responsible for the regicide in 1881, some pogromists in 1905 viewed Jews as threats to the body politic and fabric of late imperial Russian society and turned to violence to preserve the old regime.

Who were the pogromists?

In Odesa, pogromist behavior had both an ethnic and a class basis that reflected the interplay of long-term ethnic antagonisms, the structure of Odesa's economy, and short-term political catalysts. Jewish merchants' domination of the grain trade predisposed many day laborers and dockworkers, who comprised a large segment of the pogromist mobs, against the Jews, whom they conveniently saw as the source of the economic ills besetting the city. In addition, competition with Jews for scarce jobs made the situation more combustible and ripe for anti-Jewish violence. Consequently, when unemployed Russian workers sought an outlet for their frustrations and problems, they focused on Jews. Without taking into account the hostile, anti-Jewish atmosphere in Odesa, we cannot understand why Russian workers at times of economic distress chose not to attack other Russian workers who competed with them for scarce jobs or Russian employers but instead indiscriminately lashed out at all Jews, regardless of whether they were job competitors.

Ethnic and socio-economic problems alone, however, do not explain why Russian day workers decided to attack Jews in October 1905. In June, for example, Russian dockworkers and day laborers had exploded in a fit of wanton rage but chose to challenge the authorities by destroying the harbor. In October, these same workers directed their hostility and frustration against the Jews, although material conditions had not substantially changed. What had changed since the June disorders was the political atmosphere. In short, the revolutionary climate of mid-October precipitated the pogrom. Many participants in the patriotic procession of October 19 undoubtedly marched to express their support of the autocracy and disapproval of the October Manifesto.

It is worth considering, however, that many Russian workers, day laborers and dockworkers in particular, were perhaps less motivated by politics than by the opportunity to vent some frustration and collect some booty.[26] Certainly not all members of the procession and participants in the pogrom represented the extreme right of the political spectrum, as the dockworkers' and day laborers' riot in June strongly suggests. For them, the struggle between revolution and reaction, which inspired the more politically conscious, played a secondary role. Many may not have intended to assault the Jews and destroy their property but were provoked by the shooting and bomb throwing of the revolutionaries and self-defense brigades. Those actions help explain the virulence and intensity of the pogromists' attack—especially by the police—on their victims. Whatever the specific motivations of the various individuals involved in the pogrom, popular and official antisemitism thus combined with depressed economic circumstances to provide the necessary psychological and material preconditions, while the political climate of Odesa in 1905 helped trigger the pogrom.

Residential and work patterns in some neighborhoods, particularly outside the city center, may have been segregated by ethnicity, but for the most part, as Patricia Herlihy has written, "Odessa did not have neighborhoods in the sense of ethnic and social self-segregated residential areas.... Not only did the rich and poor live in propinquity, but they drank side by side as well."[27] Moreover, daily life, whether at stores, open-air markets, street stalls, and taverns, or simply walking on the streets of the city brought Russians and Jews into contact, especially in the center of Odesa, which was more ethnically heterogenous. Sociability and ethnic mixing did not mean, however, that each group did not continue to harbor prejudices. Encounters between Jews and gentiles may have erased some of the cultural differences that led to misunderstandings. Familiarity may have provided the opportunity for reduced tensions, but it also bred ethnic resentments and antagonisms, notwithstanding the cosmopolitanism of certain segments of Odesan society. This was especially true for presumably the least cosmopolitan residents of the city, unskilled workers, particularly those at the port where Russians and Jews rubbed shoulders as they competed for work during times of economic downturn.

By no means did all gentile workers participate or even sympathize with the bloodletting. Many Russian factory workers enlisted in self-defense units that patrolled the city, while others sheltered their Jewish neighbors and friends

---

[26] See Ilya Gerasimov's comment about the non-ideological motivation of pogromists ("Review").
[27] Herlihy, *Odessa: A History*, 272.

during the terror. After the pogrom, Russians who had defended Jews provided financial aid to pogrom victims and took vigorous action to punish pogromists and ensure that another pogrom would not occur.

The reluctance of these Russian factory workers to join ranks with pogromists can be attributed, in part, to the fact that they did not compete for jobs with Jews, who rarely worked in the same factories and workshops as Russians. In fact, Jews and Russians were generally not employed in the same branch of manufacturing and, unlike dockworkers and day laborers, Jews and gentiles were thus not in direct competition for employment.

Conclusion

Pogroms diverted the attention and energy of opposition forces across the empire, although workers in major cities such as Odesa, Kiev (Kyiv), St. Petersburg, and Moscow continued to challenge the tsarist government. The violence and bloodshed benefited the regime, which was able to regroup and reassert its authority and control of society. Its efforts were aided by the return of soldiers from the Russian Far East, where the war against Japan had ended. The unrest of 1905 was a public relations fiasco for the troubled autocracy, however, because it fueled belief among Western European and American governments and societies that the Russian monarchy not only condoned but also instigated attacks on its Jewish subjects.

The October 1905 pogrom in Odesa illustrates how antisemitism could become a potent force in politics. Anti-Jewish violence was part of the arsenal of conservative forces who rejected cosmopolitanism and its embrace of cultural tolerance and diversity. In 1905, speakers at meetings hosted by antisemitic organizations denounced "cosmopolitanism and other socialist teachings" as the bedfellows of political subversion. In an early version of "Russian Lives Matter," Russian nationalists advocated the view that Russians "should consider themselves masters" in their country.[28]

The pogrom served the cause of political reaction by revealing how a potentially revolutionary situation could quickly become defused when the target of the people's wrath shifted from the autocracy to the Jews, a convenient scapegoat viewed as responsible for personal difficulties and political uncertainty. The wave of pogroms that broke out in mid-October would not have occurred

---

28 Weinberg, *The Revolution of 1905 in Odessa*, 76.

without the polarized political atmosphere that had developed over the course of 1905. The issuance of the October Manifesto and the mobilization of anti-tsarist and monarchist forces in such an emotionally charged setting triggered the outbreak of bloodletting at a time of political anxiety. Fortunately, the pogrom was not a prelude to a period of sustained ethnic violence; Odesan Jews did not fall victim to another round of pogromist violence prior to the outbreak of the World War I. Ilya Gerasimov and Caroline Humphrey suggest that the 1905 pogrom provided "immunity" from future outbreaks of violence and point to "a general turning away from ethno-religious antagonism among individual citizens at the personal level,"[29] as well as the emergence of "a new cosmopolitanism of empathy" as explanations.[30] To be sure, cosmopolitanism remained alive and well in Odesa and may have strengthened according to Gerasimov and Humphrey. But antisemitic prejudices continued to co-exist with cosmopolitan values, as they did prior to 1905, and the lessening of public expression of anti-Jewish views does not explain why another pogrom did not occur. Pogroms in late imperial Russia and the early Soviet period occurred for the most part during moments of existential crises for the government. 1905 was one such moment, and the next crisis of faith did not occur until the aftermath of 1917 and World War I, when the social and political challenges facing the fledgling Bolshevik government proved fatal for tens of thousands of Jews experiencing the downfall of the Romanov dynasty.

---

29 Ilya Gerasimov, "'My ubivaem tol'ko svoikh': prestupnost' kak marker mezhetnicheskikh granits v Odesse nachala dvatsatogo veka (1907–1917)," *Ab Imperio* (January 2003); quoted in Humphrey, "Odessa: Pogroms in a Cosmopolitan City," 56.
30 Ibid.

CHAPTER 6

The Cosmopolitan Soundscape of Odesa

Anat Rubinstein

Introduction

In the past few decades, new concepts of sound have attracted the attention of musicologists, shifting the discourse from music to a wider overview of the study of sounds in relation to place and space.[1] The term *soundscape* generally refers to the entire mosaic of sounds heard in a specific location.[2] It comprises a wide array of sonorities, from the hum of traffic to the clang of church bells. The study of soundscape examines music as one of the auditory phenomena that exists in and/or between places and spaces and reflects the social, technological, economic, and political conditions of a place and aspects of culture and identity.

Cosmopolitan soundscapes refer to the transfer and diffusion of sounds among different ethnic groups beyond their specific geographical location.[3] Studies of cosmopolitanism in music attempt to decipher and theorize the constituents and forces that facilitate musical production and consumption by accommodating the local and global, as well as negotiating national versus non-national factors. Music scholars around the world continuously engage in an ongoing

---

1 See, for example, Andy Bennett, ed., *Music, Space and Place: Popular Music and Cultural Identity* (New York: Routledge, 2017); David B. Knight, *Landscapes in Music: Space, Place, and Time in the World's Great Music* (Lanham: Rowman & Littlefield, 2006); Ray Hudson, "Regions and Place: Music, Identity and Place," *Progress in Human Geography* 30, no. 5 (2006): 626–34; John Connell and Chris Gibson, *Sound Tracks: Popular Music, Identity, and Place* (London and New York: Routledge, 2003).
2 Megan E. Hill, "Soundscape," *Grove Music Online*, published online January 31, 2014, https://doi.org/10.1093/gmo/9781561592630.article.A2258182.
3 Martin Stokes, "On Musical Cosmopolitanism," *Macalester International* 21, no. 8 (2008): 3–26.

debate on this subject. Many studies of cosmopolitanism in music focus on the ways sociopolitical trends and urban modernization have affected behaviors, attitudes, and practices of composers, performers, and listeners.[4] Subsequently, these sociopolitical phenomena led to the embodiment of new aesthetics and styles that promoted "a cosmopolitan state of mind."[5]

This notion of a cosmopolitan state of mind seems especially relevant in the context of Odesa. Examination of the soundscape of Odesa in the early 1900s reveals the sonorous manifestations of cross-cultural attributes. In the case of Odesa, the city's musical soundscape was an amalgam of Russian, Jewish, and Ukrainian musical genres and foreign influences that were brought in from Italy, Greece, and other countries. This music hybridity had an inclusive potential and can thus be regarded as one of the many aspects of music cosmopolitanism, which can be viewed and explained through a wider overall perception of the city's sounds.

This relatively new approach to music/sound research can be applied also retrospectively to historical periods.[6] From the early 1800s, Odesa was famous for its prolific music making—performances, compositions, and general musical culture—in which its citizens from all social backgrounds were involved in various ways. Now, one hundred years after the civil war and Bolshevik takeover, it is timely to investigate the mutual influences in Odesa's multiethnic culture. This chapter is the first attempt to survey the musical soundscape of Odesa in the late nineteenth and early twentieth centuries in order to illustrate the city's wide range of music—from folk music and song on the Odesa streets to the rich musical harmonies that filled the opera house and sanctuaries of the city's synagogues.

The geographic, demographic, and cultural aspects of the city made it a highly attractive destination for migrants from Ukraine and the southern parts of the Russian Empire, and for Jews, Romany, Armenians, Greeks, and Italians. These newcomers arrived from countries and regions (such as the Pale of Settlement) in which all musical genres, whether folk or artistic music, vocal, or instrumental, played a role in daily life. Acknowledged as relatively "musical," these populations pursued music both as active musicians and as engaged audiences. In addition, many came from cultures in which music tutoring and apprenticeship

---

4   Sarah Collins and Dana Gooley, "Music and the New Cosmopolitanism: Problems and Possibilities," *Musical Quarterly* 99, no. 2 (2016): 139–65.
5   Cristina Magaldi, "Cosmopolitanism and World Music in Rio de Janeiro at the Turn of the Twentieth Century," *The Musical Quarterly* 92, nos. 3–4 (2009): 331.
6   See, for example, Dana Gooley, "Cosmopolitanism in the Age of Nationalism, 1848–1914," *Journal of the American Musicological Society* 66, no. 2 (2013): 523–49.

was common, where father would transmit knowledge to his son, as, for example, the Jewish *klezmer* or the Ukrainian trio (flute and two violins). These musicians formed guilds and were commissioned to perform at weddings, parties, and at cafés and restaurants. It was also common to encounter ensembles playing outdoors in parks, boulevards, and street corners. The result was music in the air—everywhere, creating the unique soundscape of Odesa.

Early years

The local press reflected Odesa's musical culture at a fairly early period. In 1822, a music periodical in French entitled *Troubadour d'Odessa* featured music critics, announcements, advertisements for concerts, and music scores.[7] A later testament to Odesa's cosmopolitan soundscape is found in an allegorical painting that commemorates the 1894 centennial anniversary of the city's founding. Flanked by other rulers and Orthodox Russian clergy, Empress Catherine the Great stands at the center of the picture behind the figure of Mother Russia, who resembles the Virgin Mary, with the holy infant in her lap. The infant, holding a boat, symbolizes the city's importance as a Black Sea port. As Iljine and Herlihy explain, the city's heterogeneous population is represented by an Italian girl holding a violin, a German girl with a guitar, a Polish girl with a lute, an Albanian girl with a triangle, a Ukrainian girl with a domra (a small string instrument of the lute family), and a Russian child with a flute.[8] Significantly, the Jews are not represented in the painting, despite their prominence among the city's population and in music making. This might reflect the hegemony of the Russian Christian culture in the 1890s.

Comprising one third of the population of the city, however, the involvement of Jews in music, both as music practitioners and as consumers, was extensive. As Steven Zipperstein notes, the economic success of Jewish merchants and the establishment of commercial ties led to Jews' participation in the city's social and cultural events and leisure activities. In addition, the advocates of the Haskalah encouraged Jews to turn to the non-Jewish world to widen their cultural, social, and economic horizons.[9] Consequently, Jews participated in many different activities in the city; for instance, they streamed to the opera and were among

---

7 Nicolas V. Iljine, ed., *Odessa Memories* (Seattle: University of Washington Press, 2003), 14.
8 Ibid., 53.
9 Steven J. Zipperstein, *The Jews of Odessa: A Cultural History, 1794–1881* (Stanford: Stanford University Press, 1985), 64–65.

Figure 1. *Pervonachal'nye vremena Odessy* (1894), black-and-white photograph.
Source: Nicholas V. Iljine, ed., *Odessa Memories* (Seattle: University of Washington Press, 2003), 53. Exhibit at Odesa Historical Regional Studies Museum. Used with permission of University of Washington Press.

its most enthusiastic spectators. Their great fondness for music also motivated them to enroll their children in music schools in the hope of cultivating a young and promising generation of musicians.

Other ethnic groups, such as Italians, Greeks, and Ukrainians, also contributed to music making. Traditional Ukrainian music, which evolved at the crossroads of Asia and Europe, was influenced by both Slavic and non-Slavic cultures. Ukrainian vocal music exhibits a wide variety of forms and a complex mix of exotic melismatic singing with Western chordal harmonies.[10] This mixture, which is also prominent in Jewish klezmer, as I will show later, generated powerful energy that stimulated the audience's intense emotional engagement. Italians brought to Odesa a rich history of music making at all levels—opera and folk, baroque finesse, and peasant dances. Italian culture impacted the city's cultural development to a great extent: Italian singers, opera impresarios, managers and players—all reflected the cultural opulence that had been left behind and the attempt to reconstruct Italy in a new land.[11]

Indoors/institutionalized music

The opera craze and classical music

Established in 1810, the city theater that housed the Odesa Opera was the main site for the performing arts in the city.[12] This was the place where Pushkin attended Rossini's operas[13] and where Franz Liszt performed his piano recitals. Many of the greatest Russian composers, including Rimsky-Korsakov and Tchaikovsky, conducted the house orchestra there. During the 1820s and

---

10 Virko Baley and Sofia Hrytsa, "Ukraine," Grove Music Online, accessed October 3, 2020, https://www.oxfordmusiconline.com/grovemusic/view/10.1093/gmo/9781561592630.001.0001/omo-9781561592630-e-0000040470; Brian A. Cherwick "Polkas on the prairies: Ukrainian music and the construction of identity" (PhD diss., University of Alberta, Canada, 1999), 19–20.

11 Anna Makolkin, *The Nineteenth Century in Odessa: One Hundred Years of Italian Culture on the Shores of the Black Sea (1794–1894)* (Lewiston: Edwin Mellen Press, 2007); Iljine, *Odessa Memories*, 15.

12 "Odessathis is how it is written on their English site National Opera and Ballet Theater," accessed August 14, 2017, https://operahouse.od.ua/en/about/history/; Herlihy, *Odessa: A History 1794–1914* (Cambridge, MA: Harvard University Press, 1986), 141.

13 As is known from Pushkin's correspondence, during his years of exile in Odesa (1823–1824), the poet became an enthusiastic fan of the Odesa Opera; Richard Taruskin, *Defining Russia Musically: Historical and Hermeneutical Essays* (Princeton: Princeton University Press, 1997), 188.

1830s, Italian operas predominated in the repertoire. Management in the first decades was also mostly Italian. As the music historian Richard Taruskin noted: "The earliest more or less continuous Italian opera enterprise in nineteenth-century Russia was based in neither capital, but in the Black Sea port city of Odessa."[14] The managers made an effort to include in the repertoire the most recent Italian operas that were being performed on other European stages. As Pinkhas Minkowsky (1859–1924), the celebrated synagogue cantor who was also an active music critic, recalled, "Every opera by Rossini, Verdi, Puccini, and Mascagni, every novel tune sanctified at the holy hall of La Scala in Milan would excite the people of Odesa and they would rush to enjoy these new works of music."[15]

At the start of the twentieth century, famous Italian opera singers arrived in Odesa every spring, spurring rivalries among passionate fans, as depicted by Minkowsky:

> Music lovers in Odesa fought each other to death. An opera singer who possessed both the talent and the skill to reach a cadence [the ending of a musical phrase] in one long breath, received the honor reserved only for kings. The crowd would carry him/her, literally, with their hands ... If this was a female singer, the diva would be the heroine of the day in Odesa, receiving endless gifts, flowers, and gems, publicly or discretely....
>
> There were times when the good Lord summoned two rival divas at the same time, each followed by a group of devoted fans willing to sacrifice their souls for their divine queen and to desecrate the name of the opponent. The city theater of Odesa would then become a battlefield. One group would carry flower bouquets, garlands, and gifts for their goddess, loudly praising and demanding an *encore*, while the other group would throw dead fish, spoiled eggs, and rotten potatoes, emitting deafening wails and whistles to show their contempt. The "battle" occasionally got out of control to such an extent that the police was forced to stop the show, lower the curtain, throw out the audience from

---

14 Ibid.
15 Pinkhas Minkowsky, "Misefer khayai" [From the book of my life], *Reshumot* 4 (1926): 135; my translation from Hebrew. On the life and work of Minkowsky, see Anat Rubinstein, "The Cantor of the Haskalah. Life, Work and Thought by Cantor Pinkhas Minkowsky (1859–1924)" [Hebrew] (PhD diss., The Hebrew University of Jerusalem, 2013).

this cave of licentiousness that they call "The Theater," and to escort the leaders of the fan groups to the holding cell until they sobered up. . . . Needless to add, among them were numerous sons of Abraham, Isaac, and Jacob.[16]

Minkowsky's reference to the Jews at the opera indicates their social mobility. As Zipperstein notes, "Local Jews, even those who had no knowledge of a foreign language, found the opera to be enjoyable, and for the mere price of a ticket (and tickets were priced quite low) they could appreciate a sense of belonging to and participating in a larger cultural milieu."[17]

Minkowsky's account highlights the connection between opera and synagogue music, both regarding aspects of performance, as I will discuss later, but also in relation to typology and classification of the audience. Seemingly, the opera house was a site for "high" culture, hence attracting an educated audience. Minkowsky's description, however, shows clearly that people from all social classes were drawn to the opera, which formed a cosmopolitan gathering place, often prone to flare up in conflicts, clashes, and rivalries. The opera embodied social, political, national, and cultural values and aesthetic codes. Representing a microcosm of the community, it also reflected points of tension. The status of the opera was similar in Italy during the nineteenth century, when people from all social strata participated as an opinionated, involved, and highly enthusiastic audience, which was sometimes difficult to control and required the authorities' intervention.[18]

In contrast to the excitement the opera aroused, concerts of instrumental classical music did not share the same success. Minkowsky describes empty concert halls. He also criticizes the people of the city for "considering themselves to be above and beyond criticism," and for neglecting other genres of art music that are considered less entertaining than the opera. Minkowsky's criticism sheds light on the repertoire played in concerts at that time:

> A sonata by Beethoven is like a language of the savages to the Odesans' ears, Bach's fugue makes them angry because they

---

16 Minkowsky, "Misefer khayai," 135–37; my translation from Hebrew. See the chapter in this volume by Mirja Lecke on Isa Kremer on the Odesa opera stage.
17 Steven J. Zipperstein, "Jewish Enlightenment in Odessa: Cultural Characteristics, 1794–1871," *Jewish Social Studies* 44, no. 1 (1982): 26.
18 Alessandra Campana, *Opera and Modern Spectatorship in Late Nineteenth-Century Italy* (Cambridge: Cambridge University Press, 2015); David R. Kimbell, *Italian Opera* (Cambridge: Cambridge University Press, 1994), 417–29.

fail to comprehend it; people have shouted at "crazy" Richard Wagner because they could not understand his music. At the first recital of Anton Rubinstein, when the gifted artist played works by Beethoven and other genuine classical composers, the city theater was half empty.... The venue was also deserted when the great Rimsky-Korsakov conducted his own symphonies. The only person whose symphonies attracted a large crowd to the hall was Peter Tchaikovsky, as he was already known to the public for his opera *Onegin*.[19]

Despite Minkowsky's complaint about opera madness and the crowd's preference for what he considered superficial musical entertainment, he saw a positive side to this frequent opera going: the continuing exposure to music contributed to the development of an exquisite musical taste, appreciation, and sensitivity to cantorial music—especially if sung by a lyrical tenor (such as Minkowsky himself). Thus, just as the crowd filled the opera house, they would, with no less enthusiasm, flock to synagogues to listen to the great tenor cantors of the city. People were attracted to the synagogues not so much for religious reasons but more often as a source of pure entertainment. Similar to the opera, Odesa's main synagogues offered a rich musical experience with high artistic standards that attracted Jews and non-Jews alike. Cantors of the Golden Age of Cantorate (from the late nineteenth century until World War I) such as Minkowsky not only led prayers but also sought to exhibit virtuosity in their singing and thus won the admiration of the audience (and spurred rivalries), similarly to their virtuoso counterparts from the opera.[20]

Synagogue Music

The two most prominent of the seventy synagogues in the city listed as active[21] were the Great Synagogue and the Brodsky/Brody Synagogue. These two were in constant rivalry over the skills of their cantors and the quality of their choirs. They were leaders of the *Khor Shul* (Choral Synagogue) liturgical style, which

---

19 Minkowsky, "Misefer khayai," 137; my translation from Hebrew.
20 Mark Slobin, *Chosen Voices: The Story of the American Cantorate* (Urbana: University of Illinois Press, 2002); Howard B. Rothman, Jose A. Diaz, and Kristen E. Vincent, "Comparing Historical and Contemporary Opera Singers with Historical and Contemporary Jewish Cantors," *Journal of Voice* 14, no. 2 (2000): 205–14.
21 Iljine, *Odessa Memories*, 67.

developed in Central and Western Europe in the second half of the nineteenth century.[22]

Ideas of aestheticization of the modern synagogue in the Russian Empire were implemented in Odesa's synagogues, following synagogues in Central Europe—mainly reform synagogues in Germany. The move towards modernization was based on the notion that a synagogue should serve not simply as a place of worship but also as a symbol of greatness and reverence. According to this view, the physical attributes of the house should also reflect moral and religious values. Order, beauty, symmetry, purity, and light were viewed not only as mere attributes of architecture but also were considered significant manifestations of the notion of religious ritual and liturgy. Hence music was intended to enhance the congregants' spiritual experience, increase their sense of belonging, and strengthen closeness to God.[23]

The Great Synagogue was Odesa's central Jewish religious institution and the established Jewish elite's place of worship. Other than for regular prayers, it served as a venue for official ceremonies held by the Jewish community in honor of the authorities. The Great Synagogue's rival—the Brody Synagogue—was the flagship of the German-model choral synagogues in the Russian Empire.

The Brody synagogue, inaugurated in 1868, was a magnificent building built in Gothic-Florentine style, which featured decorated glass windows, a dome and four-cornered towers. As Sholem Aleichem (S. N. Rabinowitz, 1859–1916) described it humorously in his Menakhem Mendel stories, "The Odessa synagogue [The Brody Synagogue] is something to see. First of all, it is called the Choir Synagogue because on top of it there's a round cap instead of a roof, and it hasn't got an East Wall. That is to say, everybody sits facing the Cantor . . ."[24] The sanctuary, as shown in figure 2, was designed according to the architectural model of the German synagogue of the mid-nineteenth century: the ark containing the Torah scrolls is in the middle of the front wall, two pillars on both sides and above them an organ and a balcony. The seats in the hall are facing the *bimah* (a raised platform) in a way that resembles rows of seats in a theater.

---

22 Abraham Z. Idelsohn, *Jewish Music: Its Historical Development* (New York: Dover, 1992), 306–07; Vladimir Levin, "Reform or Consensus? Choral Synagogues in the Russian Empire," *Arts* 9, no. 2 (2020): 1–49.

23 Michael Stanislawski, *Tsar Nicholas I and the Jews: The Transformation of Jewish Society in Russia, 1825–1855* (Philadelphia: Jewish Publication Society of America, 1983), 278–79; Michael A. Meyer, *The German Model of Religious Reform and Russian Jewry* (Cambridge, MA: Harvard University Press, 1985).

24 Sholem Aleichem (S. N. Rabinowitz), *The Adventures of Menahem-Mendl*, trans. Tamara Kahana (New York: G. P. Putnam's Sons, 1969), 34.

This design was planned for the purposes of optimal performativity. The congregants sat audience-style facing the *bimah* and watched the show, which included liturgical texts set to music, performed by the cantor and the choir.[25] The Brody Synagogue in Odesa, as well as other Russian choral synagogues, were not reform religious institutions, but they exhibited moderate structural changes in design in comparison to traditional synagogues. As Vladimir Levin emphasizes, "The majority of the changes introduced in [in Eastern European, A. R.] choral synagogues were of an *aesthetic* nature: they concerned decorum, *not the religious meaning or essence of the prayer service*."[26] Sholem Aleichem described the resemblance of the synagogue to a theater:

> I cannot understand the Jews of Odessa—why don't they go to the synagogue to pray? And even those who go to the synagogue to pray, don't pray; they sit like puppets with their fat and shiny faces; they wear top hats on their heads; their prayer shawls are small and skimpy, and—shsh!—nobody even opens his mouth. And if some Jew should venture to pray a little louder, up comes the beadle with shiny buttons and says: "Quiet, Please!" . . . Funny Jews in Odessa![27]

Upon the inauguration of the Brody synagogue, Nissan Blumenthal (1805–1903) was appointed as chief cantor; choir master and composer David Nowakowsky (1848–1921) was the music director; Rabbi David Schwebecher (1819–1888) was brought in from Germany to fill in the position of the community's spiritual leader and delivered weekly sermons in German. Blumenthal served the community for almost half a century. He was replaced by Cantor Pinkhas (Pini) Minkowsky, who held the position for thirty years (1892–1922). Nowakowsky worked alongside these two cantors as the synagogue's choirmaster. Minkowsky's collaboration with Nowakowsky in the 1890s marked the beginning of a new era in the musical history of the Brody Synagogue. It became

---

25 Ruth Hacohen-Pinczower, "Kehilot kol le'et dimdumim: Merkhavey tslil mamashiyim umedumyanim shel yahadut merkaz eropa 'im ptikhat hasha'ar ule'et ne'ilat sha'ar" [Communities of voice at times of twilight: real and imagined soundscapes of central European Jewry at the opening of the gates and the closing of the gate], in *Hadimyon haparshani: dat veomanut batarbut hayehudit behekshereyha* [The interpretive imagination: religion and art in Jewish culture in its contexts], ed. Ruth Hacohen-Pinczower, Galit Hasan-Rokem, Richard I. Cohen, and Ilana Pardes (Jerusalem: Magnes, 2016), 116–53.
26 Levin, "Reform or Consensus? Choral Synagogues in the Russian Empire," 32; my emphasis.
27 Sholem Aleichem, *Menahem-Mendl*, 34.

Figure 2. Cantor Pinkhas Minkowsky (back row, sixth from right) and the boys' choir in the Brody synagogue, Odesa, ca. 1910. Picture source: Archives of the YIVO Institute for Jewish Research, New York.

a leading musical institution in Jewish Odesa and was celebrated around the world as an important center of Jewish liturgical music. Nowakowsky also won fame in the world of Jewish music. He continued developing and perfecting his choral style and mastering polyphonic and contrapuntal techniques, which won him the nickname "the Jewish Bach."[28] In a time of Jewish cultural renaissance paved by the Haskalah movement and the rise of Jewish nationalism, innovations in music, particularly within the synagogue and the religious world, were viewed as the forefront of progress.[29]

Both Minkowsky and Nowakowsky embodied Odesa's cosmopolitan spirit. During his lifetime, Pinkhas Minkowsky was internationally known as a cantor and writer, as well as a composer and researcher of Jewish music. His vocal style was a mixture of what he referred to as "emotional singing" (*shirat haregesh*), traditional *khazanut* (cantorial singing) style, and "orderly singing" (*shirat haseder*)—Western choral style. Minkowsky belonged to both religious and non-religious worlds, true to the ideals of the Haskalah, as one can observe in his cantorial style, education, knowledge of opera and concert music, his writings, music reviews, and publications, as well as in his involvement in several Jewish national movements.[30]

During Minkowsky's tenure, an organ and a mixed-gender choir were regularly included in the services. As according to the Jewish law (Halakhah), observed by Orthodox Jews, it is forbidden to play an instrument on the Sabbath, these changes were considered radical at first. Playing an organ in synagogues was first introduced by Reform synagogues in Germany in the mid-nineteenth century to enhance performativity.[31] The Brody synagogue was not a Reform synagogue. To settle the *halakhic* conflict, a non-Jew was hired to play the organ on the Sabbath. Eventually, this performative effect became the main attraction of the synagogue. People from all around the metropolitan area flocked to the Brody Synagogue every Friday night, among them non-Jewish visitors and government officials who came to enjoy the music. The communist repression of Judaism and Jewish culture and the deaths of Minkowsky in 1924 and Nowakowsky in 1921 marked the end of the Golden Age of Odesa synagogal music.

---

28 On the life and work of David Nowakowsky, see David Lefkowitz, *The Music of David Nowakowsky, 1849–1921: Overview of Research and Practical Applications* (New York: n.p., 1994); Noreen Green, "The Forgotten Master of Jewish Music: David Nowakowsky, 1848–1921" (PhD diss., University of Southern California, 1991); Emanuel Rubin, "The Music of David Nowakowsky (1848–1921): A New Voice from Old Odessa," *Musica Judaica* 16 (2001): 20–52.
29 Levin, "Reform or Consensus? Choral Synagogues in the Russian Empire," 33–34.
30 Rubinstein, "The Cantor of the Haskalah," 29–79.
31 Tina Frühauf, *The Organ and its Music in German-Jewish Culture* (New York: Oxford University Press, 2009).

Conservatories and music education

A relatively large number of Odesa's children received music education in various forms, mainly in music schools and conservatories. Isaak Babel opens his short story "Awakening":

> Все люди нашего круга – маклеры, лавочники, служащие в банках и пароходных конторах – учили детей музыке. Отцы наши, не видя себе ходу, придумали лотерею. Они устроили ее на костях маленьких людей. Одесса была охвачена этим безумием больше других городов. И правда – в течение десятилетий наш город поставлял вундеркиндов на концертные эстрады мира. Из Одессы вышли Миша Эльман, Цимбалист, Габрилович, у нас начинал Яша Хейфец.
>
> (All the people in our circle—brokers, shopkeepers, bank clerks, and steamship office workers—taught their children music. Our fathers, seeing no future for themselves, came up with a lottery. They played it out on the bones of little people. More than any other city, Odessa was possessed with this madness. And it's true—for decades our city supplied the concert halls of the entire world with wunderkinds. Mischa Elman, Zimbalist, Gabrilowitsch came from Odessa, and Jascha Heifetz started out in our city.)[32]

The term "lottery" clearly indicates the motivation for upward social mobility and financial gain among the lower middle-class Odesa Jews—not necessarily a family tradition or love of music. Notably, none of the above-mentioned musicians was born or raised in Odesa. Jascha Heifetz visited Odesa in 1911 to give an outdoor concert that drew thousands of people. That was the summer before he started his studies with Professor Auer in St. Petersburg, which led to his subsequent worldwide career. Similarly, pianist Osip Gabrilowitsch, who was born in St. Petersburg, and violinist Efrem Zimbalist, who was born in Rostov-on-Don, may have performed in concerts in the city as young and promising musicians before the debut of their international careers.[33]

---

32 Isaak Babel', "Probuzhdenie," *Sochineniia* (Moscow: Khudozhestvennaia literatura, 1990), 2:171; Isaac Babel, "Awakening," trans. Maxim D. Shrayer, *Tablet*, April 30, 2018, https://www.tabletmag.com/sections/arts-letters/articles/awakening-short-story-isaac-babel.

33 James Loeffler, "Neither Fish nor Fowl: The Jewish Paradox of Russian Music," *Jewish Quarterly* 57, no. 2 (2010): 20–27; Galina Kopytova, *Jascha Heifetz: Early Years in Russia* (Bloomington:

One of the best-known music schools in Odesa was Pyotr Stolyarsky's violin school. Stolyarsky was an iconic teacher who developed a unique method of violin tutoring. Among his disciples was the legendary violinist David Oistrakh (1908–1974). Babel's "Awakening" provides a humorous glimpse into the "industry" in Odesa that produced violin virtuosos, run by the fictional Zagursky, clearly referring to Stolyarsky:

> Когда мальчику исполнялось четыре или пять лет – мать вела крохотное, хилое это существо к господину Загурскому. Загурский содержал фабрику вундеркиндов, фабрику еврейских карликов в кружевных воротничках и лаковых туфельках. Он выискивал их в молдаванских трущобах, в зловонных дворах Старого базара. Загурский давал первое направление, потом дети отправлялись к профессору Ауэру в Петербург....
>
> Нагруженный футляром и нотами, я три раза в неделю тащился на улицу Витте, бывшую Дворянскую, к Загурскому. Там, вдоль стен, дожидаясь очереди, сидели еврейки, истерически воспламененные. Они прижимали к слабым своим коленям скрипки, превосходившие размерами тех, кому предстояло играть в Букингэмском дворце.

(When a boy turned four or five years old, his mother took this puny, feeble creature to see Mr. Zagursky. Zagursky ran a factory of wunderkinds, a factory of Jewish dwarves in lacy collars and little patent leather shoes. He sought them out in the slums of Moldavanka, in the stinky courtyards of the Old Bazaar. Zagursky offered the initial direction, and then the children were sent to Professor Auer in St. Petersburg....

Three times a week, encumbered by my violin case and music sheets, I dragged myself to Witte Street, the former Dvoryanskaya, to Zagursky's. There, along the walls, awaiting their turn, sat Jewesses, their hysteria flaring. They pressed to their weak knees violins that exceeded the size of the children who were expected to perform at Buckingham Palace.)[34]

Indiana University Press, 2013); Roy Malan, *Efrem Zimbalist: A Life* (Pompton Plains, NJ: Amadeus Press, 2004); Harold C. Schonberg, *The Great Pianists* (New York: Simon and Schuster, 1987), 326–31.

34 Isaak Babel', "Probuzhdenie," 171–72; Babel, "Awakening."

Babel's story demonstrates the way middle-class assimilated Jews forced their sons to excel in order to attain higher social status through music. While commenting on the Jewish musical activities of the period, Yuri Slezkine mentions two significant Jewish achievements: the entry of Jews into elite professions and, accordingly, into Russian high culture.[35]

Music pedagogy in general served as a means for inculcating the younger generation with new ideologies such as the socialist movement and various national movements that were beginning to spread in the twilight years of the Russian Empire. Odesa housed the headquarters of several such groups. One of the main branches of the Zionist movement, for example, was situated in Odesa. In 1903, Odesan educator and pedagogue Noah Pines (1871–1939) published a collection of children's songs he had written, under the title "*Hazamir – shirei yeladim lezimra ulemikra*" (The nightingale—children's songs for singing and reading).[36] Pines and other Jewish intellectuals sought to create educational materials oriented towards national ideas and mastery of the Hebrew language. The *Hazamir* collection included game songs, songs of nature, and national songs that Pines deemed appropriate for children according to his pedagogical approach. In addition to Pines's songs, the collection included songs by the Hebrew poets Haim Nahman Bialik and Saul Tchernikhovsky, as well as translations of songs from other languages. The music of the songs, mostly composed by Pinkhas Minkowsky and David Nowakowsky, appeared in a separate book.

The *Hazamir* collection was a significant contribution to the Odesa culture of the time. Bialik, Tchernikhovsky, Pines, Minkowsky, and Nowakowsky, among other acclaimed Jewish writers, artists and journalists, were part of a group of Jewish intellectuals—the "Sages of Odesa"—who sought to promote the ideology of Haskalah in the revival of Jewish national culture (*tekhiya*) through art, music, literature, pedagogy, and journalism.[37] Selected poems by Bialik and Tchernikhovsky that were set to music eventually became an integral part of the evolving canonic Zionist (and later Israeli) folk song repertory.[38]

---

35 Yuri Slezkine, *The Jewish Century* (Princeton: Princeton University Press, 2004), 129.
36 Noah Pines, ed., *Hazamir* (Odesa: Moriah, 1903).
37 Dan Miron, "The Odessa Sages," in Makhve leodesa / *Homage to Odessa*, ed. Rachel Arbel (Tel Aviv: Beit Hatefutsot, 2002), 62–81.
38 Motti Regev and Edwin Seroussi, *Popular Music and National Culture in Israel* (Berkeley: University of California Press, 2004), 49–71.

Odesa was home to one of the most distinguished music conservatories in the Russian Empire. The first music school was established in 1834.[39] The Odesa Conservatory was founded in 1913 as the Odesa branch of the Imperial Russian Musical Society. It became the fourth higher education musical institution in the Russian Empire—after St. Petersburg, Moscow, and Saratov conservatories, and provided advanced musical education on European standards from its very beginning. Due to the rapid development of the Odesa institution and the high demand for music education, the conservatory hired teachers from Italy, Poland, Bohemia, Germany, Austria, St. Petersburg, and Moscow. The Polish composer, pianist, conductor, and musicologist Witold Maliszewski (1873–1939), who was Rimsky-Korsakov's disciple, became the first rector of the Odesa Conservatory.[40]

Outdoors/Non-institutionalized music making

"Odessa-mama"—Humor, satire, lust, and nostalgia

Odesa's mild climate made it possible to hold performances and concerts in the city's gardens and on the seashore promenade to entertain the passersby. Every self-respecting café had a terrace, where guests could enjoy live music. The folklore introduced by different groups of immigrants and local humor and wit poured into the urban melting pot, giving birth to a distinctive cultural and musical language. It mainly reflected the Yiddish term *di odeser gas*—the Odesan street—in popular culture, language, and song.[41] Several Odesan songs are nostalgic, addressing the city as "Odessa-mama." These songs describe the city's vibrant lifestyle and beauty, the hedonism and lawlessness of its inhabitants, and the opportunities it offers to make easy fortunes. Urban legends linked with names of Moldavanka gangsters and underworld figures are also told in nostalgic songs that were written mainly in the early Soviet era. The image of a lawless, sinful city of underworld crime nostalgically romanticized and glorified a city of the hedonistic good life alongside the poverty and distress of Moldavanka.

---

39 Iljine, *Odessa Memories*, 15.
40 "Istoriia ONMA," A. V. Nezhdanova Odessa – Odesa or Odes(s)a? National Academy of Music, accessed October 1, 2020, https://odma.edu.ua/pro-akademiyu/istoriya-onma/. On the IRMS, see Tatiana M. Kaplun, "Odesskoe otdelenie Imperatorskogo Russkogo muzykal'nogo obshchestva: stanovlenie i itogi," *Problemy muzykal'noi nauki*, no. 4 (October 2018): 127–32. On Anton Rubinstein, the IRMS, and the St. Petersburg and Moscow Conservatories, see James Loeffler, *The Most Musical Nation: Jews and Culture in the Late Russian Empire* (New Haven: Yale University Press, 2010), 15–55.
41 Iljine, *Odessa Memories*, 17–18.

Under the Soviet regime, the *blatnaia pesnia* (criminal song) offered an imaginative space that was a welcome alternative to official culture. This did not reflect reality but rather served as a representation of an idealized fantasy whose trope was Odesa.[42]

Throughout the Soviet period, nostalgia for "Odessa-mama" persisted, keeping alive the city's myth in Soviet literature, music, and cinema. One of the main figures who attached the Odesa myth to mass culture was Odesa-born jazz musician and singer Leonid Utiosov (Lazar Vaysbeyn, 1895–1982). Utiosov started his career at a young age in prerevolutionary Odesa. During the Soviet era, he introduced nostalgic Odesa as a theme in many of his songs. Using them mostly during World War II to inspire patriotism, Utiosov embodied Odesa as a symbol of the motherland. "Mishka-Odessit" was one of Utiosov's Odesa-themed smash hits.[43]

Folksongs and street music

The main folkloristic trait of music in Odesa was the *odesskii iazyk* (Odes(s)a language) that was a unique fusion of Russian, Yiddish, and Ukrainian and reflected all ethnic groups, featuring reciprocal influences.[44] Folk songs often contained Yiddish words and expressions that were translated into Russian, whereas others remained in Yiddish. Occasionally Russian words were given a Yiddish pronunciation, and syntax was adapted to the grammatical rules of Yiddish. Indeed, the local Odes(s)an Russian was often referred to as *Iudodessa* (Judeo-Odessa). Odesan Yiddish also absorbed Russian words. This was reflected in many popular songs in Yiddish, which were a mosaic of words and expressions of both languages.[45]

Numerous ballads and street songs feature topics and characters from Jewish culture and local everyday life. A good illustration is a folk song "The Rabbi of Kakhovka" (or Kakhuvk, a town located approximately two hundred kilometers to the east of Odesa):

---

42 Sophie Pinkham, "Making Deals in the Paradise of Thieves: Leonid Utesov, Arkadii Severnyi, and 'Blatnaia Pesnia,'" *Ulbandus Review* 16 (2014): 179–83.
43 Ibid.: 183–84.
44 Inna Cabanen, "Odesskii iazyk: bol'she mifa ili real'nosti?" in *Slavica Helsingiensia 40— Instrumentarium of Linguistics: Sociolinguistic Approaches to Non-Standard Russian*, ed. Arto Mustajoki, Ekaterina Protassova, and Nikolai Vakhtin (Helsinki: Helsinki University, 2010), 287–98.
45 Robert A. Rothstein, "How It Was Sung in Odessa: At the Intersection of Russian and Yiddish Folk Culture," *Slavic Review* 60, no. 4 (2001): 781–86.

В Каховке славилася дочь раввина Ента,
Такая тонкая, как шелковая лента,
Такая чистая, как мытая посуда,
Такая умная, как целый том Талмуда.

(The Rabbi's daughter, Yenta, was famous in Kakhovka/ She was as thin as a silkribbon / As clean as washed dishes / As smart as a whole volume of the Talmud.)

Yenta falls in love with a Gentile named Ivan Ivanovich—a director of a paper factory, who was handsome and tall, finely dressed in a military uniform, riding breeches and boots. One night, after the rabbi returns from the synagogue, he finds a note from his daughter with only four words: "Farewell, I've left, citizen Ivanova." The poor rabbi was so shocked that he abandoned Judaism, shaved his beard, packed his belongings, and ran away to Odesa to start a new life as a diamond merchant and to spend his leisure time at the Tango clubs.[46]

Many of the folk songs rehearse stereotypes of the Odesa myth, a city that was good and beautiful, but at the same time bad and dangerous, suggesting the good life and opportunities both to become rich fast and painfully to fall. Urban legends romanticized the gangsters of Moldavanka (fictionalized in Babel's Benia Krik and his gang). Numerous characters in the Odesan folk songs, though not necessarily associated with crime, are saturated with stereotypical Jewish names, such as: Aunt Pesia, Benia, Rabinovich, Surka (Sarah), Rosa, Berl, Leib, Yasha and Yankl. The terminology of the underworld is also rich with expressions originating from Yiddish and Hebrew. This is typical of the underworld folklore portrayed in the Odesa myth.

For instance, a popular folk song "Murka" tells the story of a woman named Murka (a nickname for Miriam or Maria), who is associated with a group of bandits. She becomes an informer who betrays the bandits and consequently is murdered by them:

Здравствуй, моя Мурка, здравствуй, дорогая,
Здравствуй, моя Мурка, и прощай,
Ты зашухарила всю нашу малину,
И теперь маслину получай.

---

46 Ibid.: 799.

(Hello, my Murka, hello, darling. / Hello, my Murka, and farewell. / You ratted on our whole operation, / So now take a slug.)

The majority of the songs about the colorful characters of the underworld are humoristic ballads, with or without a moral. Criminals are often depicted as flirtatious gentlemen who, despite their terrible crimes, show grace and manners. The comical approach leads to sublimation and refinement of their appalling acts. A song from 1917 by young Leonid Utiosov, although a little late for the timeframe discussed here, demonstrates this blend of humor and horror: Utiosov, acting the part of a paperboy, tells the audience about the latest scandal—an assault and robbery of an old lady by six bandits on Deribaskovskaia Street and the corner of Rishelievskii Boulevard, a central location downtown. The story of the robbery is told in a light and bouncy melody and in an entertaining manner. At the end, the old lady, who seems to be amused by what had just happened to her, is hoping for the bandits to return. The entertaining approach towards crime created the impression that violent acts were not a dangerous part of the daily reality in Odesa but rather a comical experience.[47]

Nostalgic Russian and Yiddish songs refer to Odesa as "Odessa-mama" (a term derived from criminal slang). The songs represent a versatile image of Odesa—a city that is proud of its wide boulevards, the seashore, the promenade, the panoramic view, the port, and the vibrant atmosphere. They portray the ambience—a fearless, carefree, hedonistic, and joyful place and highlight progressiveness and modern aspects of the city. These motifs are common to many songs that carry the title "Odessa Mama" or "Mama Ades" in different variants in Russian and Yiddish. Additionally, as pointed out by Rothstein, rhyming patterns are also common: the word "Odessa" in its Yiddish/Russian form is pronounced as *Ades/Odes*; it thus rhymes with words such as *progres* (Progress) and *farges* (forget, in Yiddish).[48] Such rhymes appear in the following stanza from Aaron Lebedev's song "Odessa Mama":[49]

> Ver es iz nokh nit geven
> in der sheyner shtot Ades
> hot di velt gor nit gezen
> un er veyst nit fun progres.

---

47 Boris Briker, "The Underworld of Benia Krik and I. Babel's 'Odessa Stories,'" *Canadian Slavonic Papers / Revue Canadienne Des Slavistes* 36, nos. 1–2 (1994): 126.
48 Rothstein, "How It Was Sung in Odessa": 789.
49 *The Best of Aaron Lebedev*, Greater Recording Company 182 (Brooklyn, 1969). This example is quoted in Rothstein, "How It Was Sung in Odessa": 789.

(Anyone who has not yet been / In the beautiful city of Ades / Hasn't seen the world at all / And he has no idea of progress.)

Klezmer, tango, and jazz—music in taverns and bars

The unique sound of the Jewish klezmer violin/fiddle played a critical role in shaping the soundscape of the city, especially in less institutional environments, both indoors and outdoors. Odesan southern klezmer style is unique compared to other klezmer styles that were prominent in other parts of Eastern Europe. In the last decades of the nineteenth century, klezmer ensembles were relatively large and included ten to fifteen players of various ages who played diverse instruments. The older and more experienced musicians were mostly fiddle, clarinet, flute, and trombone players. The younger, who were paid less, played the drums, percussion, and second fiddle and were usually hired to play at a poor family's wedding. With some help from Romany musicians, they formed small ensembles, which were barely appreciated.

Towards the turn of the century, klezmer ensembles attained a better reputation and were considered more professional. The musicians were required to demonstrate excellence and skill and to assure their clients that they were up to date with recent musical trends. As audiences expected new melodies, klezmer groups sought to expand their repertoire by introducing different musical genres and improvising on popular songs of the time. By the end of the nineteenth century, professional klezmer ensembles were expected to show virtuosic skills and were highly regarded by Jews and non-Jews alike.[50] When the imperial conservatories were opened to Jews, first in St. Petersburg and later on in Odesa, violinists who were members of a klezmer family were the first to enroll. Some of them became renowned virtuosos years later, among them Mischa Elman and David Oistrakh—both descendants of klezmer families.[51] Odesa was also a home for many virtuosos who won worldwide fame for playing other instruments, such as the clarinet and accordion. The Roma Odesa-born accordion virtuoso Misha Tsiganoff (1889–1967), for example, also known as "The Gypsy," was a non-Jew who spoke fluent Yiddish, emigrated to America, and recorded klezmer music with renowned Yiddish artists. Tsiganoff's accordion playing resembled

---

50 Walter Zev Feldman, *Klezmer: Music, History and Memory* (New York: Oxford University Press, 2016), 93–94.

51 Ibid., 98; Yale Strom, *The Book of Klezmer: The History, the Music, the Folklore* (Chicago: Chicago Review Press, 2011), 123.

playing the *bayan*—an accordion with chromatic buttons, which was a popular Ukrainian instrument.[52]

Klezmer music in Odesa flourished in conditions that were different from those in other parts of the Pale of Settlement. Whereas klezmer music in the Pale was limited to weddings and community events, in Odesa it was unrestricted. Klezmer music was present wherever Jews and non-Jews alike enjoyed listening to music. The most popular klezmer genre was the *Bulgar*, an energetic, duple-meter fast dance, with occasional triplets, often resembling the *freylekh*. The *Bulgar* originated in Bessarabia. It manifested characteristics of Bulgarian, Romanian, and Gypsy music and later became one of the most prominent klezmer genres in America.[53] The *Odesser Bulgar No. 1*, composed in 1920 by Abe Schwartz, became one of the most popular klezmer pieces in the twentieth century. The fast and bouncy *Bulgar*, combined with Hasidic dances and Russian and Ukrainian folk songs, ignited the wild, uninhibited, ecstatic atmosphere in numerous bars and taverns alongside the port area. This atmosphere is illustrated in the novella *Gambrinus* by the Russian writer Alexander Kuprin, which tells the story of Sashka, a Jewish virtuoso violinist, who played at a bar that attracted seamen of different nationalities. Klezmer music also served as a platform for the evolution of many Odesan folk songs. The relatively small ensembles that performed at bars and taverns (unlike large ensembles that performed at weddings) allowed the players to improvise on a tune and to show their talent. This improvisatory practice resembled the one found at the roots of jazz. Leonid Utiosov later claimed facetiously that Odesa, not New Orleans, was the birthplace of jazz music.[54]

Although Russian jazz emerged in prerevolutionary Odesa, Leonid Utiosov was the person who developed it into a popular genre, forming Theatro-Jazz or Soviet jazz, in the 1930s and 1940s. Although a discussion about Soviet jazz is beyond the scope of this chapter, it is important to note that the birth of jazz in Odesa is a direct outcome of the absorption and assimilation of various musical

---

52 Joshua Horowitz, "The Klezmer Accordion," *Musical Performance* 3, nos. 2–4 (2001): 143–45.
53 Walter Z. Feldman, "Bulgărească/Bulgarish/Bulgar: The Transformation of a Klezmer Dance Genre," *Ethnomusicology* 38, no. 1 (1994): 27–28; Mark Slobin, *American Klezmer: Its Roots and Offshoots* (Berkeley: University of California Press, 2002), 77, 113.
54 Iljine, *Odessa Memories*, 110. Frederick Starr, *Red and Hot: The Fate of Jazz in the Soviet Union 1917–1991* (New York: Limelight, 1994), 144–56. Utiosov was one of the first to acknowledge similarities between the development of jazz in Odesa and in New Orleans. Recent research on urban history reinforces Utiosov's claim, and also highlights other points of congruence between the two cities; see Samuel C. Ramer and Blair A. Ruble, eds., *Place, Identity, and Urban Culture: Odesa and New Orleans* (Washington, DC: Kennan Institute Occasional Papers, 2008).

trends, music cosmopolitanism, into the cultural and urban vibe of the city that had developed in the preceding decades. The improvisatory style, multifaceted sonorities, the lightness, and the bouncy manner in which jazz music erupted, perfectly matched the free and wild ambience that dominated the nightclubs in Odesa.[55] As Zeev Jabotinsky put it: "Odesa . . . has never known a tradition; for that reason, it has never been afraid to accept new forms."[56]

The appropriation of traditional Jewish music by the low culture of Odesa's bars is noted by cantor Minkowsky, who expressed his disgust upon hearing Jewish liturgical music played on gramophones in Odesa bars:

> Songs of lust and obscene language, drinking songs, and Gypsy tunes are mingled with verses from the holy prayers inside establishments of amusement, taverns and bordellos. . . . I would pass by a Greek tavern, where they would play erotic songs, songs about intoxication and theft. First, they played the *Tropak* [a Ukrainian folk dance]. Men and women would passionately hug and kiss. And all of a sudden, out of the gramophone located at the center of the bar, the *Shlosh-esreh Midot* [the thirteen attributes of God's mercy, from the Day of Atonement service] would fill the air, and all of that to the ears of drunken, gluttonous, amused men with the clinking of their toasting glasses.[57]

The desecration of sacred tunes seems to be part of Odesa's urban soundscape of street music witnessed by Mendele's eponymous protagonist in his novel *Fishke der krumer* (Fishke the lame), who encounters it in scenes of drunkenness:

> So, say you pass a boozer, well, there just is bound to be some tearful drunk inside a-sighing and a-singing a sad Ruskii song called "My Purty Li'l Miss" or some other such lovesick nonsense; whilst opposite, a Jewish gent who is no less in his cups may be giving out with Sabbath hymns or blaring "Ashes to

---

55 Starr, *Red and Hot*, 21–37.
56 Jabotinsky, *Zikhronot ben dori* [Memories of my generation] (Tel Aviv: Amikhai, 1959), 10; my translation.
57 Pinkhas Minkowsky, "Zimrat hamikdash vehagramofon" [Temple/synagogue songs and the gramophone], manuscript, National Library of Israel, archive of Pinkhas Minkowsky, MUS 16, section B, item 22, p. 5 (my translation); date unknown. More depictions of this phenomenon can be found in Minkowsky, *Moderne liturgye in undzere synagogen in rusland* [Modern liturgy in our synagogues in Russia] (Odesa: Bialik and Burishkin, 1910).

ashes, Dust to dust, twix one and t'other. Drink we must to the merry beat of a tailor's march."[58]

So we see the way non-Jews extracted only the emotional appeal of cantorial music from its sacred origin, whereas to a Jewish ear this sounded sacrilegious.

Tango—music, eroticism, and the underworld

One of the musical genres that boosted Odesa's mythical reputation for hedonism was the tango. In the second decade of the twentieth century, the tango began to spread throughout Europe like wildfire until it reached Odesa and was enthusiastically embraced by the locals of all ethnicities.[59] The dance, which is suggestive of sensuality and permissiveness, matched the ambience of the nightlife scene in Odesa.[60]

Paradoxically, the tango, a relatively moderate and restrained musical genre, served as the soundtrack for horrible, violent acts. Anecdotes about those graphic scandals were occasionally adapted to a familiar tango tune. For example, the song "На Дерибасовской открылася пивная" (A bar opened on Deribasovskaia Street) was set to the famous tango tune *El Choclo* and tells the story of a bloody fight between two gangs:[61]

> Но Костя Шмаровоз был парень пылкий:
> Чуркмену жирному он засветил бутылкой,
> Официанту засадил он в ногу вилкой,
> И началось тут славное танго.

> (But Kostia the junkman was a fiery fellow: / He blasted Chubby Churkmen with a bottle, / Jammed his fork into a waiter's leg, / And so there struck up a glorious tango.)

---

58 Mendele Moykher Sforim (S. Y. Abramovich), "Fishke the Lame," in *Tales of Mendele the Book Peddler*, ed. Dan Miron and Ken Friedman, trans. Ted Gorelick and Hillel Halkin (New York: Schocken Books, 1996), 257.
59 On the enthusiasm of Eastern European Jews for the tango, see Lloica Czackis, "TANGELE: The History of Yiddish Tango," *Jewish Quarterly* 50, no. 1 (2003): 45–52.
60 Marta Savigliano, *Tango and the Political Economy of Passion* (New York: Routledge, 2018).
61 Briker, "The Underworld of Benia Krik and I. Babel's 'Odessa Stories,'" 127.

Institutionalization of the tango occurred in the 1920s and 1930s, when it shifted from the nightclub scene to the more established arts, such as popular music, theater, and cinema.[62] In the early Soviet era, the tango became one of the most popular musical genres nationwide. Some of Utiosov's greatest hits from those decades were composed in the style of a tango. Сердце (Heart, composed by Isaac Dunaevskii, 1934) is one of the best known.

Outdoor music

Outdoor performances and live concerts took place at the well-groomed parks and along the seaside promenade. Live concerts were performed on a regular basis at the park on Deribaskovskaia Street. Haim Glicksberg, a Jewish Odesan painter and a close friend of Bialik, wrote about attending a concert in the park in his memoirs: "One summer day Bialik bought us two tickets to a symphony concert at the public park. Upon our arrival, the conductor was already standing on the podium and the concert had begun. Bialik took the program in his hands and said: 'They are now playing Grieg' ... Such is life, Grieg—let it be Grieg!"[63]

Indigent musicians with barrel organs regularly performed at the corners of the main streets. *Sharmanka*—a barrel organ that was also known as *Katerina* (from French: Charmante Catherine) was the main musical instrument seen and heard on the streets. The box had a manual revolving mechanism that contained several folk songs, popular waltzes, and opera hits. The player would stand at a corner of a street where a bar or a club was located to ambush the passersby. It was common to see an organ grinder accompanied by a little girl who was singing and dancing to the music that emerged from the sharmanka, and a pet monkey that was capering around it to attract attention.[64] As Mendele's Fishke the Lame continues strolling the streets of Odesa, he encounters street musicians playing the sharmanka:

> But, finally, this one feller managed to explain to me the entire difference between our paupers back home and their ilk here. It's the music, don't you know? That's right. For back home, a pauper eats his dry crust feeling just ever so mournful and down in the

---

62 Czackis, "TANGELE," 11.
63 Haim Glicksberg, *Bialik yom: pirkei zikhronot, tsiyurim verishumim* [Bialik everyday: memoirs, paintings, and drawings] (Tel Aviv: Dvir, 1953), 127–28; my translation.
64 Iljine, *Odessa Memories*, 111.

mouth, whereas in Odessa, he sits down to the same poor fare whilst a barrel organ[65] plays for him nearby, so he only chaws the more cheerful for it. Well, you might even say that barrel organs have gone over mighty big in Odessa as a general thing. I mean you can't turn a corner anywhere, indoors or out, without your having a barrel organ or some such wheeze box grinding away at you there. Barrel organs in the street, barrel organs at home, barrel organs in taverns, barrel organs at the circus. Why, saving your presences, sirs, but they even got the shameless gumption to be playing them things at shul [synagogues]! Ever hear of such a thing? Barrel organs at shul. Foo![66]

By associating barrel organs with synagogues, Mendele is clearly satirizing the organ at the Brody synagogue. Fishke continues, describing the music he hears on the streets, sounds he perceives as noise surrounding him from all directions: "And there is always such a great hoo-ha uproar going on in Odessa all the time on account of it, what with all them hurdy-gurdy jinglings and pipings, and folks everywhere whistling and singing along as well."[67]

"Music in the air": Odesa's soundscape as a manifestation of cosmopolitanism and cultural diversity

The cosmopolitan soundscape of Odesa is an outcome of fusion and immersion of sounds of different origins, different genres, and different languages. It also represents infusion/fusion between what was considered "low" and "high" cultures and the blurring of aesthetic and social boundaries. People of different social and economic classes were exposed to the same auditory world: most Odesans were able to afford a ticket to the opera house and most could attend a park concert. At the same time, people of all social backgrounds visited bars and night clubs, houses of worship were open to all, Jews and non-Jews flocked to services in synagogues to enjoy the music, and, of course, everyone strolled down the streets. Music was a vital commodity and Odesans were engaged as enthusiastic consumers, as active practitioners, and as a passive audience.

---

65 In the original Yiddish version, Mendele uses the word "Katerina" in reference to the barrel organ.
66 Mendele, "Fishke the Lame," 257.
67 Ibid.

Multiethnic coexistence in the harbor area created an auditory space that consisted of multiple musical genres at venues where people of different nations gathered, such as in taverns. The music that was played in those drinking houses was a mixture of genres, combining sensuality, eroticism, and emotion. Klezmer music, as one of those animated genres, was no longer exclusive to Jews. It was appropriated to some degree for playing in multinational venues. Later, it was followed by the erotic flavor of the tango.

Institutionalized multiethnic coexistence was manifested in music that was partially controlled and supervised. The opera house, in which rules and regulations were imposed and implemented and etiquette was expected (although not always observed), featured operas in different languages: Italian, Russian, French, and so on. The diversified audience included members of all ethnic groups and social backgrounds. Synagogues, mainly the Brody synagogue, served as an environment for a bi-directional flow of music from the inside to the outside and vice versa.[68] Hence it was also conceived in its heyday as a symbol of a bilateral relationship between Jews and Gentiles, in which music served as a bridge.

Odesa was not the only fast-growing port city at the time to attract a vast number of immigrants of diverse ethnicities. Although it shared many attributes with other cities,[69] its distinctiveness derived from its rich culture and musical diversity. This mixture of sounds, sights, and scents created a unique multi-sensory phenomenon—the musical myth of Odesa.

---

68 Philip Bohlman, *Jewish Music and Modernity* (New York: Oxford University Press, 2008), 99.
69 For comparison between Odesa and other port cities, see Patricia Herlihy, "Port Jews of Odessa and Trieste—A Tale of Two Cities," *Jahrbuch des Simon-Dubnow-Instituts* 2 (2003): 183–98, reprinted in Herlihy, *Odessa Recollected: The Port and the People* (Boston: Academic Studies Press, 2018), 196–208; John D. Klier, "A Port, Not a Shtetl: Reflections on the Distinctiveness of Odessa," *Jewish Culture and History* 4, no. 2 (2001): 173–178; Jarrod Tanny, *City of Rogues and Schnorrers: Russia's Jews and the Myth of Old Odessa* (Bloomington: Indiana University Press, 2011), 7–8. On the similar cultural attributes of the fast-growing Tel Aviv, see Anat Helman, *Or veyam hekifuha: Tarbut tel-avivit bitkufat hamandat 1920–1948* [Light and sea: culture of Tel Aviv during the British mandate, 1920–1948] (Haifa: University of Haifa, 2007).

CHAPTER 7

Gender, Poetry, and Song: Vera Inber and Isa Kremer in Odesa

Mirja Lecke

Introduction

During the first decades of the twentieth century, women became increasingly visible in the cultural realm of rapidly modernizing Odesa, albeit in ways that were at variance with one another. On the one hand, Odesa was the location where the first Russian women's newspaper began publication in 1912, and a local women's journal was published from 1915;[1] on the other hand, the local press frequently reported cases of rampant prostitution and human trafficking that constructed the female body as contagious.[2] These topics quickly made their way into belles lettres, for instance, in Semyon Yushkevich's *Улица* (The street) in 1911, a moralistic novella about an ill-fated young prostitute on Odesa's elegant Deribaskovskaia Street. The city's distinguished circles, by contrast, enthusiastically discussed decadent art and literature that were obsessed with sexual deviance and erotic self-destruction[3] but seemingly showed little interest in Saint Petersburg's cultural elite's "erotic utopia," which encompassed

---

1 See M. R. Bel'skii, *Gazety staroi Odessy: Spravochnik* (Odesa: VMV, 2009), 16. *Zhenskaia gazeta* was a daily newspaper dedicated to society, literature, and politics; *Zhenskoe slovo* was an illustrated journal.
2 Roshanna P. Sylvester, *Tales of Old Odessa: Crime and Civility in a City of Thieves* (DeKalb, IL: North Illinois University Press, 2005), 63–66, 81–88.
3 Ol'ga Barkovskaia, "Odessa, 1901–1941: Vystavki, zrelishcha, kontserty," in *Chernyi kvadrat nad chernym morem*, ed. A. M. Golubovski, F. D. Kokhrikht, and T. V. Shchurova (Odesa: Optimum, 2007), 15–62.

chaste marriage and philosophically sublimated new attitudes towards gender roles and homosexuality.[4]

In self-consciously modern Odesa, women constituted a growing part of the educated elites, working as teachers, academics, poets, artists, actresses, dancers, and singers. Women were active in the thriving modernist culture and in local debates on contemporary society; they were also very much involved in the multi-ethnic cultural fabric that made Odesa a cosmopolitan cultural center. In urban spaces such as associations or clubs women could legitimately interact with individuals from the region, but also from elsewhere in the Russian Empire or abroad and thus contribute to the cultural life of their hometown, although this was not true for all women of all backgrounds to the same extent. In the male-dominated world of late imperial Russia, they were marginalized by unequal gender relations, even if these relations differed greatly among the various ethnic groups and social classes. Many educated women were additionally hindered by official discrimination in tsarist times because of their Jewish ancestry; after the October 1917 Revolution, they often encountered persecution as class enemies. The communists' lip service to emancipation notwithstanding, women's contribution to the unprecedented cultural blossoming of the early twentieth century was subsequently erased from the Soviet Russian cultural historical tradition. In fact, the entire modernist movement was downplayed and tabooed during the attempt to establish a sanitized narrative about Odesa's past that presented it as a joyous port city rather than as transnationally connected and as an internally multiple cultural hub so as to align it with socialist realism, the officially prescribed mode of artistic expression. This may also explain why these women were rarely the focus of research in the Soviet Union. It is, therefore, a task for future researchers to reconstruct the manifold ways in which women shaped Odesa's cultural life at the turn of the century.

In this chapter, I will attempt to lay the foundations for a more comprehensive study by contrasting two culturally active women, the poet Vera Inber and the singer Isabella (Isa) Kremer. I chose them because they represent the enormously broad spectrum of career opportunities that allowed both women to become internationally recognized artists, for which they were arguably indebted to Odesa's open and multifaceted cultural scene in the 1910s, but also because I want to show the radically different outcomes brought about by their very slightly different life choices. Vera Inber and Isa Kremer were almost coeval (born around 1890); both came from assimilated Jewish families and made

---

[4] Olga Matich, *Erotic Utopia: The Decadent Imagination in Russia's Fin de Siècle* (Madison: University of Wisconsin Press, 2005).

their debuts in the culturally open circles of their hometown after prolonged stays abroad. Although the available sources provide no proof, the two probably knew each other. Their husbands, Nathan Inber and Israel Heifetz, had consecutively been leading figures in the liberal newspaper *Одесские новости* (Odesa news) and well-known intellectuals of the city's Literaturno-khudozhestvennoe obshchestvo (Literary-Artistic Society), known as the Literaturka, which organized poetry evenings, lectures, and discussions across the full gamut of the arts (see Guido Hausmann's chapter in this volume). Some sources state that Isa Kremer sang songs to Inber's lyrics.[5] During World War I, the October Revolution, and the civil war, both women spent time abroad in Istanbul and later returned to Odesa.

Both Inber and Kremer got divorced in the aftermath of the political turmoil of the civil war, but then they set out on different tracks. Vera Inber moved to Moscow and became one of the leading figures in Soviet literature, an acclaimed author of panegyrics on Lenin and Stalin, as well as of widely read accounts of the Leningrad blockade, which won her the Stalin prize. Isa Kremer, in contrast, built an international career in the Western hemisphere based on folksongs from many countries but, first and foremost, on Yiddish songs that she performed in concert halls around the globe. At the 1943 Teheran Conference, she performed for the gathered international leaders, among them Stalin, and dared to allude to political persecution in the Soviet Union.[6]

I will show that important elements in both women's artistic work can be traced back to the specific setting of Odesa's cultural spaces. I will concentrate on those aspects of their cultural production and careers that show traces of cultural contact, both large and small scale, between different religious and national groups. Moreover, I will show the interrelationship of their performances and overall cultural identifications with their self-positioning in the gender debates of the period. There are no sources that explicitly show either of the women's understanding of cosmopolitanism or cultural contact in multiethnic Odesa, let alone their stance toward it. However, a 1913 article series about fashion in the *Odesskie novosti* by Vera Inber allows us to infer what cosmopolitanism, or world

---

5 Isa Kremer sang songs with lyrics taken from Vera Inber's poetry volume *Горькая услада* (Bitter delight [Odesa: n.p., 1917]). See "Oni ostavili sled v istorii Odessy: Odesskii biograficheskii spravochnik, Nulevoi kilometr," accessed July 16, 2020, http://odessa-memory.info/index.php?id=327/. Some of these lyrics may be found online in Viacheslav Ogryzko, "Moe polozhenie lozhno," *Literaturnaia Rossiia* 16 (February 23, 2015), https://litrossia.ru/item/4296-oldarchive/.

6 "Kremer Iza Iakovlevna: Opernaia pevitsa s mirovoi slavoi," at Chisto odesskii sait, Odesskiy.com, accessed July 16, 2020, http://odesskiy.com/k/kremer-iza-jakovlevna.html/.

citizenship may have meant for her milieu with regard to that particular cultural realm. A *"femme de monde"* [sic], she asserts, maintaining the double meaning of the French "monde" as "world" and "high society," appropriates the entire history of clothing, ranging from Greek tunics through royal Renascence attire and Parisian silk pastoral dresses down to what she calls the street: fur coats that gild women, "colorful flowers on the city's grey asphalt," in Paris and Saint Petersburg.[7] Obviously for her, belonging to the world in the Russian Empire is tantamount to adherence to European aristocratic culture, its historical narrative included. Traveling, cultural exchange, and acquisition rather than national closure form an integral part of this socially exclusive concept that, as Jessica Berman has shown, at the time was also important in debates about new roles and aesthetic models for women as well as the enlightened ideal of the United States as a cosmopolitan nation that became eponymous for *The Cosmopolitan* magazine.[8]

Vera Inber: Bringing Odesa's past into the Soviet future

Vera Inber (born 1890)[9] is one of the few women whose active involvement in the emergence of Odesan literary modernism was acknowledged from the outset. A good indicator is a list that Yurii Olesha and Valentin Kataev compiled in 1930 to mark the "Odes(s)an period in Russian literature," in which they placed her fourth, directly after Isaak Babel, Ilia Ilf, and Evgenii Petrov, well ahead of Eduard Bagritsky, perhaps the most recognized Odesan poet, who was only ninth. Yet, Aleksandr Makarov, the author of the introduction to Vera Inber's 1965 four-volume *Collected Works*, glossed over her Odesan literary works as Inber herself did by labeling them "pre-biography."[10] In downplaying her early poetic oeuvre, Makarov followed Inber's self-presentation in her 1928 autobiography Место под солнцем (A place under the sun), in which she almost totally omitted her Odesan prerevolutionary works. Having left the city for Moscow

---

7   Vera Inber, "Tsvety na asfal'te," in *Tsvety na asfal'te* (Odessa: Druk, 2000), 7–9. Inber's expertise in fashion is also the subject of her *A Place under the Sun*; Vera Inber, *Sobranie sochinenii v chetyrekh tomakh* (Mosvka: Khudozhestvennaia literatura, 1965), 2:425–532. Unless otherwise indicated, all translations from Russian are mine—M. L.
8   Jessica Berman, *Modernist Fiction, Cosmopolitanism, and the Politics of Community* (Cambridge: Cambridge University Press, 2001), 28–53.
9   For a brief biographical overview, see "Vera Inber," in *100 velikikh Odessitov*, ed. Aleksandr Libin (Odessa: Optimum, 2009), 167–73.
10 Inber, *Sobranie sochinenii*, 1:11.

in 1922 at age thirty-two, in this book she discarded almost all previous literary activity as the fruit of a still lingering bourgeois class consciousness, the overcoming of which provided the ideological core of *A Place Under the Sun*.

Russification in the Jewish family and Ukraine's place in it

Vera Inber came from an upper middle-class Jewish family. Her father, Moisei Shpentser, had made his way from the shtetl Bobrinets to become a recognized publisher of science books in Odesa. As a vestige of his Yiddish upbringing, he would use "funny" words and phrases,[11] which his daughter Vera adored, and which may have stimulated her sensitivity to language. A heightened sense of language also came from Vera Inber's mother, Fanni Shpentser, a Russian teacher and principal of the public Jewish girls' school. In her autobiographical story "Как я была маленькая" (When I was small, 1954),[12] Inber's female narrator recalls her mother's strictly enforcing a normative concept of the Russian language (along with diligence and clear handwriting) among hundreds of Jewish girls, her daughter included; this story conveys the trauma of the imposed normative Russian. As a sign of appreciation, the mother had hung up a portrait of Konstantin D. Ushinskii, author of the widespread reading primer *Родное слово* (The native word) in their hall. "When I was still very small, I was afraid of this portrait. Konstantin Dmitrievich in his black gown and black tie on his snow-white starched shirt with his black beard and close gaze seemed very strict to me. It seemed as if he was dissatisfied with me: at that time, I still read poorly and mispronounced certain words."[13] When the narrator mastered Russian standard pronunciation and reading, however, she felt that Ushinskii's gaze changed, and she started honoring him as her mother had. As we shall see, the Russian language and its juxtaposition with its Odesan variant, as well as other languages, forms a leitmotif in Vera Inber's texts.

The imperial Russian ideas of correct language and *kul'turnost'* guided the role and function ascribed to other languages, subordinating them as mere folklore or *zhargon*. The Ukrainian presence in Odesa and its surroundings is explicitly noted in Inber's later autobiographical prose, but it is hard to judge whether this is due to her memories or out of strategic considerations. In the story

---

11 Arkadii L'vov, "Devushka iz khoroshei sem'i," in his *Kaftany i lapserdaki: Syny i pasynki: Pisateli-evrei v russkoi literature* (Moscow: Knizhniki, 2015), 435–36.
12 Inber, *Sobranie sochinenii*, 2:341–424.
13 Inber, *Sobranie sochinenii*, 2:355.

"О моем отце" (About my father, 1938) she recounts that, in the evenings, her very busy professional parents would occasionally sing Ukrainian songs.[14] Moreover, at least in her childhood stories, the family is presented as being well connected with Odesa's Ukrainian hinterland. Due to his participation in the 1880 census, her father knew Ukraine and the peasants' life there well. Inber's narrator also remembers her parents' close personal ties with Ukrainians: the family helped peasants enduring personal and economically difficult circumstances.[15]

Inber's modernism and distance from younger avant-garde Odesan authors

Because of the turmoil of the 1917 revolutions and Vera Inber's cautious reticence about her personal affairs, we know little about her career in the early twentieth century, apart from the few surviving copies of her poetry volumes and her sanitized autobiographical accounts—she largely eliminated from her literary persona the adult part of her bourgeois life and strove to distance herself from Lev Trotsky, her remote relative. At the age of twenty, she married Nathan Inber, a writer and journalist, who wrote for the *Odesskie novosti*, a newspaper headed by his father Osip.[16] During the civil war, the Inbers' house was a popular meeting place for Odesan and Moscow writers, especially while Nathan led the Literaturka and used his position there to foster modernism.[17]

Vera Inber started writing poetry early; poems for her first volume were written during a prolonged sojourn in Paris and Switzerland from 1910 to 1914. The metropolis of early twentieth-century Paris left a deep imprint on her first collection Печальное вино (Sad wine), that came out in 1914 in Paris and received favorable reviews in Russia.[18] She also published poems and articles in Odesa's local press.[19] *Sad Wine* contains remarkable poems about the perception of urban space, in which Inber assumes many different roles, including that

---

14 Ibid., 295.
15 Ibid., 296.
16 Bel'skii, *Gazety staroi Odessy*, 36.
17 Aleksandr Bisk, "Odesskaia 'Literaturka,'" *Diaspora: Novye materialy* [Paris and St. Petersburg] 1 (2001): 115–41.
18 Vera Inber, *Pechal'noe vino* (Paris: Tipografiia Rirakhovskago, 1914). It was reviewed by Razumnik Ivanov-Razumnik and Aleksandr Blok; see "Inber Vera Mikhailovna (1890–1972): Poetessa i prozaik," Oni ostavili sled v istorii Odessy: Odesskii biograficheskii spravochnik, Nulevoi kilometr, accessed July 16, 2020, http://odessa-memory.info/index.php?id=228/.
19 A collection that included Inber's "Mal'chik so skripkoi" was published in *Argus: Vse vizhu* 10 (1913): 112.

of a male speaker, displaying an interest in the interaction of gender with poetic expression. Although she contests neither sex as a universal category nor the heterosexual norm, she shows a playful approach with regard to gender and social division. Inber arranges fugitive impressions of the various senses into dense, symbolically loaded city imagery. In her poem "Фобург" (Suburb),[20] a female lyrical speaker relates an incident when steel workers on the nocturnal street blocked her way. Hit by a metal spark and a sexist remark (she writes "compliment") screamed at her, she moves on, hearing the workers' laughter. The socially underprivileged workers thus embarrass and threaten the young, privileged female, claiming the street as their, not her space.

Inber adopts a different female pose, but also one that is designed to address gender and social differences, in the earlier 1912 poem "Море" (The sea),[21] which unfolds in Odesa's port. The speaker talks with a sailor, whom she erotically desires. She is from a Christian, elitist family background, as becomes clear from an earlier visit to the pier that she recounts; she had been there with her German governess during the Lenten fast. The governess admonished her in German to stay calm—the reprimand is given untranslated, and the foreign words are particularly stressed, included in the rhyme scheme. Now, she intends to come back alone to wield her economic power; by buying the sailor's entire catch of fish, she will keep him affixed to one spot in his appealing pose, thus facilitating her erotic coming of age.

Port life is celebrated not only as a feast for the senses, however, but also as the experience of a new medium. "Я возьму с собою свой кодак / И сниму и море, и всех." (I'll bring my Kodak / and take a picture of the sea and everybody). This passage shows Inber's very early and keen awareness of the paramount role of media communication for social encounters in the modern era; she documents her experience and makes it relatable for herself and others. However, photography also demonstrates power, establishing and reaffirming the roles of the technically equipped viewer and his/her object; therefore, it is particularly noteworthy that the young woman uses a Kodak, the camera that the Romanov tsar's family (keen photographers) were known to use. As such, it seems that Inber's character is aspiring to their position as unrestricted rulers. She subjects the sailor, the port, "and everything" to her female gaze in an act of

---

20 Inber, *Pechal'noe vino*, 23; Inber, *Sobranie sochinenii*, 1:49; here the original French title is translated "Predmest'e," which erases the Western European context.
21 Inber, *Pechal'noe vino*, 41.

socially exclusive technological self-empowerment.[22] Both "Suburb" and "The Sea" clearly show that Inber in her modernist poetry is preoccupied with the interconnectedness of modern living conditions and social division, particularly with the gender aspects in cross-class encounters. The inserted foreign words function to signal the elite's connections with non-Russian cultures (French, German, etc.), beyond the confines of Russia and are thus in line with the cosmopolitan idea of *femme du monde*, who is part of a global elite rather than local ethnic groups.

In the following poetry volumes, *Горькая услада* (Bitter delight, 1917) and *Бренные слова* (Ephemeral words, 1922), she included numerous travel poems, but also fine nature lyrics, some about the seasons of the year in Odesa. While the city is either recognizable or explicitly mentioned, stylistically and in her emotional attitude, Inber keeps to a moderate modernism, employing neither daring metaphors nor anti-individualist, futuristic deconstruction. However, in a couple of light-hearted poems, she is aesthetically close to other Odesan poets; for instance, she assumes a male sailor's role, recounting erotic affairs and an alcohol-soaked life in harbor bars. "Маленький Джонни" (Little Johnny) quickly became a popular Vertinskii song and "Девушка из Нагасаки" (A girl from Nagasaki) was sung with a smoky voice by the famous Vladimir Vysotskii. Thus, by the late 1910s, Vera Inber had established the reputation of an emotionally deep and outspokenly feminine writer.[23] Yet, there were also voices criticizing her work. Literary critic Petr Pilskii considered her poetry and her entire personality affected and narcissistic and dismissed her as "a spoiled child of her thoughtless Odessa-Mama,"[24] although he wrote this bitter and misogynistic judgment later, in exile, when Inber had turned into an ardent communist.

How did Vera Inber interact with the other Odesan poets, some of whom also appear on Olesha and Kataev's list? During the peak of Inber's prerevolutionary career, Odesa had a true blossoming of avant-gardist poetry (futurist, in the authors' self-presentation), in which a frivolous tone and anti-moralist stance were typical. Following the initiatives of Petr Pilskii, and later Petr Storitsyn,

---

22 I am grateful to Yohanan Petrovsky-Shtern for pointing out to me the tsar's enthusiasm for photography; see on this Ksenia Zubacheva and Anastasiya Karagodina, "How Photography Became a Hobby of the Romanovs," *Russia Beyond*, July 4, 2017, https://www.rbth.com/arts/history/2017/07/04/how-photography-became-the-hobby-of-the-romanovs_795295; see also Charlotte Zeepvat, *The Camera and the Tsars: The Romanov Family in Photographs* (Stroud: Sutton, 2004), vi-xiv.

23 Inber's literary persona is outlined in Rina Zelenaia, "Razroznennye stranitsy," *Deribasovskaia-Rishel'evskaia* 34 (2008): 230–36 and Petr Pil'skii, "O zhemanstve," in his *Zatumanivshiisia mir* (Riga: Grāmatu Draugs, 1929), 17–19.

24 Pil'skii, "O zhemanstve," 17.

young poets held poetry readings, publishing lavishly illustrated poetry almanacs that some consider the beginning of the Odesan or "South Russian" school of writers, a significant phenomenon in twentieth-century Russian literature.[25] Yet, Inber is not mentioned in the dozens of memoirs dedicated to the era's literary life. Why is this so? The reason must be sought in the retrospective attempt to purge the Odesan avant-garde of its bourgeois cradle, the Literaturka. As the Odesan writer and critic Aleksandr Bisk recalled, Bagritsky, Olesha, and Kataev, as well as the other poets who would later form the poetry club Зеленая Лампа (the green lamp),[26] launched their careers at the Wednesday meetings of the Literaturka, then headed by Nathan Inber (who had taken over from Israel Heifetz, Isa Kremer's husband), although they denied this fact afterwards.[27]

Vera Inber herself was more open about the artistic crowd in prerevolutionary Odesa.[28] She repeatedly performed together with the Futurists on poetry evenings[29] and must have closely followed their initiatives, as she later recalled very early poems of Bagritsky that had not been published elsewhere. She was also familiar with the poets' association, The Green Lamp. Although there was contact, Vera Inber, slightly older than the others, nevertheless, did not belong to this sphere and did not socialize closely with Bagritsky's circle, and vice versa. She reported that Bagritsky visited her once in her Odesa home and did not know any of her guests. However, Valentin Kataev asked her, in 1914 or 1915, to contribute to an Odesan poetry almanac, but she never did.

Despite their shared modernist aesthetics, a cultural watershed separated Vera Inber and the poets of the Odesa School, which may have resulted from the distance between her well-to-do bourgeois status and their more modest socioeconomic backgrounds—but it even more likely derived from gender roles. In the 1910s and early 1920s, as Sergei Bondarin wrote, in Odesa, "literature was oral."[30] Spontaneously spoken, situational and ephemeral language use honored the inclusion of local Odesan language, with its deviations from the normative Russian, while circumventing the problem of the shortage of paper.

---

25 Sergei Lushchik, "Chudo v pustyne," in *Dom kniazia Gagarina: Sbornik nauchnykh statei i publikatsii* (Odesa: Plaske, 2004), 166–236.
26 On "The Green Lamp," see, for instance, Sergei Bondarin, "Kharchevnia," in *Eduard Bagritsky: Almanakh*, ed. Vladimir Narbut (Moscow: Sovetskii pisatel', 1936), 229.
27 Aleksandr Bisk, "Molodye gody Leonida Grossmana (Materialy dlia biografii)," *Novoe russkoe slovo*, January 16, 1966, 8.
28 Vera Inber, *Za mnogo let* (Moscow: Sovetskii pisatel', 1964), 221–22.
29 Alena Iavorskaia, "Eto bylo, bylo v Odesse," in *Sil'nee liubvi i smerti: Stikhotvorenia, vospominania, pis'ma*, ed. Zinaida Shishova and Dmitrii Aleskeevich Losev (Feodosiia, Moscow: Koktebel', 2011), 14, 32.
30 Bondarin, "Kharchevnia," 229.

Poetry recitations often took place while moving through city space.[31] Literary life in Odesa became associated with a male, gruff tone that privileged loud, extroverted, cocky male poets.[32] This oral culture curtailed the participation of women. We know of only two poetesses who regularly met with the younger males and were recognized by them as colleagues, Zinaida Shishova and Adelina Adalis; however, they were rarely published in the same collections with the men's poetry. Newspaper reviews and memoirs about the women's poetry performances described contributing poets as immature, naïve, and whimsical.[33] Konstantin Paustovsky reported a scandal over the recitation of the poet Lokhvitskaia's verses in 1921, which were booed as allegedly hyper-feminine "beadwork."[34] Most memoirists, including Shishova and Adalis, agreed that the witty and eccentric Eduard Bagritsky, a genius futurist of Jewish descent, was the indisputable leader in that milieu. He also stood out as a poet who published light-hearted, even slightly vulgar poems under the female pseudonym Nina Voskresenskaia and was frequently reported to have addressed contacts across ethnic lines by playing with Odesan culture's Ukrainian element, although in appearances in the public sphere, he markedly performed as a male. Compared with Inber's reluctant consideration of Ukraine, Bagritsky was much more provocative. Shishova recounted how Bagritsky performed as a Ukrainian peasant pitching prices in the market, while she, Shishova, was selling her belongings, and he also brazenly addressed a young woman in a shop in Ukrainian just for the shock effect, which shows just how socially marked the language was.[35] While, poetically, the Ukrainian element became most visible in his *Дума про Опанаса* (The lay of Opanas, 1926), Bagritsky was well aware of the performative, theatrical dimension of ethnic and social self-positioning in public space. Bagritsky, who always wanted to appear as a hero, was newly invested as a Cossack turned Soviet: "прохожие, глядя на него, на его большую голову и чуб, торчавший из-под папахи думали: вот идет бывший атаман или батько, который осоветился" (... in looking at him, his big head and forelock sticking out of his hat, the passersby thought: here comes a former Cossack leader who has turned into a Soviet man.)[36] This scene could have come out of a Babel story.

---

31 Zinaida Shishova, "O nashei molodosti," in Losev and Iavorskaia, *Sil'nee liubvi i smerti*, 91–101.
32 Konstantin Paustovskii, "Vremia bol'shikh ozhidanii," in Paustovskii, *Sobranie sochinenii*, 9 vols. (Moscow: Khudozhestvennaia literatura, 1982), 5:145.
33 See Iavorskaia, "Eto bylo," 32.
34 Paustovskii, "Vremia bol'shikh ozhidanii," 151.
35 Shishova, "O nashei molodosti," 91–101.
36 Gekht, "Vechera v zheleznodorozhnom klube," in *Bagritsky, Almanakh*, 241.

We do not have similar testimonies about female Odesan authors but, in 1918, the poet Zinaida Shishova wrote a poem about an interethnic erotic encounter in public space. It is called "Пустячек" (A trifle)[37] and sketches a short-lived love affair between a female speaker, who remains ethnically unmarked, and a Ukrainian nationalist. She ran into him on the street and—struck by the way he looked at her—took him as her lover, but subsequently, she found him ridiculous and awkward in his affection for his native Ukraine and forgot him within days. If there is any general message in this poem, it is that narrow, pettifogging nationalism is infantile, unmanly, and unattractive—that is, to contemporary women. Shishova's daring subject matter and ostentatiously negligent, individual voice must have hit a nerve because they won her the Literaturka prize.

Vera Inber and other women on Odesa's avant-garde stages

Whereas, broadly speaking, the accepted concept of gender roles at the time hindered female poets' advancement in Odesa avant-garde circles, women, among them Vera Inber, were more successful in integrating into the emerging scene of small, improvised theaters, "*teatr miniatiur*," that flourished in early twentieth-century Odesa. The famous BiBaBo established a new concept of the theater, showing several short pieces in the course of one evening and mixing dramatic scenes with music and also dance.[38] These theaters were mobile, often using basements or empty ground floor shops, making them accessible to lower social classes and people of various ethnic or religious ancestry, who could just walk in off the street. In Odesa, such miniature theaters also provided performance space for the socially marginalized, such as Jewish children from the poor district of Moldavanka, who performed in a children's opera, and artists who catered to lower-class tastes or experimented with new art forms. Here, the careers of the singer/jazz musician Leonid Utiosov and of the actor Vladimir Khenkin, who performed the role of the shtetl Jew on stage, got underway.

In the early 1920s, Vera Inber was very active in a theater of that type, named KROT, short for Konfreriia Rytsarei Ostrogo Teatra (Brotherhood of the knights of sharp theater).[39] This name is ironic and mock-aristocratic, its

---

37 Boris Bobovich et al., *Pervyi al'manakh literaturno-khudozhestvennogo kruzhka* (Odessa: n.p., 1918), 31.
38 Viktor R. Faitel'berg-Blank, "*Teatr miniatiur*," in *Serebriannyi vek iuzhnoi pal'miry*, 2 vols. (Odesa: Optimum 2004), 2:365–71.
39 This theater existed from 1921–1922; the most important sources about it are Inber, *Place under the Sun* and Zelenaia, "Razroznennye stranitsy"; see also Nataliia Sokolova, "Lidiia

acronym fittingly recalls the word "mole" as well as *krotkii*—gentle, modest,— as it was located in a simple basement. In her autobiographical *A Place under the Sun*, Inber adjusts KROT to the ideological needs of 1928 regarding ethnic plurality, class consciousness, and gender. She calls the theater SOSEP, short for: Sozvuchnyi Epokhe (Resonating with the era) and presents it as the place of her literary initiation in the midst of a diverse group of Jews, Poles, and Russians, artistically united in the search for the politically correct avant-garde, oriented towards communism,[40] a description that would have been more adequate for the group around Bagritsky, Kataev, Olesha, and Shishova. In fact, as we know, Inber had long been an accomplished poetess and what is more, the KROT theater troupe was an almost exclusively Russian Jewish enterprise. Natalia Sokolova recalls that KROT evolved from productions held on the occasion of birthdays and other family celebrations in the homes of the wealthy Bliumenfelds and Shpentsers. By turning KROT into a Union ensemble, the group funneled state resources into their productions. In KROT, writes Sokolova, Vera Inber recited poetry, the wealthy Gurfinkel daughters co-starred; in attendance were also Lidiia Ginzburg, an upcoming literary critic, and her brother, Viktor Yakovlevich Tipot (Ginzburg), as well as his wife and Inber's schoolmate, Nadezhda (née Bliumenfeld).[41]

In *A Place under the Sun*, Inber stresses the role of SOSEP's male director. By contrast, actress Rina Zelenaia recalls the KROT women (Nadezhda Bliumenfeld, Lidiia Ginzburg, and Vera Inber) as being at the heart of the ensemble.[42] The theater's repertoire was entertaining, with a varying weekly mixture of short one-act plays, songs, poetry and dance. The play *Charlstushki* involved frivolous costumes and offered a parody of western images of Russia, combined with popular local folk culture—such as the Charleston dance craze and *chastushki*, ditties or funny short, rhymed Russian songs.[43] Inber mentions one unsuccessful (and to date unpublished) antireligious satire, whose action unfolded in Noah's ark. Another of Inber's early theater plays has reached us, the jocular *Ад в раю* (Hell in paradise), performed at KROT. This is a satire on gender relations and women's emancipation in the Garden of Eden, based on the Bible. Adam wants his woman

---

Ginzburg, rodnia, znakomye: Materialy k biografii, Vospominaniia," unpublished manuscript, Russian State Archive of Literature and Arts. F3270 inv. 1 doc. 27; "Inber, Vera Mikhailovna," *Oni ostavili sled v istorii Odessy: sobranie ocherkov i biografii*, http://odessa-memory.info/index.php?id=228/.

40 Inber, *Sobranie sochinenii*, 2:485–87.
41 Sokolova, "Lidiia Ginzburg," 11, 26.
42 Zelenaia, "Razroznennye stranitsy," 233–34.
43 Sokolova, "Lidiia Ginzburg," 65–66.

to cook for him and facilitate his idle life, but first Lilith and then Eve are easily convinced by the snake to try the forbidden fruit, and both soon turn into workshy and consumption-oriented modern women: "Я умираю здесь от скуки / С небритым мужем без ребра" (I am dying of boredom here / with my ribless, unshaven husband.)[44] Inber's Lilith is remarkably different from the traditionally demonized character. In her vision, at Adam's side, any woman would turn into a Lilith, even Eve. While that play was successful in Odesa, Inber describes the play's later failure in Moscow, when a drunkard caused a disturbance that stopped the show. In the 1965 Russian edition of *A Place under the Sun*, the drunkard condemns the play as being blasphemous; in the 1930 German translation, his antisemitic outburst is quoted. But Inber does not delve into the underlying anti-Judaic sentiment or emancipatory agenda and reports the incident in an ironic, humoristic manner, criticizing the public's inability to grasp antireligious pathos.[45] Plays like *Hell in Paradise*, in combination with operetta parodies and other light genres, seem to have been the ideal sphere for Vera Inber's and other women's artistic expression in the postrevolutionary times of hunger and shortages, although Rina Zelenaia recalls that in Odesa's KROT there was a lack of contemporary satire and she knew nothing of Olesha and Kataev.[46]

After Vera Inber, along with most of the other Odesan authors, relocated to Moscow, she wrote "Васька Свист в переплете" (Vas'ka Svist in trouble, 1926), her first and only text that fits into the emerging Soviet fashion of portraying Odesan bandits in music (*blatnaia pesnia*) and literature. The poem is dramatic in form, subdivided into five parts, each with a specific tone and representing a different perspective on the death of a thief during a robbery. "Vas'ka Svist" was, and still is, a popular text, in which a modern, unconventional female character destroys a man's life. The social milieu is one of petty criminals and remains vague with regard to the gangsters' ethnic backgrounds. The hero's name is a Slavic moniker, while the female character remains unnamed, but she uses an Odesan Yiddish-Russian phrase ("пара пустяков," a couple of trifles).[47] The action described in this poem unfolds in some unidentified place in southern Ukraine around 1920, most likely in Odesa. What is remarkable is the absolutely central role of stylistics in this text; there is use of substandard language and underworld slang, as well as extremely skillful simulations of spoken language

---

44 Vera Inber, "Ad v raiu," *Deribasovskaia-Rishel'evskaia* 34 (2008): 228.
45 Inber, *Sobranie sochinenii*, 2:526–27; Vera Inber, *Der Platz an der Sonne* (Berlin: Malik, 1930), 254–55.
46 Zelenaia, "Razroznennye stranitsy," 234.
47 Inber, *Sobranie sochinenii*, 1:165.

that dominate the parts reflecting Vas'ka's perspective, distorted by alcohol and sexual desire. These long and impressive passages include the woman's incitement to commit a robbery; hence, in all parts, male perceptions dominate, whether the speech of a policeman, a medical bulletin, the last words during Vas'ka's agony, or a newspaper notice. However, "Vas'ka Svist" remained an episode and Vera Inber never became part of the Soviet period's Odesan mythmaking, with its discrete connection to subculture. Instead, she aligned completely with the repressive Soviet literary system.

Inber remembers multiethnic prerevolutionary Odesa

Famous for her Lenin odes and her account of the blockade of Leningrad, Vera Inber also wrote some little-known fine memoiristic poetry about Odesa. In her poem "Воспоминания" (Memories, 1939), which is part of the larger piece "Ovid,"[48] the autobiographically modeled speaker describes how she, as a schoolgirl, experienced the 1905 Revolution in Odesa. In the opening, her Polish cosmology teacher, Tomasz Militicki, is sketched as an odious authoritarian figure, with an annoyingly blatant Polish accent. It is symbolic that the girls first perceive the revolution during his impressive lesson about a galactic event. The lesson's "music of the spheres," its pure mathematical order, is interrupted by the actual sounds of the upheaval. The central part of the poem is a description of a demonstration turned funeral procession through the city that the girls witness, looking out onto the street through the classroom window. This scene is written in an impressionist style, the crowd metaphorically compared to a flowing river, composed of a multitude of visual and aural stimuli. The mourned victim is a student killed during a demonstration. His mother follows his corpse in a light carriage, which the speaker (in an inserted commentary) designates by the Odesan term *phaeton*. When the mourners start shouting political slogans, Cossacks quickly and forcefully disperse the gathering. In the classroom, the Polish teacher, Militicki, does the same thing to the crowd of girls observing from the window. His antiquated Russian ("Вы не внимательны суть" [You are not being attentive!]) signals his hopeless backwardness. Nonetheless, it is noteworthy that, shocked by the Cossacks' behavior, he is compassionate towards the girls and the grieving crowd. The antagonistic relationship between

---

48 Ibid., 1:466–71.

the strange old teacher and his young pupils is overcome, as they witness events of universal significance taking place in the beautiful Odesa springtime.

In the conclusion of the poem, Inber delves into the philosophical implication of this memory as a psychological process, a metamorphosis. What she offers here is no less than an alternative to the Soviet-era image of Odesa as a frivolous, criminal city. She draws a picture of Odesa's history as a sacrifice of cosmic dimensions, while referring to the Roman poet Ovid, the author of *Metamorphoses*. It is significant that Ovid was exiled to Tomi on the Black Sea, not far from Odesa. Reading Ovid, Inber's speaker is thrown back into her youth in the sun-flooded south, and she reflects on the role of language in the metamorphosis enacted by memory: "Старая мать в фаэтоне. . . . Само это слово, / Даже оно здесь сыграло какую-то роль" (The old mother in the *phaeton*. . . . The very word / Even played a certain role here).[49] In Ovid's *Metamorphoses*, Phaeton steers Phoebus's sun chariot across the sky, but loses control, causing a cosmic catastrophe.[50] This motif forms a bridge between the ending of the poem and its beginning—Militicki's astronomy lesson. Inber thus reconnects the Odesan term *phaeton* (a light carriage), which is itself derived from mythology, with the image of the sun as the grieving father (like Phoebus) and the revolution as a tragic event of universal significance. In that way, her Odesa is remembered by means of the 'metamorphosis' of a local word, moving into the realm of the Mediterranean Greek and Roman cultures associated with sun cults, which detaches Odesa from northern Russia.

Two decades later, in 1960, Inber came back to her revision of Soviet-era images of Odesa in "Я вспоминаю, из поэмы" (I remember, from a poem).[51] In this poem's opening, the process of remembering is inextricably tied to a media-worthy experience, for instance, the beginning of the twentieth century as a newspaper headline, Odesa's theater as a technologically advanced illusion machine, and the flow of visual memories: "I'd say as film frames, but this word / is too modern, / perhaps magic lantern is more appropriate."[52] In this mediated access to memory, the autobiographical speaker also embeds the subsequent image of Moldavanka, for which she names characters from Isaac Babel's *Odessa Tales*, Benia Krik and the cemetery wardens. Subsequently, she brings a stanza

---

49 Ibid., 1:471.
50 *Ovid's Metamorphoses in Latin and English*, 2 vols. (Amsterdam: Wetsteins and Smith, 1732), 1:75–90.
51 Inber, *Sobranie sochinenii*, 1:508–16; for the author herself reading the poem "Vera Inber: Ia vspominaiu . . . (chitaet avtor)" in her South Russian accent see *Odnoklassniki*, accessed July 16, 2020, https://ok.ru/video/872942209627/.
52 Inber, *Sobranie sochinenii*, 1:510.

that explains her strivings to reframe the Soviet-era cultural image of Odesa that to a large degree draws on Babel's stories: "Но мы иную знали Молдаванку, / очаг недоедания и рахита. / И, не преображенная искусством, / действительность была куда сложней" (But we knew a different Moldavanka, / a breeding ground of malnutrition and rickets. / And, not transformed by art, / the reality was much more complex.)[53]

Inber describes Babel's Odesa as an artistic metamorphosis, a pearl that nobody expected to be hidden in the misery, brought to life "Бабелевским золотым пером" (by Babel's golden quill).[54] She contrasts Babel's Odesa with an unspecified collective memory of Jewish life in the city. In the long passage that follows, the speaker recounts the assaults and unbearable living conditions that she knew about from her mother, who taught girls from Moldavanka in her Jewish school. She unfolds a complex picture of a diverse Jewish community, ranging from one family that fell into poverty when the father was fired from the opera house for taking part in an antimonarchist demonstration to fantastically rich sugar barons, approached by her mother when seeking charity. The pogroms of the early twentieth century, however, are strikingly absent from that historical picture. Inber contextualizes Jewish humor (which in the Soviet Union of 1960 had become "Odes(s)an" humor), as a survival strategy of the miserable poor. A girl sick with tuberculosis jokes about the mumps epidemic in her class: "Еще нам только свинки не хватало"[55] (All we lacked was mumps), the pun being that the colloquial *svinka* for mumps also means little pig. The subsequent nostalgic consideration of oceans that the speaker has seen is followed by memories of the city's topography and Inber's cousin Dima, who got caught in the pitfalls of revolutionary times. Here the poem breaks off.

We can only speculate about the reason why the poem remained a fragment. From the entirety of Inber's oeuvre, it seems likely that her ideological aboutturn from Odesan bourgeois *femme du monde* cosmopolitanism to unconditional loyalty to the Communist Party in the early 1920s was crucial. As a public persona and an official representative of the writers' union, Inber compromised her extreme sensitivity to social inequality and to the distinct Odesan dialect, different from the Russian norm that she had so painfully appropriated in her childhood. This led to awkward declarations such as, for instance, in her article "Великое русское слово" (The great Russian word, 1962), in which she explained the necessity for cleaning up the deteriorating Russian language. In this demand,

---

53 Ibid.
54 Ibid.
55 Inber, *Sobranie sochinenii*, 1:511.

she had numerous antecedents, among them Vladimir Lenin, Evgenii Zamiatin, and Maksim Gorky. Zamiatin and Gorky each chastised Odesans in particular for their corrupted Russian. Now Vera Inber, without the slightest sign of irony, lauds the "great Russian word" exclusively in authors whose artistic careers were inseparably connected with Odesa.

Isa Kremer: The "true daughter" of her people

The singer Isa Kremer was born in 1887 in Beltz, Bessarabia (now Bălți, Moldova).[56] When she was 12 years old, her family moved to Odesa. It was in this Black Sea metropolis that Isa Kremer became an international star with strong local ties. I will show how Isa Kremer's artistic persona embodied gender debates of her times and can be situated within what Anat Rubinstein in chapter 6 calls Odesa's cosmopolitan musical soundscape, a multifaceted phenomenon that combined local and global musical traditions while at times also allowing for national engagement.

Isa Kremer was trained as a classical opera singer in Milan. Her great success on the local as well as national opera scene notwithstanding, when she returned to Odesa in 1912,[57] she soon turned her back on classical opera roles.[58] Instead, she started to perform lighter music and operettas (at that time enormously popular) and, later on, mostly chansons with a piano accompaniment, her voice and the lyrics being the central musical elements.

It was no accident that Isa Kremer started her career in established European high-culture music that played a decisive role in creating national audiences, while at times the national identities of the composers and the performers are pushed into the background for the sake of universal harmony, and in which a singer's role is restricted to the performance of strictly prescribed and scripted music. Kremer then shifted the path of her artistic development to various genres in which the singer's persona was carefully constructed to suit the contents of the stage performance, a move that grew in importance—both as an element in the process of communicating with the audience and in terms of economic success. The most knowledgeable researcher of Isa Kremer's Russian

---

56 Unless otherwise indicated, the biographical information is taken from Judith Pinnolis' biographical sketch, "Isa Kremer," Jewniverse, last updated Novemeber 30, 2022, http://www.holoimes.jewniverse.info/isakremer/biography.htm/.
57 "Pesni dlia Stalina," Jewish.ru, September 9, 2018, https://jewish.ru/ru/people/culture/187352/.
58 Boris Savchenko, *Estrada retro* (Moscow: Iskusstvo, 1996), 152.

years, Boris I. Savchenko, shows how press reviews in 1912 attest to the success of Kremer's first opera performances, rendering her immediately the opera's best box-office draw. At that time, the Odesa opera theater, run by M. F. Bagrov, was suffering a financial crisis; many seats remained empty because of the high price of tickets. Savchenko writes that, with Isa Kremer's solo performances of entertaining music and her comic talent, the Odesan opera house conducted a general shift towards a more popular and financially viable repertoire. This shows Isa Kremer's powerful impact on her native Odesa. The antisemitic right-wing press, from the outset, however, classified Kremer as a Jewish star, which, in their eyes, automatically meant that her success was undeserved.[59]

Building on her fame performing roles of lighthearted heroines, such as the Gypsy Princess in Imre Kalman's 1912 operetta *Der Zigeunerprimas* (The gypsy band leader), the swan song of the Habsburg Empire, Isa Kremer wrote and performed solo songs. She built up an image of female sensuality and permissiveness with her famous tangos (see Anat Rubinstein's chapter),[60] and her adaptations of contemporary French Montmartre songs. But most successful were the *chansons* on erotic subjects, "интимные песенки" (intimate little songs), which became the centerpieces of Isa Kremer's prerevolutionary fame.[61] By means of her repertoire, she painted an escapist picture of the world, in all its exotic variety. As one journalist of the time noted: "She came back to us, this mistress of graceful songs, in which is revealed before us the geography of the whole globe! There is Zanzibar, sultry India, Africa with black Toms, satiated Paris, seashores, the harem of the Turkish sultan, the youthful round dance in the Russian village, and Italy with its talented singers."[62] Some of Isa Kremer's songs had colonialist and racist undertones, for instance, "Черный Том" (Black Tom) about the unhappy love of a servant for a blindingly white, unattainable lady. Her songs represented cosmopolitanism in the sense of the global mobility of the white elites with their associated tastes, very much in line with Vera Inber's interest in international fashion. While affirming the racial hierarchy of her times (and ignoring racist conceptions of Jews), she supported women's rights to erotic fulfillment, although she presented the latter in a trivial, commercialized manner, and, again not unlike Vera Inber in the poem "The Sea," she linked legitimate female sexual desire with high social status. An apt example of this is

---

59 Savchenko, *Estrada retro*, 194.
60 On Odesa as a "tango metropolis," see Inna Naroditskaia, "Is Argentine Tango Russian and How Jewish Is Russian Tango?" *Gli spazi della musica* 6, no. 2 (2017): 53–68.
61 Savchenko, *Estrada retro*, 159–73, 189.
62 Quoted in ibid., 201.

"Madame Lulu," which she wrote around 1916, in which a star with countless admirers, the eponymous Lulu, sends the men away under the pretext of fatigue, only to get together with a handsome young musician. "Мадам Лулу с ума всех сводит, глаза мерцают и горят . . . она забавы лишь хочет . . ." (Madame Lulu drives everybody crazy, her eyes shine and burn . . . she only wants to play around).

Kremer's song, which shares its title with Frank Wedekind's scandalous 1913 tragedy about a promiscuous young woman who falls victim to male fantasies, praises the diva's attitude towards life and embraces a hedonistic, modern relationship, free of moral restrictions between the sexes. It is clearly intended to blur the lines between the fictional figure in the song and Isa Kremer's performance on stage. Thus, by means of her musical repertoire, Kremer created the image of an independent, sexually active woman with a good sense of humor. She adapted the popular *estrada* format that combined singing, dancing, and other performance arts to the stage and opened highbrow opera to a less privileged audience, making her music modern, but by no means avant-gardist.

This image became all the more powerful in 1922 in its combination with a brilliant self-presentation on stage. The *New York Times* favorably reviewed her first performance in Carnegie Hall: "She is pretty and piquant, still of strongly Oriental type, in modish purple and gold, with hair midnight-black, skin lily-white, arms actively eloquent and graceful. Posed on a little raised platform with footlights and four spotlights, she made even facial expression tell the content of her songs . . . Hers is real singing rather than parlando, though her manner of the 'narrator' may often become colloquial . . . [she, M. L.] proved her skill in diction, as well as in its pantomime of moving fingers."[63]

Isa Kremer's stage presence also attracted considerable attention in the emerging mass media of the time, which becomes very clear when reading the press reviews of her performances that Savchenko collected but also in looking at the extant concert posters, photos, and reports of her performances.[64] These give an idea of Odesa's commercialized cultural sphere of the time, in which the female body is employed as eroticized surface on which the artist as recognizable individual and performer of a stage role mingle. In the *mise-en-scène*, her face (short dark hair and eyes) and the upper half of her body are always centered. In most pictures, she wears fancy, figure-hugging dresses. Visually, she presents herself as a south European, witty and sexy woman. Although the above-quoted American

---

63 "Isa Kremer Greeted," *New York Times*, October 30, 1922.
64 For an overview, see "Iza Kremer," *Informatsionnyj portal Shansona*, accessed July 16, 2020, http://russianshanson.info/?id=1042/.

observer stressed her Oriental style, in the Odesan context, her self-presentation seems more Mediterranean, in line with Odesa's image as a European, non-Russian, southern metropolis.

Her image as stereotypically Mediterranean, however, also allowed for ambivalence with regard to gender, as may be seen in a literary portrait written by a certain "Taifun," which was published in the *Одесское обозрение театров* (Odesa review of theaters). "Лицом и фигурой—типичный итальянский пикколо. / Характером напоминает его еще больше: / Весела, подвижна, жизнерадостна. / Хохочет круглый год" (With her face and her figure, she is a typical Italian piccolo. / Her character recalls one even more: / She is vivacious, agile, and cheerful. / She laughs all year round.)[65] In the many photos circulating on the internet (unfortunately, almost all undated), she is often shown in poses that present her as an emancipated modern woman, enjoying typical male pastimes such as driving a car or playing billiards; this fits the comparison Taifun draws between Isa Kremer and Odesa's famous aviation pioneer, Sergei Utochkin. Thus, Isa Kremer, in the second half of the 1910s, became the incarnation of the Odesan woman—modern, talented, witty, light-hearted, and with an insatiable lust for life.

Isa Kremer—Icon of Odesan modernism

Isa Kremer functioned as a central figure for Odesan modernism across the various arts. This becomes clear in view of the image of Isa Kremer that Isaak Babel conveyed in his sketch "Odessa" (1916): "Take, for instance, Odessan *chanteuses* (I'm talking about Isa Kremer), whose voices are small, but who brim with joy, with joy expressed artistically in their very being, with enthusiasm, with lightness and charm—with sometimes a sad, sometimes touching sense of life—a life that is good, nasty, and, *quand même et malgré tout*, extraordinarily interesting."[66] It is significant that Babel's narrator, almost paraphrasing Taifun, points out the joyfulness of her persona and of her very existence on stage and that he uses this wealth of French expressions stylistically to mark Kremer's figure as Mediterranean-European in a text that was meant to outline the messianic role of the Odes(s)an "singer of the sun" for future Russian culture. From a gender sensitive point of view, it is striking that the narrator plays down the artistic quality of Kremer's performances ("a small voice"), attributing her success

---

65 Quoted in Savchenko, *Estrada retro*, 154.
66 Isaac Babel, *Odessa Stories*, trans. Boris Dralyuk (London: Pushkin Press, 2016), 190.

rather to bodily predestination, a qualification that was not shared by experts. Babel's narrator is not alone, however, in his condescending attitude towards the Odesan star. Kornei Chukovsky wrote an epigram that also ridicules and belittles her talent: "О Иза, муза кукурузы, / К тебе так благосклонны Музы. / Ты и певунья, и плясунья, / И попрыгунья-стрекоза" (O, Isa, muse of the corn, / the muses are so well disposed toward you / You are a singer, and a dancer / and a jumping dragonfly.)[67] Babel and Chukovsky are also united in their presentation of Isa Kremer as a specifically Odesan Jewish anthropologic type of sorts, whose innovative power lies in a cheerful attitude to life.

By contrast, Isa Kremer's persona is presented as the crystallizing agent for modernist culture in Odesa in a portrait of the singer in the 1915 literary almanac, *Авто в облаках* (A car in the clouds) by Sandro Fasini (pseudonym of Srul Arnol'dovich Fainzilberg), the brother of Ilia Ilf, an important cubist painter of the period,[68] who contributed five portraits to the avant-gardist poetry volume. His portrait of Isa Kremer is a cubist pencil drawing that derives its effect from the tension between geometrically diverse squares and roundly formed elements of the human body. The female face that takes up most of surface of the composition is presented simultaneously facing forward and in profile, together with the upper part of a female body. The figure's body parts are arranged independently ("Why are Isa Kremer's eyes on her neck?" one Odesan wanted to know).[69] Eyes, nose, and mouth, all embellished with makeup, are arranged with curls, the neck and isolated female breasts as well as a stylized décolleté. This hyper-female, appearing as a dislocated image, is juxtaposed with certain male elements in the background and lower third: a top hat, a pince-nez and a pants leg out of which sticks a foot in a high-heeled shoe. Fasini's rearranged female body parts connect his drawing remarkably well to Isa Kremer's photographs from her Odesa period with their stress on her bodily presence, the upper half of the body and South European beauty. Yet, artistically and aesthetically, his drawing belongs to the avant-garde, which analyzed and critically deconstructed the emerging mass-culture of the age. In this portrait, Fasini combines not only a number of irreconcilable perspectives on the female body (typical of cubist art), but also raises the problem of the female body and the male gaze directed at it in a public space; the locus of the scene is either a theater stage (or opera, for that matter)

---

67 Kornei Chukovskii, *Dnevnik*, 3 vols. (Moscow: Prozaik, 2011), 1:191.
68 See quotations from the daily press given in Barkovskaia, "*Odessa*," 41; see also Alena Iavorskaia, "*Nezavisimyi Fazini*," in *Fazini, 1893–1944* (Moscow: Reprotsentr, 2008), 22–23.
69 "Emar: Odesskii futurism," *Iuzhnyi vestnik* 2 (1915): 27, quoted in Iavorskaia, *Fazini, 1893–1944*, 271.

or a table in a coffeehouse (the crystal glass in the lower right, perhaps on a table) or even a street (the balcony and street lamp to the left). His drawing does not raise the issue of ethnic identity nor of public visibility by means of graphic expression; rather, it deals with the sexualized body in the modern, star-centered culture. And yet, the portrait's title and its theatrical setting suggest the Odesan urban context in which the portrait circulated. Isa Kremer obviously functioned as an icon, a projection screen for very different groups; she could express modern Jewish national identity, as well as universal, modern urban entertainment and cosmopolitan leisure culture that looks towards the West.

International artist and "true daughter" of her people

Isa Kremer's ensuing world career as a markedly Jewish vocal artist was the outcome of Odesa's cosmopolitan cultural spaces that engendered her ties with Odesa's most famous Jewish intellectuals. Around 1912,[70] as I mentioned, she married the editor in chief of *Odesskie novosti*, Israel Moiseevich Heifetz,[71] to whom she had (according to some sources) sent revolutionary poems in her youth[72] and (according to another source) who had paid for her costly musical education in Milan.[73] Heifetz was the head of the Literaturka[74] and in close contact with Odesa's leading Jewish cultural activists, Haim Nahman Bialik, Mendele Moykher Sforim, Sholem Aleichem, and Mark Warshavsky. Kremer also wrote and published poetry during these years,[75] although those texts read more like song lyrics without the music.

As Isa Kremer recalled after immigrating to the US in 1923, Bialik and Mendele were regular attendees at her concerts in Odesa that were, as we have seen, socially inclusive and not nationally oriented events.[76] On these occasions they urged her to take an active role in the modern Jewish national movement. Already in the 1910s, Bialik convinced her to study Yiddish folklore and perform it on the stage as a means of strengthening cultural self-esteem among the Jews

---

70 Lois Barr, "Isa Kremer, 1887–1956," in JWA.org, last updated June 23, 2021, https://jwa.org/encyclopedia/article/kremer-isa/.
71 Bel'skii, *Gazety staroi Odessy*, 36.
72 See "Isa Kremer, 1887–1956" and the documentary film *Isa Kremer: The People's Diva*, directed by Nina Baker Feinberg and Ted Schillinger (USA, Women Make Movies, 2000), VHS.
73 Alena Gorodetskaia, "Pesni dlia Stalina," Jewish.ru., September 29, 2018, https://jewish.ru/ru/people/culture/187352/.
74 Savchenko, *Estrada retro*, 185.
75 Ibid., 187.
76 "Isa Kremer, a Child of the People," *Canadian Jewish Chronicle*, September 14, 1923, 7.

Gender, Poetry, and Song | 187

Иза Кремеръ.

Figure 3. Sandro Fasini, "Isa Kremer," *Avto v oblakakh* (1915). Photo credit: Mirja Lecke.

and bringing Yiddish songs to the attention of the general public. However, she did not restrict herself to Yiddish folklore and, adhering to the *femme du monde* paradigm, studied the folksongs of "all nations," as she stated.[77] From reviews of her later performances, we know that she performed songs in Russian, Italian, English, German, French, Romanian, and Arabic, among others. During a 1923 interview, Kremer reported her playful and somewhat erotic relationship with the elderly and serious Mendele, who credited her performances of Yiddish songs with providing a great service to the Jews and the emerging Jewish nation. He thought they successfully promoted what he called "the Jewish national idea" and lauded her for impressing this idea upon all Jewish people. This contention showed Mendele's debt to the Herderian notion of the national spirit, which Herder found best expressed in a people's folklore—a conviction Mendele shared with those Jewish musicians who were very actively constructing and promoting Yiddish folk culture in Eastern Europe to establish it as an entity distinct from the Slavic national movements around them.[78]

In fact, Kremer's Jewish songs and their public performances significantly transformed the various Jewish folk-music traditions. Jews of both genders and all social classes sang in nineteenth-century Eastern Europe; in traditional communities, however, only men were allowed to sing in front of an audience. As such, the greatest change introduced by Isa Kremer concerned gender. Moreover, the instrumentation of her songs was not traditional; Yiddish folk songs were typically sung solo and *a cappella*.[79] However, the best-known Jewish music in the Russian Empire's Pale of Settlement came from the various Jewish touring ensembles (see Anat Rubinstein's chapter), which regularly included the violin and the bass and made their way to Odesan bars. Kremer's songs, by contrast, were mostly accompanied by the piano and the violin, and sometimes by the violoncello. The piano, of course, is *the* instrument of the bourgeois age, and its use brought Kremer's songs closer to the West European chansons and coffee-house music, but with her classically trained voice also nearer to Russian romance, an immensely popular folk genre that classical composers, such as Tchaikovsky or Rimsky-Korsakov, sometimes emulated.[80] Isa Kremer's previously established popular persona underwent a significant shift when she sang

---

77 Ibid.
78 Elvira Grötzinger and Susi Hudak-Lazić, *Unser Rebbe, unser Stalin: Jiddische Lieder aus den St. Petersburger Sammlungen von Moishe Beregowski (1892–1961) und Sofia Magid (1892–1954)* (Wiesbaden: Harrassowitz, 2008), 46–64.
79 Susi Hudak-Lazić, "Die Melodien," in Grötzinger and Hudak-Lazić, *Unser Rebbe*, 101.
80 Dorothea Redepenning, "Die russische Romanze," in *Geschichte der russischen und sowjetischen Musik 1: Das 19. Jahrhundert* (Laaber: Laaber-Verlag, 1994), 38–67.

music that was recognizably Jewish but arranged for assimilated urban tastes. Moreover, Isa Kremer, the Jewish folk singer, clashed with Isa Kremer, the would-be Mediterranean Russian diva, as presented in the mass media and frivolous Russian language songs, as well as in operetta roles. Thus, an assimilated Jewess who breached traditional Jewish musical and gender conventions took on the mission of re-inventing Jewish song and lore. Such commercially driven alterations of the folk heritage did not pass without fierce resistance against this alleged falsification,[81] yet Kremer's success was not coincidental. Precisely her well-established fame in both serious and popular music styles facilitated her success as a Jewish singer performing for both Jewish *and* gentile audiences in rapidly modernizing Russia. Similar paradoxes are well known in national movements all over Europe. Folk culture needed to be adapted and adjusted to popular tastes before it could be successfully staged and become accepted by the audience as an expression of its own national identity. We thus see that Isa Kremer's remarkable artistic career became possible only in the conditions of Odesan cosmopolitan spaces and musical mind set—the presence and interaction of particular local religious and ethnic groups and their associated ideologies (the Jewish national movement and Zionism) with a more general European cultural influence (Italian opera, French chanson, Russian imperial cultural orientation towards the West).

The ambiguity of national affiliations in a cosmopolitan environment was pertinent beyond Russia's borders. Jessie Abrams, the author of the aforementioned 1923 interview article, wanted to prove that Kremer was a "true daughter" to her people. Not wanting her to be perceived as an "international Jew" (he mentions Henry Ford, alluding to the latter's antisemitic pamphlets of the early 1920s), Abrams strove to reconcile these two concepts—once again based on a Herderian set of convictions—that language and song express a people's soul. Abrams praises Isa Kremer for being a polyglot, as she offered him a choice of many different languages for the interview. However, when Abrams opted for English, she switched swiftly between English, French and Yiddish. Her first English phrase was purposely misspelled to indicate her Yiddish accent: "English I do not spik so goot." Notably, as in so many examples from Odesan culture, we are given indications of the voice and phonetics, in addition to non-normative language use, but this remains a marginal note, feeding into the childish image Abrams painted of Isa Kremer, by then a thirty-six-year-old international star.

---

81 Fritz Mordechai Kaufmann, "Die Aufführung jüdischer Volksmusik vor Westjuden," in *Jüdische Volksmusik: Eine mitteleuropäische Geistesgeschichte*, ed. Philip Bohlman (Wien: Böhlau, 2005), 151–53.

In fact, Abrams wanted to spare her from the accusation of rootless cosmopolitanism or, for that matter, of belonging to international Jewry. His argument was that, by means of performing songs in various languages, Isa Kremer was taking on the role of the daughter of each particular people—a role she played superbly, while, in fact, she was only a true child of the Jewish people. It goes without saying that he would not call her the mother of the modern Yiddish chanson.

Conclusion

Looking back at Vera Inber's early career in Odesa, the literary critic Petr Pilskii coined the phrase "одесситка, способная одесситка, хорошая одесситка, и, главное, буржуазная одесситка" (An Odesan, a talented Odesan, a good Odesan, and, most importantly, a bourgeois Odesan).[82] In its witty overemphasis on local origin and social belonging, the phrase equally suits Isa Kremer, but the two very different artistic destinies of Vera Inber and Isa Kremer also give us a more general idea of contingencies and mutual entanglements between nationalisms and cosmopolitanism in Odesa's flourishing culture, as well as their interconnections with gender and social class. Both Inber and Kremer came from the artistic upper-middle class of Odesa, for which a rather recent social advancement and family residency in Odesa were typical. They socialized with their peers from different ethnic and religious groups whose generally positive attitude towards modernization allowed for women to engage as culturally active members. Inber and Kremer could consider themselves *femmes du monde* or citizens of the world as a result of frequent and extended sojourns abroad combined with free command of several languages that complemented their consciously lived Odesan local ethnic plurality. The most important institution for Inber's and Kremer's careers was the Literaturka. While literature and the arts in the first decades of the twentieth century were heavily politicized, the Literaturka, albeit surely a socially exclusive institution, offered a forum, a marketplace of sorts, and room for various tastes, interests and ideological inclinations. This was due to the Literaturka's main objective of keeping up with contemporary developments in the arts in the Russian imperial centers and in Western Europe. This made the Literaturka the cradle of modernism in Odesa and in all of Russia for that matter. Modernism later took on its own dynamics, with its thriving interest in colorful

---

82 Pil'skii, "O zhemanstve," 18.

and light-hearted deviations from norms, futurism and anarchism, and experiments with new technologies (from the airplane to cinema).

The first two decades of the twentieth century were a time of flourishing culture, but also of commodification and crisis. In places such as the Literaturka, the opera house, and the coffeehouses in the city center, people heatedly discussed how to overcome the growing rifts that were driving society apart, both economically and with regard to national consciousness. Nationalism and cosmopolitanism, at that time often seen as opposing ways to align with a group larger than one's own, not only coexisted, but mutually enforced each other in the milieu of the Literaturka, as Isa Kremer's and Vera Inber's lives show.

Isa Kremer's career is illustrative in that respect. The decision to study vocals in Milan was a result of the Russian elite's admiration for European high culture, but Russian imperial culture also meant Russian ethnic nationalism and antisemitism, which drove some people in her milieu to opt for a specifically Jewish national identity. Kremer turned her back on the opera and on Western high culture, choosing the *estrada* that was closer to the masses' tastes and also more financially rewarding. This allowed her to become a female star with an individual persona, while maintaining the great appreciation for her masterful musical performances. This successful integration of elitist high culture and popular culture and the openness towards commercialization were typical of Odesa. At the outset, Isa Kremer's stage persona was that of the contemporary 'southern' woman: playful, sexy, and self-sufficient, but, later on, she adopted an outspokenly Jewish role, combining her "intimate little songs" with folk music and singing them in Yiddish in places where Yiddish was not the default language. She insisted on maintaining her cosmopolitan approach, however, always retaining popular songs in other languages in her repertoire. This allowed her to perform as a globally acclaimed singer, all the while promoting Jewish national aspirations—paradoxical as it may seem, a cosmopolitan with proudly displayed national roots.

One of the few certain facts about Vera Inber, by contrast, is that she never approved of nationalism. The reconstruction of her conduct in the pre- and postrevolutionary multiethnic arena remains challenging because ideological pressure and Bolshevik anti-cosmopolitanism exerted massive influence on the way in which Inber presented her life experience in poetry and memoiristic prose. While back in Odesa as well as in Leningrad and Moscow, Inber was actively involved in a multinational yet Russophone cultural fabric in which her female gender was always part of her literary persona; her most important topic in representing Odesa was social division and the space it left for modern female self-positioning. Occasionally, this included playful experimentation with male speaker positions and ethnic difference or exoticism. Taken together with her spatial orientation towards European metropolises and the sea, this gave rise to the dominant impression of a privileged female Russian.

In her later works, Odesa's Ukrainian *hinterland* and Inber's own Jewish ancestry became more visible, but these non-Russian elements were presented through internationalist lenses: the tsarist regime was to blame for exploitation and poverty that degraded people regardless of ethnic background, but fortunately it was overcome by the Revolution, in which the Russian proletariat became the leader of the world nations' emancipatory struggle. It is important to note that Inber systematically remained silent about the pogroms and outbursts of interethnic violence in view of which her displayed internationalism could have appeared questionable. By the same token, Vera Inber brushed away her bourgeois openness to other cultures that in Marxist terms only expressed the reactionary ideology of cosmopolitanism. She replaced it with a Soviet female internationalist voice speaking out against the crimes of fascism.

Inber and Kremer both projected female voices to a global audience, both had to leave Odesa behind, and both, albeit in different ways, had to adapt their Russian Jewish identities to new ways of navigating national belonging in the post-1917 world.

CHAPTER 8

The End of Cosmopolitan Time: Between Myth and Accommodation in Babel's *Odessa Stories*[1]

Efraim Sicher

Rereading the *Odessa Stories*

Isaak Babel (1894–1940) is well known for his celebration of Odesa as a hedonistic site of comic epic gangsters. Yet this common characterization in Russian literary criticism of Babel as an "Odes(s)a writer" is based on a cultural myth that all too often cites Babel as evidence. This chapter argues against the tendency to base the reading of Isaak Babel's *Odessa Stories* (1921–1932) on Odesa's reputation as a "city of rogues" and as a "criminal city"[2] or as a *topos* of postrevolutionary nostalgia for an imagined golden age of promiscuous fecundity.[3]

---

1   An earlier version of this chapter appeared as "Isaak Babel's 'Odessa Tales': Inventing Lost Time, Reshaping Memory." *Russian Review* 77, no. 1 (2018): 65–87.
2   For example, Jarrod Tanny, *City of Rogues and Schnorrers: Russia's Jews and the Myth of Old Odessa* (Bloomington: Indiana University Press, 2011). See also Roshanna P. Sylvester's study of the representation of criminality in Odessa's bourgeois press and on the stage in the early twentieth century, *Tales of Old Odessa: Crime and Civility in a City of Thieves* (DeKalb, IL: North Illinois University Press 2005). For evidence questioning the myth that crimes were characteristically committed by Jews in Odessa and comparisons with statistics from other provincial cities, see Ilya Gerasimov, "'My ubivaem tol'ko svoikh': prestupnost' kak marker mezhetnicheskikh granits v Odesse nachala dvatsatogo veka (1907–1917)," *Ab Imperio* (January 2003): 209–60. See also Patricia Herlihy, *Odessa: A History 1794–1914* (Cambridge, MA: Harvard University Press, 1986), 281–310. For the present-day legacy of "Babel's Odessa" and its discontents, see Amelia Glaser's chapter below.
3   Rebecca J. Stanton, *Isaac Babel and the Self-Invention of Odessan Modernism* (Evanston: Northwestern University Press, 2012).

Although Odesa experienced a surge of lawlessness in the civil war and early Soviet period, that is only a partial picture, which is neither precise nor balanced from the standpoint of social and cultural history.[4] Indeed, the fixation with the underworld and with the leisurely lifestyle of wealthy businessmen or its multilingual mix of nationalities only obscures any understanding of the cosmopolitan spaces which functioned before the revolution as a vibrant cultural exchange. A rich but neglected literary and artistic heritage from the prerevolutionary period, however, offers an alternate narrative. The early poetry of Bagritsky, Olesha, Kataev, Vera Inber, and Zinaida Shishova and the works of forgotten talents such as Anatoly Fioletov, Boris Bobovich, and Semyon Kesselman present a somewhat different story of prewar modernism in a cosmopolitan city, well before the birth of the "Odes(s)a school" of literature in Moscow in the 1920s.[5] Modernist art and literature was very much part of the cosmopolitan culture of prerevolutionary Odesa, at least in its intellectual and bohemian spaces, and, although Babel did not participate in the prerevolutionary blossoming of Odesa modernism, he personally knew several writers in Odesa after the civil war and later in Moscow who had made their debut in Odesa's cafes, poetry readings, and journals in 1912–18. His cultural identity emerged from Odesa's culturally diverse, multiethnic Jewish and Russian prerevolutionary environment. Indeed, the Russian and the Yiddish or Hebrew intertextuality of his work reveals how syncretically the cultural networks interacted among acculturated Jews and Russians.[6] As we shall see, what he did with the pre-existing Odessa myth is his own creation, accommodated to the exigencies of the times in which he lived and to which he fell victim.

I will argue that in his *Odessa Stories* and his writings about Odesa, Babel appropriated a familiar Odesa myth but moved from nostalgia for the prerevolutionary past to a more elegiac postrevolutionary view and, under Stalin, to the creation of a politically acceptable cultural identity. Rebecca Stanton has dated to the mid-1920s the "self-invention" of Babel and other Odesa writers after they moved to Moscow,[7] and Babel was certainly successful in reinventing himself (like Inber, as we saw in the previous chapter, and many others) as a Soviet writer on the basis of his first Odesa and Red Cavalry stories. Babel was, in fact, not the originator of Odesa literature but one of its last geniuses.

---

4   Viktor A. Savchenko, *Neofitsial'naia Odessa epokhi NEPa, mart 1921 – sentiabr' 1929* (Moscow: ROSPEN, 2012), 263–82.
5   On Odesa's literary modernism, see Mirja Lecke, "The Street: A Spatial Paradigm in Odessan Literature," *Slavonic and East European Review* 95, no. 3 (2017): 429–57.
6   Sicher, *Babel' in Context: A Study in Cultural Identity* (Boston: Academic Studies Press, 2012).
7   Stanton, *Isaac Babel and the Self-Invention of Odessan Modernism*, 33–42.

I propose revising our reading of the *Odessa Stories* and readjusting their relationship to the Odessa myth by re-examining the history of their composition and their historical context. When the stories are read together, the *Odessa Stories* apparently contain a number of inconsistencies, contradictions, and alternate modes of narration; yet they are united by a coherent historical progression from 1913 to the late 1920s and by characters who reappear in more than one story (among others, Benia Krik, Froim Grach, Tsudechkis, and Arye-Leyb). Within the larger corpus of Babel's work, the *Odessa Stories* reflect Babel's stylistic development from *Red Cavalry* to the Childhood stories as he reshaped his own cultural identity as a Russian Jew from a middle-class cosmopolitan background who was expected to display ideological and class solidarity.[8] I contend that, like other Odesa writers in the Soviet period, Babel used the Odesa myth for his own purposes, building on a nostalgia for a lost world shortly after it vanished. He then switched from identification with an imagined past to expressing an ambiguous hope for a better future despite the heavy human and cultural price exacted in the destruction of the past and in the political repression of any dissent from the Party line in the thirties, including local or regional "nationalism." I will delineate each of the phases that mark this transition from his early sketches to the first *Odessa Stories* and then to revision of the cosmopolitan past after it had been destroyed.

My account differs from previous readings of the *Odessa Stories* in that it not only rereads the stories in their historical context but also reconsiders the recovered corpus of all nine stories. The first *Odessa Stories* were written at about the same time as Babel was working on the Red Cavalry stories in 1921–23. They were clearly intended to form a cycle,[9] although only four were published together in collections of Babel's works in the 1930s and again in Soviet editions following Babel's posthumous rehabilitation during the Thaw. The Israeli edition Детство и другие рассказы (Childhood and other stories, 1979) and

---

8   I am using the terms *Odessa Stories*, Childhood stories, and Red Cavalry stories to refer to the entire cycles of these stories, including those that do not appear under this rubric in collections published in Babel's lifetime or were published posthumously. The childhood stories, for example, were intended to form a cycle called *Istoriia moei golubiatini* (Story of my dovecote) and some Red Cavalry stories were not included in the 1926 first edition of *Konarmiia (Red Cavalry)*.

9   For evidence that the *Odessa Stories* were written at the same time as *Red Cavalry*, see I. Smirin, "Na puti k *Konarmii*: Literaturnye iskaniia Babelia," *Literaturnoe nasledstvo* 74 (1965): 467–82. L. Livshits, however, claims that the composition of the *Odessa Stories* preceded the *Red Cavalry* cycle ("Materialy k tvorcheskoi biografii I. Babelia." *Voprosy literatury* 4 [1964]: 118).

some post-Soviet editions have reconstructed a cycle of nine stories. I follow the sequential order of the stories established in the Israeli edition,[10] tracing a shift in perspective from the early *Odessa Stories* to the later ones that is marked by a revision of an imagined past familiar from the Odesa myth. My reading diverges from that of most critics and commentators who, unfortunately, limit themselves to discussion of the four canonized stories, which leads them to draw doubtful conclusions about Babel's optimistic view of the Soviet regime.[11]

When the *Odessa Stories* first appeared in Odesa in 1921, and later in Moscow journals from 1923, a narrative had already been established about the city's former cosmopolitan lifestyle. The humorous sketches and anecdotes about Odesa types that were circulating from the end of the nineteenth century ensured universal familiarity with Odesa's reputation of sharp-witted, passionate characters and a leisurely café culture unlike anything in Moscow or St. Petersburg. They were taken up by satirists such as Arkadii Averchenko, who, like his fellow contributor to *Сатирикон* (Satyricon), Sasha Cherny, went into emigration after the Bolshevik takeover. It is the colorful, bustling seaport, overshadowed by the statue of the duke de Richelieu and shaken by the violence of the 1905 revolution that Cherny recalled in emigration,[12] not the "Sages of Odesa" and the Jewish cultural revival. In Alexander Kuprin's story "Большой фонтан" ("Great Fountain," 1911–1927), the protagonist Mishka Govorkov blames the bewitching effect on a northerner of Odessa's acacias for the tribulations of being married to an Odesan, in particular her atrocious Odesa *zhargon*, which she proudly defends as just as legitimate as standard Russian; absurdly, she claims Pushkin as an Odesan, because his statue stands in Odesa!

Evocations of Odesa in the Soviet period usually negotiated between nostalgic memory and political dictates when recording Odessa's present neglected and dilapidated state. For example, in 1923, Semyon Gekht, describing Odesa's deserted port and denuded parks, noted that the streets came to life only in the evening, when prostitutes and strollers listened to Rumanian musicians, but

---

10 Isaak Babel, *Detstvo i drugie rasskazy*, ed. Efraim Sicher (Jerusalem: Biblioteka Aliya, 1979), 239–317. The four-volume *Sobranie sochinenii v 4 tomakh*, ed. I. N. Sukhikh (Moscow: Vremia, 2006) respects the canonized cycle in Stalinist collections of four *Odessa Stories* but prints the remaining five in a supplementary section.

11 For standard Western readings of the four *Odessa Stories*, see Patricia Carden, *The Art of Isaac Babel* (Ithaca: Cornell University Press, 1972), 71–85; James Falen, *Isaac Babel: Russian Master of the Short Story* (Knoxville: University of Tennessee Press, 1974), 59–114; Milton Ehre, *Isaac Babel* (Boston: G. K. Hall, 1986), 46–54.

12 Sasha Cherny, "V Odesse" (1923), in *Sobranie sochinenii v piati tomakh* (Moscow: Ellis Lak, 1996), 2:103–04.

Gekht dutifully pointed to the bright proletarian future in the industrial sector of Peresyp'.[13] In a satirical sketch that conveyed something of the turmoil of Odessa's recent history, Ilia Ilf facetiously portrayed Odesa's monumental sculptures and its ruined businessmen against the background of a surreal film set peopled by Roman slaves and Petliura's combatants from the civil war.[14] Yurii Olesha emphasized his aestheticized childhood impressions of the Potemkin mutiny that conveyed to him no historical meaning, but he compensated for this apparent lack of class consciousness by declaring his gratitude to the Bolsheviks for putting into clear and politically correct perspective his memory of the tsar's visit or of the mansions of wealthy magnates.[15] Writing in 1936, at the height of the Stalinist terror, Olesha commented that Odesa's bourgeois past had been swept away, along with the untidy, dilapidated Langeron resort, to make way for a brand new stadium, the emblem, together with the figure of a young cyclist, of Odesa's future.[16]

Politically sanitized memoirs published during the Thaw by former Odessans, such as those by Konstantin Paustovsky or Lev Slavin, reinforced the mythicizing of Russian Odessa, but also rehabilitated Babel and other victims of Stalinism. As a countercultural tradition, the Odesa myth celebrated the city as a heterotopia, and, during glasnost, its representation heavily downplayed Odesa's former Jewish culture. The Ukrainian conflict from 2014, moreover, saw renewed Russian ethnic claims in Ukrainian territory, as noted in the introduction to this volume, and the Odesa myth was conscripted in order to revive the status of Odesa as a third Russian capital. The Odesa myth served political needs, and, after seventy years of communist repression and the destruction of war and the Holocaust, the myth has been absorbed into postmemory, a tertiary collective memory of what the postwar generation remembered of postrevolutionary Odesa. We therefore need to go back to the historical circumstances of the genesis and construction of Babel's Odesa text.

---

13 Semyon Gekht, "Odessa," *Ogonek*, May 6, 1923; republished in Gekht, *Izbrannoe* (Odesa: OLM, 2008), 51–52.
14 Il'ia Il'f, "Puteshestvie v Odessu," *Chudak* 13 (1929); republished in *Voprosy literatury* 1 (2004): 328–31.
15 Yurii Olesha, "Pis'mo iz Odessy," *30 dnei* 9 (1935); republished in Olesha, *Zavist', Tri tolstiaka, vospominaniia, rasskazy* (Moscow: Eksmo, 2013), 605–07.
16 Yurii Olesha, "Stadion v Odesse," *Vecherniaia Moskva*, June 2, 1936; republished in Olesha, *Zavist'*, 609–10.

An Odesa manifesto

The Odesa text ran counter to the Petersburg text as an alternative model of Westernizing influence in Russian literature.[17] The poet and essayist Bella Vernikova has defined the Odesa text in Russian literature in terms of what Yurii Lotman calls a cultural semiosphere, which (like other urban metatexts) establishes a literary tradition that draws on the entire architectural, artistic, and cultural environment.[18] The Odesa text was identified early on (in a review of a novel by the Odesa Jewish novelist Osip Rabinovich in 1849) as exotic, evoking a bourgeois, mercantile world of business and commerce for readers of *Отечественные записки* (Notes of the fatherland) in the capital St. Petersburg. The relatively tolerant and liberal cosmopolitan spaces of the sunny southern port contrasted with the political repression of the cold northern capital, an alternate source of westernization that was open to the Levant, but its bourgeois genealogy was unacceptable after the Bolshevik reoccupation of Odesa in 1921; later, the Jewish prominence in Odesa's prerevolutionary cosmopolitan culture became ideologically suspect.[19]

Despite his reputation for being the first to portray Odesa's gangsters, Babel was preceded by the Odesa prose writer Semyon Yushkevich and the local journalist Lazar Korenman ("Karmen"), both less known now than in their own day, when they were household names. They were writing about Odesa's tricksters and criminals well before Babel made Benia Krik king of the gangsters, but their portrayals are, by contrast, strikingly dark and naturalistic. Yushkevich's novel *Leon Drei* (first part, 1911; second part 1913; completed, 1917) describes an Odesa conman and swindler, a dandy who easily seduces women. Drei has none of the colorful costume and flair of Benia Krik, although he likes expensive clothes and hankers after star-spangled suspenders. He narcissistically basks in the glory of his power and self-confidently swaggers along the street. He lingers in bed enjoying the bliss of his material comforts, confident that his engagement

---

17 See Walter Koschmal, "Ein russischer Traum von Europa? Petersburg, Odessa und andere, " *Nordost-Archiv: Zeitschrift für Regionalgeschichte* 12 (2003): 43–69; Stanton, *Isaac Babel and the Self-Invention of Odessan Modernism*. On the Petersburg text, see Yurii Lotman, *Izbrannye stat'i* (Tallinn: Aleksandra, 1992); Vladimir Toporov, *Mif, ritual, simvol, obraz: issledovaniia v oblasti poeticheskogo* (Moscow: Progress, 1995). On the shaping of Petersburg's image, see Julie Buckler, *Mapping St. Petersburg: Imperial Text and Cityshape* (Princeton: Princeton University Press, 2005); Kathleen Scollins, *Acts of Logos in Pushkin and Gogol: Petersburg Texts and Subtexts* (Boston: Academic Studies Press, 2017).
18 Bella Vernikova, "Odesskii tekst," *Iz pervykh ust: odesskii tekst, istoriko-literaturnye aspekty i sovremennost'* (Moscow: Volodei, 2015), 171–206.
19 Ibid., 172–74.

to Berta Spielman, the daughter of a wealthy Odesa storekeeper, will ensure him a tidy sum in the bank. He then moves on to exploit other women, before he is caught seducing the daughter of his Russian patron, the wealthy lawyer Melnikov. Yushkevich drily observes the shallow superficiality of Odesa's Jewish bourgeoisie, the amoral, manipulative methods Jews employ to enrich themselves, and the hedonistic atmosphere of nightclubs, where chanteuses expose themselves to drunken sailors.

For his part, "Karmen" drew grim portrayals of the endless misery of Odesa's down-and-outs among the unemployed port laborers in Дикари (The savages, 1901) and На дне Одессы (At the bottom of Odesa, 1904), or the grinding poverty of a young woman who carries bricks all day in Кусок сна (A snatch of sleep, 1908). His sketches about Odessa's poor and its underworld in the local newspapers in the first years of the twentieth century give little hint of Odesa's smart shopping streets, arcades, the Palais Royal, or the Opera House. Babel, on the contrary, was reinventing a mythical past that did not exist in Yushkevich's and Karmen's brutal realism.[20]

Like Yushkevich or Vladimir Jabotinsky before him, Babel could blend into Russian literature well before the revolutions of 1917 demolished ethnic and class barriers. Babel made his debut in a liberal newspaper in 1913 in Kiev (Kyiv), where he was studying at a business college, with a contribution to the "Jewish Question," a story called "Старый Шлойме" (Old Shloime), about a Jewish family facing the choice between expulsion and apostasy.[21] The context is the antisemitic campaign leading up to the Beilis trial, which opened in September 1913, and the background is the residence restrictions on Jews in villages. Later Babel enrolled at a liberal arts college known for its revolutionary activity, the Psycho-Neurological Institute in Petrograd (as St. Petersburg was renamed during World War I), where he obtained a residence permit in October 1916 (contrary to what he later wrote in his 1924 "Autobiography").

Among the sketches and some risqué stories that Babel published in Petrograd magazines and journals before the collapse of tsarism is a call for a literary messiah from Odesa, a Russian Maupassant.[22] In "Odessa" (1916), Babel prophesied that this multiethnic port on the Black Sea could release Petersburg's icy grip on Russian literature in order to breathe life into a stifling prose full of turgid

---

20 Mirja Lecke and Efraim Sicher, "Odessa in Russian, Ukrainian, Hebrew, and Yiddish Literature," in *The Palgrave Encyclopedia of Urban Literary Studies*, ed. Jeremy Tambling (Cham: Palgrave, 2022), 1447–55.
21 "Staryi Shloime," *Ogni*, February 9, 1913, 3–4.
22 Isaak Babel, "Odessa," *Zhurnal zhurnalov* 51 (1916): 4–5.

stories of boring provincial towns in the north. In reversing north-south relations of center and periphery, Babel challenges the hegemony of the Russian literary elite and casts his poetic identity in the mold of Maupassant, his muse and acknowledged literary master, a Western model of literary realism:

> ... думается мне, что должно прийти, и скоро, плодотворное, животворящее влияние русского юга, русской Одессы, может быть (qui sait?), единственного в России города, где может родиться так нужный нам, наш национальный Мопассан.[23]

> (... it seems to me that there must come, and soon, the fruitful, life-giving influence of the Russian south, Russian Odessa, possibly—who knows?—the single city in Russia where our much-needed national Maupassant can be born).

In "Russian Odessa," Babel avers facetiously, the right conditions exist for the emergence of Russia's Maupassant—a complacent bourgeoisie, poor Jewish masses, and an antisemitic municipality, as well as a port that brings in a lot of foreigners. The sense of lightness in "Russian Odessa," Babel explains, may be partly due to the Jewish ethnic component of the city, where half the population is Jewish and where there is an ease and clarity about life, where the *luftmentshen* (literally, the people of air, the Jewish brokers who seemingly made their living out of nothing) tell racy stories about their adventures. But Babel is really talking about what Maupassant knows, what he knows (in his story "L'Aveu" [The confession], 1884) about the coachman Polyte, who is making love to the peasant girl Céleste in return for the fare. Babel is not interested, as Maupassant is, in the avarice of the Normandy peasants or the calculating response of Céleste's mother to her daughter's confession but in the life-affirming joy of the sun, which correlates with Babel's vision of Odesa cosmopolitanism. That vision idiosyncratically stresses the contribution of lower-class Jews to a hedonistic sense of joie de vivre, which Babel identifies with Maupassant's intimate knowledge of what life is really about.

Rebecca Stanton believes Babel is advancing himself as a candidate for Russia's Maupassant, its literary messiah, who claims the legitimacy of a provincial voice (and a Jewish one at that) in Russia's capital.[24] Moreover, this claim resists

---

23 Isaac Babel, "Odessa," in *Собрание сочинений*, 1:44. All translations are mine, except where otherwise indicated.
24 Stanton, *Isaac Babel and the Self-Invention of Odessan Modernism*, 31–32.

contemporary trends in literary realism, chief among them the prose fiction of Gorky and, among his protégés, Yushkevich.[25] Babel declares that Odesa's sun outshines Gorky, who figures here only as a precursor of singers of the sun. It outshines the class struggle in the smoky factories, where, Babel says, Karl Marx is going about his mundane business. Babel nevertheless refashioned his autobiography in 1924 to declare his sole debt to Gorky as his literary patron, who had sent him "into the people," and remained close to him until his death in 1936.

Babel was, however, not the first to claim Odesa's potential for reviving Russian literature by injecting southern sun into the dreary provincialism of the north. In his sketch "Odessa" (1911), the well-known journalist and critic Petr Pilskii drew attention to Odessa's literary potential (he mentions Fyodorov and Yushkevich), although he admitted (alluding to Lev Tolstoy) that it was hardly a second Yasnaia Poliana.[26] Odesa, he explained, was a city of drunken sailors straight out of Kuprin's "Gambrinus," leisurely idlers, and romantic adventurers; like Babel, he mentions the eccentric pioneer aviator Sergei Utochkin but, in contrast to Babel, ignores Odesa's Jews and the opera star Isa Kremer. We know little of Pilskii's biography, apart from his birth in 1879 in Oryol, the son of an army officer and a noblewoman, a spell in a tsarist jail for revolutionary activity, and his arrest by the Bolsheviks for expressing oppositional views in a newspaper article, after which he passed through Odesa again on his wanderings into exile, finally settling in Riga, where he died in 1941. In the 1910s, Pilskii was active in bringing futurists to prewar Odesa, including Vladimir Mayakovsky, David Burliuk, and Vasilii Kamenskii, who appeared in a cubofuturist happening in January 1914. In May 1914, Pilskii managed the first public appearances of several Odesa poets (including Eduard Bagritsky and Valentin Kataev) and sponsored Odesa's avant-garde poets. When World War I broke out, Pilskii joined the army, but Odesa's avant-garde poets continued to publish in collective volumes (*almanakhi*) or local periodicals and to meet in Café Robina or elsewhere.[27] Pilskii's article "Odessa," in a series entitled "Лика городов," (Visages of cities) appeared in the leading St. Petersburg literary journal *Пробуждение* (Awakening), and it was in the capital city that Pilskii crossed paths with Babel and other young Odessans in 1916, the year Babel published his "Odessa," also

---

25 See Vernikova, "Odesskii tekst," 242–43.
26 Petr Pil'skii, "Odessa," *Probuzhdenie*, June 1, 1911.
27 Valentin Kataev and Kornei Chukovskii remembered Pilskii as talented, but bombastic, temperamental, and manipulative; see Valentin Kataev, *Almaznyi moi venets* (Moscow: Sovetskii pisatel', 1981), 17; Kornei Chukovskii, "Kuprin," *Sobranie sochinenii* (Moscow: Terra, 2001), 5:93.

in a St. Petersburg (Petrograd) journal.[28] Like Pilskii five years before him, Babel wished to market the exoticism of Odesa in Russia's capital, playing the provincial low against the established high culture, the south against the north, but advocating ethnic difference as beneficial to the culture of the tsarist empire. Writing in Russian from Petrograd about *Russian* Odesa, Babel claims that its Western influence might revive Russian literature. Both Pilskii and Babel sought recognition for Odesa as a counterpoint to the hegemonic Petersburg text.[29] Pilskii and Babel each dutifully mention the life-affirming joy and lightheartedness of Odesa's inhabitants, who, needless to say, find life easier in Odesa's cosmopolitan atmosphere and relative freedom than in the political repression of the Russian capital.

Nor is Babel saying anything new about Odesa's spoken language (*odesskii iazyk*), which deviated from standard Russian and cultural norms—something between a dialect and a fusion of Russian, Yiddish, and Ukrainian. Russian as spoken in Odesa was notoriously "bad" or "ungrammatical," and, as Babel sarcastically notes in "Odessa," this made it a "very nasty place" ("Одесса очень скверный город"). Babel is playing a familiar tune, echoing the journalist Vlas Doroshevich's 1895 mock lecture on the language of Odesa, which describes Odesans' idiosyncratic use of Russian idiom and their carefree attitude toward the conjugation and declension of standard Russian, or their colorful turns of phrase. Such freedom, Doroshevich declares, is the essence of Odesa humor.[30] The clash of Yiddishisms or Ukrainianisms with normative Russian grammar and syntax in the speech of Babel's Odesa carters brings linguistic interference into play with comic effect.[31] However, this stylization of the speech of Odessa's carters is not characteristic of Babel's Childhood stories.

The "Odesa School"

Looking more closely at the literary material which Odesa offered in Babel's writings about the city, we notice that Odesa's cosmopolitan spaces were not all high culture. In two sketches published in March 1918, "Листки об Одессе" (Notes about Odesa), Babel described the *cafés chantants* which sprang up in

---

28 Pil'skii, *Zatumanivshiisia mir* (Riga: Grāmatu draugs, 1928).
29 On Babel's "Odessa" as a poetic manifesto, see Walter Koschmal, "Kulturbeschreibung aus der Peripherie: Babels Odessa-Poetik," *Wiener Slawistischer Almanach* 49 (1997): 311–36.
30 Vlas Doroshevich, *Odessa, odessity i odessitki* (Odessa: Yu. Sandomirskii, 1895), 48–61.
31 See examples in Efraim Sicher, *Babel in Context*, 97–102; Yohanan Petrovsky-Shtern, "Isaak Vavilonskii: Iazyk i mif 'Odesskikh rasskazov,'" *Yehupets* 13 (2003): 93–95.

the early twentieth century all around Odesa, where drag artists and conmen hung out. The cafés were more popular than the Literaturka, the literary club frequented by the intellectual elite (including Jabotinsky), or the smart cafés that catered to the middle-class bourgeoisie. Even if they did not appreciate Akhmatova and Blok there, Babel declares, this was the real Odesa of the famous singer Isa Kremer, whom Babel singles out in "Odessa" as an example of the joy (*radost'*) of Odesans, an example of life-affirming cosmopolitanism discussed in the previous chapter. Odesa, Babel writes, is a city of eccentrics and children of *luftmentshen*, who provide an inexhaustible source of interesting stories.[32] These two sketches were published in Petrograd just as Odesa fell to Austrian forces on March 13, 1918, after which Ukrainian nationalists, Petliurists, Whites, French Entente forces, and Bolsheviks fought for control of the city. Not knowing what was to befall his native city, Babel expressed the hope that, when the war ended and the officers and wealthy provincials departed, the cranes would start working again in the port and Odesa would return to its former habitual power to assimilate gesticulating Polish Jewish newcomers. The Greek coffee houses did not reopen, however, and "Rule Britannia" did not play again. By 1920, Isa Kremer and the *luftmentshen* had gone—indeed, there was no place for the *luftmentsh* in Soviet Russia. In that sense, *Еврейское счастье* (Jewish luck, 1925), a silent movie loosely based on Sholem Aleichem's Menakhem Mendel stories, for which Babel wrote the subtitles, was an obituary for both the shtetl and for the *luftmentsh*, for the Jewish traditions of Berdichev, as well as for cosmopolitan Odesa, where Menakhem Mendel sought his fortune. Nevertheless, the leading Yiddish actor Solomon Mikhoels, who starred in the film, turned the *luftmentsh* into a dreamer and a Charlie Chaplin figure (armed with umbrella instead of walking-stick), epitomizing the *kleiner mentsh* (little man) of Yiddish literature.

Little is known of Babel's participation in Odessa's cultural life in the early 1920s, when he published his first *Odessa Stories* and other stories in Odessa periodicals *Moriak*, *Izvestiia odesskogo gubispolkoma*, *Siluety*, and *Shkval*. Although he did not write poetry, Babel knew the poets in the "Green Lamp" club (whose name evoked the poets' society to which Pushkin belonged) and its successor, the "Poets' Collective." Shortly after his return from the Caucasus in January 1923, Babel read his *Odessa Stories* in the "Streams of October" writers' club, led by Bagritsky, where Gekht and other young Odessa authors discussed

---

32 Isaak Babel, "Listki ob Odesse," *Vecherniaia zvezda*, March 19 (6), 1918; March 21 (8), 1918. On the Literaturka, see the chapter by Guido Hausmann in this volume; on Isa Kremer, see the chapter by Mirja Lecke.

their work.[33] In 1923, Babel claimed an affinity between Odessa writers (including Bagritsky, Ilf, Lev Slavin, Semyon Gekht, and Valentin Kataev) in a foreword to an unpublished anthology of young Odessa authors, who were, he asserted, united by romantic dreams of exotic shores to relieve the boredom of an office job but in reality got married and settled down:

> Тут всё дело в том, что в Одессе каждый юноша – пока он не женился – хочет быть юнгой на океанском судне. И одна у нас беда – в Одессе мы женимся с необыкновенным упорством.[34]

> (Here the whole matter is that in Odessa every young fellow—until he gets married—wants to be a boatswain's mate on an ocean liner. And our only problem is that in Odesa we get married with extraordinary stubbornness.)

We should see this domesticated romanticism, however, as part of Odessa writers' aspiration to move to Moscow and Leningrad (St. Petersburg), where they hoped to gain fame as Soviet authors, and not least to earn a living. Babel, in fact, wrote letters of recommendation for the Odessa writers Gekht and Bondarin, who hoped to become successful writers in the Soviet capital.[35] Olesha and Kataev had left Odessa in 1921, fleeing hunger and Cheka terror, followed by Bagritsky and Babel himself. In a letter of April 17, 1923, to his school friend Isaak Livshits, who worked for a state publishing house in Moscow, Babel complained that he felt out of place in a provincial backwater.[36] Odessans flourished in the Moscow journals, looking back to their native town with nostalgia at a time when Odessa no longer was a center of literary modernism.

At the time, there seemed to be sufficient young talent to fulfill Babel's prophecy of an Odesan renewal of Russian literature, among them Bagritsky, Olesha, Vera Inber, Lev Slavin, and Valentin Kataev, all of whom emerged before the Bolshevik revolution. They were joined in Moscow by Konstantin Paustovsky

---

33 Alena Yavorskaya, "Semyon Gekht – uchenik Babelia," *Odessa Literary Museum*, accessed December 10, 2022, https://web.archive.org/web/20120626161316/http://museum-literature.odessa.ua/pbasic/lru/tb2/tp3/id165.
34 *Собрание сочинений*, 1:59.
35 Babel's letters of recommendation of Odessa writers to his friends Vladimir Narbut and Mikhail Kol'tsov in Moscow dated April 17, 1923 are published in S. Gekht, *Izbrannoe*, 47; see Alena Yavorskaya, "Rukopisi I. Babelia v fondakh OLM," *Dom kniazia Gagarina: Sbornik statei i publikatsii* 6, no. 2 (2011): 5–18.
36 *Pis'ma drugu: Iz arkhiva I. L. Livshitsa*, ed. Elena Pogerel'skaia (Moscow: Gosudarstvennyi literaturnyi muzei / Tri kvadrata, 2007), 16.

(who spent only a year and a half in Odesa) and Ilia (Yekhiel Lev) Fainzilberg, better known as the Jewish member of the comic duo, Ilf and Petrov. Babel and other Odesa writers became known as the *Odesskaia shkola* (Odesa School), largely as a result of Viktor Shklovsky's programmatic essay of 1933, which he entitled "South-West" (after Bagritsky's 1928 collection of verse).[37] What these romantic fellow travelers have in common, Shklovsky asserted, is their individualism and separatism and their affinity with Westernizers.[38] Shklovsky of course was interested in *siuzhetnost'* (plot-driven literature), not politics, and his recognition of an Odesa school, proposed when literature was coming under Party control and conformism was being enforced in an increasingly monolithic culture, now appears as a shortsighted and idealistic attempt to champion cultural diversity within Soviet literature, precisely when Stalin was dubbing writers the engineers of human souls, and the wraps were about to come off socialist realism. Shklovsky was soon made to recant;[39] yet his article became a touchstone for the retrospective construction after the Thaw of an "Odesa school," a notion that during the Purges was anathema, if not treasonable.[40]

Time forward?

Babel's reinvention of the past does not accord with Marxist views of the class struggle. Whereas Lenin saw time as determined by intervention in the historical dialectic, in the *Odessa Stories* the anarchic time of the gangsters intervenes in the relentless, violent cycle of pogroms and persecutions, apparently challenging the static social order, but its carnivalesque freedom does not bring change or salvation. The triumph of Soviet time, which eliminated the underworld after the civil war, also irrevocably erased the prerevolutionary past, which the *Odessa Stories* present as intrinsically Jewish and uniquely Odesan. If we follow the full cycle of nine stories, we can perceive a distinct change in the conception of time from a timeless, mythical universe to a vanished world brought to an end by revolutionary time. The four canonized stories, by contrast, do not show any significant progression beyond a timeless world, to which the narrator looks back

---

37 Viktor Shklovskii, "Yugo-zapad," *Literaturnaia gazeta*, January 5, 1933, 3.
38 Ibid.
39 Viktor Shklovskii, "Pis'mo v redaktsiiu," *Literaturnaia gazeta*, April 29, 1933.
40 The debate over the "Odessa school" continues, for example, in O. Kudrin's polemical rebuttal on nationalist grounds of claims for an "Odessa" school, "Uroki odesskoi shkoly i grebni odesskoi volny," *Voprosy literatury* 3 (2012): 9–64. See Stanton, *Isaac Babel and the Self-Invention of Odessan Modernism*, 11–15.

as a memory of a vanished way of life in Moldavanka, portrayed as a tight-knit community of tricksters and robbers. "Король" ("The King," 1921) tells how during his sister Dvoira's wedding, Benia turns the tables on the tsarist police, who intended to round up the gangsters. "Как это делалось в Одессе" ("How It Was Done in Odessa," 1923) relates the story of Benia Krik's rise to power as king of the gangsters. The broker Tsudechkis's adventures at the hands of Liubka Shneyveys in "Любка Казак" ("Liubka the Cossack," 1924) shows how a wise old Jewish broker uses his wits to win over the Amazon-like owner of the inn and become its manager. An early Odessa story that Babel did not include in the collected cycle, "Справедливость в скобках" ("Justice in Brackets," 1921), sequentially precedes "Liubka the Cossack." In it Tsudechkis tells his own story of Benia's revenge on him after he tipped off both Benia and his rival Kolia about the same job. The next tale, "Отец" ("The Father," 1924), tells how Benia seeks the hand in marriage of Basia, the daughter of the gangster Froim Grach. All these stories are set in the mythical past of prerevolutionary Odesa.

Time is the agent of cyclical change in Babel's short story "Закат" ("Sunset," written 1923–24, published posthumously 1964), on which Babel based the play of the same name. When Lyovka proposes killing their father Mendel, nicknamed "The Pogrom," Benia Krik replies:

> – Еще не время, – ответил Бенчик, – но время идет. Слушай его шаги и дай ему дорогу. Посторонись, Левка.
>
> И Левка посторонился, чтобы дать времени дорогу. Оно тронулось в путь – время, древний кассир, – и повстречалось в пути с Двойрой, сестрой Короля, с Манассе, кучером, и с русской девушкой Марусей Евтушенко.[41]

> ("It's not yet time," replied Benchik. "But the time will come. Listen out for its footsteps and make way for it. Stand aside, Lyovka."
>
> And Lyovka stood aside to make way for time. It set off, Time, the old cashier, and met on its way the King's sister Dvoira, with Menashe the driver, and with a Russian girl Marusia Evtushenko.)

Lyovka, at Benia's request, stands aside for Time to pass, until Marusia gets pregnant by the old man, who wishes to run off with her and rob his sons of their inheritance. In the story, Arye-Leyb then proceeds to tell of King David's power,

---

41 *Собрание сочинений*, 1:110.

wealth, and many wives. This local oracle seems to be suggesting that Time cannot defeat the force of life, yet, unlike the failed rebellion of King David's sons, Mendel's sons' rebellion succeeds, and they thwart the aging carter's attempt to defy the cyclical progression of generations and history. This becomes clearer in the stage version of *Sunset*, where Benia forces the old carter to accept his sabbatical retirement, declaring, "Я хочу, чтобы суббота была субботой" (I want the Sabbath to be the Sabbath).[42] The messianic time represented by the Jewish Sabbath has arrived, just as sunset inaugurates the Sabbath in the synagogue, and (unlike the Marxist view of dialectic materialism) the cycle has turned full circle. As the structured symbolism of the play makes clear, one generation succeeds another in the spirit of *Kohelet* (Ecclesiastes). Rabbi Zekhariah has the last word, expounding on the Jewish concept of cyclical time and referring (quite blasphemously) both to Joshua, who stopped the sun in the Bible, and to Jesus, who stole the sun. Rabbi Zekhariah warns that each of them thought, as Mendel did, they could stall the natural order:

> День есть день, евреи, и вечер есть вечер. День затопляет нас потом трудов наших, но вечер держит наготове веера своей божественной прохлады. Иисус Навин, остановивший солнце, был только сумасброд. Иисус из Назарета, укравший солнце, был злой безумец. И вот Мендель Крик, прихожанин нашей синагоги, оказался не умнее Иисуса Навина. Всю жизнь хотел он жариться на солнцепеке, всю жизнь хотел он стоять на том месте, где его застал полдень. Но Бог имеет городовых на каждой улице, и Мендель Крик имел сынов в своём доме. Городовые приходят и делают порядок. День есть день, и вечер есть вечер. Всё в порядке, евреи. Выпьем рюмку водки![43]

> (Day is day, Jews, and evening is evening. Day wearies us with the sweat of labor, but evening holds ready its fan of divine coolness. Joshua, who stopped the sun, was just crazy. Jesus of Nazareth, who stole the sun, was a wicked madman. And here

---

42 *Собрание сочинений*, 1:384.
43 "Zakat," *Novyi mir* 2 (1928): 35; the version in *Zakat* (Moscow: Krug, 1928) is slightly different (1: 392). The references are to Joshua 10:1–15 (where the sun stopped for Joshua) and Matthew 27:45 (where noonday went dark during the crucifixion).

> Mendel Krik, a member of our synagogue, turned out not to be wiser than Joshua. All his life he wanted to warm himself in the sun, all his life he wanted to stand where noon caught him. But God has policemen on every street, and Mendel Krik had sons in his home. The policemen come and make order. Day is day, and evening is evening. Everything is in order, Jews. Let's drink a glass of vodka!)

The historical dialectic of revolutionary time, however, swept away both Mendel the Carter and the sons who usurped him. When *Sunset* reached the Moscow stage in February 1928 for a short, unsuccessful run at the Moscow Art Theater (MkhAT), the play clearly was seriously out of step with ideological time. This was no longer the moment for nostalgic looking back to a vanished Jewish past, as Babel seemed to be doing, when the Soviet Union was gearing up for the great leap into the first Five-Year Plan and when fellow travelers were being conscripted to write about socialism under construction.

Backshadowing history

Babel was looking back to what was a politically outdated concept of time and history. Nevertheless, we can see how Babel attempted to negotiate time and history, despite his precarious position as a fellow traveler under increasing ideological attack, in the movie adaptation of the *Odessa Stories*, Беня Крик (Benia Krik, released 1927), on which Babel was working at the same time as *Sunset*. The first part of the film replays the plot of "The King" and "How It Was Done in Odessa." In the second and third parts of the film, however, we move forward to the February Revolution and the civil war. At that time, Benia's gangsters form a regiment and join the Bolsheviks, who kill Benia and Froim Grach as lawless elements after they apparently desert the front.

The film ran into trouble with the censor, as well as the critics, who accused Babel and the director Vladimir Vilner of romanticizing the bandits. Yet, unlike the *Odessa Stories*, on which it is based, the film generally conforms to an ideologically correct line, dividing Odesa between the wealthy magnate Ruvim Tartakovskii, who is indifferent to the poverty and squalor of Moldavanka, and the proletariat, represented by Sobkov, a Gorkyan master baker, who is introduced as the real hero of the film and becomes a commissar after the Bolshevik takeover. The killing of Benia Krik is framed by a scene of hardy Bolsheviks making plans at the end of the film for the future socialist city, where there is no room for bandits.⁴⁴ The socialist future apparently vindicates the destruction of the bourgeois past.

The film is much closer to historical reality than Babel's *Odessa Stories*, which perform a peculiar backshadowing of history, by which I mean the literary device of retrospectively seeing the future historical significance of past events.⁴⁵ At first glance, the fictional Benia Krik barely resembles his prototype Misha Yaponchik, the sobriquet earned by Moshe-Yaakov Vinnitskii because of his "Asiatic" eyes. Vinnitskii grew up on the tough streets of Moldavanka and was arrested on charges of burglary. Yaponchik was convicted and sentenced to twelve years imprisonment in 1908, so that at the time of the action of the first Odessa stories and the play *Sunset* (set in 1913), Vinnitskii was safely behind bars. He was released under the general amnesty granted after the February Revolution in 1917.⁴⁶

Vinnitskii liked to present himself as the enemy of the bourgeoisie and was the terror of Odesa streets during the civil war. At one point, Vinnitskii warded off a pogrom by Denikin's soldiers. During the precarious days of 1918–1919, when Odesa changed hands numerous times, he was useful to the Bolsheviks in procuring arms and munitions, as well as freeing prisoners from the city jail. Like Grigorii Kotovskii, who became a legendary civil war hero, Vinnitskii was one of many former convicts whom the Bolsheviks absorbed into their ranks as combatants.⁴⁷ The former anarchist sympathizer Vinnitskii, remarks historian Oleg Budnitskii, hoped to find common ground with the Bolsheviks in the legitimate robbing of the bourgeoisie, the exploiters of the proletariat.⁴⁸ The "three days of peaceful uprising," requested by the gangsters in "Froim Grach," were, after all, no more than what the Bolsheviks called expropriation of private property.⁴⁹ Vinnitskii's Fifty-Fourth Battalion was formed no later than May 1919, after the Soviets briefly regained control of Odesa, and it won a victory against

---

44 Ernst Wawra, "Verharren im Unentschieden: Babel's 'Helden' in *Benja Krik*," in *Glücksuchende?: Conditio Judaica im sowjetischen Film*, ed. Lilia Antipow; Matthias Dornhuber, and Jörn Petrick (Würzburg: Königshausen & Neumann, 2011), 85–102.
45 I have borrowed the term from Michael André Bernstein, *Foregone Conclusions: Against Apocalyptic History* (Berkeley: University of California Press, 1994).
46 See Oleg V. Budnitskii, "La construction d'Odessa comme 'mère du crime' ou comment Moïse Vinnitski est devenu Benia Krik," in *Kinojudaica: les représentations des juifs dans le cinéma de Russie et d'Union soviétique des années 1910 aux années 1980*, ed. Valérie Pozner and Natacha Laurent (Toulouse: Éditions Nouveau monde, 2012), 415–19.
47 Budnitskii, "La construction d'Odessa," 425–27; Saul Borovoi, *Vospominaniia* (Moscow: Evreiskii universitet v Moskve/Jerusalem: Gesharim, 1993, 1993), 76–77.
48 Budnitskii, "La construction d'Odessa," 434.
49 Собрание сочинений, 1:122.

Petliura's troops. Inexplicably, however, the Fifty-Fourth Battalion abandoned its positions without digging in and headed for Odesa. At Voznesensk, they were stopped at the railway station, and Vinnitskii was arrested. According to differing accounts, he was shot while resisting arrest or was deliberately assassinated.[50] Either way, he was buried in Voznesensk, and the celebrated cantor Pinkhas Minkowsky came from Odesa to officiate at his funeral, accompanied by the famous boys' choir from the Brody synagogue (see figure 2 in chapter 6). This detail may explain an overlooked truth in the *Odessa Stories*, for this is the factual background for the scene in "How It Was Done in Odessa" at the grave of poor Iosif, shot during a raid by Savka Butsis, whom Benia then accompanies to his grave. That scene, too, is faithfully reproduced in the film, except that in reality it was the former king of the gangsters Misha Yaponchik being buried some years later.

In backshadowing to prerevolutionary times the story of Vinnitskii's brief career as king of the gangsters in 1917–1919, Babel changes the context: the story of a Jewish gangster unfolds not during the revolution or civil war, which saw wholesale massacres of Jews in South Russia and Ukraine, but in the era of tsarist oppression and state antisemitism, which, according to communist ideology, were supposed to terminate with the revolution. This adds poignancy to the scene in "How It Was Done in Odessa," when the Jewish gangsters, under the guise of Tartakovskii's pretended funeral procession, machinegun the Slobodka thugs, who have been beating up the Jews,[51] and thus avenge the pogrom victims. To be sure, the Odessa gangsters are not all Jews, but they empower themselves at a time when the Jews had no power. Backshadowing deflects the victimhood of Jews in the pogroms of 1918–20 and projects empowerment to tsarist times, when antisemitism could be blamed on the old regime.

One may well wonder, then, what was Babel's purpose in making the Benia of the stories more of a comic than sinister villain. The gangsters' violence does not bring justice except in terms of a criminal code of honor. Benia's speech from on high at Iosif Muginshteyn's funeral in "How It Was Done in Odessa," a mock sermon on the mount claiming the poor clerk's death as a martyrdom for the working class, is a pastiche that covers up his own guilt for Muginshteyn's murder during the raid on Tartakovskii. Nor does his blackmailing of Tartakovskii into giving the bereaved aunt Pesia a pension make him into a Robin Hood.[52] Certainly, the extortion notes that Benia sends to Eikhbaum and Tartakovskii

---

50 Budnitskii, "La construction d'Odessa," 435–39.
51 *Собрание сочинений*, 1:71.
52 A common interpretation repeated by Tanny, *City of Rogues and Schnorrers*, 98.

follow the formula reported in the local press of the first years of Bolshevik rule.[53] Nevertheless, they are familiar formulas whose conventionality is foregrounded. The raids in "The King" and "How It Was Done in Odessa" are rendered as comic opera; it is thus no wonder that Benia's automobile plays arias! Perhaps we should not take the violence of Benia's henchmen too seriously: after all, they shoot in the air, because, if you don't, you might kill someone.[54] The underworld was a popular theme of Soviet Russian fiction in the twenties because transgressiveness appealed to a popular subculture that favored *blatnaia pesnia* and legends of bandits and rebels. The jazz singer Leonid Utiosov, himself an Odesa Jew, helped to popularize the Odesa underworld songs performed in the cabaret acts of Odesa's *cafés chantants* in 1917–1923, and he was seriously criticized (as was Babel) for romanticizing the bandits.[55] The *Odessa Stories* fed a longing for a lost anarchic freedom, for a libertarian excess, and a general romantic nostalgia for an abundance that could only be dreamed of in Soviet Russia.

The false memories of luxury and romantic adventure in the early Odessa stories may have been comforting for the first readers of these stories, published a mere year or so after a prolonged period of siege and civil war, during a famine that was alleviated only by sporadic shipments of foreign aid. Smuggling across the Romanian border was rife, but the fabulous goods washed up on the shores of Odesa described in "Liubka the Cossack" were surely pure wish-fulfillment:

> Всё благороднейшее из нашей контрабанды, всё, чем славна земля из края в край, делало в ту звёздную, в ту синюю ночь своё разрушительное, своё обольстительное дело.... Чёрный кок с «Плутарха», прибывшего третьего дня из Порт-Саида, вынес за таможенную черту пузатые бутылки ямайского рома, маслянистую мадеру, сигары с плантаций Пирпонта Моргана и апельсины из окрестностей Иерусалима. Вот что выносит на берег пенистый прибой одесского моря, вот что достаётся иногда одесским нищим на еврейских свадьбах.[56]

---

53 Boris Briker, "The Underworld of Benia Krik and I. Babel's Odessa Stories," *Canadian Slavonic Papers* 36, nos. 1–2 (1994): 118–22.
54 *Собрание сочинений*, 1: 63.
55 On Utiosov's songs about Odessa in the context of Stalinist cultural policy, see Matthias Stadelmann, "Von jüdischen Ganoven zu sowjetischen Helden: Odessas Wandlungen in den Liedern Leonid Utesovs," *Jahrbuch des Simon-Dubnow-Instituts* 2 (2003): 333–58; Sophie Pinkham, "Making Deals in the Paradise of Thieves: Leonid Utesov, Arkadii Severnyi, and 'Blatnaia Pesnia,'" *Ulbandus Review* 16 (2014): 177–97; Tanny, *City of Rogues and Schnorrers*, 135. See also Anat Rubinstein's chapter in this volume.
56 *Собрание сочинений*, 1:64–65.

> (The finest of our contraband, all that is famed from one end of the world to the other, exerted its destructive, luring power on that dark blue night.... The Black cook from *The Plutarch*, which had sailed into town the day before yesterday from Port Said, sneaked past customs obese bottles of Jamaica rum, oily Madeira, cigars from the plantations of Pierpont Morgan, and oranges from the outskirts of Jerusalem. This is what washes up on the foamy shore of Odessa's sea coast, this is what Odessa beggars sometimes get at Jewish weddings.)

This vision of prewar plenty must have whetted palates in famine-struck Odessa in the aftermath of the civil war and Entente blockade. For readers of the Moscow magazines (Mayakovsky's *Lef* and Voronsky's *Krasnaia nov'*), where the *Odessa Stories* were republished in 1923–24, they were exotic visions of a far-off land and a distant time.[57]

Babel's evocation of an imagined past paints a highly mythicized picture of the courtyards and streets of Odesa where life is lived to its full. In its larger-than-life colorful sensuality, these are sites of public spectatorship, as when the crowds pour into the courtyard to watch Mendel Krik being beaten up by his sons in the story "Sunset."[58] In the scene of Dvoira's wedding in "The King," the tables stretch all the way into Hospital Street—a self-contained little topography where all is hyperbolic and oversized, where sweat flows like blood and human flesh smells sweetly. The eighty-year-old Reizl is described here as traditional as a Torah scroll, and in "Liubka the Cossack," Tsudechkis is as short as the local rabbi, "our Ben-Zekhariah." The Moldavanka is "our generous mother," and it is on "our street" that Golubchik earns money matchmaking in "The Father." It is unlikely, however, that on the Sabbath, Moldavanka's day of rest, Volhynian Hasidim would be drinking wine in Liubka's inn, listening to the boastful Mendel Krik the carter with rapt attention; besides, this is a whorehouse! This is a fictional world from which traditional Judaism and the shtetl world is distanced by crime and poverty. Moldavanka's swarming paupers and ragged urchins, depicted in the film *Benia Krik* and glimpsed briefly in the childhood story "Пробуждение" ("Awakening," 1931), have been displaced by the marginal and the transgressive. Only in myth can this world be seen nostalgically because it represents an absent past that contrasts with the Soviet present.

---

57 See, for example, Konstantin Paustovskii, *Vremia bol'shikh ozhidanii* (Moscow: Sovetskii pisatel',1960), 126–27; Lev Slavin, *Ardenskie strasti* (Moscow: Sovetskii pisatel', 1960), 316.
58 *Собрание сочинений*, 1:113–14. See Petrovsky-Shtern, "Isaak Vavilonskii," 88–90.

The aesthetic distancing in the stories from a historical past correlated with an evident change in modes of narration. Babel's intention to link the Odessa stories to a narrator who is intimate with the gangsters' life can be seen in "Justice in Brackets," where Tsudechkis narrates his own misfortunes at the hands of Benia. Always the hoaxer, or *mistifikator*, Babel tested this story on an unsuspecting Paustovsky, who relates it as an incident that actually happened in a Moldavanka apartment Babel was supposedly renting (Paustovsky gives the victim's name as Tsiris, which is Yiddish for "trouble," a sure indication Babel was making this story up).[59] Using the broker Tsudechkis to connect the stories, however, would clearly not have given Babel the narratorial distance of "How It Was Done in Odessa," which he achieved by juxtaposing, through the *shamas* (synagogue beadle) Arye-Leyb, the stammering, ineffective intellectual in spectacles with the men of action, who resemble the Cossacks in the *Red Cavalry* stories with their colorful clothes, verbal exuberance, and earthy sexuality.

The intellectual in specs serves as a medium for an outsider's view, but he is also an emasculated diaspora Jew who cannot grasp the meaning of Benia's rise to be king of the gangsters—the new *Muskeljude* (Muscle Jew), who appears empowered *before* the revolution. Where there is a tsar, there cannot be a king, or so the police chief in "The King" thinks before his police station is burned down just as he was planning a raid on the gangsters. In "How It Was Done in Odessa," Tartakovskii wonders where the police end and where Benia begins; sensible people tell him Benia begins where the police end.[60] As in *Red Cavalry*, however, the figure of the intellectual in specs measures an ironic moral distance from the violence that challenges the social hierarchy.

Benia's comic adventures are best understood as the carnival laughter in Bakhtin's reading of Rabelais, the folkloric and parodic laughter of popular spectacle that resists the power of ecclesiastical and temporal authority, upending the social hierarchy and suspending historical time.[61] Just as Yushkevich's Leon Drei is a swindler who makes money by mimicking bourgeois society's ways, Benia Krik is the trickster who becomes a legendary hero by outwitting both the police and wealthy Jews. As in the transgressive time of the rogues and fools in the realist novel, which, in Bakhtin's scheme, transformed the chronotope of the adventure plot, the moral hypocrisy of society is exposed and undermined

---

59 Paustovskii, *Vremia bol'shikh ozhidanii*, 132–38.
60 Собрание сочинений, 1:75.
61 See Mikhail Bakhtin, *Tvorchestvo Fransua Rabele i narodnaia kul'tura srednevekov'ia i Renessansa* (Moscow: Khudozhestvennaia literatura, 1990), 5–23; *Rabelais and his World* (Cambridge, MA: MIT Press, 1968), 4–10.

through parody.[62] This transgressive chronotope subverts all autocratic forms of power but, in the end, it is defeated by communism, which tolerates no sentimentality for Odessa's past.

The sunset of Jewish Odesa

Such subversive laughter was more difficult to maintain under Stalin. In the later *Odessa Stories*, time feels elegiac, marking an end, rather than celebrating a lost way of life. The early days of Soviet rule in Odessa look somber in later *Odessa Stories* such as "Конец богадельни" ("The End of the Old Folk's Home," 1932). During the famine following the civil war, Arye Leyb and the other inmates of the Old Folk's Home profiteer from reuse of the same coffin in the neighboring Second Jewish Cemetery. Their revival of an ancient Jewish custom of burial solely in a shroud literally keeps them alive during a general shortage of timber for fresh coffins. But Soviet time comes in the person of Broidin, who insists on the coffin remaining in the ground at the burial of revolutionary hero Hersh Lugovoi.

The clash with Soviet time is an unequal struggle. The thirty emaciated, hungry inmates of the Old Folk's Home despair at this calamity and, when the nurse Judith Shmaiser attempts to inoculate them, they march on the cemetery to challenge its new manager Broidin. The communist Broidin marshals the political solidarity with the starving workers in Petrograd and demands to know whether Soviet power has been established or he is still working in the sweatshop on the corner of Deribaskovskaia Street. There is no room in Soviet Russia for old men and women who have outlived their time. Arye Leyb interrupts Broidin, saying that they have no time, no time to wait before they die of hunger. Despite a short-lived victory, the old folk are evicted, and the gates close after them with a finality that signals the end of old Jewish Odesa. The landscape of epidemic, death, choked paths, and stony roads contrasts with the elaborate marble monuments of Odesa's wealthy Jewish merchants and brokers, whose names resound with the history of Odesa's boom. We cannot miss the ironic note in the nostalgia for what has disappeared now that the Soviet regime has put an end to capitalist exploitation and established a new socialist order.

Another story in the *Odessa Stories* cycle, "Фроим Грач" ("Froim Grach"), composed in the late 1920s and published posthumously in 1963, is set in 1919,

---

62 See Bakhtin, *Epos i roman*, ed. S. G. Bocharov (St. Petersburg: Azbuka, 2000), 92–95.

during a brief Bolshevik rule in Odessa; it is one of five stories Babel sent back to Russia with Gorky from his temporary residence in France and Italy in 1932 in the vain hope they would restore him to favor in the Soviet Union. "Froim Grach" relates the Bolsheviks' elimination of the last gangsters, chief among them the legendary one-eyed Froim Grach, who is executed in cold blood. When the Bolsheviks refuse the bandits' demands, the gangsters raid offices and banks, and a month later the arrests begin. Someone denounces Aron Peskin as the informer and he is invited to a one-way ride, just like the informer Marants in the film *Benia Krik*. The accomplices are caught, but somehow the assailant Misha Yablochko gets away. This is when one-eyed Froim Grach walks into the headquarters of the Soviet secret police, the Cheka, and demands to see the boss, thinking he can buy him out and stop the wave of arrests. The local Cheka investigator Borovoi tells the commander Vladislav Simyon that Grach is an Odesa legend, "тут вся Одесса пройдет перед вами" (here all of Odesa passes before you).[63] But while Borovoi is explaining to the Chekists who have arrived from Moscow that Grach, not Benia Krik, is the real leader of Odessa's forty thousand thieves, Grach is executed in the backyard. A Cheka agent sent down from Moscow, Simyon cannot understand what this means to an Odessan; for him it is simply a matter of eliminating elements that have no use in a socialist society. Borovoi has to agree with that ideological perspective, but as an Odesan he knows what has been lost in the name of the socialist future:

> Он сделал усилие и прогнал от себя воспоминания. Потом, оживившись, он снова начал рассказывать чекистам, приехавшим из Москвы, о жизни Фройма Грача, об изворотливости его, неуловимости, о презрении к ближнему, все эти удивительные истории, отошедшие в прошлое . . .[64]

> (He made an effort to drive away the memories. Later, becoming more animated, he again told the Chekists from Moscow about the life of Froim Grach, about his slippery cunning and elusiveness, about his contempt for those nearest to him, all those incredible stories which receded into the past . . .)

---

63 Babel, *Собрание сочинений*, 1:126.
64 Ibid., 1:128.

Here, as in "The End of the Old Folks' Home," the chronotope of roguery and chicanery has been ruthlessly terminated, but its memory (or rather the myth of criminal Odessa) lives on in the *Odessa Tales*.

The final story in *Odessa Stories*, "Карл-Янкель" (Karl-Yankel, 1931), tells of a show trial of an Odesa *mohel* (circumciser), Naftuli, which ends with an ambivalent hope that the baby will bring together in his hyphenated name the Jewish and Marxist patriarchs. The hyphenated name, which would sound absurd to a Russian reader and ironical to a Yiddish speaker, represents an impossible fusion of ideologies and traditions in the generation after the revolution in which Jews placed their hopes in communist "internationalism." The Soviet future (the boy will be an aviator) and the friendship of the Soviet peoples (the baby suckles from a Kirghiz wet-nurse) are little more than slogans, and the story ends with the narrator's ambiguous hope that Karl-Yankel will have a better childhood than the narrator did. We thus proceed from a timeless world that lives within the cycle of the Jewish calendar and Jewish traditions in the canonical early *Odessa Stories* to the historical end of Odesa's Jewish time in the later stories. Yet there is a conspicuous absence in this story of any unambiguous inauguration of a new era, and the child's hyphenated identity is anachronistic at the time of publication. In these later stories, the Odesa past is repressed by Soviet ideology, but it resists any compromise with the new regime (in his show trial, Naftuli unmasks the lawyer Orlov under his former name Zusman, who is himself a circumcised Jew, for instance). After the revolution, the Odesa past cannot exist except as an object of nostalgia, and the later *Odessa Stories* lament a lost Jewish world whose terminal space is the cemetery.[65]

One example of how the past was mythicized and appropriated for changing political purposes is the memorable scene of the Odesa steps in Eisenstein's *Battleship Potemkin* (1925), staged as a fictionalized representation of the Potemkin mutiny.[66] It was echoed in Jean Lods' documentary film *Odessa* (1935), scripted by Babel, where Eisenstein's terrifying scene of the runaway baby carriage (the anarchic time I mentioned) is emphatically countered with a strong

---

[65] See the comparison of "The End of the Old Folk's Home" with "Cemetery in Kozin" in Maria Langleben, "Arkhetip kladbishcha v rasskazakh Babelia: 'Klabishche v Kozine' i 'Konets bogadel'ni,'" in *Tynianovskii sbornik II: Deviatye Tynianovskie chteniia*, ed. M. O. Chudakova, E. A. Toddes, and Yu. G. Tsiv'ian (Moscow: OGI, 2002.), 411–37.

[66] For a comparison of this episode with historical evidence, see Caroline Humphrey, "Violence and Urban Architecture: Events at the Ensemble of the Odessa Steps in 1904–1905," in *Locating Urban Conflicts: Ethnicity, Nationalism and the Everyday*, ed. Wendy Pullan and Britt Baillie (London: Palgrave Macmillan, 2015), 37–56. See also Rebecca J. Stanton, "A Monstrous Staircase," in *Rites of Place: Public Commemoration in Russia and Eastern Europe*, ed. Julie Buckler and Emily Johnson (Evanston: Northwestern University Press, 2013), 59–80.

image of the Soviet sailors in white uniforms, singing in unison as they march down the steps in resolute solidarity (revolutionary time). The Europeanness of Odesa stands out in this Komsomol propaganda film, which nevertheless closes with the no less iconic image of the Russian national poet laureate, Pushkin, as does Babel's 1937 story "Di Grasso," as we shall see. But this was when Babel was under pressure to write politically suitable material and was finding it difficult to get published.

Babel in Petersburg/Pushkin in Odesa

Babel's 1916 manifesto "Odessa" points southward, to the Hagia of St. Sophia in Kiev, which rivaled its namesake in Constantinople (Istanbul) in the direction of the historical Russian imperialist expansion to the Black Sea and the Levant. The conscription of a politically correct Russian nationalism to Babel's promotion of Russian Odesa, however, requires serious qualification. Not only was Babel imprecise in "Odessa" in his tendentious assessment of a move in Gogol from the bright sun of the Ukraine to the morbid darkness of St. Petersburg (as has been pointed out),[67] but also, beginning with his earliest works, Babel himself, like his beloved Maupassant, was attracted to the grotesque and extraordinary moments of everyday life—an abortion in a Petrograd bathroom ("Mama, Rimma, i Alla," 1916), voyeurism (an untitled early version of "Through the Fanlight," published in 1917), or a nurse who exposes herself to a dying soldier ("Doudou," 1917), not to mention the horrific scenes of the *Red Cavalry* stories. In "Guy de Maupassant" (written 1920–22; published 1932), the narrator muses on the consequences of an amoral hedonism in the morbid fate of Maupassant himself in a lunatic asylum. In the end, he awakens from his intoxicated infatuation with Mrs. Benderskaia to the cold, gray Petersburg morning, to the ugly face of a washerwoman, and to the general atmosphere of debauchery and corruption (there is an indirect allusion to Rasputin's murder that occurred nearby).

It seems at times that the Petersburg text darkens Babel's Odesa sun. In Babel's sketch "О лошадях" ("About Horses"),[68] from the series "Petrograd Diary" in Gorky's anti-Bolshevik newspaper *Новая жизнь* (New life), and in "Guy de Maupassant," we feel the chill of the cold sun of dying Petropolis, immortalized in Mandelstam's poetry published at this time. These were the

---

67 E. Lieber, "'Where Is the Sweet Revolution?': A Reconsideration of Gogol and Babel," *Slavic and East European Journal* 53, no. 1 (Spring 2009): 1–18.
68 Isaak Babel, "O loshadiakh," *Novaia zhizn'*, March 16 [3], 1918, 2.

apocalyptic signs of the decaying Russian capital, a motif which goes back to the foundation myth of the Petersburg text long before the city experienced the end of eschatological time in the Russian Civil War.[69] Significantly, Mandelstam's "На страшной высоте блуждающий огонь" (On a terrifying height a wandering light . . .) appeared in *Вечерная звезда* (Evening star) on March 6, 1918, just a couple of weeks before Babel's two Odesa sketches appeared in the same newspaper. On March 12, the Bolsheviks transferred the Russian capital to Moscow as the ring around Petrograd (Petersburg) tightened; those who did not flee in time suffered famine and devastation. This is the context of Babel's Petersburg story "Ходя" ("The Chinaman," 1923) and his later play *Мария* (*Maria*, repressed while in rehearsal in 1935), about the daughters of an aristocratic family who become involved with black market speculators in Petrograd in 1918. *Maria* ends on an optimistic note, as the worker's wife Elena, about to move into General Mukovnin's old apartment and about to give birth, ponders the future, filled with both hope and uncertainty, in the revolutionary city.

Gregory Freidin makes a strong case for seeing in Babel's postrevolutionary career and his personal life a turn away from the inspiration of Odesa towards the grim realities of revolutionary Petrograd and the horrors of the civil war, culminating in an apparent accommodation to Soviet reality in the play *Maria*.[70] I do not concur that this indicates Babel was selling out the aesthetics of "Odessa." The transition from the comic hyperbole of the *Odessa Stories* to the stark realism of the collectivization and later Childhood stories entailed a concomitant reassessment of cultural identity, shared with many other assimilated Russian Jews, who looked to Pushkin as the icon of Russian culture. Pushkin, Yuri Slezkine reminds us, was emblematic for Russian Jews as the entry ticket for cultural assimilation. The test that the boy undergoes in "История моей голубятни" ("Story of My Dovecote," 1925), when he hysterically declaims Pushkin in order to enter the *gimnaziia*, was a typical *rite de passage* that becomes a paradigmatic case in Slezkine's presentation of Russian Jewish identity in the twentieth century.[71]

The Pushkinian line in the Russian tradition adheres to a western orientation, as did the Odesa writers. Babel could locate himself comfortably within the paradigm of assimilated Russian-speaking Jews for whom cosmopolitanism,

---

69 Valerii Tiupa, "Mytho-Tectonics of the Petersburgian Hypertext of Russian Literature," *Russian Literature* 62 (2007): 99–112.
70 Gregory Freidin, "Two Babels—Two Aphrodites: Autobiography in *Maria* and Babel's Petersburg Myth," in *The Enigma of Isaac Babel: Biography, History, Context*, ed. Gregory Freidin (Stanford: Stanford University Press, 2009), 16–56.
71 Yuri Slezkine, *The Jewish Century* (Princeton: Princeton University Press, 2004), 131–36.

understood as the aspiration of many Russian Jews to belong to a multiethnic society), was receding as a viable option of cultural identity when Soviet "internationalism" was beginning to look more like adoption of Russian national identity. The national laureate Pushkin, by the 1930s canonized as the founding father of the Russian literary language, embodied humanistic values and realism, but he became increasingly a vehicle of Soviet Russian chauvinism under Stalin.

Pushkin enthused about the multiethnic diversity of Odessa in lines intended for book 7–8 of Евгений Онегин (*Eugene Onegin*, 1823–30), although he excluded the Jews, already a visible presence in Odesa, from his list of exotic foreigners. For Pushkin, the city breathed Europe, although (like Petersburg in "The Bronze Horseman") it was periodically flooded, and the dust turned to mud. In the fragments from *Eugene Onegin*, Pushkin conveniently cemented Odesa into his vision of European Russia as a city of art and music, Ausonia (the classic Greek name often applied as a poetic term for Italy).[72] Stanton suggests that Babel, like Olesha and Kataev, was appropriating the Russian literary tradition identified with Pushkin, whom Odesans associated with their city because he wrote *Eugene Onegin* there (although the lines devoted to Odesa were written elsewhere).[73] Pushkin is ubiquitous in the Russian version of the Odesa myth and in the poetry that was published in prerevolutionary Odesa, as young poets melded modernism with a Russian literary tradition in which they strove for acceptance.

In "Di Grasso," which belongs to Babel's Childhood series, the Italian tragedian's passionate performance provides the opportunity for the young boy to discover the meaning of true art. Maupassant gives way to the clarity of Pushkin's prose style. The immediate context of the publication of "Di Grasso" in the satirical magazine *Ogonyok* (The little lamp) in 1937 was the centenary of Pushkin's death, which the Party manipulated to distract from the Terror, when intellectuals and ordinary citizens alike were being arrested. Writers (including Babel) were called to account in the "anti-Formalist" campaign against Western modernism, particularly Proust and Joyce. The "anti-Formalist" campaign to weed out any remaining vestiges of non-conformism began with a public attack on the composer Dmitri Shostakovich in *Pravda* in early 1936, followed by criticism

---

72 Alexander Pushkin, *Eugene Onegin A Novel in Verse*, trans. Vladimir Nabokov, 2nd ed. (Princeton: Princeton University Press, 1990), 334. See Anna Makolkin, "City-Icon in a Poetic Geography: Pushkin's Odessa," in *Writing the City: Eden, Babylon and the New Jerusalem*, ed. Peter Preston and Paul Simpson-Housley (London: Routledge, 1994), 95–108.
73 Stanton, *Isaac Babel and the Self-Invention of Odessan Modernism*, 27, 38–41.

of Eisenstein and the theater director Vsevolod Meyerhold.[74] In the wake of the new Soviet constitution, Stalin wished to consolidate his grip on a society unified around a single "All-Union" cultural identity. Although Mayakovsky (who committed suicide in 1930) had thrown Pushkin overboard from the Futurist ship of poetry, the communist leadership found in Pushkin a convenient figure for mobilizing support.[75] Time was no longer to be seen as the historical disjuncture of the revolution or the Futurists' messianic looking to the future; instead, the Pushkin jubilee signaled a conservatism grounded in the present. Paradoxically, time was both monumental and eschatological. The carefully stage-managed and strictly supervised celebration of Pushkin as the immortal fighter for freedom (although he was peripheral to the Decembrist revolt and was reconciled with the tsar) made the Russian national bard contemporary with socialist heroes and the common citizen.[76]

Babel, in my opinion, pays more than mere lip service to the figure of Pushkin in the epiphany of "Di Grasso," underscoring an aesthetic point at a time he looked to both Pushkin and Tolstoy for a clearer prose style.[77] Clarity of vision is likewise the watchword in Babel's manifesto "Odessa." "Di Grasso" also makes a statement about cultural identity just as, at the close of "Karl-Yankel," the narrator looks out the window at Pushkin Street, diverging from the Russian Jewish symbiosis on Malo-Arnautskaia Street, where the Hebrew poet Haim Nahman Bialik used to live.[78] "Di Grasso" locates the city in a Russian, not Jewish, cultural space, and, like many evocations of Odesa in the Soviet period, it negotiates between a repressed or nostalgic memory and political dictates. The story ends,

---

74 See Solomon Volkov, *Shostakovich and Stalin: The Extraordinary Relationship between the Great Composer and the Brutal Dictator*, trans. Antonina W. Bouis (New York: Knopf, 2004), 99–117; see also the intelligence reports and official directives in Katerina Clark and Evgeny Dobrenko, eds., *Soviet Culture and Power: A History in Documents, 1917–1953* (New Haven: Yale University Press, 2007), 229–48.
75 Nicholas S. Timasheff, *The Great Retreat: The Growth and Decline of Communist Russia* (New York: Dutton, 1946), 176–77; Stephanie Sandler, *Commemorating Pushkin: Russia's Myth of a National Poet* (Stanford: Stanford University Press, 2004), 107–19; Karen Petrone, *Life Has Become More Joyous, Comrades: Celebrations in the Time of Stalin* (Bloomington: Indiana University Press, 2000), 113–47; Volkov, *Shostakovich and Stalin*, 20–22. Jonathan B. Platt has challenged the view that the Pushkin centenary was meant to cover up the Purges ("Pushkin Now and Then: Images of Temporal Paradox in the 1937 Pushkin Jubilee," *Russian Review* 67, no. 4 [October 2008]: 638–60).
76 Jonathan B. Platt. *Greetings, Pushkin! Stalinist Cultural Politics and the Russian National Bard* (Pittsburgh: University of Pittsburgh Press, 2016), 144–55; Evgeny Dobrenko, "Pushkin in Soviet and Post-Soviet Culture," in *The Cambridge Companion to Pushkin*, ed. Andrew Kahn (Cambridge: Cambridge University Press, 2006), 206–12.
77 See Babel's comments in 1937 on Tolstoy in Собрание сочинений, 3:398.
78 Sicher, *Babel in Context*, 127. I am grateful to Hamutal Bar-Yosef for pointing out the allusion.

significantly, not with an evocation of a lost cosmopolitan past of Western culture, typified by the Sicilian tragedian Giovanni Grasso's Russian tour in winter 1908–09,[79] nor with fond memories of Odesa's unforgettable Jewish characters, but it closes with an artistic inspiration which the narrator identifies with Pushkin. The story concludes:

> . . . я остался один и вдруг, с такой ясностью, какой никогда не испытывал до тех пор, увидел уходившие ввысь колонны Думы, освещённую листву на бульваре, бронзовую голову Пушкина с неярким отблеском луны на ней, увидел в первый раз окружавшее меня таким, каким оно было на самом деле, – затихшим и невыразимо прекрасным.[80]

> (... I was left on my own, and suddenly, with such clarity as I had never previously experienced, I saw the columns of the Duma rising upwards, the leaves in the light on the boulevard, Pushkin's bronze head with the moon's blurred reflection on it, I saw for the first time what was around me as it was in actual fact—tranquil and inexpressibly splendid.)

This story, published at the height of the Stalinist Terror, marks the distance the author has traveled both in his aesthetics and in his cultural identity. Babel has placed the Odesa myth securely within the Russian literary tradition, enshrined in the canonical figure of Pushkin as an icon of Russian cultural identity, but he has also dedicated his art to an ideal clarity of vision.

---

79 In December 1908, Babel attended performances by Grasso in Odesa (Elena Pogorelskaia and Stiv Levin, *Isaak Babel: Zhineopisanie* [Moscow: Vita-Nova, 2020], 37–40). Gregory Freidin identifies the performance described in the story as *Feodalesimo*, reworked for Grasso by a Catalan dramatist Angel Guimera from his own play *Maria-Rosa* ("Fat Tuesday in Odessa: Isaak Babel's 'Di Grasso' as Testament and Manifesto," *Russian Review* 40, no. 2 [1981]: 109–10).
80 *Собрание сочинений*, 1:208.

CHAPTER 9

Where the Steppe Meets the Sea: Odesa in the Ukrainian City Text

Oleksandr Zabirko

Introduction

In a sense, the cultural myth of Odesa, one of the biggest cities in Ukraine, is larger than life, yet its multiethnic, multireligious, and multicultural image has a basis in historical fact. For instance, it was a hotbed of Jewish Enlightenment (Haskalah) and of the Greek national revival (manifested by the secret society founded in Odesa in 1814, "Filiki Eteria"). At the same time, the notion of *Odessity* (in Russian, *odesskost'*) as "a state of mind, a memory, and a literary image"[1] was and arguably still is firmly integrated into the Russian imperial heritage and, by extension, into the literature produced in the Russian language.

Within Russian cultural space, Odesa acquired its own urban text, similar to the somewhat more prominent St. Petersburg text, generating a more or less stable set of characteristics and narrative techniques that reinforced the city's cultural uniqueness and visibility. Overshadowed by Russian cultural domination, the image of Odesa in Ukrainian literature and culture may certainly be described as less clear-cut and less recognizable. Nevertheless, Ukrainian authors, while challenging Russian imperial culture's understanding of *Odessity*, managed to produce a distinct city text in its own right, thus reclaiming and modeling Odesa's Ukrainian element.

---

1 Joachim Schlör, "Odessity: In Search of Transnational Odessa," *Quest: Issues in Contemporary Jewish History* 9 (October 2011): 124. On the Petersburg text, see the chapter by Efraim Sicher in this volume.

The city's unique position in the cultural concepts of Russian imperial space, where it functioned as a less hostile mirror image of St. Petersburg,[2] certainly provided a window of opportunity for integrating Odesa into the imagined geographies of Ukrainian literature. At the same time, however, both Odesa and St. Petersburg shared one particular feature of a Russian imperial metropolis: their sheer existence and growth epitomized the victory of Culture over Nature. Like St. Petersburg's literary image as an architectonic miracle built on hostile marshes, Odesa's spectacular rise as a boom town, in a supposedly uninhabitable region, in its own way contributed to the prestige of the Russian imperial project. One of the earliest poetic texts about Odesa, an ode written in 1806 by an author with the enigmatic pseudonym P. F. B. already interprets Odesa's growth as a triumph against the wild and empty steppe:

> Где степи лишь одно унылу мысль рождали
> И странника где взор предела их не зрел . . .
> Там ныне здания огромные явились,
> Обилие во всем и вкус, и красота,
> Народы разных вер и стран там водворились.
> Где дикие места, где делась пустота? . . .[3]

> (Where the steppes had only one sad thought, / And where a wanderer could not see their limits . . . / There are now huge buildings, / Abundance in everything, good taste and beauty, / Peoples of various faiths and countries settled there. / Where are the wild places and where did all the emptiness go? . . .)

Almost three decades later, in his *Отрывки из путешествия Онегина* (Fragments from Onegin's journey, 1830), Aleksandr Pushkin, while painting a romantic image of a still very young metropolis, suggested, however, that the triumph of high culture against the hostile surroundings was not fully accomplished, as the presence of the uncultivated steppe was noticeable everywhere in Odesa: "Все хорошо, но дело в том / Что степь нагая там кругом" (Everything is fine [here], but the problem is // That there is a bare steppe all around the

---

2 Rebecca J. Stanton, *Isaac Babel and the Self-Invention of Odessan Modernism* (Evanston: Northwestern University Press, 2012), 4, 17.
3 Quoted in Saul Borovoi, "Puteshestvie Onegina i odesskaia tema v russkoi literature pervoi treti XIX veka," in *Pushkin na iuge: Trudy Pushkinskikh konferentsii Odessy i Kishineva*, ed. Z. A. Borinevich-Babaitseva, I. K. Vartichan, and G. F. Bogach (Kishinev: Shtiintsa, 1961), 2:268.

place). What unites these two poetic texts is, among other things, the conceptualization of the city as a hermetic universe in the middle of nowhere; this poetic strategy follows the desire to literally strip the space around the city of its cultural layer and to present the steppe as a naked, uncivilized tabula rasa, an area of emptiness (*pustota*) and wildness (*dikost'*).

Although not explicitly hostile towards the idea of Ukraine's ethnic and cultural difference, the early Russian myth of Odes(s)a obviously originated from the imperial drive to colonize and transform endless expanses, while conceptualizing the initial, pre-imperial state as endlessly dull or at least unremarkable. This myth downgraded the steppe landscape along the northern Black Sea coast to the status of *provintsiia*, an imperial backwater, thus relegating it to the wild, uncultivated realm of Nature, rather than to the refined sphere of Culture. This particular side of the Odesa myth would soon become a challenge for Ukrainian literature which, in the nineteenth century, not merely rediscovered the steppe as an area full of life but also valorized it as a cradle of Ukrainian national culture.

This potential conflict notwithstanding, traveling to the southern city became a major theme both in folkloristic and belletristic texts composed in the Ukrainian language during the late nineteenth century. Thus, in prerevolutionary Ukrainian folklore, Odesa was occasionally depicted as a place of boundless opportunities and upward social mobility. For instance, in the songs of the *chumaks* (a particular stratum of goods peddlers, who were probably the most mobile population in the Ukrainian rural community), the image of Odesa is deliberately contrasted with the routines of rural life:

> А в Одесі добре жити,
> Мішком хліба не носити,
> На панщину не ходити,
> Подушного не платити,
> Ні за плугом, ні за ралом
> Називають мене паном![4]

> (It is good to live in Odesa, / [where] You do not need to carry grain in a sack, / [where] You do not have to work on the lords' fields, / [where] You do not need to pay poll tax, / Or to walk behind the plow, / And where everybody calls you "Sir"!)

---

4   Tetiana Liptukha, "A v Odesi dobre zhyty...," *Dom kniazia Gagarina: Sbornik nauchnykh statei i publikacii* 7 (2016): 17.

While the folkloristic perception of Odesa focuses mainly on the highs and lows of the peasants' (usually grain peddlers) arrival at a vivacious, multiethnic city, for the professional Ukrainian writers, Odesa epitomized a maritime exoticism and, therefore, functioned as a major source of lyrical inspiration. One of the most vivid manifestations of such literary quests for the unknown is the collection *Подорож до моря* (A journey to the sea, 1888) by Lesia Ukraiinka.[5] This volume offers a poetic travelogue that starts from the author's native region, Volhynia (in today's northwestern Ukraine), goes through the picturesque steppe landscapes of Podolia (aptly connoted Ukraine's beauty), to a southern seaport—which remains unnamed throughout the course of the journey but is described as being undeniably impressive and joyful, although also as a strikingly alien environment: "Великеє місто. Будинки високі, . . . І все чужина!" (Great city, tall houses, . . . And everything is foreign!). Yet, Odesa's foreignness is neither hostile nor threatening but, rather, both friendly and inviting: "добрії люди мене привітали / В далекій країні" (Good people greeted me / In that faraway country).[6] The aesthetics of a non-hostile foreignness alongside ethics of hospitality (which is central for the discourse on cosmopolitanism from Kant to Derrida) mark Lesia Ukraiinka's Odesa as a cosmopolitan space without, however, mentioning the term "cosmopolitanism" as such. At the same time, considering the Odesa region to be a distant and exotic place leaves no doubt that, in Lesia Ukraiinka's collection, the city of Odesa and its surroundings are perceived as non-Ukrainian territory. This poetic construct of the Odesa region reaches its climax at the ruins of the Ottoman fortress in Akkerman, where a flower growing on the floor of one of the towers inspires a romantic story about a Ukrainian Cossack who must have died there in captivity—a story that culminates in the traveler's wish to bring the flower "back to Ukraine": "Чи гадав той козаченько, йдучи на чужину, / Що вернеться з його серця квітка на Вкраїну?" (When he went off to foreign lands, could that Cossack have ever thought / that a flower grown from his heart would return to Ukraine?)[7]

Despite the familiar images of Odesa, Lesia Ukraiinka's poetic journey is ultimately a journey "далі від душного міста" (away from the sultry city)[8] to the seemingly endless and untamed space of the sea; therefore, the author predominantly focuses on the features of Nature, rather than on those of Culture. Nevertheless, references to Ukrainian cultural life in Odesa may already be

---

5   Lesia Ukraiinka, *Lisova pisnia* (Kharkov: Folio, 2017), 43–50.
6   Ibid., 45.
7   Ibid., 48.
8   Ibid.

found in the very first lines of Lesia Ukraiinka's volume, manifested in its dedication to the family of Mykhailo Komarov—a prominent figure in the Ukrainian national movement of the late nineteenth century.[9]

Cosmopolitanism as a challenge: Odesa in the texts of Ivan Nechui-Levyts'kyi

Komarov, who made a name for himself due to his efforts to develop education for the Ukrainian population, was not only a remarkable Odesan resident but also a probable prototype for Viktor Komashko, the protagonist of one of the central Odesan texts in Ukrainian literature, the novel *Над Чорним морем* (On the Black Sea, 1890), by Ivan Nechui-Levyts'kyi. This novel focuses on a love story between two young Ukrainians—a teacher named Viktor Komashko and a bank clerk called Oleksandra (Sania) Navrots'ka. The latter, though not a teacher by profession, is an educated woman, who dedicates her free time to teaching in the local women's schools. Whereas Komashko is concerned about the education of the Ukrainian lower classes and dreams of a Ukrainian national revival, Sania is preoccupied with educating "the most oppressed representatives of the most oppressed nation," Jewish women. Although described as the noble endeavor of a young, idealistic spirit, Sania's decision is put to the test throughout the novel and is judged to be less pragmatic, and ultimately less valuable, than the strategy pursued by Komashko.

Thus, apart from the love story, *On the Black Sea* offers a fictionalized treatise on the uneasy relations and direct competition between Ukrainian nationalism and European cosmopolitanism. Odesa, the thriving young metropolis, offers an appropriate setting for such a discussion. Unlike other urban centers in the Russian Empire's "Southwest," in Odesa, the Ukrainian national awakening had to come to terms not only with Russian cultural dominance but also with the cosmopolitan culture in the city.

As a contested area, the Odesa region presented both opportunities and threats to the Ukrainian national movement. On multiple occasions, Nechui emphasizes the serene beauty of both the city and its seaside resorts, the Malyi and Velykyi Fontan, where a large part of the story unfolds and most of the conversations take place. The city, which Nechui calls Odes, using a masculine gender noun, is neither a foreign nor a hostile place but rather a hospitable venue for

---

9   See chapter 2 above by Yohanan Petrovsky-Shtern.

multinational residents and visitors. Its exoticism is not alien, but all too familiar, and is sometimes revealed as nothing more than an exalted self-fashioning by the city dwellers, as evidenced by a description of a Jewish merchant woman "made up and painted like an Indian idol."[10]

Though not too prominent in Nechui's oeuvre, the Jewish theme, combined with an Odesan motif, also features in one of his earlier works, a short novel *Burlachka* (A barge hauler, 1880)—a text with barely disguised antisemitic rhetoric, epitomized in the figure of a tavern keeper and moneylender, Leizor Rabinenko, who drew the local Ukrainian peasants into his web of lies and intrigues and, by doing so, "sucked the money out of their pockets just like a spider sucks the blood out of the flies." The image of a Jewish bloodsucker culminates in the metaphorical description of the Jewish state within a state, with Odesa (Odes) as its capital:

> В Лейзора в Одесі були свої ще вищі начальники: жидівські губернатори і міністри, котрим він подавав звістку за все і приставляв їм пашню. То були міністри пшениці, жита, міністри гречки й проса й навіть міністри свинячого сала, олії й дьогтю: то були взагалі українські губернатори мужицького поту та сліз, міністри людської кривавиці.[11]
>
> (In Odes, Leizor had his even higher superiors—Jewish governors and ministers, to whom he reported everything. These were ministers of wheat [and] rye, ministers of buckwheat and millet, even ministers of lard, oil and tar; in general, they were Ukrainian governors of peasant sweat and tears, ministers of the people's bloody wounds.)

A rural dweller himself, Leizor gives the impression of an easygoing man, whose manners are not much different from those of his Ukrainian neighbors; yet, at the same time, he is constantly climbing the ladder of the supposed, secret Jewish hierarchy and is certain soon to reach the unofficial rank of "Jewish Governor of Ukraine" ("йому небагато зосталось дослужувати до уряду жидівського губернатора України").

To be sure, in his work, Nechui does not portray all Jews as villains (some are exploiters, others are victims); yet, it is undeniable that the author does not

---

10 Ivan Nechui-Levyts'kyi, *Nad Chornym morem* (Kharkov: Folio, 2008), 39.
11 Ivan Nechui-Levyts'kyi, "Burlachka," in *Tvory v triokh tomakh* (Kyiv: Dnipro, 1988), 2:188.

shy away from articulating some negative stereotypes regarding Jewish life and culture. Similarly, in *On the Black Sea*, the enlightened liberals Viktor Komashko and Sania Navrots'ka exchange some widespread clichés about the life and status of Jewish women and, ultimately, about the horrible smell in the classrooms of the Jewish school where Sania works. Moreover, Sania's efforts on behalf of the Jewish communities of Odesa and Kishinev do not result in a definitive understanding of the importance of a Jewish-Ukrainian alliance in the face of Russian imperial domination. During the conversation between Sania and Komashko, the cooperation of minority ethnic groups gives way to competitive victimhood and loyalty to one's own people:

> Жидівська женщина найбільше загнана в неволю, не має навіть права молитись вкупі з мужчинами, сісти за стіл з ними . . . А поки жидівська дівчина не вийде заміж, не має права ногою ступити в синагогу; її вважають не за людину . . .
> — А народ наш ще більше, – перебив її Комашко . . .
> — Я ладна служити хоч би й в народній школі. Тоді б я знала принаймні, що я щось роблю, а не чевріюю, як чевріють без діла й нудьгують сотні й тисячі молодих паннів.[12]

> (A Jewish woman is most enslaved; she does not even have the right to pray with men, or to sit at the table with them. . . . Until a Jewish girl gets married, she has no right to set foot in the synagogue; she is not considered a human being. . . .
> "And our people are enslaved even worse," Komashko interrupted. . . .
> "I am ready to work in a public school, as well. Then, at least I would know that I am doing something useful and not just wasting away like hundreds and thousands of young girls are wasting away in idleness and boredom.")

The idea of a political alliance between Ukrainians and Jews later gained momentum in the writing of Odesan Zionist writer Vladimir Jabotinsky roughly two decades after the publication of Nechui's novel (as Yohanan Petrovsky-Shtern explains in chapter 2 of this volume). For the author of *On the Black Sea*, on the contrary, the merits of the Ukrainian-Jewish dialogue are anything but obvious,

---

12 Nechui-Levyts'kyi, *Nad Chornym morem*, 129.

thus, in the novel, the close co-existence of Jewish and Ukrainian emancipatory agendas turn Odesa to a terrain of their implicit contestation.

Nevertheless, *On the Black Sea* refers to Odesa not as a threatening but a welcoming environment. If there is any menace behind the façade of the flamboyant seaport, it is the menace of cosmopolitanism, which, along with social mobility and the overall attraction of the city, easily draws upwardly mobile Ukrainians to abandon their own culture, language, and traditions. This potential threat justifies the juxtaposition of nationalism and cosmopolitanism in Nechui's novel: if the "national awakening" of the Ukrainians is perceived here as an ideal goal, then cosmopolitanism and social mobility acquire the quality of a political accusation as two interconnected forces, which may lead to denationalization and assimilation of the Ukrainian educated class. The dangers of denationalization are manifested in the novel by two negative characters—a Ukrainian trader, Fesenko, and a Greek banker, Arystyd Selabros. While Fesenko is portrayed as a ruthless and narrow-minded careerist, who renounces his Ukrainian ancestry and cultural background in favor of the supposedly superior Russian imperial culture, Selabros confidently identifies himself as a cosmopolitan Odesan. An ardent admirer of Sania's closest friend, Nadia Murashkova (who is of mixed Greek and Ukrainian origin), he is also described as a very talkative poseur, who seduces Nadia, only to dump her soon afterwards.

The somewhat simple-minded plot of the novel notwithstanding, the competition between cosmopolitanism and nationalism is not reduced to a simple black-and-white panorama, where good and honest nationalists are juxtaposed with bad and treacherous cosmopolitans. Indeed, the novel's protagonists reject Selabros's Odesan cosmopolitanism; however, they do not reject it as such, but rather identify it as a cover for money-grabbing, hedonism, and lax morals. More importantly, the Ukrainian cultural nationalism advocated by Komashko and eagerly embraced by Sania is neither a parochial idea of belonging to an idyllic rural community, nor an aggressive ideology of "blood and soil," but encompasses all the cultural groups living in Ukraine. In the novel, this openness is illustrated by the figure of Mavrodin, Viktor Komashko's best friend and another character of Greek ancestry, who, however, also embraces Ukrainian language and culture without rejecting his Greek background.

This bland-sounding resolution of clashing ideologies results primarily from the form and style of Nechui's narrative. The characters in *On the Black Sea* are not ideologues, nor does the narrator seek to deliver a political message; the simple plot of the novel is driven by human foibles and virtues, with humor and satire, rather than with conclusive lessons. If there is a message in the narrator's attempts to ridicule the high-flying rhetoric of the self-proclaimed cosmopolitans, then it is most likely a plea to keep one's feet on the ground. In a similarly ironic way, Sania's feminist views may be depicted as honest and progressive; yet, at the end of the novel, this staunch feminist still must learn how to cook borscht properly for her future husband.

Nechui was often criticized as being conservative, even reactionary, because of his ironic attitude towards some of the newest intellectual trends reaching Ukraine from Western Europe. That assessment, however, requires further clarification. Nechui identifies the mixture of national groups (combined with Russian language education) as a breeding ground for cosmopolitan ideas that could potentially impede the development of Ukrainian culture. In one of his earlier texts, the short novel *Khmary* (The clouds, 1874), set mainly in Kyiv, cosmopolitanism is just a disguise for *velykorusshyna* (Great Russian nationalism), while the pernicious mechanism that promotes both these ideas is the Russian-language high school.[13] Despite this potential threat, Nechui does not call for the defeat, let alone eradication, of ethnic diversity but painstakingly asserts the Ukrainian presence among the multinational residents of Odesa and other cities in Ukraine.[14] Nevertheless, this presence easily turns into a claim. Although Ukraine had not existed as an independent country in his lifetime, Nechui attributes an existential reality and permanence to it; thus, in his novel, the ports of the Black Sea coast are explicitly mentioned as "our ports," where "our" certainly does not refer to the Russian Empire.

Furthermore, here, Odesa's status as a Ukrainian city is not only claimed but also deliberately modeled. Although Nechui does not hide the fact that the language his multiethnic characters speak to each other is, in most cases, Russian—in all the scenes and episodes, he assiduously translates their speech into Ukrainian. What might easily be misinterpreted as the unifying zeal of cultural nationalism is, in fact, an attempt to showcase the potency of a linguistic variety, which was at that time routinely identified as the Little Russian dialect, a language in which the imperial authorities ultimately banned publishing, when the Ems Ukaz, issued in 1876, prohibited the use of Ukrainian in print. Placing the Ukrainian language within Odesa's urban scenery meant expanding its registers and spheres of use; as such, a tongue predominantly associated with the uneducated rural strata, effectively functions in the novel as a language of "abstractions and aberrations," of ideological arguments and political debates, as well as the language of chit-chat over coffee, at family dinners, while picnicking,

---

13 Maxim Tarnawsky, *The All-Encompassing Eye of Ukraine: Ivan Nechui-Levyts'kyi's Realist Prose* (Toronto: University of Toronto Press, 2015), 210.
14 Ibid., 85.

or in popular music, that is, as a language compatible with modern European ideas and an urban lifestyle.

The relationship between the place and its inhabitants was not limited to the idea of Odesa as a natural space for cosmopolitanism. On a larger scale, Odesa's scenic villas and warm, humid sunshine, mixed with cool sea breezes, evoked a holiday spirit, which the narrator upholds throughout the course of the novel, but which is also presented as an ambivalent factor, in terms of its influence on the characters. For some, Odesa's relaxed atmosphere easily becomes an excuse for intellectual laziness, cowardice, and ethical complacency (frequently camouflaged as an expression of cosmopolitan spirit).[15] Others, however, rise to the challenge and use Odesa's urban setting as an opportunity for emancipation and personal growth.

The latter is definitely Sania's case: "a girl without a dowry," who is seeking a different path than most women of her age; but it also suits Komashko, a peasant's son, who "grew up in the steppe" and comes to the city to pursue his almost messianic goal of "serving the people." In the middle of the novel, Komashko's lengthy monologue, filled with his childhood memories of fishing with his grandfather in the picturesque Dniester estuary, offers an important lyrical pause in the otherwise strictly plot-driven narration. This retrospective monologue illustrates the emotional experience that the protagonist brings to Odesa:

> Буду вчитись співати або грати; я люблю музику, – ворушилось в моїй думці. – Або вивчусь лучче малярства, буду малювати; змалюю ту красу, що в небі, що на лимані, – думав я, – або . . . буду писати вірші, складу віршами книжку, таку, як "Катерина" . . . Напишу про діда Хтодося . . . про безщасних, прибитих бідою. . . . Про їх, про їх![16]

> ("I'll learn how to sing or play an instrument. I love music," stirred in my soul. "Or, better yet, I'll learn to paint, I'll paint! I will paint this beauty that's in the heavens, at the estuary," I thought, ". . . or . . . I'll write poetry, I'll amass a book of poems, like [Taras Shevshenko's poem] 'Kateryna.' I will write about Grandpa Khtodos', about the unfortunate, about those who are crushed by poverty. Yes, about them! About them!")

---

15 Ibid., 93.
16 Nechui-Levyts'kyi, *Nad Chornym morem*, 77; the English translation is taken from Tarnawsky's, *The All-Encompassing Eye*, 97.

This catalogue of the protagonist's artistic ambitions provides an allegoric image of Ukrainian literature and arts maturing from the "natural poetic sentiment" to socially conscious realism. In the novel, this development acquires an important spatial dimension: the creative enthusiasm that once sparkled in Komashko's early life amid the Ukrainian steppe unfolds in the entirely different, urban environment of Odesa, where the peculiar mixture of Nature and Culture results in the specific notion of freedom (or rather in a sort of inner liberation):

> Молодий хлопець одкривав свою душу. Над широким морем, на вільній волі, далеко од свого домашнього й службового клопоту в його душа стала одкритою, як буває часом в дорозі. . . . І серце тоді любе дужче, й приятельство стає міцніше, й слово – щиріше.[17]

> (The young man was baring his soul. Upon the wide sea, in free surroundings, far from his domestic and business worries, his soul became open, as it sometimes happens, when one is on the road. . . . And in times like this, the heart starts loving harder, and friendship becomes stronger, and the words become more sincere.)

As a liminal space between the native steppe and the exotic realm of the sea, Odesa presents a rite of passage for the young Ukrainian protagonists. While Sania Navrots'ka and Viktor Komashko would preserve their love and their marriage through the hardships of persecution, exile, and pressure from the imperial authorities, they would eventually return to Odesa to continue their mission in the field of popular education. However, the novel ends not with the story of their success but with its tragic counterpart—the fate of Nadia Murashkova. Seduced and dumped by Selabros, Nadia ultimately chooses the same path of popular nationalism as Komashko and joins the Ukrainian populists (*narodovci*) in their campaign of "going to the people." She is teaching in a rural school but is soon fired from her position "без объяснения причин" (without explanation)—an expression from Russian imperial officialese, which remains untranslated in Nechui's otherwise strictly Ukrainian narration. Broken and exhausted, Nadia returns to her native Kishinev and dies soon thereafter.

---

17 Nechui-Levyts'kyi, *Nad Chornym morem*, 70.

Despite all their differences (in gender, temperament, and so forth), it is Komashko and Murashkova who exemplify the highs and lows of the Ukrainian intelligentsia in the late Russian Empire. Unsurprisingly, at the end of the novel, their names are pronounced together several times and ultimately become both collective and cratylic names "Komashkos and Murashkos" (Комашки та Мурашки),[18] in other words, "insects and ants." Thus, in the eyes of their ideological enemies, they are vermin that cause problems by carrying and spreading the "disease" of Ukrainian nationalism while, in the eyes of their supporters, they are tireless soldiers of enlightenment and national emancipation, who (while serving the imperial state) sacrifice their time, health, and energies to the national cause.

Towards the modernist urban text: The Soviet Odesa of Ivan Mykytenko

Even if *On the Black Sea* is not one of the most successful or widely mentioned works by Nechui-Levyts'kyi (let alone of Ukrainian prose as a whole), it offers several key elements of the literary modeling of Odesa that were reintroduced into Ukrainian literature in the 1920s by an entirely different generation of writers in an entirely different political and aesthetic context. Paradoxically, these very elements reappeared within new modernist trends, which Nechui had sharply criticized as being inappropriate for a developing Ukrainian culture. For their part, representatives of Ukrainian modernism occasionally portrayed him as a narrow-minded realist writer of the older generation. Against this background, the idea of a literary tradition or intergenerational continuity at the genesis of the Ukrainian literary representation of Odesa seems rather improbable; nevertheless, at least in terms of plot structure and its themes, the modernists' Odesa text of the 1920s echoes *On the Black Sea* when it presents its own variations on a story about a young Ukrainian steppe-dweller who travels to the southern seaport in search of intellectual or artistic challenges.

Despite this common feature shared with Nechui's novel, a modernist urban text is, first and foremost, a product of the early Soviet era and, here, most notably, an offspring of the so-called "Literary Discussion," which facilitated a fairly new understanding of Ukrainian national identity, freed from ethnic and folkloristic inveteracy and open to the cultural avant-garde coupled with European

---

18 Ibid., 201–03.

modernism. Initiated by novelist Mykola Khvyl'ovyi in the early 1920s, this wide-ranging debate on the national status of Ukrainian culture coincided with the implementation of *korenizatsiia*, an affirmative Soviet policy towards non-Russian nationalities.[19] Although the main idea of korenizatsiia was to cultivate communist cadres for every nationality and in each newly established Soviet republic, in Ukraine this policy helped to raise the literacy of the Ukrainophone rural population, while stimulating the unprecedented development of Ukrainian print media and literary production.[20] Borrowing extensively from West-European traditions, the vanguard of Ukrainian literature of the 1920s seized the opportunity to distinguish their identity from that of their Polish and Russian neighbors. Yet, in a somewhat paradoxical opposition towards the Soviet concept of korenizatsiia as strengthening the ethnic roots of the indigenous cultures, the authors of Ukrainian literature in the 1920s looked to urban spaces, such as Odesa, in order to go beyond the ethnic limits of their "culture of steppe-dwellers" and to gain access to a broader European heritage; as such, their literary works were saturated with maritime motifs and a cosmopolitan atmosphere of the Black Sea metropolis.

The idea of Ukraine's cultural sovereignty attracted people with very different political, ethnic, and aesthetic backgrounds, and so, too, the modernist Odesan text appears as a collective production of authors whose aesthetic orientations ranged from realism to neo-romanticism and to futurism. At the realist end of this range, we encounter the short novel (*povist'*) *Vurkahany* (The thugs, 1928) by Ivan Mykytenko, whom contemporary Ukrainian scholarship regards as a conformist Soviet writer and a harbinger of socialist realism. Mykytenko was indeed a member of the presidium of the First Soviet Writers' Congress (1934), where socialist realism was endorsed as the only official method of literary production. His career ended dramatically in 1937, however, when he was accused

---

19 Olena Palko, "Between Two Powers: The Soviet Ukrainian Writer Mykola Khvyl'ovyi," *Jahrbücher für Geschichte Osteuropas*, no. 4 (2016): 575–98.
20 On the all-Soviet policy of *korenizatsiia*, see Terry D. Martin, *The Affirmative Action Empire: Nations and Nationalism in the Soviet Union, 1923–1939* (Ithaca, NY: Cornell University Press, 2001); Francine Hirsch, *Empire of Nations: Ethnographic Knowledge and the Making of the Soviet Union* (Ithaca, NY: Cornell University Press, 2005). On the Ukrainian dimension of *korenizatsiia*, see Matthew D. Pauly, *Breaking the Tongue: Language, Education, and Power in Soviet Ukraine, 1923–1934* (Toronto: University of Toronto Press, 2014); Olena Palko, *Making Ukraine Soviet: Literature and Cultural Politics under Lenin and Stalin* (London: Bloomsbury, 2020). On the issue of literacy and reading public in Ukraine during *korenizatsiia*, see Myroslav Shkandrij, "The Ukrainian Reading Public in the 1920s: Real, Implied, and Ideal," *Canadian Slavonic Papers* 58, no. 2 (2016): 160–83.

of Trotskyism and expelled from the Communist Party. Soon afterwards, he was found dead on the outskirts of Kharkiv.

The author's ideological background notwithstanding, *The Thugs* addresses some prominent topics in European literature of that time: the theme of the artist as the other; the experience of solitude and painful alienation as the price of creative genius, and, ultimately, the (im)possibility of the physical or mental survival of an artist in a pragmatic and cruel society.[21] The novel focuses on the hard-luck story of a Ukrainian teenager with a markedly Russian name, Alyosha—an orphan who grew up in an unspecified rural area and was brought to a city orphanage by a villager. This beautiful, southern city on the seashore, although unnamed throughout the novel's plot, is still easily identifiable as Odesa. Naturally, for a homeless child who spends his days on the streets and nights in the orphanage, the street becomes a central paradigm for conceptualizing the unfamiliar urban setting.[22] Less obvious, however, is the fact that, for Alyosha, strolling about the streets of Odesa becomes synonymous with joie de vivre, providing perpetual excitement:

> Вулиці, повні гарячої снаги, переливаються в сонячнім тремтінні, грають велетенськими шибами, киплять у шварканні черевиків, зітхають стомлено під тінню дерев. Візники, підпершись батожинами, закам'яніли на своїх високих сидіннях. Близько будинку пролітають трамваї, виблискуючи райдугами скла в золотих рамцях. Дзвонять дрібно, тривожно, часто. "Дзінь-дзінь! Дзінь-дзінь!" – відгукується до них Альошине серце, налите вщерть незнаною радістю життя. Він одбігає од воріт, кидається в широкі розгони.[23]

> (The streets, full of heat, shimmer and tremble under the sun, they play with giant windows, boil in the squeaking of shoes, sigh wearily under the shade of trees. The coachmen, propped up with whips, are frozen in their high seats. Trams fly near the

---

21 Two other major Ukrainian texts that tackle the issues of madness and the social isolation of mentally ill persons appeared roughly during the same period: the novel *Sanatoriina zona* (Sanatorium zone, 1924) by Mykola Khvyl'ovyi and the play *Narodnyi Malakhiy* (The People's Malachy, 1927) by Mykola Kulish. On Mykytenko, see Tetiana Sverbilova, Natalia Maliutina, and Liudmyla Skoryna, *Vid modernu do avanhardu: Zhanrovo-styliova paradygma Ukraiins'koii dramaturhii pershoii tretyny XX st* (Cherkasy: Yu. A. Chabanenko, 2009), 369–80.
22 On the *topos* of the street in Russophone texts about Odesa, see Mirja Lecke, "The Street: A Spatial Paradigm in Odessan Literature," *Slavonic and East European Review* 95, no. 3 (July 2017): 4–29.
23 Ivan Mykytenko, *Vurkahany* (Kharkov: Ukraiins'kyi robitnyk, 1927), 9.

house, sparkling with rainbows of glass in golden frames. They ring shrilly, anxiously, and frequently. Alyosha's heart, filled to the brim with the unknown joy of life, responds to them: "Ding-ding! Ding-ding!" He runs away from the gate [of the orphanage] and dives into the wide-open spaces [of the city].)

Furthermore, the cityscape of Odesa is marked by the presence of natural elements, the sea and rocks around the port. While the sea has an overwhelming and long-lasting effect on a steppe child, the hills and the rocks provide him with clay—the material he needs for his artistic endeavors. Alyosha, who appears to be a gifted and aspiring sculptor, uses the clay to create a statuette of the devil, which initiates dramatic events in the orphanage. The fight over the statuette escalates and ends with a knifing in which one of the orphans is wounded. Alyosha's best friend, a teenager nicknamed Matros (Seaman) flees, and the protagonist himself suffers a nervous breakdown and is transferred to a mental hospital.

While both the hospital and the orphanage are described as humane and progressive institutions, on the plot level they are associated with restrictions and uniformity and, as such, provide an aesthetic opposition to the free and creative environment of Odesa's streets. In the clinic, Alyosha encounters a young man named Roman, who, in his condition of acute mental illness, paints enigmatic and captivating pictures that draw the attention of both the patients and the medical staff. After Roman's recovery, his talent disappears, and he produces only mediocre, amateurish paintings, much to the delight of his doctor, who declares that, as a sane person, Roman will now be able to paint fences and, thus, will serve society.

This unifying force of Soviet modernity is tackled and presented in all its ambivalence in another Odesan text written by Mykytenko, the play *Kadry* (Cadres, 1930), where the Soviet educational conveyor belt defines and shapes the life of students who are in Odesa for "accelerated" courses of study. In the final scene, a train full of young professionals departs the Odesa railway station, while other trains with new arrivals are approaching the city. Similarly, in *The Thugs*, Alyosha, who fortunately retained his talent after medical treatment, leaves Odesa on his way to Kharkiv (then the capital of Soviet Ukraine), where he hopes to enter art school.

It is noteworthy that leaving Odesa for eastern Ukraine appears as a recurrent motif in the Ukrainian literature of the 1920s; for example, in the poem "Odesa-Kharkiv" by Ivan Malovichko,[24] bourgeois Odesa is left behind both

---

24 Ivan Malovichko, "Odesa-Kharkiv," in *Ukraiins'ka avanhardna poeziia: Antolohiia 1910–1930*, ed. Oleh Kotsarev and Iuliia Stakhivs'ka (Kyiv: Smoloskyp, 2014), 346.

geographically and mentally in favor of the futuristic and proletarian capital city. In Oleksandr Soroka's poem "Na Donbas" (To Donbas), young Odesans travel to the coal mines on the Russian-Ukrainian borderland in order to become shock workers (*udarniki*).[25] As in Russian literature, where Odesa occupies an intermediate position between the provinces and the historical capitals (Moscow and St. Petersburg), in Ukrainian literature of the 1920s, Odesa's liminality acquires additional dimensions as a space between Kharkiv and Kyiv, on the one hand, and the steppe terrain of southern and eastern Ukraine, on the other.

Although the Ukrainian avant-garde poets occasionally defined Odesa as a "big nil," compared to thriving and modern "KhRK,"[26] in Mykytenko's *The Thugs*, the author subtly juxtaposes the two cities by integrating into the narrative a description of certain songs being played. At the end of the novel, leaving Alyosha back in Odesa, the narrator proposes a short detour to Kharkiv, where the reader is immediately greeted by a military march glorifying Bolshevik exploits in the recent war against Poland. This march is performed by young Komsomol members at the city's central square (described as an impressive conglomeration of asphalt and concrete, framed by high-rise buildings and red banners). In contrast, the song that accompanies Alyosha in Odesa (and which he learns by heart) is a popular song about two criminals' escape from the municipal prison, a song performed in Russian thieves' cant, infused with words of Yiddish, Greek, and Ukrainian origin. While numerous variations of this song exist, with Leonid Utiosov's "С Одесского кичмана" (The Odesa slammer) arguably being the most prominent of them, Mykytenko offers a peculiarly Ukrainian or rather Ukrainianized version of the song's lyrics:

>Йшлі два вуркагана
>з адєского кічмана . . .
>. . . з адєского кічмана
>дамой..
>Товариш мой вєрний,
>болять мої рани . . .
>Болять мої рани
>на груді.
>Одна заживаїть,

---

25 Oleksandr Soroka, "Na Donbas," in Kotsarev and Stakhivs'ka, *Ukraiins'ka avanhardna poeziia*, 521.
26 Also see Sava Holovanivs'kyi, "Tysnu ruku!" in Kotsarev and Stakhivs'ka, *Ukraiins'ka avanhardna poeziia*, 206.

другая начинаїть . . .
А третя откриваїться
внутрі . . .[27]

(Two thugs fled / the Odesa slammer / [they fled] the Odessa slammer / and were heading home / My dear comrade, / my wounds are hurting / the wounds / on my chest [are hurting] / One wound is healing, / another one starts [hurting], / And the third one opens up / inside. . . .)

By foregrounding criminal slang, which he incorporates into the title of the novel, Mykytenko aims at a representation of Odesan language which, in *The Thugs*, also features *surzhyk* (a mixture of Ukrainian and Russian, hardly definable in linguistic terms),[28] and various sociolects of the lower classes. Mykytenko's main strategy here is the phonetic and graphemic integration of Russian linguistic elements into the Ukrainian main text. For instance, the word адєскій (Odesan) reflects the Russian pronunciation by means of Ukrainian graphemes, while the word заживать occupies a middle ground between the two standard variants (standard Russian: заживает; standard Ukrainian: заживає). This technique resembles a post-colonial mimicry of Russian, which would become prominent in Ukrainian literature only in the 1990s and would be applied by the pioneers of Ukrainian post-modernism (Oksana Zabuzhko, Iurii Andrukhovych, etc.). In Mykytenko's text, this graphemic representation of non-Ukrainian lexemes marks a specific Odesan dialect, which is integrated into the Ukrainian main text. Within the context of the standard Ukrainian language of the narrator and the educated characters in the novel (medical personnel, Komsomol activists, artists, and others), the Odesan language loses its status as a non-standard variety of Russian and appears as non-standard Ukrainian, thus making Odesa an integral part of the Ukrainian cultural universe.

The opposition between Odesa and Kharkiv is delineated not only through linguistic and aesthetic details but also on the plot level. In contrast to Kharkiv's patriotic grandeur, the petty-bourgeois coziness and the ideological liminality of Odesa serve a particular purpose—they transform the cityscape into the sublime space of parenthood and family that nurtures an orphan boy (Alyosha) and

---

27 Mykytenko, *Vurkahany*, 39.
28 Swedish linguist Niklas Bernsand defines *surzhyk* as "norm-breaking, non-obedience to, or non-awareness of the rules of the Ukrainian and Russian standard languages" ("Surzhyk and National Identity in Ukrainian Nationalist Language Ideology," *Berliner Osteuropa Info*, no.17 [2001]: 40).

helps him attain sanity and a full life. As such, after leaving the mental hospital, Alyosha roams around the city in search of shelter and finally sets himself up for a night's sleep on the pedestal of one of the monuments, which can be easily recognized as the monument to Odesa's founder, Joseph de Ribas (1749–1800). Covered by the warm summer air and protected by the statue of the old general, the future sculptor falls into "a deep and sweet sleep."[29]

A Poet between love and death: Odesa in the works of Volodymyr Sosiura

Although purely fictitious, in many ways Mykytenko's novel about the homeless child Alyosha echoes the autobiographical text of one of the most remarkable Ukrainian steppe-dwellers to appear in Odesa in the 1920s—the young poet, Volodymyr Sosiura. He had been serving in the ranks of the Ukrainian Army led by Symon Petliura, when, in late 1919, he was taken prisoner by a military unit of the White Army. While in captivity, he contracted typhus and was transferred to a hospital in nearby Odesa. In February 1920, when the Red Army occupied the city, Sosiura went over to the Bolsheviks and joined the ranks of the First Black Sea Division, which consisted mainly of former Petliurans. These twists in a soldier's life and fate provided the basic narrative for Sosiura's autobiographical novel *Tretia rota* (The third company, 1926–30), an odyssey of a young hero in and around war-torn Ukraine. In this novel, Sosiura does not dwell much on ideology nor reveal clear political sympathies. Yet, if one can speak of a single political sentiment that pervades the entire text, it is that of the poet's deep attachment to his country, which leads him to barely concealed attempts to resolve the conflict between nationalism and communism, a recurrent motif in Sosiura's poetry, as well.[30]

Sosiura's account of the Russian Civil War (1917–1922) is full of macabre atrocities that he witnessed: the changing battle scenes, executions, and the references to the infamous pogrom in Proskuriv (now Khmelnytsky, Ukraine). These episodes occasionally are interrupted by erotic dreams and actual love affairs, which cause the entire narrative to trace a thin line between love and death, or rather between the symbolic poles of Eros and Thanatos. The clash of ideologically motivated violence and erotically driven passion culminates in those chapters of the novel that take place in Odesa.

---

29 Mykytenko, *Vurkahany*, 116–17.
30 George S. N. Luckyj, "A Lyricist's Record of the Revolution: A Note on an Unpublished Collection of Verses by Volodymyr Sosyura," *Canadian Slavonic Papers* 3 (1958): 103–08.

Unsurprisingly, after joining the Bolsheviks, Sosiura does not rush to the front of the ongoing war but grasps the chance to stay in Odesa as a cadet (*politkursant*) for a "course of political lectures."[31]

> І я лишився на курсах.
> Було синє й чудесне море. На лекціях казали, що «бытие определяет сознание», що душа «продукт производственных отношений . . .» І мені страшно стало, що я, людина, яка керує своїми думками й поступками, раптом підлягаю якійсь табуретці і взагалі мертвим речам.
> Мені перестало хотітися жити, і я умовився з однією курсанткою повіситись . . .
> Але море було таке чудесне, і увечері на Дерибасівській вулиці золотою ниткою тремтіли в небі ліхтарі, а повітря було ніжне, тепле й бархатне, і я роздумав умирати. Я познайомився з одеськими поетами, вони прийняли мене в свій гурток.
>
> (So, I stayed to attend the courses.
> The sea was blue and beautiful. During the lectures, they taught us that "being determines consciousness" and that a soul is "a product of industrial relations." And I got so scared that I, a person who controls my thoughts and actions, suddenly became subordinate to a [classroom] stool or any other inanimate object.
> I stopped wanting to live, so I talked to a lady cadet and we decided to hang ourselves . . . But the sea was so wonderful, the lights of Deribasovskaia Street trembled like a golden thread in the evening sky, and the air was tender, warm, and velvety, that I decided not to die. I met Odesa poets; they accepted me into their circle.)

This circle is the famous "Kollektiv poetov," where Sosiura enjoyed the patronage of Yurii Olesha and Eduard Bagritsky and made his literary debut on stage, promptly followed by a debut in the Soviet press in the newspaper *Odesskii Kommunist*, where he published his first poems under the pseudonym Smurnyi. More importantly, in Odesa, Sosiura became not just a poet, but a Ukrainian poet. A native of Donbas, he was fluent both in Ukrainian and in Russian, which produced a tension particularly visible in *Tretia rota*, where the language of

---

31 Volodymyr Sosiura, *Tretia rota*, in *Vybrani tvory v dvokh tomakh* (Kyiv: Naukova dumka, 2000), 2: 406.

narration is Ukrainian, while the language of the characters is often Russian. According to Bagritsky's biographer, Mikhail Zagrebel'nyi, it was Bagritsky, who encouraged Sosiura to switch exclusively to the Ukrainian language.[32] Furthermore, in the 1930s Bagritsky translated several of Sosiura's poems into Russian. However, in *Tretia rota*, it was the editors of the newspaper *Visti*, Volodymyr Koriak and Vasyl' Blakytnyi, who offered the columns in their newspaper for Sosiura's Ukrainian poetry, thus determining his language choice.

Although the launch of his poetic career was definitely a major event in the life of the twenty-two-year-old protagonist, in *Tretia rota* it is not just the poetry but rather erotic encounters and, ultimately, carnal pleasures that bring him back to life:

> Одного разу я читав вірші, а через піаніно на мене дивилася смуглява дівчина в буржуазному вбранні, у неї на шиї було янтарне намисто. Взагалі на мене дивилося багато дівчат, і од того мені було соромно ще дужче. Дівчина з янтарним намистом попросила в мене прикурити. Я їй простягаю запалену цигарку через піаніно, але вона не бере, а хоче, щоб я їй дав прикурити з рота. Я взяв цигарку в рот і перехилився до неї через піаніно, а вона до мене, й наші очі майже зійшлися... Коли її цигарка загорілася, вона сказала:
>
> – Как хорошо жить![33]
>
> (One day, I was reading poetry, while a dark-skinned girl in a bourgeois dress with an amber necklace around her neck was looking at me over the piano. In general, many girls looked at me at that time, and I was ashamed of it even more. The girl with the amber necklace asked me to light a cigarette. So, I handed her a lit cigarette over the piano, but she didn't take it; instead, she wanted me to light it from the cigarette in my mouth. So, I took my cigarette and leaned over towards her, she leaned over to me, and our eyes met.... When her cigarette lit up, she said:
>
> "Life is such a good thing!" [this last phrase is in Russian—O. Z.])

---

32 Mikhail Zagrebel'nyi, *Eduard Bagritskii* (Kharkiv: Folio, 2012), 41–48.
33 Sosiura, *Tretia rota*, 407.

The return to life in Odesa comes with the omnipresence of the sea, which not only provides scenery but also influences the feelings and emotions of the characters:

> Мене зовсім не було. Були тільки розширені очі Ольги, її швидке дихання, і все... А потім ми знову почали цілуватись і тремтіти. Це було щось божевільне. Я аж злякався. Може, це од моря?[34]

> (I was completely absent. There were only Olha's wide eyes, her rapid breathing and all... And then we started kissing and trembling again. It was something crazy. I was scared. Maybe it was because of the sea?)

Having been brought to Odesa as a prisoner, the protagonist of *Tretia rota* willingly remains in the "sweet captivity" (солодкий полон) of the city, although, near the end of the novel, memories of his native steppe and the banks of the Donets River become more frequent and persistent.

Although Sosiura spent only a few years in Odesa, against the backdrop of the events described in *Tretia rota*, Odesa was destined to become a major memorable place in his literary oeuvre. Some of these memories were about the start of his literary career or, more frequently, about becoming a faithful communist and a party member.[35] Other references to Odesa, however, appear in literary works written for the drawer (not intended for publication because of Soviet censorship). Along with *Tretia rota*, published only posthumously in 1988, Odesa features in the poem "Розстріляне безсмертя" (Executed immortality), which was finished in 1960 but also remained unpublished until 1988. This lengthy poem starts with an attempt to reconstruct yet another text, the poem "Makhno" (about the Ukrainian anarchist leader and head of an insurrectionary army in 1917–20), which Sosiura probably completed in the late 1920s but which was confiscated by the Soviet Secret Police (GPU) and was never returned to the author. Unable to recollect the original text of "Makhno," in "Executed Immortality," Sosiura first tries to reconstruct the events of the Russian Civil War (such as the massacre of one of the Makhno units by the Petliuran regiments) before addressing his friends and fellow writers, to whom he had presented or declaimed his unpublished poem back in the 1920s.

---

34 Ibid., 408.
35 See, for example, Volodymyr Sosiura, *Vybrani poezii* (Kyiv: Radians'kyi pys'mennyk, 1975), 251.

Most of these friends succumbed to Stalinist purges, were executed, assassinated, or perished in prisons and labor camps; the poem thus turns into a seemingly endless catalogue of deceased writers whose names had been obliterated from the annals of Soviet literature and who would later enter Ukrainian literary history under the collective designation of the "Executed Renaissance" (Розстріляне Відродження). Sosiura's objective of recalling the names of the deceased writers and thus securing their posthumous existence in a literary text explains the somewhat paradoxical title of the poem—"Executed Immortality." This lofty goal required an appropriate format and narrative style; therefore, the majority of the stanzas strike an uplifting tone, balancing eulogy and martyrology. This model is disrupted several times, however, most notably in those episodes taking place in Odesa:

> Як жалко Бабеля! Я з ним
> іще в Одесі був знайомий
> в двадцятім році, молодим.
> Йому "Махна" в двадцять четвертім
> (я був тоді таким упертим!.)
> читав. Одсовувавсь од мене
> він, а у вікна – день, блакить . . .
> проказуючи: "Буде бить . . ."
> Як серце билося шалене!
> О ні, мій Бабелю, не я!
> Не я, не я, не я, не я!
> Не буду бить, не бив я зроду
> синів єврейського народу . . .[36]

(How sorry I feel for Babel! / I got acquainted with him / in Odesa, back in 1920, / when I was young. / I read him "Makhno" in twenty-four / (I was so stubborn then!) / He started moving away from me [to the window], / and by the window's—daylight and blue [skies] . . . / saying: "He's up for a fight . . ." / My heart was beating madly! / Oh no, my [dear] Babel, not me! / Not me, not me, not me, not me! / I will not hit [you], I never raised my hand / against the sons of the Jewish people . . .)

---

36 Volodymyr Sosiura, "Rozstriliane bezsmertia," in *Vybrani tvory v dvokh tomakh*, 2:207.

The reference to Isaak Babel's execution fits into the elegiac tone of the poem, but once Odesa is mentioned, the setting suddenly changes and, instead of the expected elegy, the reader is confronted with an anecdote about Babel's misunderstanding (either real or feigned) of young Sosiura's intentions in reciting lines about Makhno, whose soldiers raped and murdered Jews in the civil war.

The second Odesan episode that appears in the poem is a love affair, albeit an abortive one. During his stay in Odesa, Sosiura fell in love with Natalia Zabila (who would later become a leading author of Ukrainian children's literature) and, in line with the tension between love and death, invited her for a romantic date at night in a cemetery. However, Zabila (who was a married woman) arrived in the company of her friend and colleague Mariia Pryhara, who helped brush off the unlucky admirer:

> Наталю! Чи ж забула ти
> той тихий цвинтар і хрести,
> що поруч університету,
> де "гарбуза" дала поету,
> закоханому в тебе, ти? [. . .]
> Та, може, й краще так. Так треба.
> Бо я поет, ти – поетеса,
> з тобою нас сварила б преса.
> Сварились ми б і ночі й дні,
> тобі я б заздрив, ти – мені.
> Пригара. Літо. Ніч. Одеса.[37]

(Natalia! Did you forget / That quiet cemetery with crosses, / Near the university, / Where you rejected a poet [lit., gave a "pumpkin" to a poet], / Who was in love with you? . . . / But perhaps that was for the better. That was how it should be. / Because I am a poet, and you are a poetess, / The press would have torn us apart. / We would have quarreled night and day. / I would have envied you, and you would have envied me. / Pryhara. Summer. Night. Odesa.)

Let's not forget that "Executed Immortality" is, first and foremost, a text dedicated to his late friends and colleagues, but it is also an appeal against the

---

37 Ibid., 2:230.

persecution of artists and for creative freedom. The references to Odesa function as lyrical or humoristic intermezzos in an otherwise serious poetic testament of an aging writer.

Interrupted experiment: Iurii Ianovs'kyi's cinematographic prose

The construction of an urban text within Ukrainian modernist writing reached its climax in the experimental prose of the 1920s, at which time Odesa features prominently in the novel *Майстер корабля* (The shipmaster, 1928) by Iurii Ianovs'kyi. This novel may be defined as a fictionalized memoir, a skillful combination of autobiographical and fictitious, sometimes utterly fantastic, elements.

The first and last chapters of the novel frame the entire text and are set in the imagined future of the 1970s, while the bulk of the story takes place fifty years earlier, in the 1920s. The opening passages present the aging narrator To-Ma-Ki watching home movies, transmitted via radio waves from the National Film Archive to his television set. The narrator's exotic name, which sounds both oriental and futuristic, is derived from the first syllables of his honorary title, "Товариш Майстер Кіно" or Comrade Master of Cinema. The cryptic names of other characters thinly veil the identities of some leading 1920s Ukrainian artists and writers. Apart from Ianovs'kyi's alter ego, To-Ma-Ki, the two other protagonists are Sev, a film director, whose character is based on Oleksandr Dovzhenko, and the dancer, Taiakh, whose prototype was the actress and ballerina Ida Penzo. In a pas de trois between friendship and a love triangle, their relations provide the narrative background for an otherwise nonlinear, plotless novel, exhibiting a collage of heterogeneous elements, including personal letters from characters to the narrator, a ship's log, a painting, a ballet performance, and a circus act.

Similar to their real-life prototypes, this trio of protagonists is preoccupied with film production at a local movie studio resembling the Odesan premises of the All-Ukrainian Photo and Cinema Administration (VUFKU). In the 1920s, VUFKU developed into a magnet for Ukrainian futurists. The new artistic medium of cinema attracted the vanguard of Ukrainian art and literary production, including the writers Mykhail' Semenko, Nik Bazhan, Maik Iohansen, Geo Shkurupii, and the theater directors Les' Kurbas and Favst Lopatyns'kyi. In 1925, Mykhail' Semenko, the unofficial leader of Ukrainian futurists and then editor-in-chief of the Scenario Department at VUFKU studios, invited the writer Ianovs'kyi to work as an editor.[38] Within two years at VUFKU, Ianovs'kyi had himself risen to the position of editor-in-chief and was responsible for writing movie scripts, composing intertitles, and overseeing film production.

The Shipmaster, written soon after Ianovs'kyi's residence in Odesa, provides a vivid example of cinematographic techniques applied to a literary text. The use of different grammatical tenses marks the shifts between the events witnessed by To-Ma-Ki (which are narrated in the historic present) and those retrospective stories told by other characters (usually rendered in the past tense), whereas the nominal sentences without verbal predicates simulate a camera-eye perspective, creating the striking effect of immediate narration, thus surpassing the past-ness and distancing of traditional autobiographical fiction.[39] For instance, To-Ma-Ki's first meeting with Taiakh is narrated as follows:

> Тайах танцює в захваті. . . . Одіж на ній лиш підкреслює довершеність жіночих форм, її обличчя бліде навіть крізь пудру. . . . Я виходжу на вулицю й іду. "Оце вже вона. Тепер мені не викрутитись." Я констатую, що й викручуватись мені не дуже хочеться. Підходжу до пам'ятника, звідки видно огні порту й море.[40]
>
> (Taiakh is dancing ecstatically. . . . The clothes only emphasize the perfection of the female form; her face is pale (which one can see) even through the powder. . . . I go outside and walk away. "That's her. Now I can't get out." I recognize that I don't really want to get out. I approach the monument, from where you can see the lights of the port and the sea.)

Although cinema has a strong impact on the narrative techniques applied here, *The Shipmaster* goes beyond the simple imitation of cinematic aesthetics. In constructing his memoir/novel, Ianovs'kyi unites two seemingly incompatible sides of cinema production, the depiction of real life and the artistic transformation of factual material. In lengthy metafictional comments, the narrator justifies the artistic editing of life and the modification of factually filmed material

---

38 Oleh S. Ilnytzkyj, *Ukrainian Futurism, 1914–1930* (Cambridge, MA: Harvard University Press, 1997), 103–04.

39 Anna Chukur, "Film Aesthetic in the Ukrainian Novel of the 1920s: The Novel as Experiment" (PhD diss., University of Toronto, 2016), 84–88, http://hdl.handle.net/1807/92672/.

40 Iurii Ianovs'kyi, *Maister korablia* (Kharkov: Knyhospilka, 1928), 17.

through montage. Typically for the novel's outspokenly self-reflexive character, the outcome of this metafictional discussion is manifested in practice when Sev and To-Ma-Ki are planning to make a film about an uprising on a ship, as told to them by a seafarer named Bohdan, who claims to be the only survivor after the rebel ship was gunned down by a Turkish cruiser. Nonetheless, Sev decides to add his own invented narrative to embellish Bohdan's story:

> Мені потрібний цей епізод у трюмі, і я його хочу розповісти вам так, як я його роблю. Богдан про нього не розповідав, але я беру не так, як було, а так, як могло бути. Ви слухаєте?[41]

> (I need this episode in the hold, so I'd like to explain to you how I'm producing it. Bohdan didn't recount it, but I'm presenting it not how it happened, but how it could have happened. Are you listening?)

Sev instructs the cameraman shooting this newsreel to film the arrival of the Turkish cruiser *Ismet* at the Odesa seaport and plans to use the shots of the cruiser greeting the Soviet delegation with cannon shots for an utterly different purpose. Through a process of montage, he intends to present the Turkish cruiser as attacking Bohdan's ship, a sequence contrary to the true intention of the cruiser's amicable visit, thus completely reversing the message of the newsreel by portraying friend as foe.[42] More importantly, blending facts with fiction occurs on yet another level, as the arrival of the Turkish delegation refers to a well-known historical episode—the meeting between the Turkish foreign minister and the Soviet Commissar for Foreign Affairs, which took place in Odesa in November 1926. The specific notion of poetic truth and the overall interest in the constructivity of a work of art (which goes back to Shklovsky and Russian formalism) prevail over facts and easily outweigh history, ideology, and politics alike.

Ianovs'kyi's ambivalent attitude towards ideology may be illustrated by the references in the opening chapter of the novel to a film masterpiece *The Birth of the Internation* [a title with a neologism—"інтернація"—that sounds strange even in the original Ukrainian] and its director, Semper Travytsia. It is possible to decipher the relationship of the names of the fictional director and film to a real work of art: with regard to the former, the combination of the Latin word

---

41 Ibid., 178.
42 Chukur, "Film Aesthetic," 113.

"semper" with the Ukrainian word "travytsia" (grass) may be translated as evergreen, whereas the movie title refers to an evergreen film, *The Birth of a Nation* (1915) by D. W. Griffith. A landmark in film history and by far the most complex movie made up to that date, *The Birth of a Nation* is also an undisguised homage to the Ku Klux Klan and a hymn to racial intolerance. By slightly altering the title of the film (from "nation" to "internation"), the narrator of *The Shipmaster* does not try to diminish the controversial character of the movie nor to make it compatible with the Soviet idea of internationalism. He rather emphasizes that the plot of the movie is less important than the techniques and methods used by the director. In other words, the question: "How was this film made?" appears far more important than the question: "What is the film about?"

With the same creative vigor, *The Shipmaster* aims at constructing a new understanding of Ukrainian culture. The topography of this novel features "the City" (recognizable as Odesa) and "the Republic" (recognizable as Soviet Ukraine) as being the starting points for journeys towards exotic lands. Setting the story in a port city enables Ianovs'kyi to redefine the spatial horizons of Ukrainian literature, to surpass the ethnic limits of Ukrainian culture, and, ultimately, to gain access to a broader European heritage. Whereas the epigraphs, quoted in their original Russian, German, English, and Latin, place the novel within the European literary tradition, the text itself expands the Western canon with stories of travels to East Asia, Oceania, and South America, and references to Oriental cultures or the use of Malay and Javanese vocabulary. Departing from the shores of the four imperial languages (and, by extension, from the port of the former imperial city), the novel literally goes overseas in order to articulate a sense of a world culture, which incorporates all of humanity's cultural output and which therefore can be described as cosmopolitan.

In the 1920s, neoromantic, nautical adventure fiction becomes prominent in Russian literature, too, most notably in the works of Aleksandr Grin (for example, *Scarlet Sails*, 1923; *She Who Runs on the Waves*, 1928) and later in the texts of Konstantin Paustovsky and Valentin Kataev. However, Ianovs'kyi's novel, while sharing some stylistic similarities with the prose of his Russian contemporaries (for instance, the maritime theme, exaggerated symbolism, paradoxical metaphors, etc.), also differs both from Paustovsky's or Kataev's realism as well as from Grin's fantastic universe. Instead, Ianovs'kyi offers a roman à clef, where real people and real places are overlaid with futuristic or romantic elements. While Grin situates his alternative, maritime culture in a fairyland (often referred to as Grinlandia by fans) and strips it of any Russianness, the narrator of *The Shipmaster* is very clear about his ambition to create a new national culture for his Ukraine of the future. Thus, the novel saturates the traditional Ukrainian "culture of the steppe-dwellers" with maritime exoticism and the multicultural atmosphere of the Black Sea metropolis, effectively turning Odesa into a mediator between tradition (epitomized by the steppe) and radical innovation (represented by the sea). In his insightful review of the novel, Valer'ian Pidmohyln'yi interprets this spatial model as a departure from the literary practices of older generations:

> . . . дивно стає, що нація, яка століттями сиділа коло моря, яка пускалась навіть у одчайдушні морські походи, так довго не помічала його в своїй літературі, заворожена чорною, нерухомою землею своїх степів! І здається цілком закономірним, що тепер, підводячи нарешті втуплений у землю погляд, література наша зареагувала на море якраз романтично – воно, таке близьке й безпосередньо корисне, від раптового знайдення стало трохи ірреальне, бо не відчуте воно ще, не оповане й не здобуте в нашій творчості, бо вражає своєю новиною, непережитою знадою далеких обріїв.[43]

> (. . . one cannot but marvel that a nation that sat by the sea for centuries, and which even set off on daring sea expeditions, did not notice it in its literature for such a long time, fascinated as it was with the black, motionless soil of its steppes! And it seems perfectly natural that now, finally raising its gaze, which was fixed on the ground, our literature has responded to the sea precisely in a romantic way—being so close and directly useful, [the sea] became slightly unreal from this sudden discovery because it is not yet sensed, nor mastered, nor conquered in our literature and because it dazzles with its novelty and the unexperienced temptation of distant horizons.)

The work of Pidmohyln'yi, whose Kyiv-based novel *Misto* (The city, 1928) set the benchmark for the new Ukrainian urban prose, exemplifies the desire of an entire generation of writers to change the beaten track of Ukrainian literature— an ambitious project that abruptly was cut short. A victim of Stalinist terror, Pidmohyln'yi headed a seemingly endless list of Ukrainian literati who did not survive the 1930s. Many of them (including Semenko, Iohansen, Kurbas, and

---

43 Quoted in Chukur, "Film Aesthetic," 76.

Shkurupii) were in one way or another attached to Odesa, in general, and to the Odesan VUFKU, in particular.

Against this background, the narrative setting of *The Shipmaster* acquires a tragic, if not prophetic, significance. Imagining himself fifty years later seems a rather unusual choice of perspective for a young author, who was just twenty-six years old when he wrote *The Shipmaster*. The novel's exaggerated optimism and futurist aesthetics barely camouflage the sentimental tone of farewell to both Odesa and the cinema, a theme which Ianovs'kyi would reiterate in his essay collection Голівуд на березі Чорного моря (Hollywood on the Black Sea shore, 1929–30). To be sure, the protagonists of his novel, or rather their real-life prototypes, survived the Stalinist purges, but each of them would pay the price: Ida Penzo spent several years of her life in the Gulag and never returned to the stage; Oleksandr Dovzhenko's impressive career reached its peak in 1930, when his masterpiece, the silent movie *Earth*, was suddenly banned by Soviet authorities; and, finally, Iurii Ianovs'kyi by the early 1930s was routinely accused of nationalism by Soviet literary critics and gradually forced himself into a Procrustean bed of socialist realism.

Final remarks

The Shipmaster manifests an interrupted attempt to challenge both the imperial/colonial legacy of Ukraine and the ethnic rootedness of Ukrainian cultural tradition, but it also illustrates the efforts made to redefine Ukraine in regional and global terms. What remains of this interrupted experiment is a model envisaging Ukraine as a part of Europe and the world, with cities like Odesa being conceptualized as crossroads of artistic trends, and cultural developments. Coupled with an idea of Ukraine's emancipation from Russian cultural and political dominance, this aestheticized model is, in its own way, both national and cosmopolitan, as it painstakingly highlights a universal background of national particularity. Furthermore, this model provides a viable opposition to Soviet and, more recently, to Russian neo-imperial appropriation of Odesa. One thinks here of Ivan Kozlenko's novel *Tanger* (2017), where a literary variation on the relationships between Iurii Ianovs'kyi and Oleksandr Dovzhenko deliberately challenges the imperial myth of Odesa as a Russian city.

Although the literary production of the 1920s remains central for the development and consolidation of the Odesa text of Ukrainian literature, the roots of this city text obviously go back to the nineteenth century, where Odesa functions as an epitome of exoticism (for example in Lesia Ukraiinka's poetic travelogue) or as a scene of ideological and national contestations (as in Nechui's realist novel). Capitalizing on these earlier literary works, the modernist urban text emphasizes Odesa's liminality by creating a story of a young Ukrainian newcomer in the southern port city. His encounters in his new surroundings fluctuate between opportunities and temptations, chances and threats, and include a love story or rather the constant tension between love and death (often amplified with motifs of criminality or eroticism). Finally, the protagonist leaves Odesa in order to pursue a career in one of the cultural capitals of Soviet Ukraine (Kharkiv or Kyiv). From this point on, Odesa functions in the story as a site of nostalgic memory (for instance, in the works of Sosiura) or as a point of imagined return.

The underlying notions of mobility and place provide Odesa with a strong sense of translocality, thus constructing an image of a spatial entity, which programmatically transcends boundaries, including those of a national culture, but which also evades the ethnic hierarchies of an imperial metropolis. From this perspective, it may be argued that Ukrainian modernist literature constructs Odesa first and foremost as a cosmopolitan space. While reclaiming Odesa's Ukrainian element, this literature also offers an alternative, pluralistic image of a space of intellectual and artistic freedom, a site of opportunities for newcomers, where tradition meets innovation and where the steppe meets the sea.

CHAPTER 10

The Ukrainization of Odes(s)a? On the Languages of Odesa and Their Use

Abel Polese

There [in Odesa] the Russian jostles a Turk, a Frenchman, an Arab, an Englishman, an Armenian, an Italian, a Bulgarian or Wallachian, a Pole, a Circassian, a Hungarian, a Persian or Bokharan

—Daniel Wegelin.[1]

Introduction: Is it possible to de-politicize language?

At a Ukrainian studies conference in 2014, a Ukrainian scholar based in Kyiv, in a naive attempt to give me some feedback after my intervention about Odesa, came up to me and said: "I could feel that they kind of brainwashed you out there, convincing you that in Odesa people do not speak Ukrainian." I long reflected about this exchange and why I felt so uncomfortable after it. I was annoyed by the association of language usage with a political position, which was not necessarily the case here and was very far from the scope of my paper. The association was understandable, though, given that the conference took place a few months after Putin's annexation of Crimea. Moreover, every and any issue, and especially the language issue, can be politicized. This is what ethnic entrepreneurs are looking for in order to attain consensus.[2] What I love about academia, however, is that

---

1   Quoted in Patricia Herlihy, *Odessa Recollected: The Port and the People* (Boston: Academic Studies Press, 2019), 117.
2   David Horowitz, *Ethnic Groups in Conflict* (Berkeley: University of California Press, 1986).

one can take a step back and reflect on things beyond their political meaning. After all, my interest at that time, and in this chapter, was not which language should be spoken in a particular Ukrainian city, but what happens at the everyday level when, in a multilingual city in the twenty-first century, people are requested to suddenly change their language usage habits. This question is all the more important due to the cosmopolitan nature of Odesa. As elaborated in the introduction to this volume, we are not talking here of a city featuring some mere Russian versus Ukrainian cultural competition. We are talking of a place in which histories and cultures have always overlapped.[3] This is why Guido Hausmann in his chapter discusses the term "translocality" as an attempt to move away from a Eurocentric view and refer to a "multiethnic constellation" with the goal of evading the Eurocentric connotations of cosmopolitanism.[4] From this angle, it becomes possible to look at Odesa as a "space," here interpreted as folded into social relations through everyday practices, paving the way to an idea of space as undergoing continual construction as a result of the agency of things encountering each other in more or less organized circulations.[5]

The way Odesans inhabited multiethnic spaces in mixed neighborhoods. These were environments where everyday experience leads to mutual recognition, feelings of solidarity with strangers and members of other local groups did not necessarily denote mobile elites and a large spatial framework—as the Kantian understanding of cosmopolitanism implies—making possible the relative freedom of Odesa's cosmopolitan spaces.[6] Accordingly, the notion of cosmopolitanism allows us to refer to a reality that is well beyond the dichotomy between Russian and Ukrainian cultures, identities, and nations. The choice of a language is not always or necessarily political, then; but it may be interpreted in the framework of the tense relationship between continuity and change.[7] For several reasons, throughout Ukraine's post-Soviet independence, Odesa was a city where the majority of its inhabitants tended to use Russian for daily communication. This, in spite of the myriad of languages spoken in its courtyards,

---

3   Patricia Herlihy, *Odessa: A History, 1794–1914* (Cambridge, MA: Harvard University Press, 1986); Patricia Herlihy, "How Ukrainian is Odessa? From Odessa to Odesa," in *Odessa Recollected: The Port and the People* (Boston: Academic Studies Press, 2018), 74–82.
4   Ulrike Freitag and Achim von Oppen, "Translocality: An Approach to Connection and Transfer in Area Studies," in *Translocality: The Study of Globalising Processes from a Southern Perspective*, ed. Ulrike Freitag and Achim von Oppen (Leiden: Brill, 2010), 3.
5   Henri Lefebvre, *The Production of Space* (Cambridge, MA: Blackwell, 1991), 32. See also David Harvey, *Justice, Nature and the Geography of Difference* (Oxford: Basil Blackwell, 1996).
6   See introduction to this volume, 00–00.
7   James March, "Continuity and Change in Theories of Organizational Action," *Administrative Science Quarterly* 41, no. 2 (1996), 278–87.

where, for example, Jewish, Russian, Bulgarian, and Armenian religious or cultural events were celebrated. In short, the city's inhabitants exchanged cultural information and learned words in numerous languages from diverse traditions and cultures.

In the early 1990s, the rebuilding of the Ukrainian nation was framed as a kind of "internationalist cosmopolitanism" that had endorsed Russian as a language of communication during the nineteenth and throughout the twentieth century. The Ukrainian language was then chosen as an integral component of national identity construction. The message of the 1996 constitution, as well as subsequent legislation, was clear: "the native language of Ukrainians is Ukrainian"—at least in theory. Two questions follow from this, however: What happens when someone is expected to show their loyalty to a national project by supporting the use of a language that few people have used so far in certain contexts and cities? To what extent are individuals willing to change their language practices and behavioral patterns??

Odesa is administratively in Ukraine (in spite of the current attempts by the Kremlin to annex the east of the country at the time of writing), accordingly my experience is that people unfamiliar with the region frequently say that "Odesa is in Ukraine, so people speak Ukrainian." Yet those I have met who are more aware of the complex story of the country often assume that Russian is widely spoken or ask about the relationship between Russian and Ukrainian language usage in the city. This is an important point in my claim for scientific validity for this chapter beyond its historical moment. The language(s) of Odesa have constantly changed since its inception. French and Italian were widely spoken in the nineteenth century, but so too were Greek, Romanian, Gagauz, Yiddish, and Ukrainian; and, of course, Russian was the official language of the city under both tsarist and Soviet rule. After Ukrainian independence in 1991, the city remained multilingual with Ukrainian gradually gaining importance as an administrative language and therefore the language of instruction in the education system. The language of the everyday remained Russian, however, although language choice has been affected by subsequent political events.

The 2004 Orange Revolution saw many individuals deliberately deciding to use Ukrainian for their daily life for ideological reasons.[8] Odesa was possibly less affected than other cities, but the Kremlin's 2014 annexation of Crimea, and even more so the Russian army's invasion of Ukraine in February 2022

---

8   Abel Polese, "Une version alternative de la «révolution orange»: Transformations identitaires et 'nation building spontané,'" *Socio-logos* 4 (2009), https://journals.openedition.org/socio-logos/2315.

transformed the use of Ukrainian from a practical question to a political statement. For one thing, I observed day by day an increased use of Ukrainian in social media by friends and colleagues whom I knew to be Russian speakers (in the sense that they used to prefer Russian for everyday communication). However, what has been put in simplistic terms as the Russian-Ukrainian divide is for Odesa far more complex. True, switching to Ukrainian may be regarded as a way to identify with the Ukrainian state. Continuing to use Russian, however, does not automatically mean a pro-Russia position, and questioning this assumption was at the core of my conference presentation and remains so in this chapter. Beyond political statements, what happens when the language your state demands that you speak is not the one you want to speak or habitually use in your daily life? Many factors will influence the synergy between the way you're supposed to behave and the way you end up behaving.

This chapter's dual goal lies at the intersection of Odesa's multilingual settings and the language question. Empirically, it documents a part of a transition from Russian to Ukrainian in the 2000s in some spheres of the city's public life and the latent tensions that emerged. This is not an isolated issue. A large variety of citizens of the former USSR underwent similar experiences when the city in which they were living adopted another language; it sometimes led, to a sense of alienation from the very place where they had grown up.[9] This chapter seeks to both enter into a dialogue with the rest of the chapters in this volume by engaging with modes of constructing cosmopolitanism and to examine a question that arose in almost all post-Soviet capitals and possibly elsewhere: What is the outcome of competition between two or more languages in a single space?

When you are requested, or at least expected, to use a language that you consider secondary or non-preferred for a certain kind of communication,[10] or you simply do not have a preference at all, you have three options: adapt, reject, or tacitly reject—that is, officially accept the new rules but engage in what Kotkin calls a "tactic of the habitat"[11] to avoid complying with the rule. This can also be related to Scott's concept of everyday resistance that is somehow "invisible," silent, or performed discretely so as not to challenge the symbolic

---

9 David Laitin, *Identity in Formation: The Russian-Speaking Populations in the New Abroad* (Ithaca, NY: Cornell University Press, 1998).
10 Dominique Arel, "Language Politics in Independent Ukraine: Towards One or Two State Languages?" *Nationalities Papers* 23, no. 3 (1995): 597–622.
11 Stephen Kotkin, *Magnetic Mountain Stalinism as a Civilization* (Los Angeles: University of California Press, 1997).

power of the state;[12] it may occur through the creation of a constant "state of exception,"[13] something that happens "only here, only now, only once." In our case, this happens when an Odesan decides, in a situation where they would be requested to speak Ukrainian, to use Russian rather than Ukrainian. But when such a situation repeats itself throughout days and months, it becomes the norm. This informal and allegedly exceptional use of Russian in the everyday operates on two distinct levels: the individual, which may be dictated by mere convenience or personal preferences, and the political, which may eventually result from the synergy of originally nonpolitical actions. We may regard resistance as something visible and consisting of strong and assertive actions performed by a multitude of individuals, but it is also informal, invisible, silent, and situational.[14] It may consist of apparently insignificant actions performed, sometimes unconsciously, by thousands of individuals on a regular basis.[15] The study of the everyday[16] can help us single out actions that are performed only "here and now" and widen the range of actors that need to be taken into account for the construction of the political.[17]

In the region of the former Soviet Union, attention to the everyday has led to identifying the deployment of several "tactics of the habitat,"[18] including "avoidance" and "bricolage," to renegotiate the individual's relationship with the state.[19] As a result, the everyday served to identify and explain negotiations and possible contradictions between state intentions and results[20] or between

---

12 Sarah Murru and Abel Polese, eds., *Resistances: Between Theories and the Field* (New York: Rowman & Littlefield Publishers, 2020).
13 Giorgio Agamben, *State of Exception*, trans. Kevin Attell (Chicago: University of Chicago Press, 2003).
14 James C. Scott, *Weapons of the Weak: Everyday Forms of Peasant Resistance* (New Haven: Yale University Press, 1985).
15 Scott, *Two Cheers for Anarchism: Six Easy Pieces on Autonomy, Dignity, and Meaningful Work and Play* (Princeton: Princeton University Press, 2012).
16 Michael Skey, "The National in Everyday Life: A Critical Engagement with Michael Billig's Thesis of Banal Nationalism," *Sociological Review* 57, no. 2 (2009): 331–46; Tim Edensor, "Reconsidering National Temporalities," *European Journal of Social Theory* 9, no. 4 (2006): 525–45; Tim Edensor, *National Identity, Popular Culture and Everyday Life, National Identity, Popular Culture and Everyday Life* (London and New York: Routledge, 2020).
17 Yael Navaro-Yashin, *Faces of the State: Secularism and Public Life in Turkey* (Princeton: Princeton University Press, 2002).
18 Kotkin, *Magnetic Mountain Stalinism*.
19 Timothy Johnston, *Being Soviet: Identity, Rumour, and Everyday Life under Stalin 1939–1953* (Oxford: Oxford University Press, 2011).
20 Abel Polese, "The Formal and the Informal: Exploring 'Ukrainian' Education in Ukraine, Scenes from Odessa," *Comparative Education*, 46 (2010): 47–62.

official state narratives and the way ordinary citizens ended up living them.[21] The everyday applied to Odesa can be regarded as a mode of resistance that includes visible and invisible actions, often performed individually and without coordination. Yet, they are reproduced by a significant number of individuals, thus eventually affecting the dynamics and mechanisms of the society in which these actions are embedded.[22] We can refer here to the broad gray zone between unorganized resistance, individually conceived and carried out by members of a community—or citizens—with little awareness of—or even interest in— similar actions and the gathering of a substantial amount of members of an individual (social or political) movement that challenges, nationally or transnationally, a decision made by the authorities.[23] This approach, which has been used in the past for the study of national identity, looks at the "banal" elements that nonetheless become part of the cultural load of citizens when they eventually construct their linguistic and ethnic identity.[24]

Methodological approaches to the study of everyday cosmopolitanism

What made Odesa a more interesting case to me than Ukraine's eastern regions, where Russian was also widely spoken, was its history, its essence as a contradictory site of multiple cosmopolitanism that slowly transformed and shaped its merchant class until the October Revolution and continued as socialist cosmopolitanism, or what Humphrey and Skvirskaya describe as cosmopolitan heritage

---

21 Emilia Pawłusz and Oleksandra Seliverstova, "Everyday Nation-Building in the Post-Soviet Space. Methodological Reflections," *Studies of Transition States and Societies* 8, no. 1 (2016): 69–86; Rico Isaacs and Abel Polese, "(Re)Imagining or Imagined Nation-Building? Nation-Building and Identity in the Post-Soviet Space: New Tools and Approaches," in Rico Isaacs and Abel Polese, *Nation-Building and Identity in the Post-Soviet Space: New Tools an Approaches* (New York: Routledge, 2016), 1–23; Polese et al., "Conclusion: When Post-Socialism Meets the Everyday," in *Informal Nationalism after Communism: The Everyday Construction of Post-Socialist Identities*, edited by Polese et al. (London: Tauris, 2018), 183–87.
22 Polese et al., "Negotiating Spaces and the Public–Private Boundary: Language Policies Versus Language Use Practices in Odessa," *Space and Culture* 22, no. 3 (2019): 263–79.
23 Abel Polese, Lela Rekhviashvili, and Jeremy Morris (2016) "Informal Governance in Urban Spaces: Power, Negotiation and Resistance among Georgian Street Vendors," *Geography Research Forum* 36, no. 2 (2016): 15–32.
24 Thomas Hylland Eriksen, "Formal and Informal Nationalism," *Ethnic and Racial Studies* 16, no. 1 (1993): 1–25; Polese et al., *Identity and Nation Building in Everyday Post-Socialist Life* (London and New York: Routledge, 2019); Jon E. Fox, "The Edges of the Nation: A Research Agenda for Uncovering the Taken-for-Granted Foundations of Everyday Nationhood," *Nations and Nationalism* 23, no. 1 (2017): 26–47.

in the Soviet Union.[25] However, this can also be understood as the pragmatic cosmopolitanism of daily life in which diverse social groups get along under dire economic circumstances.[26] Odesa was the city I came to know; it was the city I had fallen in love with during my first year with the Civic Education Project and then during my PhD research. As a popular song goes, "Odesa is not a city but a fiancée." It was the city I explored, courtyard by courtyard, during endless walks. It was the city I came to love even more when I learned about its past through Patricia Herlihy's densely researched articles and books.[27] This tiny settlement, founded by the Russians at Hadzhibey in 1794, became a commercial metropolis in about half a century and its population increased by 259% between 1811 and 1861. By 1914, it had 630,000 inhabitants, most of whom were migrants from all over the world. Indeed, according to the 1897 census, Odesa was host to people from fifty-five language groups and from more than thirty countries, including the US, China, and Japan.[28] Odesans spoke many languages. Already in the nineteenth century, and ignoring the Ukrainian and Jewish populations, Kohl wrote: "In the streets [of Odesa] one can hear Russian, English, Italian, German, Tartar, Polish, Turkish, Greek, Armenian, Moldovan, Bulgarian, Hungarian, Dalmatian, French, Swedish, Spanish, and these languages are not spoken by foreigners but by the regular inhabitants of the city."[29]

During my doctoral work, Odesans continued to speak many languages. Russian was a sort of lingua franca for communication, but one could hear anything else from Gagauzian to Romanian or Bulgarian, Greek and German and, of course, Ukrainian. When these speakers converged on the city and interacted, they usually used Russian; but by no means does this imply that Odesa speaks only Russian. In each Ukrainian city, or even micro-environment, there's a sort of peer pressure to use either Russian or Ukrainian. If Odesa is a Russian-language city primarily, Odesans also speak Ukrainian and everything else, including German and Korean—languages that are supported through international grants seeking to give ethnic populations the chance to "maintain their language."

---

25 Caroline Humphrey, "Odessa: Pogroms in a Cosmopolitan City," in *Post-Cosmopolitan Cities: Explorations of Urban Coexistence*, ed. Caroline Humphrey and Vera Skvirskaja (New York: Berhahn, 2012), 17–64.
26 Vera Skvirskaja, "At the City's Social Margins: Selective Cosmopolitanism in Odessa," in Humphrey and Skvirskaja, *Post-Cosmopolitan Cities*, 94–112.
27 Herlihy, *Odessa: A History*; *Odessa Recollected*.
28 Patricia Herlihy, "Death in Odessa: A Study of Population Movements in a Nineteenth-Century City," in Herlihy, *Odessa Recollected*, 100–16.
29 Kohl, cited in Herlihy, *Odessa Recollected*, 17.

A big challenge thus emerges: How to capture this manifestation of cosmopolitanism? How to experience, and then convey to the reader, the unique diversity of an environment or of a family with a particular ethnicity? How to go beyond the Russian-Ukrainian dichotomy to explore the languages of the city and their use? And how to "blend into" these environments so that individuals will not feel forced to act in a certain manner and give the interviewer the response they think is expected? The resulting complex triangulation emerged out of trial and error, experiments that were informed by an attempt to live the city in all its intricacy. I spent a year as a visiting professor at Odesa National University prior to the research and it gave me a sufficient number of initial contacts. I was also lucky to meet, at a few Odesa-related conferences, some colleagues who would soon become friends and accompany me in this adventure. Through these contacts, I managed to get a position as a visiting professor at a small local university that offered a small salary (I had no scholarship or other source of income back then) and a one-room apartment in the administration building. Located in the historical Moldavanka area, the university is in walking distance of the center of the city; and the job introduced me to colleagues and students from whom I could get more contacts, as well as giving me access to an everyday environment that could provide data.

I spent the first months of my fieldwork building a solid network. I started with institutions at the margins of the language debate; after all, as Odesa is much more than a Russian-Ukrainian dichotomy, I thought it worthwhile to see how people who do not occupy one of these poles saw the use of language and identity. Liaising with, inter alia, Jewish, Korean, Bulgarian, Greek, and Gagauz communities, as well as Old Believers, was a way to explore various parallel worlds coexisting in the city. I created a second contact point by visiting schools. Sometimes I just dropped in and asked to talk to the principal; on other occasions, I was introduced by someone. A third contact point was created by attending a variety of events until I felt I had enough contacts to begin conducting in-depth interviews (forty-nine in total) with people with whom I forged trusting relations over several months. At the end of an interview, I would ask the interviewee to put me in touch with their parents and/or offspring so that I could gain the perspective of at least two generations and explore intergenerational changes of habits and attitudes. This process lasted around twelve months, during which time I also monitored the use of languages in public and private spaces and the occasions at which people would be expected, or willing, to use one language rather than another. I first interacted with the city in 2003; however, I continued my relationship with it by visiting until 2020. The year 2009 was the last time I conducted fieldwork in Odesa, which is also the reason why I prefer to concentrate on the dynamics of language use rather than engage in the more political (and politicized) Russia versus Ukraine debate.

The language of Ukraine and the languages of Odesa

The language (or languages) question in Ukraine has received a great deal of attention since Ukrainian independence.[30] Scholars have compared the different uses of, and attitudes towards, languages across various Ukrainian regions[31] and suggested that Russian will remain a major language for a long time.[32] The persistence of Russian is the result of the fractioned origins of the Ukrainian state, which came to encompass areas that had been subject to the rule of various entities and, consequently, hosted a multiplicity of languages (Polish, Romanian, Russian, Ukrainian, to mention but the main ones). The interrelationship of politics and language has been explored in terms of politics (both higher echelon and everyday),[33] the rewriting of history,[34] the politics of memory,[35] and the creation and discovery of national identity.[36] Some scholars have examined the transition of the political elite from a predominantly Russian-language environment to a gradually more Ukrainian one.[37] The understanding of language of preference starts from the politics of the everyday in looking at the attitude of different segments of the population and of regions towards language

---

30 Dominique Arel, "Interpreting 'Nationality' and 'Language' in the 2001 Ukrainian Census," *Post-Soviet Affairs* 18, no. 3 (2002): 213–49. Dominique Arel, "Language Politics in Independent Ukraine: Towards One or Two State Languages?" *Nationalities Papers* 23, no. 3 (1995): 597–622.; Taras Kuzio, "History, Memory and Nation Building in the Post-Soviet Colonial Space," *Nationalities Papers* 30, no. 2 (2002): 241–64.
31 Anna Fournier, "Mapping Identities: Russian Resistance to Linguistic Ukrainisation in Central and Eastern Ukraine," *Europe–Asia Studies* 54, no. 3 (2002): 415–33.
32 Paul S. Pirie, "National Identity and Politics in Southern and Eastern Ukraine," *Europe–Asia Studies* 48, no. 7 (1996): 1079–1104.
33 Jan Germen Janmaat, "The Ethnic 'Other' in Ukrainian History Textbooks: The Case of Russia and the Russians," *Compare* 37, no. 3 (2007): 307–24.
34 Katerzyna Wolczuk, "History, Europe and the 'National Idea': The 'Official' Narrative of National Identity in Ukraine," *Nationalities Papers* 28, no. 4 (2000): 671–94; Jan Germen Janmaat, "Ethnic and Civic Conceptions of the Nation in Ukraine's History Textbooks," *European Education* 37, no. 3 (2005): 20–37.
35 Tanya Richardson, *Kaleidoscopic Odessa: History and Place in Contemporary Ukraine* (Toronto: University of Toronto Press, 2008).
36 Taras Kuzio, "National Identity and History Writing in Ukraine," *Nationalities Papers* 34, no. 4 (2006): 407–27.
37 Dominique Arel, "How Ukraine Has Become More Ukrainian," *Post-Soviet Affairs* 34, no. 2–3 (2018): 186–189; Kuzio, "National Identity and History Writing in Ukraine."

use.[38] Some correlation has, then, been sought between language and political preferences,[39] as that information and manipulation of media can be influenced by the source (and thus language) employed. This has drawn considerable attention—there was particularly intense interest in the 1990s and 2000s—to the study of the ethno-linguistic composition of the country.[40] The coexistence of languages and cultures facilitated research on linguistics and language use which studied the environments and spaces where one language tended to prevail over another and the by no means unique phenomenon throughout Ukraine of *surzhyk*.[41] This pidgin language is a mix of Russian and Ukrainian that sometimes becomes a marker of identity in some areas of the country and that has been provocatively defined as "the real national language of Ukraine" in the incarnation of the Ukrainian popular figure Verka Serdiuchka, the drag persona of Ukrainian comedian and pop singer Andriy Danylko.[42] In terms of chronology, attempts to give more space and importance to Ukrainian in both the public and political life of the country are noteworthy. In line with Ukraine's implementation of its 1996 constitution, Russian was downgraded to the status of minority language and slowly phased out from various spheres of public life. From 1989 through 2001, the number of pre-schools and schools officially using Ukrainian as a means of instruction climbed from 51% and 49% up to 76% and 70% respectively. Elite schools, such as a lyceums and gymnasiums, as well as colleges which enable students to enrol in university without taking entrance exams, were targeted in an attempt to encourage present and future generations to use Ukrainian.[43] At least theoretically, Ukrainian schools were received textbooks before other schools and tax cuts were applied for the publication of books and textbooks in Ukrainian.[44]

---

38 Fournier, "Mapping Identities"; Fournier, "Patriotism, Order and Articulations of the Nation in Kyiv High Schools before and after the Orange Revolution," *Journal of Communist Studies and Transition Politics* 23, no. 1 (2007): 101–17.
39 Dominique Arel, "La face cachée de la Révolution orange: L'Ukraine et le déni de son problème régional," *Revue d'Etudes Comparatives Est-Ouest* 37, no. 4 (2006), https://doi.org/10.3406/receo.2006.1788.
40 Andrew Wilson, "Elements of a Theory of Ukrainian Ethno-National Identities," *Nations and Nationalism* 8, no. 1 (2002): 31–54.
41 Laada Bilaniuk, *Contested Tongues: Language Politics and Cultural Correction in Ukraine* (Ithaca, NY: Cornell University Press, 2006); Patrick Sériot, "Diglossie, Bilinguisme ou Mélange de Langues: Le Cas du Surżyk en Ukraine," *Linguistique* 41, no. 2 (2005): 37–52.
42 Joseph James Crescente, "Performing Post-Sovietness: Verka Serdiuchka and the Hybridization of Post-Soviet Identity in Ukraine," *Ab Imperio* no. 2 (2007): 405–30.
43 Nancy Popson, "The Ukrainian History Textbook: Introducing Children to the 'Ukrainian Nation,'" *Nationalities Papers* 29, no. 2 (2001): 325–50.
44 Stephen Shulman, "Ukrainian Nation-Building under Kuchma," *Problems of Post-Communism* 52, no. 5 (2005): 32–47.

Russian language and literature were phased out in Ukraine's state schools by 1997. Additionally, Ukrainization was promoted by trying to change attitudes towards the Ukrainian language by introducing school subjects such as "We, the citizens of Ukraine" and "Ukraine's European Choice." The term *ridna mova* (native language) was used to refer to Ukrainian, a move that signaled that the language would be the native tongue of all Ukrainians. The reaction of the population was mixed. On the one hand, some regions used language as an excuse to distance themselves from the capital; on the other, many Ukrainians adapted, believing that knowing Ukrainian could be an advantage in the job market for themselves or for their children.

Taken together, these measures indicate that, although coercive measures to expedite the use of Ukrainian were not really in place, the state message regarding the use of languages was strong and relatively clear. Ukrainian was the sole state language and the "native language" of the country's citizens. The message was not necessarily received in the case of Odesa, where it was possible to note a potential conflict between top-level forces, pushing for the Ukrainization of public spaces, and lower-level ones, with a significant number of citizens silently resisting and trying to adhere to Russian-language communication as much as possible.[45] Statistics reveal this only partially, as the census grouped the city with its oblast, which also hosts a number of Ukrainian villages. A glance at a historical comparison of language use (see table 3) and the ethnic composition of Odesa (see table 4) helps clarify the linguistic situation.

Table 3. Linguistic structure of Ukraine in historical comparison (by percentage)[46]

Linguistic groups	1991–1994	1995–1999	2000–2003
Ukrainian-speaking Ukrainians	41.2	46.3	45.4
Russian-speaking Ukrainians	32.6	28.2	30.9
Russian-speaking Russians	19.7	17.0	16.5
Other	6.5	8.5	7.2
Total	100	100	100

---

45 Polese, "Between 'Official' and 'Unofficial' Temperatures: Introducing a Complication to the Hot and Cold Ethnicity Theory from Odessa," *Journal of Multilingual and Multicultural Development* 35, no. 1 (2014): 59–75.

46 Valerii Khmelko, *Lingvo-etnichna struktura Ukrainy: Rehionalni osoblyvosti i tendentsii zmin za roky nezalezhnosti* [The linguistic and ethnic composition of Ukraine: Regional specificities and tendencies in the years of independence] (Kyiv: International Institute of Sociology, 2004), accessed January 1, 2023, http://ekmair.ukma.edu.ua/bitstream/handle/123456789/8098/Khmelko_Linhvo-etnichna_struktura_Ukrainy.pdf.

Table 4. Ethnic composition of Odesa in 1989 and 2001[47]

1989		2001		% speaking their national language
Ukrainians	(48.9%)	Ukrainians	(61.6%)	71.6%
Russians	(39.4%)	Russians	(29.0%)	97.0%
Bulgarians	(5.9%)	Bulgarians	(1.3%)	77.8%
Jews	(1.5%)	Jews	(1.2%)	3.6%

With regard to the relationship between language and identity, the census offers a further hint. More people classified as Ukrainians speak Russian than those classified as ethnic Russians who speak Ukrainian. Russians and Ukrainians are, however, not distributed homogeneously throughout the country, but each group is present in a stronger concentration in some areas of each oblast. Data for Odesa are available only as an aggregate of the city with the oblast, which is very diverse. At present, the methodology of the census has been under considerable scrutiny. Critical analysis of the results of national censuses suggested that the methodology adopted led to an increase in the figures of ethnic Ukrainians and Ukrainian speakers living in the country.[48] Even self-identification as Ukrainian or Ukrainian speaker was affected by possible ideological support for the Ukrainian state, according to some interpretations.[49]

Table 5. Language spoken by the two main national groups[50]

Ukrainians	85.2% (Ukrainian speakers)	14.8% (Russian speakers)	0
Russians	95.9% (Russian speakers)	3.9% (Ukrainian speakers)	0.2% (speak another language)

These data suggest a picture where Odesa and, in general, its region displayed some preferences for the use of Russian language but where Ukrainian is still present, spoken, and in general accepted.[51] Overall, ascertaining precisely how

---

47 Source: State Statistics Committee of Ukraine, *2001 All-Ukrainian Population Census*, accessed December 7, 2022, http://2001.ukrcensus.gov.ua/eng/.
48 Ihor Stebelsky, "Ethnic Self-Identification in Ukraine, 1989–2001: Why More Ukrainians and Fewer Russians?" *Canadian Slavonic Papers* 51, no. 1 (2009): 77–100.
49 Oxana Shevel, "Nationality in Ukraine: Some Rules of Engagement," *East European Politics and Societies: and Cultures* 16, no. 2 (2002), 2 (2002), https://doi.org/10.1177/0888832540201600203.
50 Source: *2001 All-Ukrainian Population Census*, http://2001.ukrcensus.gov.ua/eng/.
51 Polese and A. Wylegala, "Odessa and Lvov or Odesa and Lviv: How Important Is a Letter? Reflections on the "Other" in Two Ukrainian Cities," *Nationalities Papers* 36, no 5 (2008): 787–814.

many Russians or Russian speakers live in Odesa may be challenging. It is not, however, really a relevant question for a qualitative analysis based on the identification of dynamics, rather than figures. At this stage, it might be reasonable to formulate two hypotheses. First, the number of Russian speakers in the city is high enough to pose a question about the use of Ukrainian: if the state imposes Ukrainian as the language of communication, we can reasonably assume that a large majority of people will not really welcome this measure. Second, the peer-pressure language in Odesa is Russian. Each Ukrainian city has a primary and secondary language. In some, you would expect to hear mostly Ukrainian and would be surprised if you were addressed in Russian; in others, it is the opposite. The peer-pressure language could also be defined as the language that a bilingual Ukrainian citizen would choose to use to feel comfortable in a given city. Kyiv can be regarded as in between, and the use of Ukrainian has increased significantly year by year. In Odesa, one would expect Russian to be predominant in that a significant number of Ukrainian speakers would make an effort to speak Russian when addressing someone unknown. Ukrainian could still be used, but at the beginning of an official speech or meeting there might also be an opportunity to switch to Russian as soon as someone declared their inability to understand or work in Ukrainian.

London may be multicultural, but have you ever met a Gagauz out there?

In many respects, I found Odesa the ideal setting to study the tension between Ukrainization and the use of Russian, between what we should do and what we ultimately do. Whereas Ukraine's eastern regions are a hybrid space because of the number of ethnic Russians and Russian speakers who arrived as a result of Soviet massive relocation policies, Odesa was in between. The city's strong identity and long multiethnic history ensured that Odessans would go beyond the Russian-Ukrainian dichotomy; or, as popular wisdom put it, "my mother is Greek, my father is Russian, I am Odesan." My informants often recalled childhood scenes of mingling in the famous Odesa courtyards with children from other ethnic backgrounds. They celebrated Jewish, Bulgarian, and any other national holidays in addition to Soviet ones, heard words in other languages, and enjoyed an extremely open environment where switching and overlapping identities were almost the norm. A local ethnographer once claimed to know a "Bulgarian village" where about half of the population was ethnically Greek but classified as Bulgarian. In Soviet terms, he said, Russian would be the favorite nationality, but Slavic was still better than non-Slavic; Greeks, then, would declare themselves Bulgarian in the national census, just in case, to avoid any trouble that might arise because of their non-Slavic identity.

When the administrative director of the institute where I was teaching told me that "Odessa does not, and will not, speak Ukrainian," I did not interpret this as a political position. This meant, rather, "We've spoken Russian all our lives, why should we change that?" or even, "if everyone is speaking Russian in a place, I will not be the one sticking out by speaking Ukrainian." Yet, there were exceptions and Ukrainian or hybrid spaces. When official signs in streets, museums, and other public places were in need of replacement, they were replaced with Ukrainian or bilingual ones, eventually creating the odd situation where most Odesa streets had three names: the new one, often written both in Russian and Ukrainian, and the old one, often different, that people remembered from Soviet times.[52] During fieldwork, I witnessed a gradual but steady increase in the use of Ukrainian for official communication, at least at the beginning of an official speech. Officials would introduce themselves in Ukrainian and then switch to Russian, if the situation allowed it, or stick to Ukrainian. During an official opening in Kiliia (near the Romanian and Moldovan borders), the locals explicitly asked the rector of Odesa National University to switch to Russian because they were uncomfortable listening to Ukrainian. Russian continued to be the language of daily communication within the university when going for tea or even conducting internal business. But Ukrainian, or at least a hint of it, would be the starting point for official openings, especially for high-level officials. Another interviewee once said, half-joking, that he would use Ukrainian when he went to a city office for a document; after all, as no ordinary Odesan used Ukrainian in public offices, speaking the national language, in his view, would give civil servants the impression that he was someone important and thus possibly speed up things.

These phenomena explain why the city as a whole does not, perhaps, speak Ukrainian, but Odesans, taken individually, speak Ukrainian in principle. This was one of the things that most struck me during my fieldwork. It was as if knowledge of Ukrainian was the hidden treasure of the Odesans; they would display it only on particular occasions, such as when they rediscovered their Ukrainianness during a trip abroad or when something emotionally touching

---

52 Abel Polese, "Where Marx Meets Ekaterina (the Great): The Dichotomy between National and Plural Identities in Odessa," paper presented at the Annual Convention of the Association for the Study of Nationalities, New York, 2007.

happened.[53] Indeed, the Orange Revolution of 2004 was this kind of emotionally charged moment—and much changed. I have primarily documented this with regard to Kyiv, where some families and institutions switched from Russian to Ukrainian for their daily language almost overnight.[54] The change was not limited to Kyiv, however. The city that I knew before and after 2004 had undergone subtle, perhaps silent, but significant transformation. Ukrainian was not widely spoken, but the attitude towards the language had changed. I was particularly surprised when I saw some of my interviewees, whom I had known as Russian speakers, using Ukrainian in their daily lives and for social media posts. Another informant reported: "Yes, I am a Russian speaker but, you know, during the 2004 events, I would wake up and while washing dishes try to remember, and sing, the words of the Ukrainian national anthem."

In some respects, even more striking was the fact that, despite their daily use of Russian, some informants declared themselves fluent in Ukrainian. Some would confuse words or construct the sentence according to Russian grammar while using Ukrainian words, but they were somehow convinced that they spoke Ukrainian properly and routinely.[55] Some went as far as to state that they spoke Ukrainian better than western Ukrainians, who "had unfortunately had their language contaminated by Polish and were mixing the languages, whereas in regions such as Odesa, Ukrainian had remained free from foreign influence." Eventually, a tendency emerged in front of my eyes: the great majority of my informants declared that they spoke Ukrainian but preferred Russian for communication. Few of them, if any, could remember where they had learned it: some recalled childhood summers spent at the grandmother's Ukrainian village; others believed that it was during travel to the west of the country; and a number said that they started reading in Ukrainian, as if one could one day just start reading in a foreign language. What is important to a social scientist is that, taken together, a series of casual events, defines a tendency. If each informant "learned" Ukrainian in a different way, I conclude that there are various means of language exposure and that, regardless of one's actual language fluency, one's perception of fluency was important. Odesans would have learned Ukrainian at some time in their lives and, regardless of the fact that they barely used it or that

---

53 Polese, "Une version alternative de la 'révolution orange': transformations identitaires et 'nation building spontané,'" *Socio-Logos: Revue de l'association Française de Sociologie* 4 (2009), https://journals.openedition.org/socio-logos/2315.
54 Polese, "Can Nation Building Be 'Spontaneous'? A (Belated) Ethnography of the Orange Revolution," in Polese et al., *Identity and Nation Building in Everyday Post-Socialist Life*, 161–75.
55 Polese and A. Wylegala, "Sprache und Identität: Reflexionen aus Odessa und Lwiw," *Ukraine-Analysen*, no. 3 (2008): 13–17.

they might be prone to errors in usage, they had constructed a narrative affirming that they spoke it fluently. The question was not whether Odesans speak Ukrainian, then, but how they decide when and whether to switch languages.

Ukrainian could be heard sporadically at a bazaar (for instance, if a seller was from a Ukrainian village) or at high-level official meetings but not at lower-level ones (for instance, a university departmental meeting). I noticed that regardless of their first language, state officials would make more of an effort to use Ukrainian for official occasions. People exhibited some flexibility, switching to Russian if, for instance, in a court, the defendant did not understand Ukrainian well. Other occasions would include the meeting of two civil servants, who would start in Ukrainian and then switch to Russian by tacit agreement once they realized that their interlocutor was more comfortable with Russian; or, possibly, communication between a local administration and the central one in Kyiv, where Ukrainian was more frequently used. Overall, the tensions between the two languages and the way Odesans constructed a space that could be regarded as a compromise between "Ukrainian," as dictated by the central administration, and "Russian," as sometimes perceived by external observers or politicians concerned about the extensive use of Russian in the city.

Languages of socialization and communication

Two assumptions guided the choice of one of the main observation points during fieldwork. First, when trying to promote the use of a new language, younger generations are easier to mold than elder ones, who have a long and consolidated practice in language use. Schools, therefore, are likely to become one of the main places for rolling out Ukrainization policies.[56] The second is that efforts to Ukrainianize schools could depend on the strategic importance of the school to the Ukrainian nation-building project. I had learned that education authorities quickly converted elite schools (i.e., a lyceum) to Ukrainian-language education while introducing a more relaxed plan to more standard schools. If this was accurate, the most important schools in Odesa would receive greater pressure to comply with Ukrainian-language requirements than other schools and definitely more than Russian schools (these are Ukrainian schools where Russian is the main language of instruction). I therefore assumed that the tensions,

---

56 Peter W. Rodgers, "'Compliance or Contradiction'? Teaching 'History' in the 'New' Ukraine. A View from Ukraine's Eastern Borderlands," *Europe–Asia Studies* 59, no. 3 (2007): 503–19; Richardson, *Kaleidoscopic Odessa*, 48, 227.

and the difference, between various educational institutions and their requirements, would be particularly visible when comparing the way elite schools adapted to Ukrainian-language requirements and the way standard schools did. Of the six schools selected for intensive observation, three were considered elite schools. Their pupils went to the best universities, often without entrance exam requirements.[57] The other three were standard schools with no particular specialization and one of them had Russian as the main language of instruction. Nevertheless, all the administrative documents had to be completed, at least theoretically, in Ukrainian. The program still had to comply with the requirements of the Ukrainian Ministry of Education. But it would be delivered, except for Ukrainian language and literature subjects, in Russian.

The way teachers, the administration, and pupils interacted had a lot in common regardless of whether or not the school was elite. Some differences emerged between Russian and Ukrainian schools, and slightly different tendencies were visible depending on the age of the pupils. First, it seemed that it was easier for younger pupils to adapt to Ukrainian-language activities. Second—and this may simply be my sense of things—in the Russian-language school the tension between languages was lower than in Ukrainian-language ones for the simple fact that there was no gap between the language teachers and pupils were expected to speak and the one they spoke ordinarily.

The first point refers to the performance of rituals, holiday celebrations, and collective activities such as reading poetry or singing songs in public on special days. Notwithstanding the language spoken during daily interaction, there was a tacit understanding that the performance language would be Ukrainian. This was somehow lived as a state of exception, a language for official communication. In some respects, pupils learning socialization at school would also learn the way to socialize through language. For official occasions, they would be trained to use Ukrainian, smile and recite a poem or sing as their parents would do at their age (but in Russian). Older pupils seemed less at ease, not with Ukrainian itself, but with the use of Ukrainian, whereas younger pupils had possibly come to consider the school as "the place where you officially speak Ukrainian." Older pupils, who had already studied several years in the same institution and had not experienced any formal pressure to use Ukrainian, now had to adapt.

Place is important and, as the OPOL (one parent one language) approach suggests, language can also be associated with place and space. In a school, there are several spaces, or environments, of socialization: the classroom with the teacher,

---

57 Abel Polese "The Formal and the Informal: Exploring 'Ukrainian' Education in Ukraine, Scenes from Odessa," *Comparative Education* 46, no. 1 (2010): 45–62.

private talks with the teacher, communication with friends, and communication with the class. Each of them has its own register, favorite words, tone, and slang, or technical words. Even adhering to a single language, the vocabulary used in each of these situations will be different. To request the use of Ukrainian (and a certain kind of Ukrainian) might, then, be perfectly acceptable. It is just a matter of educating, or training, the target group. This brings us to the second point, that is, language use and the tension between the two languages. Language interaction in the schools also involved adults who had been using Russian most of their life and associated it not only with the classroom and school but, possibly, with each aspect and sphere of their personal and professional life. Consequently, the creation of new habits was filtered through the capacity of teachers to "adapt" to the new environment and expectations. This adaptation is at the roots of an imprecise language attitude that could be observed inside and outside the classroom. When entering the classroom, the teacher would greet pupils in Ukrainian, but the environment might be disrupted in several ways—for example, if some of the pupils did not remain silent and the teacher needed to call for order. In another instance, when some administrative information (about forthcoming events, holidays, and so forth) needed to be delivered, Russian would then usually be preferred.

Change would occur when "official time" began and the teacher started instruction. The teacher sometimes even translated into Ukrainian comments made by pupils in Russian—a practice that that served a double function. First, it helped those with weak Ukrainian to learn new words and, second, it showed that official comments need to be in Ukrainian. In fact, pupils tended to use either Russian or Ukrainian for their intervention depending on whether they said something they had read in the textbook (usually in Ukrainian) or simply guessed the answer to a question. Teachers might strive to deliver their class in Ukrainian, but they often used a mix of the two languages; if a Russian word came to a teacher more quickly, they would then promptly "Ukrainize" it for the occasion. At times, Russian was widely used until, at the end of the class, the teacher switched back to Ukrainian to thank the students for their attention and say goodbye to them. Russian was also the language for disciplining pupils who talked or joked too much during the lesson. In such a case, the register moved to the everyday one, with the teacher speaking to the child in a one-to-one personal communication fashion.

Textbooks were, in principle, in Ukrainian, but the transition period took longer than expected, and not all schools had received them at the time of the fieldwork. In some other cases, the teacher would prefer to use a Russian textbook or even Russian material taken from the internet. They justified this by saying that there was no textbook available or that pupils did not read well in Ukrainian.

The teacher might point to my presence as the main reason why the class was conducted in Russian. This was allegedly based on the (wrong) assumption that I did not understand Ukrainian, perhaps because our first interaction with the director was in Russian. At any rate, my presence was one of the many reasons to impose a constant state of exception ("just this time, just today, just here"). In search of the borders of this state of exception, I was genuinely surprised when I found that Ukrainian sounded odd when used to teach "the history of Odes(s)a." After all, the history of the city is mostly in Russian. The teacher then affirmed that Russian was the only language in which that class could possibly be delivered. She was pulled back to official reality, however, by my request to visit that class. The deputy principal did not allow the state of exception for delivering "only this lecture" in Russian although the course was formally being conducted in Ukrainian. From that point on, she started renegotiating her statement, implying that, after all, the teacher was using Ukrainian and only sporadically Russian—when this was absolutely necessary.

Another state of exception emerged during an interview with a civil servant. She told me that Russian was widely used for all sorts of communication in her building, and added that panic would ensue when they needed to send an official message to Kyiv. They would get the one Ukrainian speaker in the office to check the message. This made me think of the Soviet saying: "They claim to be paying us, and we claim to be working for them," where the above dynamic is enabled by a sufficient degree of complicity between the two parts. Odesans strive to present an appearance of Ukrainianness, and the state does not burrow under the surface.

In many respects, the tensions between the official version of a nation of Ukrainian speakers and the everyday reality becomes more visible on the job market. Schools and public offices have a version of how things should work. The economy is about how things are now, today. In Estonia and Latvia, where Russian is not particularly encouraged by state policies, some jobs require fluency in both the national language and Russian, whereas others only require Russian and some degree of knowledge of the national language. In Odesa, the majority of jobs require the ability to speak Russian whereas only a fraction of them require fluency in Ukrainian.

Switching between ideological, pragmatic, and policy considerations, Odesans constantly renegotiate the meaning of public space and official state narratives. On the one hand, one can see the state and its desire to homogenize and harmonize,[58] sometimes disrupting habits and requesting new attitudes.

---

58 James C. Scott, *Seeing like a State: How Certain Schemes to Improve the Human Condition Have Failed* (New Haven: Yale University Press, 1998).

On the other hand, however, this becomes feasible only so long as citizens (or a substantial majority) comply with these rules. Whilst not openly challenging state narratives or its symbolic order, they resist de facto by not complying with some state instructions. The Ukrainian state somehow projects an ideal version of what being Ukrainian means but Ukrainians all across Ukraine have different ways of accepting or renegotiating it. Some accept a number of identity boundaries without taking the whole package but display a sufficient degree of devotion to the state. In turn, the state accepts what they offer, does not coerce or punish people, and leaves them relatively free to choose their version of Ukrainianness.

Conclusion

The Odesan-Russian dictionary defines *molodoi* (young) as anyone from ten to ninety-nine years. Likewise, and in a way typical of Odesa's flexibility, speaking Ukrainian in the city is possible but there is little need for it in reality. This may or may not, of course, be regarded as a political position. After all, if you ask someone to switch to a new path and behave differently, they will comply without protesting or mistakenly take the old path a few times more. Even if you stress the fact that good citizens ought to change their habits, the conflict between individual and state morality does not always allow the state to prevail;[59] individuals living through historical changes are often caught between what the state expects and what they are comfortable with. Bourdieu speaks of the convenience of morality,[60] meaning that we will act morally as long as it suits us. Ariely talks of the "construction of honesty": individuals build an image of themselves such that, no matter what they do, they will not be able to imagine themselves as honest.[61] My informants rarely, if ever, associated themselves 100% with Russia, but they did not champion Ukraine either. They showed some kind of allegiance to the state, but also to themselves, their identity, their credos. Rejection of the state can be associated with the politicization of the language issue, something that has emerged in other parts of the country and has led to political confrontation; but a desire to engage in contentious politics also depends on where you are supposed to use the language and how often. To what extent is the governing

---

59 Abel Polese, "Too Much Corruption or Simply too Much Talk of . . . Corruption . . . ?" *Transitions*, November 11, 2016, https://tol.org/client/article/26474-too-much-corruption-or-simply-too-much-talk-of-corruption.html?print.
60 Pierre Bourdieu, *Outline of a Theory of Practice*, trans. Richard Nice (Cambridge: University of Cambridge Press, 1977).
61 Dan Ariely, *The Honest Truth about Dishonesty* (New York: Harper Perennial, 2012).

entity choosing for you? And what do you lose and gain when switching language? At this stage, the degree of everyday resistance and compromise in Odesa seems to suit the population and has largely resulted in the avoidance of direct confrontation. This situation has, of course, been dramatically affected by the annexation of Crimea in 2014 and then the invasion by Russia in 2022. Both events have prompted a dramatic revival in the use of Ukrainian language. However, an analysis of the effects of the war goes beyond the scope of this chapter (and could be a subject for a subsequent study), where the main goal was to discuss the existence of mechanisms mediating Ukrainization policies without necessarily openly opposing them. What are the mechanisms, tactics, and strategies used when you are requested to change your linguistic habits to satisfy the needs of an emerging sovereign state? In some respects, this state of affairs sounds almost like something from another century, when a change of ruler required people to instantaneously learn and adapt to another language. History has shown that, with enough effort and resources, whole populations can be "converted"; they will then forget some elements of their history and culture and adopt others.[62] This can take a more violent or peaceful form, but whole peoples change language, culture, and identity, as seminal studies on national identity have documented.[63] The choices of language(s) in a place are a result of a random sequence of events that is affected by internal and external dynamics, synergies, and chance. Claims that "this place only speaks this language" or that "we came here before so this is our land" can certainly have emotional appeal but are difficult to back up scientifically. At the time of my fieldwork, Russian was generally preferred, at least in some contexts. I was also lucky to witness attempts to transition towards a broader use of Ukrainian. But what the future holds for us nobody can predict, and whatever language Odesa will speak in the future cannot erase its cosmopolitan origins and its fascinating history so far.

---

[62] Ernest Gellner, *Nations and Nationalisms* (Oxford: Blackwell, 2006).
[63] Anthony D. Smith, *Nationalism and Modernism: A Critical Survey of Recent Theories of Nations and Nationalism* (London and New York: Routledge, 2013).

CHAPTER 11

Rereading Babel in Post-Maidan Odesa: Boris Khersonsky's Critical Cosmopolitanism

Amelia M. Glaser

In 2010, the poet Boris Khersonsky dedicated a poem to the Russian writer Isaak Babel, presenting Babel's oeuvre, as well as films that it inspired, as tragic remnants of the Soviet regime. The poem opens:

> Товарищ Исаак Бабель пишет историю города О.,
> крупной жемчужины у Черного м.
> По этому тексту будут снимать кино,
> товарищ Бабель величает товарища Сталина, но
> Бабеля расстреляют – полностью и насовсем.[1]

> Comrade Isaak Babel writes the history of the city O.,
> the great pearl by the Black Sea.

---

1 Khersonsky, "Tovarishch Isaak Babel' pishet istoriiu goroda O.," in *Odesskaia Intelligentsia* (Kharkov: Folio, 2017), 422. Khersonsky published this poem on his LiveJournal page the day the monument was erected in Odesa, dating it 2010—accessed November 27, 2020, https://borkhers.livejournal.com/1119672.html. He recalls, in this post, that Boris Vladimirsky (who went on to direct a large Russian Jewish émigré cultural center in California) shared a handmade edition of Babel's stories with him. Khersonsky is likely referencing Babel's scripting of the voiceover for director Jean Lods' film *Odessa* (Komosomol'skaia kinofabrika, Odesa, 1935). I am grateful to Gregory Freidin for this and other contextual points in this essay.

> They'll make a movie from this text,
> Comrade Babel exalts comrade Stalin, though
> They will shoot Babel—completely and eternally.

The poem constitutes a rare criticism of a writer who is widely read as the embodiment of Odes(s)a humor in Russian literature. By questioning Babel's legacy, Khersonsky seeks to imagine a different Odesa, one that is no longer beholden to the Soviet mixture of Russian imperialism and multinationalism promoted in the name of communist internationalism, but to a post-Soviet, Ukrainian vision of cosmopolitanism.

Khersonsky reposted this poem to his LiveJournal page in 2011, on the day a monument to Babel was installed in a small plaza in Odesa, on the corner of Rishelievskaia and Zhukovskaia streets. The *Всемирный Клуб Одесситов / Всесвітній клуб одеситів* (Worldwide Club of Odes(s)ans) raised the funds for the statue, administered a contest for its design, and commissioned the celebrated Moscow-based artist, Georgy Frangulian, who worked in collaboration with the Odesa sculptor Mikhail Reva. Frangulian portrayed Babel seated, a notebook and pen on his knee. A few feet away rests a large wheel bearing Babel's name, a symbol which, Frangulian has asserted, viewers can interpret for themselves:

> Кто-то увидит в нём колесо тачанки из "Конармии," кто-то услышит стук колёс по булыжной мостовой транспортного средства "Извозопромышленного предприятия Мендель Крик и Сыновья," для кого-то – это будет колесом истории, которое в то жестокое время перемалывало судьбы людей.[2]

> (Someone will see in it the *tachanka* [machine-gun cart] wheel from *Red Cavalry*, someone else will hear the wheels of the "Mendel Krik and Sons Industrial Transport Enterprise" vehicle clattering on the cobblestones; for someone else this will be the wheel of history, which in that cruel time pulverized people's fates.)

---

2 Georgy Frangulian, "Pamiatnik Isaaku Babel'iu," georgy-frangulian.ru, accessed August 25, 2020, http://georgy-frangulyan.ru/ru/gallery/pamyatnik-isaaku-babelyu-v-odesse/. Frangulian has created monuments to Pushkin, Okudzhava, Brodsky, Einstein, and Yeltsin (among others).

Babel promised, in his 1916 essay "Odessa," that the city would produce the "Литературный Мессия, которого ждут столь долго и столь бесплодно" (Literary Messiah, for whom they've been waiting so long and so fruitlessly).[3] If Babel did not become Russian literature's savior, his *Одесские рассказы* (*Odessa Stories*) and *Конармия* (*Red Cavalry*) did secure his place as a major writer for the Soviet era and his *Odessa Stories* became prooftexts for modern Odesa. At the monument's unveiling, the Odesa-born Moscow stand-up comedian Mikhail Zhvanetsky (1934–2020) declared that Babel triumphed over Stalin: "Великий тиран гнобил великого писателя. . . . Помнят обоих, чтят одного" (A great tyrant defiled a great writer. . . . They'll remember both but honor only one).[4] The Odesa-based satirist Valery Khait, who initiated the project, wrote, "Исаак Бабель – великий сын Одессы: он многим обязан ей, равно как и она – ему" (Isaak Babel is Odesa's glorious son: he is greatly indebted to the city, just as the city is to him).[5] Babel has long personified the myth of Odesa for residents and non-residents of the city. For some, he is the progenitor of a lost Soviet humor, for others, a folk historian of Odesa's underworld, a Russian writer commemorating a Jewish past, or a testimony as a victim of Stalin's purges.

In his 2011 LiveJournal post, Khersonsky included a postscript to his poem about Babel, where he fondly recalls discovering Babel's erotic stories, printed in samizdat during the Thaw, adding that, at the time, he and his friends did not know "О связи Бабеля с карательными органами, о его присутствии на допросах с применением пыток во время гражданской войны" (of the connection between Babel and the state organs of repression, about his participation in interrogations where torture was applied during the civil war).[6] This claim about torture is uncited and historical sources do not corroborate it. However, over the past decade, Khersonsky has become increasingly critical of Babel's role in Odesa mythology, and has, in fact, used him as a convenient symbol for his own increasing animosity toward Russian culture. After all, as Gregory Freidin has stated, "Одесса обязана ему своим мифом" (Odesa owes its myth to him).[7] The author who immortalized the Jewish bandit Mikhail Vinnitskii, widely known

---

3   Isaak Babel, "Moi listki: Odessa," *Zhurnal zhurnalov*, no. 51 (1916): 4–5.
4   Aleksei Khalanskii, "Zhvanetskii i Pozner otkryli v Odesse pamiatnik Babel'iu," *Novye izvestiia*, September 5, 2011, https://newizv.ru/news/culture/05-09-2011/150660-zhvaneckij-i-pozner-otkryli-v-odesse-pamjatnik-babelju.
5   Aleksandr Riabkov (blog post), "Pamiatnik Babel'iu," histodessa.ru, July 9, 2018, https://histodessa.ru/pamyatnik-babelyu/.
6   Boris Khersonsky, LiveJournal, accessed November 27, 2020, https://borkhers.livejournal.com/1119672.html.
7   Gregory Freidin, "Forma soderzhaniia: Odessa-mama Isaaka Babelia," *Neprikosnovennyi zapas* 4 (2011): 11.

as Mishka Yaponchik, in the figure of Benia Krik has remained for Khersonsky too Soviet and too god-like, inhibiting and criminalizing the city's post-Soviet cultural development. Khersonsky (born in 1950), a poet and psychotherapist, is one of Ukraine's best known contemporary Russian-language poets, and his writing is as layered as Babel's. Born in Chernivtsi in 1950, Khersonsky attended medical school in Odesa and built a distinguished career there as a clinical and academic psychologist. A Russian speaker who became well known as a Soviet dissident poet, Khersonsky has written to broad acclaim about his Jewish ancestry and the theology of the Russian Orthodox church, into which he was baptized as an adult. He has also shifted from expressing pride in Odesa's literary history toward frustration with the joint forces of Soviet literary history and the Russian presence in Ukraine.

In his Russian-language poetry, Khersonsky merges the styles and languages of past writers, borrowing from Babel, Brodsky, Blok, Bagritsky, and biblical texts while simultaneously rejecting the canonical authority of all these influences. Khersonsky has sought, in his writing, to resist nearly every dominant voice in post-Soviet Ukraine, from its local oligarchy to the Soviet nostalgia of a Russian neo-imperialist narrative. To better understand the complex, enduring role of the Odesa myth in the city itself, I will focus, in this chapter, on Khersonsky's deconstruction of this myth. I propose in the following section that Khersonsky prompts us to read Odesa as a post-cosmopolitan city. I will then examine how Soviet Odesa literature, which emerged as an internationalist iteration of pre-Soviet cosmopolitanism, has continued to color post-Soviet literature in and about Odesa. I will conclude this chapter with a close look at Khersonsky's 2018 "Notes of a Madman," a satirical novella that portrays the stagnant Odesa myth through a doomed metaphorical relationship between the Odesa intelligentsia and the alienated writer. In this satirical treatment of his city, Khersonsky offers a literary approximation of the ironic visual art produced by his friend and contemporary, the postmodern painter Aleksandr Roitburd. A reading of Khersonsky's recent work helps us to understand the artistic legacy of Odesa, a city that has had difficulty escaping a specifically Soviet image of cosmopolitanism.

Post-cosmopolitan Odesa

Russian-language writers who came of age in the early twentieth century are associated with stories and poems of Odesa's criminal underground and with creative mixtures of Russian, Ukrainian, and Yiddish. Babel, along with Yurii

Olesha, Eduard Bagritsky, Vera Inber, Ilya Ilf, and Yevgeni Petrov, continued to represent the city in Soviet literature after leaving Odesa. Khersonsky claims to have turned his back on the *Odesskaia shkola* (Odesa School). In a 2017 Facebook post, he asserted, "Бо вони були майже усі (за виключенням Жаботинського й Катаєва останніх років його життя) талановитими, але радянськими письменниками" (They were all, with the exception of Jabotinsky and Kataev at the end of his life, talented, but Soviet, writers).[8] Some critics view Khersonsky, a vocal supporter of the 2013–14 Euromaidan with a strong social media presence, as closer to Kyiv than to his native city.

Khersonsky's public critique of Babel's place in Odesa mythology helps to explain a cultural divide in Ukraine that became apparent in the aftermath of the Euromaidan protests, which led to the ouster of then-President Yanukovych over his corruption and rejection of closer ties to the European Union. This divide, which deepened with the outbreak of the war in Donbas in 2014, became an irreparable rift following Russia's full-scale invasion of Ukraine in 2022. Odesa experienced an early painful schism when, on May 2, 2014, conflicts between pro-Russian and pro-Kyiv demonstrators led to the death of over forty people (most of them supporters of Russia) in a fire at the Trade Union House in Odesa. Although Khersonsky's position is common among Ukrainian-language writers and artists, he was, until 2022, in a minority of Odesa writers in direct opposition to Russia's attempt to exercise what Anibal Quijano has called a "coloniality of power."[9] In addition to criticizing Russia's military intervention in Ukraine, Khersonsky has, since 2014, increasingly written poetry in his non-native Ukrainian in protest against the Russian state's political and cultural presence in Ukraine.

Khersonsky's reassessment of Soviet Russian literature exposes two competing and politically charged visions of identity in early twenty-first-century Odesa. During the first eight years of the Russian-Ukrainian War, one dominant Odesa ideology continued to place Moscow at the center of an internationalist struggle against fascism, whereas another rejected Russia's influence in the region, seeking non-Soviet models, including Western Europe, Ottoman history, and imperial Russian history, to understand Ukrainian identity.

---

8 Khersonsky, Facebook post, December 12, 2017, https://www.facebook.com/borkhers/posts/1788632214504930.

9 Anibal Quijano, "Coloniality of Power, Eurocentrism, and Latin America," *Nepantla: Views from the South* 1, no. 3 (2000): 533–80. See Walter D. Mignolo, "The Many Faces of Cosmopolis: Border Thinking and Critical Cosmopolitanism," in *Cosmopolitanism*, ed. Dipesh Chakrabarty, Homi K. Bhabha, Sheldon Pollock, and Carol A. Breckenridge (Durham, NC: Duke University Press, 2002), 157–88.

Russia's full-scale invasion of Ukraine in 2022 has led to new unity among Odesa's residents, uniting former adversaries in a struggle to maintain the country's independence. However, the cultural division between, largely, Russian- and Ukrainian-speakers in Odesa until 2022 presents a case study in understanding how Ukrainians have struggled to reconcile competing pasts with competing visions of the future.[10] In this chapter, I read Khersonsky as a practitioner of what Walter Mignolo has called "critical cosmopolitanism." Mignolo discusses the supposedly cosmopolitan narratives that position themselves as either managerial or emancipatory but are in actuality often "oblivious to the saying of the people that are supposed to be emancipated."[11] In the twenty-first century, Mignolo observes, "cosmopolitanism (and democracy) can no longer be articulated from one point of view, within a single logic, a mono-logic (if benevolent) discourse from the political right or left." Mignolo warns against mistaking colonial rhetoric for cosmopolitanism and calls attention to the "coloniality of power and the colonial difference produced, reproduced, and maintained by global designs."[12]

Khersonsky, in his simultaneous engagement of the Soviet internationalist narrative, Jewish collective memory, and Ukrainian national narrative can be read as a practitioner of critical cosmopolitanism, one who embodies what Rebecca Walkowitz has described as a "double consciousness, comparison, negation, and persistent self-reflection: an 'unwillingness to rest,' the attempt to operate 'in the world' . . . [while] preserving a posture of resistance."[13] Khersonsky is resisting a complex post-Soviet constellation of power, which includes, simultaneously, the Soviet-style cultural imperialism of Russia and the Ukrainian post-Soviet oligarchy. It is important to note that Khersonsky's critique is seldom directed at Babel's work but rather takes aim at the figure of Babel in Odesa's cultural memory. An examination of Khersonsky's post-Soviet critique of Babel's role in Odesa mythology helps to clarify how the competing claims became sharper amid the rising tensions between Russia and Ukraine in the decade leading up to 2022.

Frangulian's Babel statue is one of many in a city physically layered in memory. Francesco Boffo and Avram Melnikov's 1828 statue of the Duc de Richelieu overlooks the Potemkin steps. Friedrich Brugger's 1863 statue of Count Vorontsov stands on Odesa's Cathedral Square. Yuri Dmitrenko's 1900 monument to

---

10 See, for example, "Odessa Finds Its Ukrainian Identity Ahead of Russian Advance," *Economist*, March 7, 2022, https://www.economist.com/europe/2022/03/07/odessa-finds-its-ukrainian-identity-ahead-of-a-russian-advance.
11 Walter D. Mignolo, "The Many Faces," 159.
12 Mignolo, "The Many Faces," 179.
13 Rebecca Walkowitz, *Cosmopolitan Style* (New York: Columbia University Press, 2006), 2.

Catherine the Great, surrounded by her fellow founders of the city, long stood in the city center, on Katerynyns'ka (Ekaterininskaia) Square (it was dismantled in 1920, replaced by a bust of Marx, and was restored in 2007, only to be dismantled again in 2022). Along the Black Sea shore is a 1960 Obelisk to the Unknown Sailor, a 1965 monument to the mutiny aboard the battleship *Potemkin*, and a 1984 monument to the air force. A 1984 war memorial in the city center commemorates the Odesans who fought against the city's fascist German and Romanian occupiers in 1941. Beginning in the early 1990s, a Holocaust memorial complex was built in Prokhorovka Park (Prokhorovsky Square) that includes sculptures by the well-known Moscow artist Zurab Tsereteli. Fiction has merged with history on the streets of post-Soviet Odesa: a 2004 plaque commemorates the death of the infamous Jewish gangster, Mikhail Vinnitskii, widely known as Mishka Yaponchik. Mikhail Reva designed a 1999 monument to Ilf and Petrov's "twelfth chair." Aleksander Tokarev's statues of Pushkin, Utiosov, Utochkin and Gotsman (the hero in a Soviet-era TV program) were installed in 1999, 2000, and 2008, respectively. In 2002, the city installed Tokarev's monument to the unknown wives of sailors. The 1995 monument to "Rabinovich," the ubiquitous butt of Jewish jokes, has spawned the disconcertingly antisemitic tradition of rubbing its ear for financial luck.[14] Other monuments, such as the memorial to the eighteenth-century Cossack Antin Holovaty represent attempts to nationalize a Ukrainian memory-scape. Taken collectively, the sculptures advertise Odesa's claims to fame in twentieth-century culture as a city known for its early Soviet humor and a city that heroically survived World War II. This Russian-centered memoryscape can be read as a form of "restorative nostalgia," which, Svetlana Boym explains: "evokes national past and future, unlike "reflective nostalgia [which] is more about individual and cultural memory." Indeed, even as Odesa commemorates national and Soviet traditions, memories of Odesa's pre-Soviet past are disappearing. In 2015, UNESCO changed Odesa's status as a world heritage site, revising its categorization from C (historical city) to D (area of historical buildings). The Greek section, for example, has been lost to modern construction, largely due to the desire among the city's nouveaux riches to design new residences in the city center. The physical city, privileging a "restorative" form of nostalgia, preserves collective memories that were formed during the Soviet period. It is this artistic and political form of nostalgia against which Khersonsky is pushing.

---

14 "Monument Rabinovich, Odessa," IGotoWorld, accessed November 24, 2020, https://ua.igotoworld.com/en/poi_object/78200_pamyatnik-rabinovichu-odessa.htm.

Iconoclasm is part of Khersonsky's literary identity. In one poem, he writes proudly of the many apparent contradictions in his identity, from his dual allegiances to Russian and Ukrainian, to his Christian/Jewish faith: "Я вихрестився колись – то ж гоніть мене юдеї! / Но остался евреем в глубине христианской идеи" (I once was baptized, so persecute me Jews / but remained a Jew in the depths of Christian thought). The poem ends with the provocation: "Я живу в Одесі. Убийте мене, одесити." (I live in Odesa. Kill me, Odesans). Khersonsky's pride in his seeming inconsistencies may be read as a manifesto on his rejection of monolithic and monoethnic ideas.[15] The form of the poem, in addition to its content, displays a multiethnic identity, as Khersonsky mixes Russian words and syntax into his Ukrainian lines. Khersonsky here is openly displaying his opposition to both Soviet nostalgia and ethnic and religious purism. When Khersonsky shared this poem in a Facebook post, one of his contacts commented approvingly on Khersonsky's unwillingness to conform to any party line, "So you are not only a cosmopolitan, but you're also a religious anarchist and an Odesan *Nonconformist*!!!" By calling Khersonsky a "cosmopolitan," this commentator is simultaneously referencing Stalin's antisemitic campaign against cosmopolitanism and Khersonsky's rejection of nationalist doctrine. Khersonsky's persistent advocacy of an idealized, hybrid and local identity, presents a concrete vision for a distinctly anti-imperialist twenty-first-century Odesa cosmopolitanism. His provocation to "Odesans" (*odessity*) calls attention to his role as an outsider in his own city, as well as his distance from official portrayals of Odesa culture (including the Worldwide Club of Odes[s]ans).

Odesa is still a city of many cultures: it continues to draw migrants from within and outside Ukraine, including Afghan, Turkish, and migrant Roma populations. Vera Skvirskaja examines "the marginality of a historically local (or 'internal') Other, the Gypsy; and the marginality of the recent foreign migrants, who have become omnipresent in Odesa's marketplaces but less so in other public realms."[16] Odesa still has a visible Jewish community, which has restored synagogues and cultural centers. The city's Ukrainian-speaking minority has also become more visible over the past few years. Recent Ukrainian-language initiatives have helped to connect Odesa to other Ukrainian cities. A Ukrainian-language bookstore-I (Knyharnia-kav'iarnia) on Katerynynska

---

15 Boris Khersonsky, "Ia rozmovliaiu rosiis'koiu s zhinkoi ta naodyntsi," posted to Facebook on March 26, 2020, https://www.facebook.com/photo?fbid=3154906684544136&set=a.174157859285715.

16 Vera Skvirskaja, "At the City's Social Margins: Selective Cosmopolitans in Odessa," in *Post-Cosmopolitan Cities: Explorations of Urban Coexistence*, ed. Caroline Humphrey and Vera Skvirskaja (New York: Berghahn Books, 2012), 68.

Street stocks new literary publications and hosts events. More established institutions, including the Odesa Hrushevsky Library and Odesa's Museum of Fine Art, have worked to promote contemporary Ukrainian literature and art, although not without visible public discord. The painter Aleksandr Roitburd assumed directorship in 2018, an appointment that many progressive, intellectual, and younger Ukrainians welcomed. However, attempts to establish a bridge between Odesa and the capital city Kyiv have been tenuous since the outbreak of the war in Donbas, and the global Covid-19 pandemic has further limited these new venues' activities. A year after Roitburd's appointment as museum director, for example, the city's regional council dismissed him because of his involvement in the 2013–2014 Euromaidan protests in Kyiv.[17] The largely Russian-speaking city of Odesa has remained a contrast to the Ukrainian-language culture steadily gaining ground in Kyiv and throughout much of Ukraine.[18] Efforts to disrupt Russia's cultural influence and political power in the city have repeatedly been met with mistrust, if not violence.

In an April 12, 2019, interview with the poet Iya Kiva in *Shoizdat* (a blog connected to the Kyiv publisher Sho), Khersonsky commented:

> Якщо визнати, ніби Одеса – це більше ніж місто, це країна, то столицею (культурною) цієї країни є і буде Москва. Мовою Одеси буде скалічена на кшталт їдишу російська. Біблією будуть "Одеські оповідання" Бабеля, а офіційним гімном – "С Одеського кічмана втекли два уркани."[19]

> (If you admit that Odesa is more than a city, that it's a country, then the capital (cultural) of this country is and will be Moscow. The language of Odesa will be twisted in the image of Yiddish Russian. The Bible will be Babel's *Odessa Stories*, and the official anthem is "Two Crooks Fled from the Odessa Slammer.")

---

17 See Konstantin Akinsha, "Culture Wars, Odessa Style," *Atlantic Council*, September 24, 2019, https://www.atlanticcouncil.org/blogs/ukrainealert/culture-wars-odessa-style/.

18 According to Ievgen Vorobiov, a May 2015 poll revealed that almost 60 percent of the population prefer to use Ukrainian in "everyday conversation" ("Why Ukrainians Are Speaking More Ukrainian," June 26, 2015, https://foreignpolicy.com/2015/06/26/why-ukrainians-are-speaking-more-ukrainian/). See Abel Polese's chapter above.

19 Iya Kiva, "Boris Khersonskii: 'Odesa – tse zavzhdy zhyttia v podviinomu prostori'" (interview with Boris Khersonsky), *Shoizdat*, April 12, 2019, https://shoizdat.com/boris-khersonskii-odesa-tse-zavzhdi/. Here, Khersonsky is referencing Boris Timofeev's and F. Kel'man's (Mikhail Ferkel'man) Russian song "S odesskogo kichmana" (From an Odessa slammer), made famous by the singer Leonid Utiosov.

Here, Khersonsky implies that the humorous role of Yiddish-inflected Russian is part of what has relegated Odesa culture to the margins of—not Ukraine but Russia. (The language of Odes(s)a, to Khersonsky's ear, conspicuously excludes Ukrainian.) Odesa, burdened by its place in Russian history, has been unable to move beyond its Soviet role. In the *Shoizdat* interview, Khersonsky asserts that Odesans should not only embrace the city's imperial past but also welcome the future, while working to remove the Soviet military monuments to a "hero-city." If Babel introduced Odesa as a model for Russia's "literary messiah" in his 1916 "Odessa," Khersonsky seeks to undermine this gospel in twenty-first-century Ukraine.

Between imperial cosmopolitanism and Soviet internationalism

Nineteenth-century Odesa was a place of refuge, where individuals sought fortune and autonomy. The city was mythologized as such in literary accounts. Its banks were known to pay high interest rates. Its status as a *porto franco*, or free port, from 1819 to 1858 made it a privileged, deterritorialized urban center. In the early Soviet period, literary portrayals of Odesa's multiethnicity still reflected the city's history of multiethnic exchange, but it fit into a larger picture of Soviet multiethnicity. Just as the Leninist project of indigenization (*korenizatsiia*) was swiftly abandoned under Stalin for a form of Soviet Russian-centered nationalism, so, too, did cosmopolitan Odesa disappear in comparison to the Soviet administrative centers. At the turn of the twentieth century, Odesa was larger than Kyiv, yet by the end of the 1930s it was smaller than both Kyiv and Kharkiv.[20] In the Soviet period, Odesa, with its beaches, coastline, warm climate, and myth, was a popular tourist destination.[21] Rebecca Stanton observes in her study of early Soviet Odesa fiction that the city offered a contrast not only to the rural image of Soviet Ukraine, but also "constituted itself as a site of nostalgic and playful resistance to the 'homogenizing impulse' emanating from

---

20 As Zvi Gitelman and others have noted, the post-Soviet period saw a return to ethnic identities, also among urban Jewish communities (Gitelman, "A Jagged Circle: From Ethnicity to Internationalism to Cosmopolitanism—and Back," in *Cosmopolitanism, Nationalism and the Jews of East Central Europe*, ed. Michael L. Miller and Scott Ury [New York: Routledge, 2016], 191); see Roman Szporluk, *Russia, Ukraine, and the Breakup of the Soviet Union* (Stanford: Hoover Institution Press, 2000), xxix, 76.
21 Tanya Richardson, *Kaleidoscopic Odessa: History and Place in Contemporary Ukraine* (Toronto: University of Toronto Press, 2008), 33.

Moscow." Odesa thieves and smugglers became mainstays of Soviet Odesa modernism.[22] In Bagritsky's oft-cited "Контрабандисты" (Smugglers, 1927), Odesa's smugglers are foreigners and give the city color:

Три грека в Одессу
Везут контрабанду.[23]

(Three Greeks smuggle / Contraband into Odesa.)

The myth of the Odesa criminal helped to engender a Soviet counterculture, but at the same time, the myth of an Odesa underworld eventually entered Soviet mainstream literature and cast a shadow over the city.[24] Odesa's carnivalesque mystique provided a controlled respite from Soviet socialism, while ultimately helping to uphold it. The Soviet Odesa rogue might be likened to the medieval church carnival, which, as Bakhtin observed, "celebrated temporary liberation from the prevailing truth."[25] The Odesa hooligan became a Soviet commodity, a symbol of a cosmopolitan port city that enriched the Moscow-centered socialist international utopia. The comical Odesa trickster conjured a provincial celebration that, while destabilizing the top-down proletarian project, ultimately reinforced proletarian internationalism—a Soviet reimagining of cosmopolitanism that looked toward Moscow. Moreover, when the comic Odesa writers of the Soviet period migrated to Moscow and Leningrad (St. Petersburg), their Odesa subject matter traveled with them, rendering Russia proper an imperial authority over the southwestern periphery.

If, as Khersonsky has suggested, early twenty-first-century Odesa still served Moscow as a source of culture and comedy, this relationship helps us to understand the complex relationship between Russia as a regional imperial presence and with Ukraine's efforts to define itself as a multiethnic, democratic state.

Tanya Richardson described Ukraine's struggle against Russia's post-Soviet claim to regional dominance masquerading as internationalism: "The claims

---

22 Rebecca Stanton, *Isaac Babel and the Self-Invention of Odessan Modernism* (Evanston: Northwestern University Press, 2012), 19.
23 Eduard Bagritsky, "Kontrabandisty," culture.ru, accessed September 2, 2022, https://www.culture.ru/poems/47376/kontrabandisty. My translation.
24 Jarrod Tanny suggests that Odesa's roguish reputation resulted in the myth surviving into the Soviet period "despite the puritanically transformative intentions of Soviet Communism and its many ideologues" (*City of Rogues and Schnorrers*, 82).
25 Mikhail Bakhtin, *Rabelais and His World*, trans. Helene Izwolsky (Bloomington: Indiana University Press, 1984), 10.

that Odesa is internationalist and 'not Ukrainian' can be understood when considered in relation to shifting political spaces, demographic and ideological relationships between country and city, and the politics of generating and defining high and low culture."[26] Odesa became provincial in the Soviet period; its cosmopolitanism was reconfigured into stories that supported a Soviet version of communist internationalism, reworking an imperialist idea as the friendship of Soviet peoples. In post-Soviet Russian rhetoric, the term "international" has become shorthand for pro-Russian, feeding a Kremlin-fueled idea that the former Soviet states, in their break with Moscow, have become dangerously nationalist.

In the early years of the twenty-first century, scholars, indeed, observed a rise in forms of East European nationalism. Ronald Suny, in his 1993 book *Revenge of the Past*, proposes that the breakup of the Soviet Union resulted partly from Soviet nationalities policy, under which, "nationality . . . had taken on a new importance as an indicator of membership in a relevant social and cultural community."[27] This assertion of national agency included not only state nationalisms, but also minority cultures.[28] Khersonsky, in his writing during the Donbas War, suggested that both Ukrainian national pride and a revival of Jewish cultural traditions depend on a rejection of the Russian imperialist narrative that has continued to claim itself as the heir to Soviet internationalism.[29]

Can Odesa continue to grow as a cosmopolitan cultural center, or has the myth of modern Odesa made the city irreversibly dependent on its past? Bruce Robbins's assertion that cosmopolitanism itself is changing—that it has a "new cast of characters"—offers some promise of rejuvenation for Ukraine's cities, including Odesa. The political scientist Volodymyr Kulyk has argued that since the Euromaidan protests, the meaning of "Ukrainian" has begun to change from an ethnic identity to a civic one, based on culture. According to Kulyk, in a 2017 survey, more self-identified Ukrainian citizens identified as speakers of both Russian and Ukrainian than they had in 2012 or 2014.[30] Karyna Korostelina has observed that many supporters of the Euromaidan "believe that Ukraine should build its

---

26 Richardson, *Kaleidoscopic Odessa*, 172.
27 Ronald Suny, *The Revenge of the Past* (Stanford, CA: Stanford University Press, 1993), 121.
28 Zvi Gitelman, among others, has noted the post-Soviet period return to ethnic identities, including urban Jewish communities (Gitelman, "A Jagged Circle," 187–204).
29 According to an OECD report, the population in Odesa due to migration increased by only 0.2 percent between 2011 and 2016. On the general population growth and migration in Ukraine since 2011, see *OECD Multi-level Governance Studies Maintaining the Momentum of Decentralisation in Ukraine* (Paris: OECD Multi-level Governance Studies, 2018), 54–55.
30 The number of Ukrainians who identified Ukrainian as their native language went up by 6 percent between 2012 and 2017; Volodymyr Kulyk, "Shedding Russianness, Recasting

own civic identity and civic society." For Korostelina, this "civic-multicultural narrative" represents a new shift away from both a Ukrainian national narrative, which doesn't leave room for the civic, and the Soviet-influenced neo-imperialist narrative, which relies "on collective consciousness, with imperial values influenced by Russia."[31] Vitaly Chernetsky has considered this shift in light of literary and cultural transformations, noting: "As this civic identity gains greater relevance and importance in post-Maidan Ukraine, Russophone writing is coming into its own as a form of Ukrainian literature."[32] Khersonsky, who has long written poetry in Russian that rejects a Russian nationalist narrative, is a leader in this broadening of Ukrainian literature. Dirk Uffelman has described Khersonsky's ironic embrace of the anti-Ukrainian term, "Russophobe," citing the poet's reclamation of a string of seemingly conflicting epithets—"cosmopolite-Russophobe-graphomaniac-Jewbanderovites."[33] The term "Jewbanderovite" (*Zhidobanderovets*) ironically combines Jews with the followers of Stepan Bandera, a Ukrainian nationalist leader who, during World War II, briefly collaborated with the Nazis as a means of furthering his anti-Soviet agenda. During the 2014 Euromaidan, the Russian and anti-Maidan media frequently accused the Maidan activists of being nationalist "Banderites." Now, the pro-Kremlin media has accused all those fighting for an independent Ukraine of aligning themselves with nationalism akin to the antisemitism of Bandera's followers. The term "cosmopolitan," on the other hand, became a derogatory antisemitic slur in the Soviet Union. Thus, by combining the concept of the Ukrainian nationalist "Banderite" with the berated "cosmopolitan," Khersonsky unites two diametrically opposed thorns in the side of Russian-Soviet nationalism—Ukrainian nationalists and Jewish cosmopolitans.

Ukrainianness: The post-Euromaidan Dynamics of Ethnonational Identifications in Ukraine," *Post-Soviet Affairs* 34, no. 1 (March 2018): 130. See the chapter by Abel Polese in this volume.

31 Karina V. Korostelina, "Conflict of National Narratives of Ukraine: Euromaidan and Beyond," *Die Friedens-Warte* 89, nos. 1–2 (2014): 277.

32 Vitaly Chernetsky, "Russophone Writing in Ukraine," in *Global Russian Cultures*, ed. Kevin M. F. Platt (Madison, WI: University of Wisconsin Press, 2019), 50. See Chernetsky, "Multidirectional Memory as Challenge and Promise," talk streamed live on September 23, 2020, accessed October 21, 2020, https://www.youtube.com/watch?v=Ch8qy7e2hLY&-fbclid=IwAR3IPv7_tTxwCFq6hkY67q0I2RFXSFVihyS-mcTs6IlOL-mPSZOyW8kxArw. Marko Pavlyshyn has also taken up this theme of the civic turn in Ukrainian identity, "Literary History as Provocation of National Identity, National Identity as Provocation of Literary History: The Case of Ukraine," *Thesis Eleven* 136, no 1 (October 5, 2016): 74–89.

33 Dirk Uffelman, "Is There Any Such Thing as Russophone Russophobia?: When Russian Speakers Speak out against Russia[n] in the Ukrainian Internet," in Platt, *Global Russian Cultures*, 225. Uffelman cites Boris Khersonskii, Livejournal post, December 4, 2014, https://www.borkhers.livejournal.com/2014/12/04.

Khersonsky's turn away from Soviet literature is an act of resistance to a dominant Russian Odesa literary paradigm. Absorption of Russian culture became a mark of Jewish assimilation even before the revolution. Isaak Babel's school-aged protagonist in "The Story of my Dovecot" (1925) enters a trance-like state as he shouts Pushkin's verse at his examiners in his bid to beat the anti-Jewish quota. Vladimir Jabotinsky recalled, "When I was not yet fourteen, and even today, it would be difficult to find a verse of Pushkin that I would not know and could not complete."[34] Yuri Slezkine has remarked on the importance of Russian high culture to Soviet Jewish identity. Citing Jabotinsky, Slezkine observes that "assimilated Jews found themselves in the role of the only public bearers and propagandists of Russian culture, [with no choice but] "to honor Pushkin . . . in total isolation."[35] Although Jabotinsky greatly exaggerates the role of Jews as Pushkin's sole champions, the relationship between Russian culture and assimilation is important (as Efraim Sicher explains in chapter 8 in this volume). The bond forged, beginning in late tsarist times, between Russian modernization and Jewish cultural identity has remained important to Russia's pride as a victor over fascism. In the present struggle between Russia and Ukraine, supporters of the Kremlin have seized upon historical conflicts between Jews and Ukrainians. Khersonsky's provocation has been to identify publicly as a Russian-speaking Jew who aligns himself with Kyiv and rejects present-day Russia, with its claim to internationalism.

Khersonsky was already questioning the seemingly unbreakable bond between Jewish culture and the Russian canon in his 2006 novel in verse *Семейный архив* (Family archive) a collection of salvaged family history, told in the present tense chronologically from the prerevolutionary Pale to 1990s Odesa. Characters are evoked through stories, photographs, and the towns where they lived. Khersonsky writes of ashes and burials, postcards and love affairs. "Odessa 1932" tells of Nadia and Solomon, who teach in a Yiddish high school. Mendele Moykher Sforim, the "grandfather" of Yiddish literature provides a Jewish subtext to accompany their household quarrels.

> Надя легла. Из угла – всхлипы и бормотанье.
> Соломон открывает книгу. Менделе Мойхер-Сфорим.
> Бытовая история. Юмор под пеленой печали,

---

[34] Vladimir Jabotinsky, *Vladimir Jabotinsky's The Story of My Life*, ed. Brian Horowitz and Leonid Katsis (Detroit: Wayne State University Press, 2016), 44.
[35] Yuri Slezkine, *The Jewish Century* (Princeton: Princeton University Press, 2004), 71.

получается тоже скорее не чтенье, а причитанье.
Боже, о чем мы спорим? Боже, о чем мы спорим?³⁶

(Nadia went to bed. From the corner come sobs and muttering. / Solomon opens a book: Mendele Moykher Sforim, / A quotidian history. Humor behind a veil of sadness, / sounds more like a lamentation than reading. / God, what are we fighting about? God, what are we fighting about?)

The couple's estrangement from each other mirrors the gradual estrangement of Jews from Soviet culture in the early years of Stalin's rule. At the end of their lives, the couple is buried in a Christian cemetery. The Soviet Union, despite its purported internationalism has, we see in this vignette, become increasingly dominated by Christian Slavs. In an ironic reference to this practice (which is anything but international), Khersonsky writes, simply: "Христианское кладбище в тридцатые годы / было интернациональным"³⁷ (The Christian cemetery, in the thirties, was international). Throughout this cycle, Khersonsky integrates Jewish and Ukrainian history. Pavel Kriuchkov has called him a "воскреситель, реаниматор родовой памяти, беспрерывно уходящей в небытие"³⁸ (resurrector, a reanimator of ancestral memory, which keeps disappearing into oblivion). Indeed, describing the language and practices of his Jewish ancestors is a means of reviving a cultural history that was buried in an "international cemetery." The poet Arkadii Shtypel, in his preface to this volume, pronounces Khersonsky's achievement as the documentation of his ancestors' lives. "Праведников и грешников, циников и идеалистов, мудрецов и сумасшедших – всех их объединяет одно: они были"³⁹ (Saints and sinners, cynics and idealists, sages and madmen—one thing unites all of them: they were). In addition to verifying and validating the lives of these ancestors, however, Khersonsky gives them

---

36 Khersonsky, *Semeinyi Arkhiv*, accessed March 31, 2021, http://www.vavilon.ru/texts/khersonsky1.html. My translation consults Boris Khersonsky, *Family Archive*, dalehobson.org, accessed November 29, 2022, https://www.dalehobson.org/khersonsky/archive.html.
37 Boris Khersonsky, *Semeinyi Arkhiv*, accessed March 31, 2021, http://www.vavilon.ru/texts/khersonsky1.html. My translation consults Ruth Kreutzer and Dale Hobson's translation, dalehobson.org, accessed November 29, 2022, https://www.dalehobson.org/khersonsky/archive.html.
38 Pavel Kriuchkov, "Bogu vidnee," *Parallel 7*, no. 32, March 11, 2007, https://45parallel.net/boris_khersonskiy/.
39 Arkadii Shtypel, "Predislovie," in Boris Khersonsky, *Semeinyi arkhiv* (Moscow: Novoe literaturnoe obozrenie, 2006), 5–8.

fragments of textual heritage that fall outside the usual definitions of Russian Jewish identity.

Parts of the cycle are phrased as rabbinic disputes. In "Одесса 1915: Две фотографии" (Odessa 1915: Two photographs) we find a rabbinic debate over secular culture:

> Ребе Ицхак Леви говорил:
> "Не удивительно, что евреи
> усваивают премудрость народов
> столь успешно, на зависть внешним.
> Ибо после того,
> как они отринули Тору,
> пустота в их сердцах и разуме
> столь велика, что туда
> вместится все что угодно."
>
> Также ребе Шрага Мендлович
> отвечал:
> "Удивляться нечему
> и, увы, нечем гордиться.
> Гордился бы Иеремия,
> если б ему сказали,
> что еврейские мастера
> изготовили золоченое
> изображение Ваал-Фегора
> лучше чем хананеяне?"[40]

(Rabbi Itskhak Levi said: / "It's not surprising that Jews / assimilate the wisdom of the world's nations / so well, to the envy of outsiders. / For after / rejecting the Torah, / the emptiness in their hearts and minds / was so great, that it could fit / anything in it." / And Rabbi Shraga Mendlowitz / would answer: / "Nothing surprising there / and, alas, nothing to be proud of. / Would Jeremiah be proud / if they told him / that Jewish sculptors / had carved a golden idol / of Ba'al Pe'or better / than the Canaanites?")

---

40 My translation consults Kreutzer and Hobson's translation, dalehobson.org, accessed November 29, 2022, http://www.dalehobson.org/khersonsky/boriscon.html.

This Jewish story of apostasy and cultural loss is also a reclamation of cosmopolitanism. By describing characters who read Mendele Moykher Sforim and engage in rabbinic disputes, Khersonsky is offering a literary alternative to the tradition of Soviet Odesa humor. He is also suggesting the possibility of a cultural alternative to a Soviet Jewish assimilation narrative.

Odesa's peripheral literary legacy

The literary critic Vinay Dharwadker described world literature as "a montage of overlapping maps in motion."[41] Odesa, a city on the periphery of the former tsarist, Ottoman, and Austro-Hungarian empires, reflects this kind of cultural montage, and as such, has provided a counterpoint to established world cultural centers, through literary production in Russian, Ukrainian, Yiddish, or Hebrew. Odesa, a culturally marginal space on the frontiers of the tsarist empire and Soviet Union, provided a crucial counterpoint to the more monolithic centers of government. In the early Soviet period, the center to which Russian-language Odesa writers turned was almost exclusively Moscow. The Soviet geopolitical hierarchy established Odesa, with its peripheral Russian accent and its history of multicultural exchange, and its legendary criminal underworld, as a source of comedy. Since Ukraine's 1991 declaration of independence, Odesa has remained on the periphery of Russian culture, but the political center has shifted from Moscow to Kyiv. Tanya Richardson has observed that "implicitly, contemporary representations of Jewish Odesa reinforce the idea that Odesa is situated in Russian cultural geographies but not Ukrainian ones."[42] Given the cultural role of Odesa in the Soviet Union, is it possible for this peripheral space to either reorient to a different center or to reinvent its identity as a post-Soviet city?

This Russophone Ukrainian city continues to have a role in Russian popular culture thirty years after the breakup of the Soviet Union.[43] The Odesa-born, Moscow-based satirist, Mikhail Zhvanetsky was known for his one-liners about life in the USSR.[44] Odesa, in Zhvanetsky's jokes, is funny because of his favored

---

41 Vinay Dharwadker, *Cosmopolitan Geographies: New Locations in Literature and Culture* (London and New York: Routledge, 2001), 3.
42 Richardson, *Kaleidoscopic Odessa*, 197.
43 On the proposal that Odesa should join Russia, see "Khar'kovu, Odesse i Nikolaevu nuzhno vossoedinit'sia s Rossiei," *EurAsia Daily*, June 17, 2020, https://eadaily.com/ru/news/2020/06/17/harkovu-odesse-i-nikolaevu-nuzhno-vossoedinitsya-s-rossiey-politolog.
44 On the "anthropological" orientation of Zhvanetsky's writing, see Olga Tabachnikova, *Russian Irrationalism from Pushkin to Brodsky: Seven Essays in Literature* (New York and London: Bloomsbury, 2015), 263.

combination of Ukrainian and Jewish Russian—two outsider cultures that are close enough to be central to Russian, but far enough away to make the Russian capital appear a stable center. He opens his vignette "Приезжий в Одессе" (A visitor in Odessa) with a conversation between two strangers. The visitor, who needs to send a letter, asks the Odesan where the post office is. The native Odesan invites the visitor to follow him. However, whereas in Odesa parlance the phrase "Пошлите со мной" means "let's go together," in standard Russian it means "Send it with me." The joke develops from a protracted miscommunication.[45]

Zhvanetsky's joke may be nominally at the expense of the Muscovite visitor, but it pokes fun at the Odesa dialect, exposing it as a backward, albeit endearing, manner of speaking that enriches the Russian language and Russian comedy through its idiosyncrasies. Zhvanetsky, who signed a letter condemning Russia's annexation of Crimea in 2014, did not align himself with Russian neo-imperialism. Nevertheless, his comedy perpetuates the trenchant cultural imperialism that Russia has sought to maintain in Ukraine and which denies the significance of Ukraine in the Russian cultural landscape. For Khersonsky, who, in his 2019 *Shoizdat* interview with Iya Kiva, called Zhvanetsky "the protagonist of Odesa," Zhvanetsky and the Worldwide Club of Odes(s)ans have helped to render Odesa a commemorative city, forging a tighter bond between contemporary Odesa and Odes(s)a-born Russian-speakers who have left the city.

Khersonsky has lamented the departure of Odesa's most creative writers, from Babel to Zhvanetsky, who commented, "Художники из Одессы уезжают. Ее надо заканчивать, как школу" (Artists leave Odessa. You have to finish it, like school).[46] Those left behind, Khersonsky observes, have steeped themselves in a mythology based on the work of these former Odesans:

> – З одного боку, ти живеш у місті з великими літературними традиціями, з підліткового віку перебуваючи в ореолі славетних імен Бабеля, Багрицького, Ільфа та Петрова, Катаєва. З іншого – ти поступово починаєш розуміти, в чому саме полягають ці традиції: місто народжує талановитих людей, але не піклується про них і не виховує, а навпаки – виштовхує.

---

45 Mikhail Zhvanetsky, *Sobranie proizvedenii v chetyrekh tomakh* (Moscow: Vremia, 2001); see http://www.jvanetsky.ru/data/text/t5/5tom_Priezzhij_v_Odesse/.

46 Mikhail Zhvanetsky, "Odessa," in *Sobranie proizvedenii v chetyrekh tomakh*, t. 1 (Moscow: Vremia, 2001); see oddesskiy.com, accessed January 2, 2023, http://odesskiy.com/zhvanetskiy-tom-1/odessa.html.

Знані імена здебільшого належать тим, хто виїхав з Одеси: спочатку – до Парижа, потім – до Москви, зараз іноді – до Києва.[47]

(On the one hand, you live in a city with great literary traditions, from childhood you're in the aura of the famous names of Babel, Bagritsky, Ilf and Petrov, Kataev. On the other hand, you gradually come to understand these traditions: the city gives birth to talented people but does not care for them and does not educate them, but on the contrary—pushes them out. The best-known names are mostly people who left Odesa: at first for Paris, then Moscow, and now sometimes Kyiv.)

The abandoning of Odesa is a recurrent theme in the work of younger Russophone Odesa writers who came of age after Ukraine's independence: "Мы – бегущие по волнам ломаные песчинки, / Невесомое крошево солнца на улице Веры И" (We are the broken grains of sand running in the waves, / The weightless crumbs of sun on Vera I. Street), writes Elena Borishpolets, a poet born in Odesa in 1980.[48] The Odesa that Borishpolets describes is a remnant, lingering after others have departed, bearing names of nearly forgotten Soviet poets such as Vera Inber. The poetic persona struggles against a Kunderan "lightness of being": life, bereft of the heavy ideology of Cold War communism, has been cast adrift. The poem ends with a return to this unsettling weightlessness and immobility:

> Завтра с рассветом выйду и поверну направо,
> Я ничего не вешу, а мне очень нужен вес.
> Боже, когда мне ехать? Боже, куда мне надо?
> И Боже тихонько скажет: ты остаёшься здесь.

(Tomorrow at dawn I'll go out and turn to the right, / I don't weigh anything, but I really need weight. / God, when should I leave? God where should I go? / And God will quietly say: you'll stay right here.)

---

47 Iya Kiva, interview with Boris Khersonsky.
48 Elena Borishpolets, "Iuzhnaia storona" *45parallel*, accessed November 30, 2022, https://45parallel.net/elena_borishpolets/stihi/#yuzhnaya_storona.

Borishpolets highlights the struggle between an oppressive past and a stagnant present. The divine command that ends the poem echoes in descriptions of the city, including its gritty courtyards and prying neighbors.

Borishpolets published her first book, *Голубая звезда* (Blue star), in 2015, under the auspices of the "Green Lamp" literary club, which is part of the Worldwide Club of Odes(s)ans. Another member of the "Green Lamp" group, Taisia (Taia) Naidenko, a poet and journalist born in 1982, has enjoyed some acclaim among Russian literary critics. Like Borishpolets, Naidenko meditates on hypothetical departures. One poem begins, "Супермен проживает в Одессе. Вторую осень / Уклоняется он от призыва. Под психа косит" (Superman has been living in Odesa. For the second autumn / he's evaded the draft. Faking madness). In the final stanza, Superman lifts off to the sky, as the persona watches, unable to follow. "Город шепчет 'Останься. . . .' / И я всегда остаюсь" (The city whispers, "Stay." . . . / And I always remain . . .).[49]

Naidenko is very much a poet of contemporary Odessa. She has spoken out publicly against the current Russian regime and discussed the difficulty of writing in Russian as a Ukrainian. Simultaneously, she has embraced a sartorial similarity to the poet Anna Akhmatova (1889–1966) in her clothing and hairstyle. In a review of Naidenko's book launch at the Worldwide Club of Odes(s)ans, Evgeny Golubovsky jokes about Naidenko's resemblance to her famous Odesa-born forebear:

> Верите ли вы в реинкарнацию? И я не верил. До тех пор пока . . . Так вот я вчера проводил презентацию первой книги Анны Ахматовой «Вечер», 1912 год. Перед первой мировой.[50]
>
> (Do you believe in reincarnation? Neither did I. Until now. . . . So yesterday I led a presentation of Anna Akhmatova's first book, her 1912 *Evening*. Before World War I.)

The Russian author, journalist, and literary critic Dmitry Bykov discussed Naidenko in a radio editorial devoted to Ukraine, which aired on the Moscow station Ekho Moskvy in August 2017. Even as he attempts to differentiate

---

49 Taia Naidenko, "Supermen v Odesse" (from her collection *Zapakh chaek i moria krik*), *Almanakh Deribasovskaia Rishel'evskaia*, no. 74 (2014): 219. The poem was republished in *Vse D(a)no* (Odesa: Zelenaia lampa, 2019), 13.
50 Evgeny Golubovsky, "'Vse dano,' Taia Naidenko. Vyshla v svet debiutnaia kniga avtora," odessitclub.org, March 20, 2019, https://www.odessitclub.org/index.php/novosti-i-publikatsii/2702-vsjo-dano-verite-li-vy-v-reinkarnatsiyu.

Naidenko from Akhmatova, the comparison leads Bykov into the trappings of literary sexism, wherein the woman poet's crime, to cite Adrienne Rich, is "only to cast too bold a shadow."[51] In Bykov's words,

> Найденко . . . нашла очень быстро свою дорогу. И невзирая на то, что она внешне так похожа на Ахматову. . . . В одном только они похожи – в таком некотором бесстыдстве. Но ее поэма, ну, или цикл большой о современной Одессе – это такой новый одесский эпос, попытка создать новую одесскую культуру, как бы написать ее поверх всех этих бабелевских и катаевских текстов, попытка действительно создать современный одесский миф.[52]

> (Naidenko . . . has quickly found her own way, despite looking so much like Akhmatova. They are similar in only one way—they share a certain shamelessness. But her *poema*, or long cycle about contemporary Odesa—is a new Odesa epic, an attempt to create a new Odesa culture, as if to write it over all those Babel and Kataev texts, an attempt truly to create a contemporary Odesa myth.)

Bykov, who undermines his own observations by characterizing both poets as "shameless," nonetheless observes the extent to which Naidenko, as she works to find her voice as a poet, is constricted by the scaffolding of Russian culture, including those Soviet writers who have linked Odesa to the Russian language— Babel, Kataev, and others. Akhmatova, whose connection to the city is limited to her biography, nevertheless bestows associative literary capital on Naidenko, which has helped to make her legible in Russian literature. The sheer enormity of Odesa's Russian literary history makes it difficult to escape Russia's cultural orbit. Pascale Casanova, in her center/periphery model, acknowledges the myth of "peaceful internationalism, a world of free and equal access in which literary recognition is available to all writers, an enchanted world that exists outside time and space and so escapes the mundane conflicts of human history."[53] To dismantle the myth of a peaceful exchange of literature between center and periphery

---

51 Adrienne Rich, *Snapshots of a Daughter in Law* (New York: Norton, 1967), 24.
52 Dmitry Bykov, "Odin," *Ekho Moskvy*, August 4, 2017, https://echo.msk.ru/programs/odin/2030070-echo/.
53 Pascale Casanova, *The World Republic of Letters*, trans. M. B. DeBevoise (Cambridge, MA: Harvard University Press, 2004), 43.

would require desacralizing the tradition of Russian high culture and its deeply talented Odesa practitioners. The Russophone Odesa writers who work under the auspices of the Worldwide Club of Odes(s)ans have had difficulty escaping a twentieth-century Odesa literary tradition. Khersonsky, although thirty years older than Naidenko and Borishpolets, has resisted—sometimes to the point of self-parody—any connection between his own poetry and Soviet Odesa.

Boris Khersonsky's anamnesis

Whereas, in his earlier work, Khersonsky unearthed family memories hidden since the revolution, in the years since the 2013–2014 Euromaidan, he has attacked the Soviet Odesa myth more directly. In a July 2017 poem addressed to Isaak Babel, Khersonsky offers a pastiche of language reminiscent of Mayakovsky, Brodsky, and Blok to combine images from Babel's *Red Cavalry* tales with the exploits of Benia Krik, the gangster king of *Odessa Stories*:

> Слышу крики "ура!" и звон буденовских сабель.
> Слышу разбойничий свист на улицах Молдаванки.
> Тише ораторы! Ваше слово, товарищ Бабель!
> Жизнь – поддельный брюлик, но хорошей огранки.
> Итальянская ария с черноморских подмостков
> отзовется в парадных ля-минорной блатною песней
> в исполнении под гитару группой пьяных подростков.
> Революция – это прекрасно, ограбления – интересней
> Ибо вор в законе – тот же царь на престоле.[54]

(I hear the "Hurrahs" and the clangor of sabers from Budenny's ranks. / I hear the robber's whistle on the Moldavanka streets. / Hush, orators! You have the floor, Comrade Babel! / Life is a fake diamond, but a good cut. / An Italian aria from the Black Sea stage / will echo in the thief's song in A-minor performed / on the landing by a bunch of drunk teenagers with a guitar / accompaniment. / Revolution is great, robbery is more interesting / For a crime lord is the same as a tsar on his throne.)

---

54 Boris Khersonsky, "Den' rozhdeniia Isaaka Babelia," Facebook post, July 12, 2020, https://www.facebook.com/borkhers/posts/3451296364905165. The poem is dated July 13, 2017.

In his ongoing engagement with Babel's legacy, Khersonsky criticizes the immobility of Odesa's literary culture. More importantly, he creates his own fictionalized Babel as a convenient means of likening the continued celebration of revolution and war to the exaltation of bandits. The accusation is not entirely fair or accurate: Babel was critical of violence and ironical about the weapon-wielding Cossacks in *Red Cavalry* and bandits of his *Odessa Stories* (though his narrators admire their masculinity and prowess). What we find in Khersonsky, then, is a fictionalized Babel, which allows Khersonsky simultaneously to differentiate himself from one of his literary models and undermine the pro-Russian mythology in Odesa. When asked whether it is possible for Odesa's literary culture to move beyond its Soviet myth, Khersonsky proposed that the Odesa myth must first be "decriminalized." "Mishka Yaponchik and Sonka Zolotaia Ruchka cannot be the city's symbols."[55] By rejecting Babel's fictionalized status as an Odesa patriarch, he is calling for a different kind of cosmopolitan Odesa culture, one that might replace the hegemonic status of the Russian literary canon.

Khersonsky's 2017 book *Одесская интеллигенция* (Odessa intelligentsia) is arguably his most biting satire of Odesa literary culture. The book includes the satirical novella *Записки безумца* (Notes of a madman) and poems dedicated to the city, all of which take aim at the ossified nature of Odesa literary culture. *Notes of a Madman* opens with a declaration: "Это было так давно, что Одессу еще не переименовали в пгт [поселок городского типа] Одессочка" (This happened such a long time ago that Odessa had not yet been renamed the rural township of Odessochka).[56] The figure of the "Odessa Intelligentsia" ("O. I.") wanders throughout the book: it is a "молодящаяся дама, склонная к полноте, от природы кудрявая и страстная. Ее мама – Одесса, папа неизвестен, ибо мама та еще. . . . Сама О.И. считает, что ее папа – Исаак Бабель, который во всем признался перед расстрелом"[57] (. . . a lady who attempts to appear young, with a tendency to put on weight, passionate, with natural curls. Her mother is Odes(s)a, her father is unknown because mama is such a. . . . O. I. herself believes her dad may be Isaak Babel, who confessed to everything before he was executed). This singular figure, a misogynistic embodiment of the "Odessa Mama," haunts the waking and dreaming psyche of the first-person narrator. Her close friend is the similarly anthropomorphized Odes(s)a Literary Community, who resents the narrator "за то, что я выкладываю много стихов в Фейсбуке"[58]

---

55 Iya Kiva, interview with Boris Khersonsky.
56 Boris Khersonsky, *Odesskaia Intelligentsiia* (Kharkov: Folio, 2017), 11.
57 Ibid., 13.
58 Ibid., 224.

(because I post too many poems on Facebook). O. I. carries a Chinese fan in her muff of "three silver fox tails," where she also keeps a copy of Babel's *Odessa Tales*. She meets the narrator on the city streets, knocks on his door in the middle of the night, and disturbs his dreams. The narrator, for his part, haunts and taunts the Odes(s)a Intelligentsia in equal measure. Yet, as the narrator repeats multiple times, "Я сошел с ума от любви к Одесской Интеллигенции"[59] (I fell madly in love with the Odessa Intelligentsia).

The "Odessa Intelligentsia" is heir to the city's culture, arbiter of taste, object of desire, and friend of the city's literary community. In one episode, the narrator describes a group congregating outside a literary club, where a woman in uniform admits them one by one, using a set of Odesa-themed passwords:

> Пароль – Леонид. Отзыв – Утесов. Пароль – Исаак. Отзыв – Бабель. Один пожилой дядя ответил – Иаков, и его не пустили. Пароль – Одесса. Отзыв – Жемчужина. Пароль – Каштан. Отзыв – Платан.[60]

> (Password: Leonid. Response: Utiosov. Password: Isaak. Response: Babel. One old fellow answered Jacob, and they did not let him in. Password: Odessa. Response: Pearl. Password: Chestnut. Response: Sycamore.)

The narrator recognizes the bouncer to be the Odes(s)a Intelligentsia. She looks at him and promptly closes the door behind her. Из полуподвала раздались аплодисменты. Там начинался поэтический спам, ох, извините, слэм[61] (From the basement came applause. The poetry spam—oops, slam—had begun). Intelligentsia's literary taste is bound to the Soviet canon: she recites poetry by Anna Akhmatova and Vera Inber and defends the honor of Isaak Babel.

Self-psychoanalysis meets the time-honored tradition of literary parody: O. I., who is perpetually spurning or scolding the narrator, is an object of desire and disgust. In one exchange, the narrator recites a satirical couplet that pokes fun at what he characterizes as the shtetl nostalgia of the Soviet Jewish writers Ilya Ehrenburg and Vera Inber:

---

59 Ibid., 50.
60 Ibid., 18.
61 Ibid.

Дико воет Эренбург, повторяет Инбер дичь его,
ни Москва, ни Петербург не заменят им Бердичева.⁶²

(Ehrenburg is howling wildly, Inber follows suit, / neither Moscow, nor Petersburg will replace Berdichev for them.)

Odes(s)a Intelligentsia, upon hearing this, accuses the narrator of antisemitism. When reminded that she isn't even Jewish, O. I. responds, "– Я интернациональная. Спроси у кого угодно, и тебе ответят: Одесская Интеллигенция интернациональна!"⁶³ (I am international. Ask anyone, and they will tell you that the Odes(s)a Intelligentsia is international!). Here, international, which so often appeared in the Soviet Union as code for assimilated Jews, is an ironic reference to the persistent myth of Soviet Odesa multiculturalism. By claiming internationalism, the non-Jewish O. I. is able to accuse the Jewish, pro-Ukrainian narrator of antisemitism, thereby mirroring and parodying the popular Kremlin-aligned view that Ukrainians who resist Russia's dominance are aligned with fascists. The narrator concludes that, sadly, this was a dream. "Эротический сон, героиней которого я так и не смог овладеть ни во сне, ни наяву. . ."⁶⁴ (An erotic dream, with a heroine I could never possess in a dream or in real life . . .). The dysfunctional relationship is burdened by the perpetual possibility of intimacy. Later, when the narrator describes propositioning O. I., she explains that he is too Jewish:

– Понимаешь, ты, конечно, не обрезан, но в остальном у тебя типично еврейская внешность.
– В чем проблема? Ты же интернациональна!
– Да, я интернациональна! Но я потенциальная наследница Одесской Аристократии. Поэтому у себя дома я должна быть хоть немного антисемиткой . . .⁶⁵

("You see, of course you aren't circumcised, but in every other way you have a typical Jewish appearance.
"What's the problem? You're international, after all!

---

62 Ibid., 27.
63 Ibid.
64 Ibid.
65 Ibid.

"Yes, I'm international! But I'm a potential heir to the Odes(s)a Aristocracy. Therefore, in private I have to be at least a little bit antisemitic...")

The encounters between the culturally disenfranchised narrator and O. I. take place over a span of decades. There was, we learn, a time when the two frequently met. Their friendly conversations, visits to the beach, and meetings in dreams tend to end in philosophical stalemates. O. I. and her friends, Odes(s)a Literary Community and Odes(s)a Agency have conversations that could, in theory, have taken place in the Soviet period, on topics such as Brezhnev, bathing suits, and Akhmatova. They do not like to discuss religion or joke about Isaak Babel. Inevitably, the narrator quarrels with Odes(s)a Intelligentsia. Among his other offenses, the narrator learns that he has been rejected for calling Babel's Benia Krik a bandit.[66] Tortured by O. I.'s rejection, the narrator unfriends her on Facebook.

The elusive O. I. occupies a place in the narrator's psyche between mother and lover. Toward the end of the novella, the narrator dreams of the heroine's attempt (unsuccessfully) to suckle newborn Odessa "Не берет!" (She won't take it!), O. I. cries. When the narrator responds, "Дай мне, я возьму!" (Give it to me, I'll take it!), he is spurned: "Ни капли моего молока предателю Одессы!"[67] (Not a drop of milk for the traitor to Odessa!). Syntactically, this statement is ambiguous: the narrator could just as easily be offering to take Baby Odes(s)a for O. I. as to offer to take her breast. But to Odes(s)a Intelligentsia, he is unambiguously a spurned child. The novella can be read as a manifesto in which Boris Khersonsky gleefully embraces his role as Odesa's renegade son. Symbolically loaded characters mix, fall in and out of love, and utter platitudes. These include the Odes(s)a Agency, the narrator's wife Lusia (Khersonsky's actual wife, Ludmila Khersonskaia, is also called Lusia), the black cat, Basia, Major Valerevich, and Fidel and Raul Castro, who eventually make their way to visit Odesa via Lviv. An artist resembling Aleksandr Roitburd—dubbed here "Краснобородер" (Redbeard)—enters the book as a figure who offends public taste. In one conversation, O. I. asks the narrator about the artist's work:

---

66 Ibid., 225.
67 Ibid.

— А правда, что художник Краснобородер рисует Шевченко, "Битлз," Пушкина и Достоевского с ... (тут она немного смутилась) – с писями?
— Не с писями, а с пейсами! – наставительно сказал я.
— Ой, это еще хуже! – побледнев, сказала Одесская Интеллигенция.[68]

("Is it true that the artist Krasnoboroder is depicting Shevchenko, the 'Beatles,' Pushkin, and Dostoevsky with ... (here she was a bit embarrassed)—with penises?
"Not with penises, but with *peyos*!" [sidelocks]—I explained.
"Oy, that's even worse!" said the Odessa Intelligentsia, turning pale.)

Roitburd, apart from appearing in fictionalized cameos in the novella, wrote a preface for the book in which he describes Khersonsky's "anamnesis"—the obsessive recollection of memories, or a patient's account of their own medical history:

Одесским поэтам положено воспевать Одессу и одесситов. Херсонский обследует город и его обитателей как врач, вскрывая язвы, проникая в глубины бессознательного, диагностируя тяжелые и зачастую неизлечимые заболевания. Там, где у других – краеведение, у Херсонского – анамнез.[69]

(Odessa poets are supposed to glorify Odessa and Odessans. Khersonsky examines the city and its residents as a doctor, discovering ulcers, penetrating the depths of the unconscious, diagnosing difficult and often incurable diseases. Where others have local history, Khersonsky has anamnesis.)

Odesa's real ulcers, Roitburd observes, show up in thinly veiled ciphers for those familiar with the city's history: the corner of Babel and Bebel streets is the historical KGB building. Roitburd observes further that the bizarre anti-Ukrainian slogans such as "We won't believe the evil fool who plays on the bandura," and "Those who wear an embroidered shirt, must answer to a Russian tank" appeared

---

68 Ibid., 248.
69 Ibid., 4.

in pro-Russian demonstrations in Odesa in the spring of 2014.[70] Roitburd, naming the political antagonism that inspired *Notes of a Madman*, helps to lay bare the division between one Odesa that aligns itself with Russia and another that aligns itself with Ukraine. Roitburd and Khersonsky, despite being Russophone artists who are influenced by Russian art and literature, have firmly cast their lot with Kyiv.

Roitburd's ironic treatment of post-Soviet Ukraine desacralizes post-Soviet nostalgia and serves as a natural illustration of Khersonsky's work. Khersonsky, in fact, includes several of Aleksandr Roitburd's paintings from the 2016 series "Metaphysics of Myth" in *Odessa Intelligentsiia*. Roitburd similarly desacralized Odesa nostalgia in his visual art. The cycle depicts famous city landmarks invaded by sea creatures. The architecture of the Odesa pier, Pushkin's bust, and the train station are underwater. The statue of Duc de Richelieu is covered in sea snails (figure 1).

Figure 4. Aleksandr Roitburd, "Вид Толедо в Ненастье" (View of Toledo in Bad Weather), from *Метафизика Мифа* (Metaphysics of Myth), oil on canvas, 150 × 200 cm), 2016. Reproduced with permission of the artist.

---

70 Ibid.

Odesa in Roitburd's series has been metaphysically invaded, its mythical status made irrelevant and ridiculous by swamp creatures. In this cycle, the slowly eroding city yields to creatures and darkness. Roitburd, who is a practitioner of the trans-avant-garde school, has long created works that, like the postmodern conceptualist art of the late and post-Soviet period, unsettle the sacred texts of Soviet culture. His 1998 short video project, "Psychedelic Invasion of the Battleship *Potemkin* into Sergei Eisenstein's Tautological Hallucinations," refigures Eisenstein's sober image of the mother holding her wounded child before the tsar's officers as two figures, dressed in the masks of beasts, on the iconic Potemkin steps (figure 2).

Figure 5. Aleksandr Roitburd, "Psychedelic Invasion of the Battleship *Potemkin* into Sergei Eisenstein's Tautological Hallucinations," still from black-and-white video, 1998, Museum of Modern Art, New York. Reproduced with permission of the artist.

Khersonsky's rejection of Odesa's Soviet-centered culture is more comprehensible in light of Roitburd's visual art. Both artists actively supported the Euromaidan and both then devoted much of their work to publicly rejecting a Russia-centered vision of Odesa. Although both Khersonsky and Roitburd have garnered praise and prizes nationally and internationally, both remain an enigma in their home city. Roitburd was temporarily dismissed from his position as director of the Museum of Fine Arts in 2018, following controversy over his participation in the Maidan, and reinstated following a large demonstration against his dismissal. Khersonsky has similarly sparked outrage over his grotesque treatments of sacred memories. In a 2008 poem, which Khersonsky posted to Facebook on May 8, 2019, the day before the May 9th celebration of Victory in Europe Day, he takes aim at the Soviet commemoration of World War II.

> Будет Коля жив – без ноги, но с медалью,
> Будет пить в подвале со всякой швалью.
> Будет пить-гулять, наливать соседу
> Будет песни петь про войну-победу.[71]

(Kolia will survive—without a leg, but with a medal, / He'll drink in the basement with any old riffraff. / He'll wander drunk, pour up for his neighbor, / He'll sing songs of the war-victory.)

Khersonsky's rejection of the ossified war narrative about heroes, like his rejection of the ossified Babel myth, exposes a desire to remove Odesa from the Soviet sphere. The bloggers at "Timer" called Khersonsky's May 9 posts scandalous.

Khersonsky, in response, redoubled his criticism of his native city. In a Facebook post on July 5, 2020, he attributed the sharp decline in the level of literary life in the provinces and in Odesa in particular to several factors, including "Гибель редактуры и критики" (the death of editing and criticism), the noise of mass media, the "Odesa myth," and the divisive effects of the Donbas War.[72] How viable or lasting is the Odesa myth in the twenty-first century, particularly amidst a war between Ukraine and Russia?

Khersonsky, like Roitburd, came of age in the Soviet dissident generation, a generation that, recognizing the inconsistencies of the Soviet project, bastardized socialist realism and high culture alike in works of *sots-art*: Vitaly Komar and Alexander Melamid, in their 1982 satire, "Yalta Conference," replaced the iconic portrait of Roosevelt, Stalin, and Churchill with an image of E. T., Stalin, and (huddled in the shadows behind them) Hitler. Classic writers were not exempt

---

71 Boris Khersonsky, "Edut tanki po chernomu poliu," Facebook post, May 8, 2019), https://www.facebook.com/borkhers/posts/2470916126276532.

72 Boris Khersonsky, Facebook post, July 5, 2020 https://www.facebook.com/borkhers/posts/pfbid021FhYPLktGasG9ZSY5jgoC4zhPd2XYtCBZVKdN6YCyMcs7tYacV6Nzn8N23L2C-Gqgl.

from this kind of satire. Boris Orlov, in his 1989 "Totem National, A. S. Pushkin in Marshal's Uniform," displayed a bust of Pushkin covered in several dozen Soviet military medals, and writers such as Dmitry Prigov and Vladimir Sorokin have taken aim at the Russian canon. These ironic interpretations of Soviet icons of high culture suggest that military and cultural images have already morphed into objects of kitsch in their official presentations.

To some extent, Khersonsky's desacralizing treatment of the mythical image of Babel approximates this critical conceptualist tradition. Khersonsky, however, explicitly distances his project from the Russian Moscow-based Sots Art movement-art. At the end of *Notes of a Madman*, the narrator describes an armed guard at the state art warehouse who asks visitors to renounce postmodernism. A friend made it into the warehouse in hopes of seeing the dead corpse of socialist realism. "Но оказалось, что покойник жив, называет себя Соц-артом, попивает чилийское вино 'Пиночет' (или 'Пинонечет'? – вечно я все путаю)" (But it turns out that the deceased is alive, it calls itself sots-art, and it is drinking the Chilean wine Pinochet (or is it 'Pinot-no' [Пинонечет, lit. Pinot-odd number]?—I always mix everything up . . .). By dismissing sots-art on the penultimate page of his novella, Khersonsky also rejects late Soviet satirical iconography which, while bastardizing socialist realism, nonetheless repurposes it as high kitsch that is too close to a Soviet aesthetic.

In a 2016 poem included in *Odessa Intelligentsia*, Khersonsky writes of the incompatibility of the Odesa myth with the city's reality.

> В мире есть только Одесса. Но и Одесса не та.
> Формы ее расплылись и поблекли цвета.
>
> Эх, взял бы я в руки тросточку, и надел канотье,
> спел бы прохожим песенку о нашем житье-бытье,
> о двадцать третьем трамвае, который давно не маршрут,
> о запертом накрепко рае, куда никого не берут,
> о тех, кто свалили отсюда и не вспоминают о нас,
> о лицах приезжего люда, о толпах трудящихся масс . . .[73]

(In the world there is only Odessa. But Odessa isn't the same. / Her forms are blurred, and her color has faded. / Eh, I would pick up a cane and don a boater hat, / I would sing a song to

---

73 Khersonsky, *Odesskaia Intelligentsiia*, 306.

passersby of our life and livelihood, / of tram 23, which long since stopped running, / of the tightly locked heaven, where nobody is admitted, / of the ones who took off and don't remember us, / of the faces of the visitors, of the crowds of the working masses . . .)

In this poem, Odesa continues to flout an ill-fitting myth. The singer that the poet longs to become is the same singer that he rejects, the Odesa-born writer who continues to paint a commemorative picture of a forgotten, peripheral Odesa. Instead, the poet sings of a city that has ceased to move, that has become disconnected from the very cosmopolitanism it once epitomized. Those Ukrainians who have embraced a civic understanding of nationhood have arguably moved toward a new form of multiethnic cosmopolitanism, which, to borrow Martha Nussbaum's formulation of the Kantian cosmopolitan ideal, can be defined as the expression of "allegiance . . . to the community of human beings in the entire world."[74] Khersonsky paints a picture of an Odesa that has been left behind, a victim of a failed Soviet internationalist project that, as Khersonsky presents it, now masquerades as Russian cultural imperialism.

At times, Khersonsky's ironic rejection of Odes(s)a comes uncannily close to the tradition he claims to resist. Babel, after all, began his 1916 essay "Odessa" mocking the revulsion a Russian from the capital felt towards Odesa Russian: "Одесса очень скверный город" (Odesa is a terrible city).[75] Khersonsky, a longtime reader of Babel, is aware of Babel's ideological complexities. Efraim Sicher, in his reading of Babel's incomplete collectivization stories, observes that Babel "knew the truth about Stalinism" and, moreover, "[p]ossibly, we will never know how much of that truth he managed to tell in the stories that have been lost to us."[76] Khersonsky's quarrel, after all, is not really with the writer he once loved but with the national supremacy and neo-imperialism that encroached upon literary freedom by the late 1920s. If Babel sought to renew the stultified Russian canon with his *Odessa Stories*—a bible for Soviet modernism,—Khersonsky's rejection of Babel's Odesa myth constitutes a form of apostasy. For Khersonsky, the nostalgic celebration of Soviet Odesa culture, albeit with a heavy dose of irony, is a threat to a state still fighting for its independence from Russia.

---

74 Martha Nussbaum, "Patriotism and Cosmopolitanism," *Boston Review*, October 1, 1994, https://www.bostonreview.net/articles/martha-nussbaum-patriotism-and-cosmopolitanism/.
75 Isaak Babel, "Moi listki: Odessa."
76 Efraim Sicher, *Babel in Context: A Study in Cultural Identity* (Boston: Academic Studies Press, 2012), 227.

Contributors

Amelia M. Glaser's work lies at the intersection of Russian, Ukrainian, and Jewish literatures. She is the author of *Jews and Ukrainians in Russia's Literary Borderlands* (Northwestern University Press, 2012) and *Songs in Dark Times: Yiddish Poetry of Struggle from Scottsboro to Palestine* (Harvard University Press, 2020), the editor of *Stories of Khmelnytsky: Competing Literary Legacies of the 1648 Ukrainian Cossack Uprising* (Stanford University Press, 2015), *Comintern Aesthetics* (with Steven S. Lee, University of Toronto Press, 2020), and the translator of *Proletpen: America's Rebel Yiddish Poets* (University of Wisconsin Press, 2005). She teaches Russian and Comparative Literature at the University of California—San Diego, where she holds the endowed Chair in Judaic Studies.

Guido Hausmann is professor of East and Southeast European history at the University of Regensburg, Germany, and head of the history division at the Leibniz Institute for East and Southeast European Studies, Regensburg. He is the author of *Universität und städtische Gesellschaft in Odessa, 1865–1917. Soziale und nationale Selbstorganisation an der Peripherie des Zarenreiches.* (Steiner Verlag, 1998) and of *Mütterchen Wolga. Ein Fluss als Erinnerungsort vom 16. bis zum frühen 20 Jahrhundert* (Campus Verlag, 2009).

Brian Horowitz is the Sizeler Family Professor of Jewish Studies at Tulane University in New Orleans. He is the author of many books and articles on East European Jewish history. His study *Vladimir Jabotinsky's Russia Years, 1900–1925* appeared in 2020 (Indiana University Press). He has also edited with Leonid Katsis *Jabotinsky's Story of My Life* (Wayne State University Press, 2016).

Mirja Lecke (co-editor) is chair of the Department of Slavic Literatures and Cultures at the University of Regensburg, Germany. Her academic interests include Russian literature of the imperial and post-Soviet periods in postcolonial perspective and Polish literature of the Enlightenment and postcommunist eras. She is the author of *Westland. Polen und die Ukraine in der russischen Literatur von Puškin bis Babel'* (Peter Lang, 2015), a monograph about the representation of the Western borderlands in Russian imperial literature, and with Elena Chkhaidze she co-edited *Rossiia – Gruziia posle imperii*

[Russia—Georgia after empire] (NLO, 2018), a volume on Russian-Georgian literary relations in the post-Soviet era.

Svetlana Natkovich is a senior lecturer in the Department of Jewish History at the University of Haifa. Her interests include issues of Jewish modernization in Eastern Europe, the history of early Zionism, the intersection between history and literature, and the cultural history of capitalism. She is the author of *Among Radiant Clouds: The Fiction of Vladimir (Ze'ev) Jabotinsky in Its Social Context* [Hebrew] (Magnes Press, 2015) and editor of *Vilna Casanova: Three Autobiographical Texts by Abraham Uri Kovner* [Hebrew] (Dvir, 2017).

Yohanan Petrovsky-Shtern is the Crown Family Professor of Jewish Studies and a professor of Jewish history in the History Department at Northwestern University. Petrovsky-Shtern is a Fulbright Specialist on Eastern Europe, and a fellow at the Harvard Ukrainian Research Institute. He has been a full professor at the Free Ukrainian University in Munich; a regular visiting professor at the Ukrainian Catholic University in Lviv; Lady Davis Professor at the Hebrew University of Jerusalem; and the Kosciuszko Visiting Professor at Warsaw University. He has been awarded an honorary doctorate of the National University Kyiv-Mohyla Academy in Kyiv. He has published more than one hundred articles and seven books, including *The Jews in the Russian Army: Drafted into Modernity* (Cambridge University Press, 2008; 2nd ed., 2014); *The Anti-Imperial Choice: the Making of the Ukrainian Jew* (Yale University Press, 2009); *Lenin's Jewish Question* (Yale University Press, 2010); *Jews and Ukrainians*, special issue of *Polin* 26 (Littman Library of Jewish Civilization, 2011, co-edited with Antony Polonsky); *Cultural Interference of Jews and Ukrainians: A Field in the Making* (Kyiv-Mohyla Academy, 2014); *The Golden Age Shtetl: A New History of Jewish Life in East Europe* (Princeton University Press, 2014; 2nd ed. 2015); *Jews and Ukrainians: A Millennium of Co-Existence* (University of Toronto Press, 2016, co-authored with Paul Robert Magocsi; 2nd ed. 2018). His works have been translated into Russian, Polish, Ukrainian, French, Spanish, German, and Hebrew.

Abel Polese is a scholar and development worker who divides his time between Europe, the former USSR, and Southeast Asia. His doctoral dissertation was titled "Dynamics of Nation Building and Identity Construction: A Case Study of Odessa" (Free University of Brussels, 2009). He was principal investigator of SHADOW a four-year project beginning in 2018, funded through Marie Curie RISE, a research and training program designed to develop strategic intelligence on the region and train specialists on informality in post-Soviet spaces. His project "Sustainable Development in Cultural Diversity" received the Council of Europe's Global Education Award in 2011. He is a member of the Global Young Academy, uniting scholars active in research policy and dialogue with non-academic institutions and has been a visiting fellow at the University of Toronto, Harvard University, Renmin University, China, Tbilisi State University, Jawarlahal Nehru University, Tezpur University, Corvinus University, the University of Cagliari, and the Moscow Higher School of Economics. In 2020–21, he was a visiting professor at the Graduate School of Core Ethics and Frontier Sciences, Ritsumeikan University in Kyoto, Japan. He has published seventeen books, over one hundred peer-reviewed chapters and articles and designed capacity building and training programs in the Caucasus, Central Asia, Eastern Europe, Southeast Asia, and Latin America.

Anat Rubinstein is a choral director and musicologist who specializes in the research and performance of Jewish choral music. She completed her PhD in musicology at the Hebrew University of Jerusalem in 2013 on the life and works of Cantor Pinkhas Minkowsky (1859–1924), who was a significant and influential figure in early twentieth-century Jewish music in Odesa. Dr. Rubinstein has established and conducted various choirs in Israel and the USA and has organized choral events and workshops at the community and university level. She is currently the conductor and music director of the Hebrew University Students' Choir in Jerusalem, Israel, and a lecturer at the External Studies Institute at the Jerusalem Academy of Music and Dance.

Efraim Sicher (co-editor) is emeritus professor of Comparative Literature at Ben-Gurion University of the Negev, Israel. He has published widely on modern Jewish culture, including *Jews in Russian Literature after the October Revolution: Writers and Artists Between Apostasy and Hope* (Cambridge University Press, 1995), and has edited the unexpurgated stories of Isaak Babel in Russian, English, and Hebrew. His book *Babel in Context* was published by Academic Studies Press in 2012. Among his recent books are *The Jew's Daughter: A Cultural History of a Conversion Narrative* (Lexington Books, 2017); *Re-Envisioning Jewishness: Reflections on Identity in Contemporary Jewish Culture* (Brill, 2021); *Postmodern Love in the Contemporary Jewish Imagination: Negotiating Identities and Spaces* (Routledge, 2022). His new book (with Daniel Feldman), *Poesis in Extremis: Literature Witnessing the Holocaust*, is forthcoming from Bloomsbury.

Robert Weinberg is Isaac H. Clothier Professor of History and International Relations at Swarthmore College. He is the author of *The Revolution of 1905 in*

Odessa: Blood on the Steps (Indiana University Press, 1993); *Stalin's Forgotten Zion: Birobidzhan and the Making of a Soviet Jewish Homeland* (University of California Press, 1998); *Revolutionary Russia: A History in Documents* (with Laurie Bernstein; Oxford University Press, 2010); *Ritual Murder in Late Imperial Russia: The Trial of Mendel Beilis* (Indiana University Press, 2013). He is also co-editor of *Ritual Murder in Russia, Eastern Europe, and Beyond* (Indiana University Press, 2017) and has published articles on antisemitism; the Jewish labor movement; ethnic violence in late imperial Russia; anti-Judaism in the early Soviet period; and efforts to productivize Russian and Soviet Jews.

Oleksandr Zabirko studied literature and linguistics at the University of Luhansk (Ukraine) and the University of Duisburg-Essen (Germany). Currently, he is a researcher in the Slavic Department of the University of Regensburg. His major fields of research are literary models of spatial and political order, contemporary literature(s) from Russia and Ukraine, and fantastic literature in general. His most recent publication is the monograph *Literarische Formen der Geopolitik: Raum – und Ordnungsmodellierung in der russischen und ukrainischen Gegenwartsliteratur* (Literary Forms of Geopolitics: The Modelling of Spatial and Political Order in Contemporary Russian and Ukrainian literature [University of Münster Press, 2021]).

Bibliography

Aberbach, David. *Bialik*. New York: Grove Press, 1988.

Adam, Thomas. *Buying Respectability: Philanthropy and Urban Society in Transnational Perspective, 1840s to 1930s*. Bloomington: Indiana University Press, 2009.

Agamben, Giorgio. *State of Exception*. Translated by Kevin Attell. Chicago: University of Chicago Press, 2003.

Ahad Ha'am (Asher Zvi Hirsch Ginsberg). "Rech' Akhad-Gaama na soveshchaniiakh OPE v Odesse, 15 maia 1902 g." *Nedel'naia khronika voskhoda*, June 21, 1902, 488–89.

Akinsha, Konstantin. "Culture Wars, Odessa Style." *Atlantic Council*, September 24, 2019. https://www.atlanticcouncil.org/blogs/ukrainealert/culture-wars-odesa-style/.

Andriewsky, Olga. "'Medved' iz berlogi': Vladimir Jabotinsky and the Ukrainian question, 1904–1914." *Harvard Ukrainian Studies* 14, no. 3–4 (1990): 249–67.

Appiah, Kwame Anthony. "Cosmopolitan Patriots." In *Cosmopolitics: Thinking and Feeling beyond the Nation*, edited by Pheng Chea and Bruce Robins, 91–114. Minneapolis: University of Minnesota Press, 1998.

Archykova, O. G., et al. *Dzherela pam'iati: kataloh vystavky do 90-richchia Ukrains'koho tovarystva "Prosvita" v Odesi (1905–1909)*. Odesa: n.p., 1995.

Arel, Dominique. "La face cachée de la Révolution orange: L'Ukraine et le déni de son problème régional." *Revue d'Etudes Comparatives Est-Ouest* 37, no. 4 (2006): 11–48.

———. "How Ukraine Has Become More Ukrainian." *Post-Soviet Affairs* 34, no. 2–3 (2018): 186–189.

———. "Interpreting 'Nationality' and 'Language' in the 2001 Ukrainian Census." *Post-Soviet Affairs* 18, no. 3 (2002): 213–49.

———. "Language Politics in Independent Ukraine: Towards One or Two State Languages?" *Nationalities Papers* 23, no. 3 (1995): 597–622.

Ariely, Dan. *The Honest Truth about Dishonesty*. New York: Harper Perennial, 2012.

Ascher, Abraham. *The Revolution of 1905: Russia in Disarray*. Stanford: Stanford University Press, 1988.

Ascherson, Neal. *Black Sea: The Birthplace of Civilisation and Barbarism*. New ed. London: Vintage, 2007.

Atlas, Doroteia. *Staraia Odessa, ee druz'ia i nedrugi*. Odesa: Tipo-litografiia Tekhnik, 1911.

Avrutin, Gene and Elissa Bemporad, eds. *Pogroms: A Documentary History of Anti-Jewish Violence*. Oxford: Oxford University Press, 2021.

Azadovskii, Konstantin. "Aleksandr Bisk i Odesskaia 'Literaturka.'" *Diaspora* [Paris and St. Petersburg] 1 (2001): 95–115.

Babel, Isaak. "Awakening." Translated by Maxim D. Shrayer. *Tablet*, May 1, 2018. https://www.tabletmag.com/sections/arts-letters/articles/awakening-short-story-isaac-babel.

———. *Detstvo i drugie rasskazy*. Edited by Efraim Sicher. Jerusalem: Biblioteka Aliya, 1979.

———. "Listki ob Odesse." *Vecherniaia zvezda*, March 19 [6], 1918; March 21 [8], 1918.

———. "O loshadiakh." *Novaia zhizn'*, March 16 [3], 1918, 2.
———. "Odessa." *Zhurnal zhurnalov* 51 (1916): 4–5.
———. *Odessa Stories*. Translated by Boris Dralyuk. London: Pushkin Press, 2016.
———. *Pis'ma drugu: Iz arkhiva I. L. Livshitsa*. Edited by Elena Pogerel'skaia. Moscow: Gosudarstvennyi literaturnyi muzei / Tri kvadrata, 2007.
———. *Sobranie sochinenii v 4 tomakh*. Edited by I. N. Sukhikh. Moscow: Vremia, 2006.
———. *Sochineniia*. 2 vols. Moscow: Khudozhestvennaia literatura, 1990.
———. "Staryi Shloime." *Ogni*, February 9, 1913, 3–4.
———. *Zakat*. Moscow: Krug, 1928.
Bakhtin, Mikhail. *Epos i roman*. Edited by S. G. Bocharov. St. Petersburg: Azbuka, 2000.
———. *Rabelais and his World*. Translated by Helene Izwolsky. Cambridge, MA: MIT Press, 1968; Bloomington: Indiana University Press, 1984.
———. *Tvorchestvo Fransua Rabele i narodnaia kul'tura srednevekov'ia i Renessansa*. Moscow: Khudozhestvennaia literatura, 1990.
Baley, Virko, and Sofia Hrytsa. "Ukraine." Grove Music Online. Oxford University Press. 2001. https://www.oxfordmusiconline.com/grovemusic/view/10.1093/gmo/9781561592630.001.0001/omo-9781561592630-e-0000040470.
Banbaji, Amir. *Mendele vehasipur haleumi* [Mendele and the national narrative]. Or Yehudah: Kinneret Zmora Beitan Dvir, 2009.
Banbaji, Amir, and Hannan Hever, eds. *Sifrut vema'amad* [Literature and class]. Jerusalem: Van Leer Institute, 2014.
Barkovskaia, Ol'ga. "Odessa, 1901–1941: Vystavki, zrelishcha, kontserty." In *Chernyi kvadrat nad chernym more*, edited by A. M. Golubovskii, F. D. Kokhrikht, and T. V. Shchurova, 15–62. Odesa: Optimum, 2007.
Barr, Lois. "Isa Kremer. 1887–1956." In Jewish Women: A Comprehensive Historical Encyclopedia. Jewish Women's Archive. Last updated June 23, 2021. https://jwa.org/encyclopedia/article/kremer-isa/.
Bartal, Israel, Jonathan Dekel-Chen, David Gaunt, and Natan M. Meir, eds. *Anti-Jewish Violence: Rethinking the Pogrom in East European History*. Bloomington: Indiana University Press, 2011.
Bauer, Henning, Andreas Kappeler, and Brigitte Roth, eds. *Die Nationalitäten des Russischen Reiches in der Volkszählung von 1897*. 2 vols. Stuttgart: Steiner Verlag, 1991.
Bel'skii, M. R. *Gazety staroi Odessy: Spravochnik*. Odesa: VMV, 2009.
Beliavskaia, Nadezhda. "Vaynshteyn Grigorii Emmanuilovich." Odesskii Biograficheskii Spravochnik. Accessed June 1, 2020. http://odessa-memory.info/index.php?id=457.
Belousova, Lilia. "Integratsiia Evreev v Rossiiskoe soslovnoe obschestvo: Pochetnye grazhdane goroda Odessy Evreiskogo proiskhozhdeniia," *Moria* 5 (2006): 6–23.
"Ben-Ami" [Mark Rabinovich]. "Moi snosheniia s M. Dragomanovym i rabota v *Vol'nom slove*." *Evreiskaia starina* 3–4 (1915): 347–66.
"Ben-David" [Y. L. Dovidovitz]. "Mikhtavim meodesa." [Letters from Odesa]. *Hamelits*, October 9, 1889, 2.
Ben-Yehuda, Eliezer. *A Dream Come True*. Edited by George Mandel. Translated by T. Muraoka. Boulder: Westview Press, 1993.
Bennett, Andy. *Music, Space and Place: Popular Music and Cultural Identity*. New York: Routledge, 2017.
Berkowitz, Isaak Dov. *Harishonim kevnei adam* [The first generations seen personally]. Vol. 2. Tel Aviv: Dvir, 1958.

Bermann, Jessica. *Modernist Fiction, Cosmopolitanism and the Politics of Community*. Cambridge: Cambridge University Press, 2001.

Bernsand, Niklas. "Surzhyk and National Identity in Ukrainian Nationalist Language Ideology." *Berliner Osteuropa Info* no. 17 (2001): 38–47.

Bernstein, Michael André. *Foregone Conclusions: Against Apocalyptic History*. Berkeley: University of California Press, 1994.

Bialik, Haim Nahman. "Hasokher." [The merchant]. In *Sipurim* [Stories], 281–96. Tel Aviv: Dvir, 1953.

Bilaniuk, Laada. *Contested Tongues: Language Politics and Cultural Correction in Ukraine*. Ithaca, NY: Cornell University Press, 2006.

Bilousova, Lilia. "Natsional'ni tovarystva v Odesi v XIX – na pochatku XX st." *Ukrains'kyi istorychnyi zhurnal* 2 (2017): 46–63.

Bilyk, Anna. "Teatral'no-kriticheskaia elita Odesskogo listka." *Almanakh Deribasovskaia-Rishel'evskaia* 30 (2007): 230–38.

Bisk, Aleksandr. "Molodye gody Leonida Grossmana (Materialy dlia biografii)." *Novoe russkoe slovo*, no. 19305, January 16, 1966.

———. "Odesskaia 'Literaturka.'" *Diaspora* [Paris and St. Petersburg] 1 (2001): 115–141.

Bobovich, Boris, Sergei Gol'denfel'd, Georgii Dolinov, Lanta Dunichevskaia, Petr Ershov, Yurii Olesha, Mariia Svirchevskaia, Leonid Siviaver, Ol'ga Slominskaia, Emil' Shirman, and Zinaida Shishova. *Pervyi al'manakh literaturno-khudozhestvennogo kruzhka*. Odesa: n.p., 1918.

Bohlman, Philip. *Jewish Music and Modernity*. Oxford: Oxford University Press, 2012.

Boldyrev, Oleksandr. *Odes'ka Hromada: Istorychnyi narys pro ukrains'ke national'ne vidrodzhennia v Odesi u 70-ti rr. XIX – pochat. XX st*. Odesa: Maiak, 1994.

Bondarin, Sergei. "Kharchevnia." In *Eduard Bagritsky: Almanakh*, edited by Vladimir Narbut, 229–34. Moskva: Sovetskii pisatel', 1936.

Borenstein, Elliot. *Plots against Russia: Conspiracy and Fantasy after Socialism*. Ithaca, NY: Cornell University Press, 2019.

Borishpolets, Elena. "Iuzhnaia storona." 45parallel. Accessed December 12, 2022. https://45parallel.net/elena_borishpolets/stihi/#yuzhnaya_storona.

Borovoi, Saul. "A fargesener nihilist (Yehudah Leib Lerner)" [A forgotten nihilist, Yehudah Leib Lerner]. *Filologishe Shriftn* 3 (1929): 473–84.

———. "Puteshestvie Onegina i odesskaia tema v russkoi literature pervoi treti XIX veka." In *Pushkin na iuge: Trudy Pushkinskikh konferentsii Odessy i Kishineva*, edited by Z. A. Borinevich-Babaitseva, I. K. Vartichan, and G. F. Bogach, 2:265–88. Kishinev: Shtiintsa, 1961.

———. *Vospominaniia*. Moscow: Evreiskii universitet v Moskve/Jerusalem: Gesharim, 1993.

Bourdieu, Pierre. *The Field of Cultural Production*. Edited by Randal Johnson. Cambridge: Polity Press, 1993.

———. *Outline of a Theory of Practice*. Translated by Richard Nice. Cambridge: Cambridge University Press, 1977.

Boym, Svetlana. *The Future of Nostalgia*. New York: Basic Books, 2001.

Bradley, Joseph. *Voluntary Associations in Tsarist Russia: Science, Patriotism, and Civil Society*. Cambridge, MA: Harvard University Press, 2009.

Briker, Boris. "The Underworld of Benia Krik and I. Babel's Odessa Stories." *Canadian Slavonic Papers* 36, no. 1–2 (1994): 115–134.

Brodets'ka, N. A.; Yatsun, N. O. *Biblioteka M. F. Komarova: kataloh kolektsii Odes'koi natsional'noi naukovoi biblioteky imeni M. Gor'koho*. Odesa: Brovkin, 2014.

Buckler, Julie. *Mapping St. Petersburg: Imperial Text and Cityshape*. Princeton: Princeton University Press, 2005.

Budnitskii, O. V. "La construction d'Odessa comme 'mère du crime' ou comment Moïse Vinnitski est devenu Benia Krik." In *Kinojudaica: les représentations des juifs dans le cinéma de Russie et d'Union soviétique des années 1910 aux années 1980*, edited by Valérie Pozner and Natacha Laurent, 411–439. Toulouse: Éditions Nouveau monde, 2012.

Bykov, Dmitry. "Odin." *Ekho Moskvy*, August 4, 2017. https://echo.msk.ru/programs/odin/2030070-echo/.

Cabanen, Inna. "Odesskii iazyk: bol'she mifa ili real'nosti?" In *Slavica Helsingiensia 40—Instrumentarium of Linguistics: Sociolinguistic Approaches to Non-Standard Russian*, edited by Arto Mustajoki, Ekaterina Protassova, and Nikolai Vakhtin, 287–298. Helsinki: Helsinki University, 2010.

Campana, Alessandra. *Opera and Modern Spectatorship in Late Nineteenth-Century Italy*. Cambridge: Cambridge University Press, 2015.

Carden, Patricia. *The Art of Isaac Babel*. Ithaca: Cornell University Press, 1972.

Casanova, Pascale. *The World Republic of Letters*. Translated by M. B. DeBevoise. Cambridge, MA: Harvard University Press, 2004.

Central Zionist Archives, Jerusalem: Z3: Jabotinsky's Papers.

Cesarani, David, ed. *Port Jews: Jewish Communities in Cosmopolitan Maritime Trading Centres, 1550–1950*. Southampton: Frank Cass and the Parkes Centre, University of Southampton, 2001.

Cheah, Pheng. "Introduction Part II: The Cosmopolitical—Today." In *Cosmopolitics: Thinking and Feeling beyond the Nation*, edited by Pheng Cheah and Bruce Robins, 20–41. Minneapolis: University of Minnesota Press, 1998.

Chekhovich, Pavel Semenovich, and A. M. Dragana. *Novaia khlebnaia gavan' v Odesse*. Kiev [Kyiv]: n.p., 1906.

Chernetsky, Vitaly. "Multidirectional Memory as Challenge and Promise." Posocomes. September 23, 2020. Lecture, 1:31:18. https://www.youtube.com/watch?v=Ch8qy7e2hLY&fbclid=IwAR3IPv7_tTxwCFq6hkY67q0I2RFXSFVihyS-mcTs6IlOL-mPSZOyW8kxArw.

———. "Russophone Writing in Ukraine." In *Global Russian Cultures*, edited by Kevin M. F. Platt, 48–68. Madison, WI: University of Wisconsin Press, 2019.

Chernilo, Daniel. "Cosmopolitanism and the Question of Universalism." In *Routledge Handbook of Cosmopolitanism Studies*, edited by Gerard Delanty, 47–59. London: Routledge, 2012.

Chernyi, Sasha. *Sobranie sochinenii v piati tomakh*. Moscow: Ellis Lak, 1996.

Cherwick, Brian A. "Polkas on the Prairies: Ukrainian Music and the Construction of Identity." PhD diss., University of Alberta, 1999.

Chmyr, S. G. "Odes'ka hromada v ukrains'komu natsional'nomu rusi (kinets' XIX – pochatok XX st.)." *Pivdenna Ukraina XX stolittia: Zapysky naukovo-doslidnyts'koi laboratorii istorii Pivdennoi Ukrainy ZDU* 1, no. 4 (1998): 107–14.

Chukovskii, Kornei. *Dnevnik*. 3 vols. Moskva: Prozaik, 2011.

———. "Dva slova o kosmopolitizme i natsionalizme. Iz pis'ma k odnomu antisionistu." *Iuzhnye zapiski*, no. 17 (May 16, 1903): 701–703.

———. "Kuprin." *Sobranie sochinenii*. Moscow: Terra, 2001. 5:77–107.

———. *Serebrianyi gerb*. Moscow: Detskaia literatura, 1961.

———. "Shevchenko." *Russkaia mysl'* 4 (1911): 86–101 (2nd pagination); 5 (1911): 99–110 (2nd pagination). Reprinted, edited and with preface by Miron Petrovsky in *Raduga* 3 (1989): 121–36.

———. "Sluchainye zametki." *Evreiskaia zhizn'* 11 (1904): 177–82.

———. *Sobranie sochnenii v piatnadtsati tomakh*. Moscow: Terra-Knizhnyi klub, 2001–2009.

Chukur, Anna. "Film Aesthetic in the Ukrainian Novel of the 1920s: The Novel as Experiment." PhD diss., University of Toronto, 2016. http://hdl.handle.net/1807/92672/.

Chykalenko, Yevhen. *Shchodennyk, 1907–1917*. Kyiv: Tempora, 2011.

Clark, Katerina, and Evgeny Dobrenko, eds. *Soviet Culture and Power: A History in Documents, 1917–1953*. New Haven: Yale University Press, 2007.

Clover, Joshua. "Retcon: Value and Temporality in Poetics." *Representations* 126, no. 1 (2014): 9–30.

Collins, Sarah, and Dana Gooley. "Music and the New Cosmopolitanism: Problems and Possibilities." *The Musical Quarterly* 99, no. 2 (2016): 139–65.

Connell, John, and Chris Gibson. *Sound Tracks: Popular Music Identity and Place*. New York: Routledge, 2003.

Crescente, Joseph James. "Performing Post-Sovietness: Verka Serdiuchka and the Hybridization of Post-Soviet Identity in Ukraine." *Ab Imperio*, no. 2 (2007): 405–30.

Czackis, Lloica. "TANGELE: The History of Yiddish Tango." *Jewish Quarterly* 50, no. 1 (2003): 45–52.

De Ribas, Aleksandr. *Staraia Odessa. Istoricheskie ocherki i vospominaniia*. Odesa: n.p., 1913.

Dharwadker, Vinay, ed. *Cosmopolitan Geographies: New Locations in Literature and Culture*. London: Routledge, 2001.

Dmitriev-Mamonov, Vasilii, ed. *Ukazatel' deistvuiushchikh v imperii aktsionernykh predpriiatii i torgovykh domov*. St. Petersburg: E. Vern, 1905.

Dobrenko, Evgeny. "Pushkin in Soviet and Post-Soviet Culture." In *The Cambridge Companion to Pushkin*, edited by Andrew Kahn, 206–12. Cambridge: Cambridge University Press, 2006.

Doroshevich, Vlas. *Odessa, odessity i odessitki*. Odesa: Yu. Sandomirskii, 1895.

D-ov, V. "Iubilei 'Prosveshcheniia': O dvadtsatiletnei deiatel'nosti Odesskogo otdeleniia Obshchestva rasprostraneniia prosveshcheniia mezhdu evreiami Rossii (1867–1892)." *Voskhod* 7 (July 1893): part 2, 12.

Drews, Peter. *Herder und die Slaven: Materialien zur Wirkungsgeschichte bis zur Mitte des 19. Jahrhunderts*. Munich: Sagner, 1990.

Dubin, Lois C. "'Wings on their feet . . . and wings on their head': Reflections on the Study of Port Jews." *Jewish Culture and History* 7, no. 1–2 (2004): 14–30.

Dubnow, Simon. "O natsional'nom vospitanii." *Nedel'naia khronika voskhoda*, January 1, 1902, 10–13.

———. *Kniga Zhizni: Materialy dlia istorii moego vremeni: Vospominaniia i razmyshleniia*. St. Petersburg: Peterburgskoe vostokovedenie, 1998.

Dziuba, Ivan. "Z orlynoiu pechal'iu na choli . . ." In *Vladimir (Zeev) Zhabotyns'kyi i ukrains'ke pytannia. Vseliuds'kist' u shatakh natsionalizmu*, edited by Izrail Kleiner, 7–26. Edmonton: Kanads'kyi Instytut Ukrains'kykh Studii, 1995.

Edensor, Tim. *National Identity, Popular Culture and Everyday Life*. London: Routledge, 2020.

———. "Reconsidering National Temporalities." *European Journal of Social Theory* 9, no. 4 (2006): 525–45.

Eggel, Dominic, et al., "Was Herder a Nationalist?" *The Review of Politics* 69, no. 1 (2007): 48–78.

Ehre, Milton. *Isaac Babel*. Boston: G. K. Hall, 1986.

El'iashevich, Dmitrii. *Pravitel'stvennaia politika i evreiskaia pechat' v Rossii, 1797–1917*. St. Petersburg: Mosty kul'tury, 1999.

Eriksen, Thomas Hylland. "Formal and Informal Nationalism." *Ethnic and Racial Studies* 16, no. 1 (1993): 1–25.

Evreiskaia narodnaia partiia. St. Petersburg: n.p., 1907.

Faitel'berg-Blank, Viktor R. "Teatr miniatiur." In *Serebrianyi vek iuzhnoi pal'miry* 2:365–71. Odesa: Optimum, 2004.

Falen, James. *Isaac Babel: Russian Master of the Short Story*. Knoxville: University of Tennessee Press, 1974.

Fedina, Olga. *What Every Russian Knows (And You Don't)*. London: Anaconda Editions, 2013.

Feldman, Walter Zev. "Bulgărească/Bulgarish/Bulgar: The Transformation of a Klezmer Dance Genre." *Ethnomusicology* 38, no. 1 (1994): 1–35.

———. *Klezmer: Music, History, and Memory*. New York: Oxford University Press, 2016.

Fichmann, Ya'akov. *Amat habinyan: sofrei odesa* [The foundation of the building: Odessa's authors]. Jerusalem: Mossad Bialik, 1951.

———. *Rukhot menaganot: sofrei polin* [The tune of the winds: Polish authors] Jerusalem: Mossad Bialik, 1952.

Fournier, Anna. "Mapping Identities: Russian Resistance to Linguistic Ukrainisation in Central and Eastern Ukraine." *Europe–Asia Studies* 54, no. 3 (2002): 415–33.

———. "Patriotism, Order and Articulations of the Nation in Kyiv High Schools before and after the Orange Revolution." *Journal of Communist Studies and Transition Politics* 23, no. 1 (2007): 101–17.

Fox, Jon E. "The Edges of the Nation: A Research Agenda for Uncovering the Taken-for-Granted Foundations of Everyday Nationhood." *Nations and Nationalism* 23, no. 1 (2017): 26–47.

Frankel, Jonathan. *Prophecy and Politics: Socialism, Nationalism, and Russian Jews, 1862–1917*. Cambridge: Cambridge University Press, 1981.

Freidenberg, Mikhail. *Nakhodchivyi redaktor i evreiskii vopros*. Odesa: n.p., 1885.

Freidin, Gregory. "Fat Tuesday in Odessa: Isaak Babel's 'Di Grasso' as Testament and Manifesto." *Russian Review* 40, no. 2 (1981): 101–21.

———. "Two Babels—Two Aphrodites: Autobiography in *Maria* and Babel's Petersburg Myth." In *The Enigma of Isaac Babel: Biography, History, Context*, edited by Freidin, 16–56. Stanford: Stanford University Press, 2009.

———. "Forma soderzhaniia: Odessa – mama Isaaka Babelia." *Neprikosnovennyi zapas* (2011): 1–11.

Freitag, Ulrike, and Achim von Oppen. In *Translocality: The Study of Globalising Processes from a Southern Perspective*, edited by Freitag and von Oppen, 1–21. Leiden: Brill, 2010.

Frühauf, Tina. *The Organ and Its Music in German-Jewish Culture*. New York: Oxford University Press, 2009.

Gekht, Semyon. "Vechera v zheleznodorozhnom klube." In *Eduard Bagritskii. Almanakh*, edited by Vladimir Narbut, 235–43. Moskva: Sovetskii pisatel', 1936.

———. *Izbrannoe*. Odesa: OLM, 2008.

Gelbin, Cathy S., and Sander L. Gilman. *Cosmopolitanisms and the Jews*. Ann Arbor: University of Michigan Press, 2017.

Gellner, Ernest. *Nations and Nationalisms*. Oxford: Basil Blackwell, 2006.

Gerasimov, Ilya. "'My ubivaem tol'ko svoikh': prestupnost' kak marker mezhetnicheskikh granits v Odesse nachala dvatsatogo veka (1907–1917)." *Ab Imperio* (January 2003): 209–60.

———. *Plebeian Modernity. Social Practices, Illegality, and the Urban Poor in Russia, 1906–1916*. Rochester, NY: University of Rochester Press. 2018.

Giessen, Iosif. *V dvukh vekakh: Zhiznennyi otchet*. Berlin: Speer & Schmidt, 1937.

Gitelman, Zvi. "A Jagged Circle: From Ethnicity to Internationalism to Cosmopolitanism—And Back." In *Cosmopolitanism, Nationalism and the Jews of East Central Europe*, edited by Michael L. Miller and Scott Ury, 187–204. New York: Routledge, 2016.

Glicksberg, Haim. *Bialik yom: pirkei zikhronot, tsiyurim verishumim* [Bialik everyday: memories, paintings and drawings]. Tel Aviv: Dvir, 1953.

"God deiatel'nosti Odesskogo Obshchestva Vspomoshchestvovania Evreiam v Palestine." In *Sion: Evreisko-Palestinskii Sbornik*, 209–272. St. Petersburg: n.p., 1892.

Goldstein, Yossi. *Anu khayinu harishonim: toldot khibbat tsion, 1881–1918* [We were the first: The history of the Hibbat Tsion movement]. Jerusalem: Mossad Bialik, 2015.

Golubovsky, Evgeny. "'Vse dano,' Taia Naidenko. Vyshla v svet debiutnaia kniga avtora." *Vsesvitnii klub Odessitov*, March 20, 2019. https://www.odessitclub.org/index.php/novosti-i-publikatsii/2702-vsjo-dano-verite-li-vy-v-reinkarnatsiyu.

Gooley, Dana, Ryan Minor, Katherine K. Preston, and Jann Pasler. "Cosmopolitanism in the Age of Nationalism, 1848–1914." *Journal of the American Musicological Society* 66, no. 2 (2013): 523–49.

Gorodskoe Obshchestvennoe Upravlenie. *Odessa 1794–1894*. Odesa: n.p., 1895.

Green, Noreen. "The Forgotten Master of Jewish Music: David Nowakowsky, 1848–1921." PhD diss., University of Southern California, 1991.

Grötzinger, Elvira, and Susi Hudak-Lazić. *Unser Rebbe, Unser Stalin: Jiddische Lieder aus den St. Petersburger Sammlungen von Moishe Beregowski (1892–1961) und Sofia Magid (1892–1954)*. Wiesbaden: Harrassowitz, 2008.

Gruzenberg, Saul. "Po povodu odesskogo sobraniia obshchestva prosveshcheniia." *Budushchnost'*, June 21, 1902, 488–89.

Gubar', Oleg. *Ocherki rannei istorii evreev Odessy*. Odesa: BMB, 2013.

———. "Valikhovskii priiut i Koganovskie ucherezhdeniia." *Almanakh Deribasovskaia-Rishel'evskaia* 24 (2006): 6–13.

Hacohen-Pinczower, Ruth. "Kehilot kol le'et dimdumim: Merkhavey tslil mamashiyim umedumyanim shel yahadut merkaz eropa 'im ptikhat hasha'ar ule'et ne'ilat sha'ar" [Communities of voice at times of twilight: Real and imagined soundscapes of Central European Jewry at the opening of the gate and the closing of the gate]. In *Hadimyon haparshani: dat veomanut batarbut hayehudit behekshereyha* [The interpretive imagination: Religion and art in Jewish culture in its contexts], edited by Ruth Hacohen-Pinczower, Galit Hasan-Rokem, Richard I. Cohen, and Ilana Pardes, 116–53. Jerusalem: Magnes, 2016.

Haitner, Uri. "Hamiskhak batfisato hakalkalit vehakhevratit shel zhabotinski" [Play in Jabotinsky's social and economic thinking]. *Haumah* 160 (2005): 35–39.

Haramati, Shlomo. "Halashon ha'ivrit bamishnato shel zeev zhabotinsky" [The Hebrew language in Zeev Jabotinsky's thought]. *Leshonenu la'am* 32, nos. 3–5 [313–315] (1981): 67–152.

Harvey, David. *Justice, Nature and the Geography of Difference*. Oxford: Basil Blackwell, 1996.

Hausmann, Guido. "Paradise Anticipated: The Jews of Odessa in the 19th and 20th Centuries." *Jahrbuch des Simon-Dubnow-Instituts* 2 (2003): 151–81.

———. *Universität und städtische Gesellschaft in Odessa, 1865—1917: Soziale und nationale Selbstorganisation an der Peripherie des Zarenreiches*. Stuttgart: Franz Steiner, 1998.

———. "Die wohlhabenden Odessaer Kaufleute und Unternehmer. Zur Herausbildung bürgerlicher Identitäten im ausgehenden Zarenreich." *Jahrbücher für Geschichte Osteuropas* 48 (2000): 41–65.

Helman, Anat. *Or veyam hekifuha: tarbut tel-avivit bitkufat hamandat 1920–1948* [Light and sea: The culture of Tel Aviv during the British Mandate, 1920–1948]. Haifa: University of Haifa, 2007.

Herlihy, Patricia. "The Ethnic Composition of the City of Odessa in the Nineteenth Century." *Harvard Ukrainian Studies* 1 (1977): 53–78.

———. *Odessa. A History, 1794–1914*. Cambridge, MA: Harvard University Press, 1986.

———. *Odessa Recollected: The Port and the People*. Boston: Harvard Ukrainian Research Institute and Academic Studies Press, 2018.

———. "Port Jews of Odessa and Trieste: A Tale of Two Cities." *Jahrbuch des Simon-Dubnow-Instituts* 2 (2003): 183–98. Reprinted in Patricia Herlihy, *Odessa Recollected: The Port and the People* (Boston: Academic Studies Press, 2018).

Hill, Megan E. "Soundscape." Grove Music Online. Oxford University Press. January 31, 2014. https://www.oxfordmusiconline.com/grovemusic/view/10.1093/gmo/9781561592630.001.0001/omo-9781561592630-e-1002258182.

Hoerder, Dirk. "Migration and Cultural Interaction across the Centuries: German History in a European Perspective." *German Politics and Society* 26, no. 2 [87] (2008): 1–23.

Hofmeister, Alexis. *Selbstorganisation und Bürgerlichkeit. Jüdisches Vereinswesen in Odessa um 1900*. Göttingen: Vandenhoeck & Ruprecht, 2007.

Hirsch, Francine. *Empire of Nations: Ethnographic Knowledge and the Making of the Soviet Union*. Ithaca, NY: Cornell University Press, 2005.

Holovanivs'kyi, Sava. "Tysnu ruku!" In *Ukraiins'ka avanhardna poeziia: Antolohiia, 1910–1930*, edited by Oleh Kotsarev and Iuliia Stakhivs'ka, 205–6. Kyiv: Smoloskyp, 2014.

Holtzman, Avner. *Hayim Nahman Bialik: Poet of Hebrew*. New Haven, CN: Yale University Press, 2017.

Horowitz, Brian. *Jewish Philanthropy and Enlightenment in Late-Tsarist Russia*. Seattle: University of Washington Press, 2009.

———. *The Russian-Jewish Tradition: Intellectuals, Historians, Revolutionaries*. Boston: Academic Studies Press, 2017.

———. *Vladimir Jabotinsky's Russian Years, 1900–1925*. Bloomington: Indiana University Press, 2020.

Horowitz, David. *Ethnic Groups in Conflict*. Berkeley: University of California Press, 1986.

Horowitz, Joshua, "The Klezmer Accordion." *Musical Performance* 3, nos. 2–4 (2001): 143–45.

Hudson, Ray. "Regions and Place: Music, Identity and Place." *Progress in Human Geography* 30, no. 5 (2006): 626–34.

Humphrey, Caroline. "Odessa: Pogroms in a Cosmopolitan City." In *Post-Cosmopolitan Cities: Explorations of Urban Coexistence*, edited by Humphrey and Vera Skvirskaja, 17–64. New York: Berghahn Books, 2012.

———. "Violence and Urban Architecture: Events at the Ensemble of the Odessa Steps in 1904–1905." In *Locating Urban Conflicts: Ethnicity, Nationalism and the Everyday*, edited by Wendy Pullan and Britt Baillie, 37–64. London: Palgrave Macmillan, 2015.

Ianovs'kyi, Yurii. *Maister korablia*. Kharkiv: Knyhospilka, 1928.

Iavorskaia, Elena (Alena). "Eto bylo, bylo v Odesse." In *Sil'nee liubvi i smerti: Stikhotvoreniia, vospominaniia, pis'ma*, by Zinaida Shishova, edited by Dmitrii A. Losev and Alena Iavorskaia, 13–33. Feodosiia and Moscow: Koktebel', 2011.

———. "Nezavisimyi Fazini." In *Fazini, 1893–1944*, 7–41. Moscow: Reprotsentr, 2008.

———. "Semyon Gekht—uchenik Babelia." Odesa Literary Museum. Accessed December 10, 2022. https://web.archive.org/web/20120626161316/http://museum-literature.odessa.ua/pbasic/lru/tb2/tp3/id165.

———. "Rukopisi I. Babelia v fondakh OLM." *Dom kniazia Gagarina: Sbornik statei i publikatsii* 6, no. 2 (2011): 5–18.

Idelsohn, Abraham Z. *Jewish Music: Its Historical Development*. New York: Dover, 1992.

Ilany, Ofri. *In Search of the Hebrew People: Bible and Nation in the German Enlightenment*. Bloomington: Indiana University Press, 2018.

Il'f, Il'ia. "Puteshestvie v Odessu." *Chudak* 13 (1929). Republished in *Voprosy literatury* 1 (2004): 328–31.

Iljine, Nicolas V., ed. *Odessa Memories*. Seattle: University of Washington Press, 2003.

Ilnytzkyj, Oleh. *Ukrainian Futurism, 1914–1930*. Cambridge, MA: Harvard University Press, 1997.

Inber, Vera. *Ad v raiu. Deribasovskaia-Rishel'evskaia: Odesskii al'manakh* 34 (2008): 214–30.

———. "Mal'chik so skripkoi." *Argus: Vse vizhu* 10 (1913): 112.

———. *Der Platz an der Sonne*. Translated by Elena Frank. Berlin: Malik, 1930.

———. *Sobranie Sochinenii v chetyrekh tomakh*. Vols. 1–2. Moscow: Khudozhestvennaia literatura, 1965.

———. *Tsvety na asfal'te*. Odesa: Druk, 2000.

———. *Za mnogo let*. Moskva: Sovetskii pisatel', 1964.

"Inber, Vera Mikhailovna." *Oni ostavili sled v istorii Odessy: sobranie ocherkov i biografii*. http://odessa-memory.info/index.php?id=228/.

"Isa Kremer: A Child of the People." *Canadian Jewish Chronicle*, September 14, 1923.

"Isa Kremer Greeted." *New York Times*, October 30, 1922.

Isaacs, Rico, and Abel Polese. *(Re)Imagining or Imagined Nation-Building? Nation-Building and Identity in the Post-Soviet Space: New Tools and Approaches*. London: Routledge, 2016.

"Istoriia ONMA." Odes'ka Natsional'na Muzichna Akademiia. Accessed October 1, 2020. https://odma.edu.ua/pro-akademiyu/istoriya-onma/.

Ivanov, Sergei. "Ukrokhamy v Odesse – okkupanty, unichtozhaiushchie kul'turu." *EurAsia Daily*, November 11, 2022. https://eadaily.com/ru/news/2022/11/28/ukrohamy-v-odesse-okkupanty-unichtozhayushchie-kulturu.

Ivanova, Evgeniia, ed. *Chukovskii i Zhabotinskii*. Moscow and Jerusalem: Mosty kultury/Gesharim, 2005.

"Iza Kremer na saite 'Informatsionnyi portal zhanra russkii shanson.'" Informatsionnyi portal zhanra "Shanson." Accessed July 16, 2020. http://russianshanson.info/?id=1042/.

Izgoev, Aleksandr S. "Pis'ma o sionisme," *Yuzhnoe obozrenie*, July 11, 1899.

Jabotinsky Institute, Tel Aviv. F. 912: Jabotinsky Archives.

Jabotinsky, Vladimir. *Causeries. Pravda ob ostrove Tristan da Run'ia*. 2nd ed. Paris: Tipografiia d'Art Voltaire, 1930.

———. *The Five: A Novel of Jewish Life in Turn-of-the-Century Odessa*. Translated by Michael R. Katz. Introduction by Michael Stanislawski. Ithaca, NY: Cornell University Press, 2005.

———. "Otpor." *Razsvet*, March 15, 1913; March 22, 1913; 14–15 April 4, 1913.

——— [Altalena]. *Piatero*. New York: Rausen Broth & Jabotinsky Foundation, 1947.

———. "Pis'ma o natsional'nostiakh i oblastiakh. Evreistvo i ego nastroeniia." *Russkaia mysl'* 32, no. 1 (1911): 95–114.

———. *Povest' moikh dnei*. Jerusalem: Biblioteka Aliya, 1989.
———. "Priezzhii." *Odesskie novosti*, December 23 [January 5] 1911, 3–4.
———. "Samoupravlenie natsional'nogo men'shinstva." Jabotinsky Institute, f. 901/1913.
———. *Sochineniia v deviati tomakh*. Minsk: Met, 2007.
———. "So storony." *Odesskie novosti*, October 29, 1910.
———. "Struve i ukrainskii vopros." *Odesskie novosti*, March 2, 1912.
———. "Tochka nad i." *Ukrainskii vestnik*, July 2, 1906.
———. "Toska o patriotizme." *Iuzhnye zapiski*, May 16, 1903.
———. "Traktat po filologii." *Odesskie novosti*, July 23, 1912.
———. "Traktat po pedagogike." *Odesskie novosti*, July 8, 1912.
———. "Urok iubilieia Shevchenki." *Odesskie novosti*, February 27, 1911.
———. *Vladimir Jabotinsky's Story of my Life*. Edited by Brian Horowitz and Leonid Katsis. Detroit: Wayne University Press, 2016.
———. *Zikhronot ben dori* [Memories of My Generation]. Tel Aviv: Amikhai, 1959.
Janmaat, Jan Germen. "Ethnic and Civic Conceptions of the Nation in Ukraine's History Textbooks." *European Education* 37, no. 3 (2005): 20–37.
———. "The Ethnic 'Other' in Ukrainian History Textbooks: The Case of Russia and the Russians." *Compare* 37, no. 3 (2007): 307–24.
Johnston, Timothy. *Being Soviet: Identity, Rumour, and Everyday Life under Stalin 1939–1953*. Oxford: Oxford University Press, 2011.
Kal'ian, Serhii. "Natsional'na polityka V. Zhabotyns'koho u kontektsi odes'koho periodu ioho diial'nosti." In *Odessa i evreiskaia tsivilizatsiia: k 100-letiiu so dnia rozhdeniia Saula Borovogo*, edited by Mikhail Rashkovetskii, et al., 167–73. Odesa: Negotsiant, 2004.
Kanunnikova, Ol'ga. "Khudozhnik i okrestnosti." *Novyi mir* 4 (2002): 175–79.
Kaplun, Tatiana M. "Odesskoe otdelenie Imperatorskogo Russkogo muzykal'nogo obshchestva: stanovlenie i itogi." *Problemy muzykal'noi nauki*, no. 4 (2018): 127–32.
Kataev, Valentin. *Almaznyi moi venets*. Moscow: Sovetskii pisatel', 1981.
Kaufmann, Fritz Mordechai. "Die Aufführung jüdischer Volksmusik vor Westjuden." In *Jüdische Volksmusik: Eine mitteleuropäische Geistesgeschichte*, edited by Philip Bohlman, 143–56. Vienna: Böhlau, 2005.
Khag yovel: Di iubilei faierung im 17-ten november 1890 in odesa dem folkes shraiber yitskhok yoel linetskii [The Jubilee celebration of the people's writer Yitskhok Yoel Linetskii, November 17, 1890 in Odesa]. Odesa: n.p., 1890.
Khalanskii, Aleksei. "Zhvanetskii i Pozner otkryli v Odesse pamiatnik Babel'iu." *Novye izvestiia*, September 5, 2011. https://newizv.ru/news/culture/05-09-2011/150660-zhvaneckij-i-pozner-otkryli-v-odesse-pamjatnik-babelju.
"Khar'kovu, Odesse i Nikolaevu nuzhno vossoedinit'sia s Rossiei." *EurAsia Daily*, June 17, 2020. https://eadaily.com/ru/news/2020/06/17/harkovu-odesse-i-nikolaevu-nuzhno-vossoedinitsya-s-rossiey-politolog.
Khersonsky, Boris. *Family Archive*. Translated by Ruth Kruezer and Dale Hobson [1996]. Accessed October 8, 2020. http://www.dalehobson.org/khersonsky/boriscon.html.
———. "Nenavizhu vse russkoe?" LiveJournal, December 4, 2014. https://borkhers.livejournal.com/2014/12/04.
———. *Odesskaia Intelligentsiia*. Kharkiv: Folio, 2017.
———. *Semeinyi arkhiv*. Moscow: Novoe literaturnoe obozrenie, 2006.

———. "Tovarishch Isaak Babel' pishet istoriiu goroda O." LiveJournal, September 4, 2011. https://borkhers.livejournal.com/1119672.html.

Khmelko, Valerii. *Lingvo-etnichna struktura Ukraini: Rehional'ni osoblyvosti i tendentsii zmin za roki nezalezhnosti.* 2004. Accessed December 7, 2022. http://ekmair.ukma.edu.ua/bitstream/handle/123456789/8098/Khmelko_Linhvo-etnichna_struktura_Ukrainy.pdf.

Kimbell, David R. *Italian Opera.* New York: Cambridge University Press, 1994.

King, Charles. *The Black Sea.* Oxford: Oxford University Press, 2005.

———. *Odessa: Genius and Death in a City of Dreams.* New York: Norton, 2011.

Kirpichnikov, Aleksandr I., and Aleksei I. Markevich. *Proshloe i nastoiashchee Odessy.* Odesa: n.p., 1894.

Kitanina, Taisia. *Khlebnaia torgovlia Rossii v 1875–1914.* Leningrad: Nauka, 1978.

Kiva, Iya. "Boris Khersonskii: 'Odesa – tse zavzhdy zhyttia v podviinomu prostori.'" *Shoizdat*, April 12, 2019. https://shoizdat.com/boris-khersonskii-odesa-tse-zavzhdi/.

Klausner, Yosef. *Opozitsiyah lehertzl* [Opposition to Herzl]. Jerusalem: Hotsaat Akhi'ever, 1960.

Kleiner, Israel. *From Nationalism to Universalism: Vladimir (Ze'ev) Jabotinsky and the Ukrainian Question.* Edmonton: Canadian Institute of Ukrainian Studies Press, 2000.

Kleinman, Moshe, ed. *Entsiklopediyah letsiyonut* [Encyclopedia of Zionism]. Tel Aviv: Chechik Press, 1947.

Klier, John. *Imperial Russia's Jewish Question, 1855–1881.* Cambridge: Cambridge University Press, 1995.

———. "A Port, Not a Shtetl: Reflections on the Distinctiveness of Odessa." *Jewish Culture and History* 4, no. 2 (2001): 173–78.

Knight, David B. *Landscapes in Music: Space, Place, and Time in the World's Great Music.* Lanham: Rowman & Littlefield Publishers, 2006.

Kopelman, Zoia. "Zhabotinskii i ivrit." In *Zhabotinskii i Rossiia: sbornik trudov Mezhdunarodnoi konferentsii "Russian Jabotinsky: Jabotinsky and Russia,"* 207–36. Stanford: Department of Slavic Languages and Literature, Stanford University, 2013.

Kopytova, Galina. *Jascha Heifetz: Early Years in Russia.* Bloomington: Indiana University Press, 2013.

Kornbluh, Anna. *Realizing Capital.* New York: Fordham University Press, 2014.

Korolev, Andrei, and Elena Poliakovskaia. "Vspominaia vareniki 'z vishnei.'" Radio Svoboda. Accessed May 4, 20212. https://www.svoboda.org/a/27560521.html.

Korostelina, Karina V. "Conflict of National Narratives of Ukraine: Euromaidan and Beyond." *Die Friedens-Warte* 89, nos. 1–2 (2014): 269–90.

Koschmal, Walter. "Kulturbeschreibung aus der Peripherie: Babels Odessa-Poetik." *Wiener Slawistischer Almanach* 49 (1997): 311–36.

———. "Ein russischer Traum von Europa? Petersburg, Odessa und andere." *Nordost-Archiv. Zeitschrift für Regionalgeschichte* 12 (2003): 43–69.

Kostusyev, Aleksei, et. al. *Odessa Economic and Social Development Strategy 2022.* City of Odesa, Odesa, Ukraine. Accessed December 7, 2022. https://omr.gov.ua/images/File/DODATKI2013/strategia_eng.pdf.

Kotkin, Stephen. *Magnetic Mountain: Stalinism as a Civilization.* Los Angeles: University of California Press, 1997.

Kozlenko, Ivan. *Tanzher.* Kyiv: Komora, 2017.

Kratkii Otchet Imperatorskogo Novorossiiskogo Universiteta. Odesa: n.p., 1882.

"Kremer, Iza Iakovlevna (1887–1956)." Oni ostavili sled v istorii Odessy: Odesskii biograficheskii spravochnik. Accessed July 16, 2020. http://odessa-memory.info/index.php?id=327/.

"Kremer Iza Iakovlevna: Opernaia pevitsa s mirovoi slavoi." odesskiy.com. Accessed July 16, 2020. http://odesskiy.com/k/kremer-iza-jakovlevna.html/.

Kressel, Getzel. *Leksikon hasifrut ha'ivrit badorot haakhronim* [Lexicon of Hebrew literature in recent generations]. 2 vols. Merhavia: Sifriyat poalim, 1965.

Kriksunov, Piotr. "Tainy Samsona Nazoreia: Razmyshleniia nad perevodom *Samsona Nazoreia* Zhabotinskogo." In *Zhabotinskii i Rossiia: sbornik trudov mezhdunarodnoi konferentsii "Russian Jabotinsky: Jabotinsky and Russia,"* edited by Leonid Katsis and Helena Tolstoy, 184–195. Stanford: Department of Slavic Languages and Literature, Stanford University, 2013.

Kriuchkov, Pavel. "Bogu vidnee." 45Parallel, March 11, 2007. https://45parallel.net/boris_khersonskiy/.

Kudrin, O. "Uroki odesskoi shkoly i grebni odesskoi volny." *Voprosy literatury* 3 (2012): 9–64.

Kulyk, Volodymyr. "Shedding Russianness, Recasting Ukrainianness: The Post-Euromaidan Dynamics of Ethnonational Identifications in Ukraine." *Post-Soviet Affairs* 34, nos. 2–3 (2018): 119–38.

Kuzar, Ron. *Hebrew and Zionism: A Discourse*. Berlin: De Gruyter, 2001.

Kuzio, Taras. "History, Memory and Nation Building in the Post-Soviet Colonial Space." *Nationalities Papers* 30, no. 2 (2002): 241–64.

———. "National Identity and History Writing in Ukraine." *Nationalities Papers* 34, no. 4 (2006): 407–27.

Laitin, David. *Identity in Formation: The Russian-Speaking Populations in the New Abroad*. Ithaca, NY: Cornell University Press, 1998.

Langleben, Maria. "Arkhetip kladbishcha v rasskazakh Babelia: 'Klabishche v Kozine' i 'Konets bogadel'ni.'" In *Tynianovskii sbornik II: Deviatye Tynianovskie chteniia*, edited by M. O. Chudakova, E. A. Toddes, and Yu. G. Tsiv'ian, 411–37. Moscow: OGI, 2002.

Lecke, Mirja. "The Street: A Spatial Paradigm in Odessan Literature." *Slavonic and East European Review* 95, no. 3 (July 2017): 429–57.

Lecke, Mirja and Efraim Sicher. "Odessa in Russian, Ukrainian, Hebrew, and Yiddish Literature." In *The Palgrave Encyclopedia of Urban Literary Studies*, edited by Jeremy Tambling, 1447–55. Cham: Palgrave, 2022.

Lederhendler, Eli. *The Road to Modern Jewish Politics: Political Tradition and Political Reconstruction in the Jewish Community of Tsarist Russia*. New York: Oxford University Press, 1989.

Lefebvre, Henri. *The Production of Space*. Oxford: Basil Blackwell, 1991.

Lefkowitz, David. *The Music of David Nowakowsky, 1849–1921: Overview of Research and Practical Applications*. New York: n.p., 1994.

Lesia Ukraiinka [Larysa Petrivna Kosach-Kvitka]. *Lisova pisnia*. Kharkiv: Folio, 2017.

Levin, Vladimir. "Reform or Consensus? Choral Synagogues in the Russian Empire." *Arts* 9, no. 2 (2020): 1–49.

Libin, Aleksandr. "Vera Inber." In *100 velikikh Odessitov*, edited by Aleksandr Libin, 167–73. Odesa: Optimum, 2009.

Lieber, Emma. "'Where Is the Sweet Revolution?': A Reconsideration of Gogol and Babel." *Slavic and East European Journal* 53, no. 1 (Spring 2009): 1–18.

Lilienblum, Moshe Leib. *Khatot ne'urim, o, vidui hagadol shel ekhad hasofrim ha'ivrim* [Sins of my youth, or the great confession of one of the Hebrew writers]. Vienna: Buchdruckerei von Georg Brög, 1876.

———. *Ktavim otobiografiyim* [Autobiographical writings]. Jerusalem: Mossad Bialik, 1970.
Liptukha, Tetiana. "A v Odesi dobre zhyty . . ." *Dom kniazia Gagarina. Sbornik nauchnykh statei i publikatsii* 7 (2016): 15–22.
"V literaturno-artisticheskom klube." *Odesskie novosti*, January 1, 1913.
Litvak, Olga. *Haskalah: The Romantic Movement in Judaism*. New Brunswick: Rutgers University Press, 2012.
Livshits, L. "Materialy k tvorcheskoi biografii I. Babelia." *Voprosy literatury* 4 (1964): 110–35.
Ljuboja, Dušan. "Herder's Ideas and the Pan-Slavism: A Conceptual-Historical Approach." *Pro&Contra* 2, no. 2 (2018): 67–85.
L'nyavskiy, Svetlana. "Odesa in Diachronic and Synchronic Studies of Urban Linguistic Landscapes of Ukraine Conducted Between 2015 and 2019." *East West* 9, no. 2 (2022): 93–143.
Loeffler, James Benjamin. *The Most Musical Nation: Jews and Culture in the Late Russian Empire*. New Haven: Yale University Press, 2010.
———. "Neither Fish nor Fowl: The Jewish Paradox of Russian Music." *Jewish Quarterly* 57, no. 2 (2010): 20–27.
Lotman, Yurii. *Izbrannye stat'i*. Tallinn: Aleksandra, 1992.
Luckyj, George. "A Lyricist's Record of the Revolution: A Note on an Unpublished Collection of Verses by Volodymyr Sosyura." *Canadian Slavonic Papers* 3 (1958): 103–08.
Lur'e, Samuil. "Ne plakat', ne smeiat'sia." In *Knigi nashego detstva*, by Miron Petrovsky, 416–21. St. Petersburg: Ivan Limbakh, 2006.
Lushchik, Sergei. "Chudo v pustyne." In *Dom kniazia Gagarina: Sbornik nauchnykh statei i publikatsii*, 166–236. Odesa: Plaske, 2004.
L'vov, Arkadii. *Kaftany i lapserdaki, Syny i pasynki: Pisateli-evrei v russkoi literature* Moskva: Knizhniki, 2015.
Lyon, Janet. "Cosmopolitanism and Modernism." In *The Oxford Handbook of Global Modernisms*, edited by Mark Wollaeger and Matt Eatough, 388–415. Oxford: Oxford University Press, 2012.
Magaldi, Cristina. "Cosmopolitanism and World Music in Rio de Janeiro at the Turn of the Twentieth Century." *Musical Quarterly* 92, no. 3–4 (2009): 329–64.
Magocsi, Paul Robert, and Yohanan Petrovsky-Shtern. *Jews and Ukrainians: A Millennium of Coexistence*. 2nd rev. ed. Toronto: University of Toronto Press, 2018.
Makolkin, Anna. "City-Icon in a Poetic Geography: Pushkin's Odessa." In *Writing the City: Eden, Babylon and the New Jerusalem*, edited by Peter Preston and Paul Simpson-Housley, 95–108. London: Routledge, 1994.
———. *The Nineteenth Century in Odessa: One Hundred Years of Italian Culture on the Shores of the Black Sea, 1794–1894*. Lewiston: Edwin Mellen Press, 2007.
Malan, Roy. *Efrem Zimbalist: A Life*. Pompton Plains, NJ: Amadeus Press, 2004.
Malovichko, Ivan. "Odesa-Kharkiv." In *Ukraiins'ka avanhardna poeziia: Antolohiia, 1910–1930*, edited by Oleh Kotsarev and Iuliia Stakhivs'ka, 346–49. Kyiv: Smoloskyp, 2014.
March, James. "Continuity and Change in Theories of Organizational Action." *Administrative Science Quarterly* 41, no. 2 (1996): 278–87.
Marek, Pinkhus. "Natsionalizatsiia vospitaniia i evreiskie uchebnye zavedeniia." *Evreiskaia Shkola* 3 (1904): 5–8.
Markevich, Aleksei I. "E. Zolia kak belletrist." *Yuzhno-russkii al'manakh* [Odesa] 5 (1899): 1.
———. "O literaturnoi deiatel'nosti Emilia Zolia." In *Otchet pravleniia*, 9. Odesa: n.p., 1899.

Martin, Terry D. *The Affirmative Action Empire: Nations and Nationalism in the Soviet Union, 1923–1939*. Ithaca, NY: Cornell University Press, 2001.

Materialy k istorii russkoi kontr-revoliutsii. Tom. 1, Pogromy po ofitsial'nym dokumentam. St. Petersburg: Tipografiia tovarishchestva "obshchestvennaia pol'za," 1908.

Matich, Olga. *Erotic Utopia: The Decadent Imagination in Russia's Fin de Siècle*. Madison: University of Wisconsin Press, 2005.

Maxwell, Alexander. "Herder, Kollár, and the Origins of Slavic Ethnography." *Traditiones* 40, no. 2 (2011): 79–95.

McReynolds, Louise. "V.M. Doroshevich: The Newspaper Journalist and the Development of Public Opinion in Civil Society." In *Between Tsar and People. Educated Society and the Quest for Public Identity in Late Imperial Russia*, edited by Edith W. Clowes, Samuel D. Kassow, and James L. West, 233–247. Princeton: Princeton University Press, 1991.

Mel'nychuk, I. "Natsional'ni pohliady V. Zhabotyns'koho, 224–28." In *Evrei v Ukraini: istoriia i suchasnist'*. Zhytomyr: ZhDU, 2009.

Mendele Moykher Sforim [S. Y Abramovich)]. "Biymei hara'ash" [In the days of tumult]. *Pardes* 2 (1894): 31–59.

———. *Fishke der Krumer* [Fishke the lame]. Odesa: n.p., 1888.

———. "Fishke the Lame." In *Tales of Mendele the Book Peddler*, edited by Dan Miron and Ken Friedman and translated from Yiddish by Ted Gorelick and Hillel Halkin. 3–298. New York: Schocken Books, 1996.

Meyer, Michael A. *The German Model of Religious Reform and Russian Jewry*. Cambridge, MA: Harvard University Press, 1985.

Mignolo, Walter D. "The Many Faces of Cosmo-polis: Border Thinking and Critical Cosmopolitanism." In *Cosmopolitanism*, edited by Dipesh Chakrabarty, Homi K. Bhabha, Sheldon Pollock, and Carol A. Breckenridge, 157–188. Durham, NC: Duke University Press, 2002.

Miller, Michael L., and Scott Ury. "Dangerous Liaisons: Jews and Cosmopolitanism in Modern Times." In *The Routledge Handbook of Cosmopolitanism Studies*, edited by Gerard Delanty, 550–62. London: Routledge, 2012.

———. "Cosmopolitanism: The End of Jewishness?" *European Review of History* 17, no. 3 (2010): 337–359.

Ministerstvo torgovli i promyshlennosti. Otdel torgovych portov. *Opisanie Odesskago porta*. St. Petersburg: n.p., 1913.

Minkowsky, Pinkhas. "Misefer khayai" [From the book of my life]. *Reshumot* 4 (1926): 123–44.

———. *Moderne liturgye in undzere synagogen in rusland* [Modern liturgy in our synagogues in Russia]. Odesa: Bialik and Burishkin, 1910.

———. "Zimrat hamikdash vehagramofon" [Temple/synagogue songs and the gramophone.] Manuscript. National Library of Israel, Archive of Pinkhas Minkowsky, MUS 16, section B, item 22, p. 5. N.d.

Miron, Dan. "'Al khakhmei odesa / The Odessa Sages." In *Mekhvah leodesa / Homage to Odessa*, edited by Rahel Arbel, 33–37; 62–81. Tel Aviv: Beit Hatfutsot, 2002.

———. *Bodedim bemo'adam: ledyokanah shel harepublikah hasifrutit ha'ivrit betekhilat hameah ha'esrim* [When loners come together]. Tel Aviv: Am Oved, 1987.

"Monument Rabinovich, Odessa." IGotoWorld.com. Accessed December 7, 2022. https://ua.igotoworld.com/en/poi_object/78200_pamyatnik-rabinovichu-odesa.htm.

Morgulis, Mikhail. "Mnenie komiteta odesskogo otdeleniia Obshchestva rasprostraneniia prosveshcheniia o evreiskoi narodnoi shkole." *Ezhenedel'naia khronika voskhoda*, April 19, 1902, 6–8.
———. "Nationalizatsiia i assimiliatsiia." *Voskhod* 5 (May 1902): 99–115.
———. "Sushchnost' iudaizma." *Voskhod* 1 (January 1891): 75–89.
Morozan, Vladimir. "Krupneishie torgovo-bankirskie doma Odessy XIX vek." *Ekonomicheskaia istoria. Ezhegodnik* 9 (2007): 137–92.
———. *Delovaya zhizn' na iuge Rossii v XIX-nachale XX veka*. St. Petersburg: Dmitri Bulanin, 2014.
Moshenskii, Sergei. *Rynok tsennykh bumag Rossiiskoi imperii*. Moscow: Ekonomika, 2014.
Murru, Sarah, and Abel Polese, eds. *Resistances: Between Theories and the Field*. New York: Rowman & Littlefield Publishers, 2020.
Muzychko, Oleksandr. "Rid Smolens'kykh v istoriohrafichnomu protsesi seredyny XIX – pershoi tretyny XX st." In *Zapysky istorychnoho fakul'tetu*, 20:266–83. Odesa: Odes'kyi natsional'nyi universytet, 2009.
———. "Vladimir Zhabotinskii i Dmitrii Dontsov: nekotorye paralleli k istorii ukrainskogo i evreiskogo natsional'nykh dvizhenii v pervoi polovine XX veka." In *Piataia Mezhdunarodnaia konferentsiia "Odessa i evreiskaia tsivilizatsiia,"* edited by Mikhail Rashkovetskii, et al., 42–49. Odesa: Negotsiant, 2007.
Mykytenko, Ivan. *Vurkahany*. Kharkiv: Ukraiins'kyi robitnyk, 1927.
Myronets, Nadia. "G. Shvyd'ko, *Mykhailo Komarov i Katerynoslavshchyna*." *Ukrains'kyi arkheohrafichnyi shchorichnyk*, nos. 16–17 [19–20] (2012): 659–66.
Naidenko, Taia. "Zapakh chaek i moria krik." In *Almanakh Deribasovskaia Rishel'evskaia*, no. 74 (2014): 214–20.
———. *Vse dano*. Odesa: Zelenaia lampa, 2019.
Nakhimovsky, Alice. "Mikhail Zhvanetskii: The Last Russian-Jewish Joker." In *Forging Modern Jewish Identities: Public Faces and Private Struggles*, edited by Michael Berkowitz, Susan L. Tananbaum, and Sam W. Bloom, 156–79. London: Vallentine Mitchell, 2003.
Naroditskaia, Inna. "Is Argentine Tango Russian and How Jewish Is Russian Tango?" In *Gli spazi della musica* 6, no. 2 (2017): 53–68.
Nathans, Benjamin. *Beyond the Pale: The Jewish Encounter with Late Imperial Russia*. Berkeley: University of California Press, 2002.
Natkovich, Svetlana. "Odessa as 'Point de Capital': Economics, History, and Time in Odessa Fiction." *Slavic Review* 75, no. 4 (2016): 847–71.
———. "*Samson*, the Hebrew Novel: The History of the Writing and Reception of Jabotinsky's Novel and the Consolidation of the Norms of Realism in Hebrew Literature." *Jewish Quarterly Review* 110, no. 4 (2020): 733–55.
———. "'What is Permitted to Jupiter is not Permitted to an Ox': *Maskilim* as a Class Phenomenon." *Jewish Social Studies* 27, no. 3 (Fall 2022): 158–88.
Navaro-Yashin, Yael. *Faces of the State: Secularism and Public Life in Turkey*. Princeton: Princeton University Press, 2002.
Nechui-Levyts'kyi, Ivan. "Burlachka." In *Tvory v triokh tomakh*. Vol. 2. Kyiv: Dnipro, 1988.
———. *Nad Chornym morem*. Kharkiv: Folio, 2008.
Nussbaum, Martha. "Kant and Cosmopolitanism." In *The Cosmopolitanism Reader*, edited by Garrett W. Brown and David Held, 27–44. Cambridge: Polity, 2010.
———. "Patriotism and Cosmopolitanism." *Boston Review*, October 1, 1994. http://bostonreview.net/martha-nussbaum-patriotism-and-cosmopolitanism.

"Obshchestvo 'Prosvita' v Odesse." *Kievskaia starina*, November–December (1905): 105–16.
"Odessa Finds Its Ukrainian Identity Ahead of Russian Advance." *Economist*, March 7, 2022. https://www.economist.com/europe/2022/03/07/odessa-finds-its-ukrainian-identity-ahead-of-a-russian-advance
Odesskii pogrom i samooborona. Paris: Izdanie zapadnogo tsentral'nogo komiteta Po'ale-Tsion, 1906.
Ogryzko, Viacheslav. "Moe polozhenie lozhno." *Literaturnaia Rossia*, February 23, 2015. https://litrossia.ru/item/4296-oldarchive/.
Olesha, Yurii. *Zavist', Tri tolstiaka, vospominaniia, rasskazy*. Moscow: Eksmo, 2013.
Organization for Economic Cooperation and Development (OECD). *Maintaining the Momentum of Decentralisation in Ukraine*. Paris: OECD Multi-level Governance Studies, 2018.
Otchet o deiatel'nosti komiteta odesskogo otdeleniia Obshchestva dlia rasprostraneniia prosveshcheniia mezhdu evreiami v Rossii v 1901 g. Odesa: Obshchestva dlia rasprostraneniia prosveshcheniia, 1902.
Otchet pravleniia Odesskago literaturno-artisticheskago kluba za 1914-i god. Odesa: n.p., 1915.
Otchet pravleniia Odesskago literaturno-artisticheskago kluba za 1915-i god. Odesa: n.p., 1916.
Otchet pravleniia Odesskago literaturno-khudozhestvennogo obshchestva za 1898 g. Odesa: n.p., 1899.
Otchet pravleniia Odesskago literaturno-khudozhestvennogo obshchestva za 1903 g. Odesa: n.p., 1904.
Ovidius Naso, Publius. *Ovid's Metamorphoses in Latin and English*. Vol. 1. Amsterdam: Wettsteins and Smith, 1732.
Palko, Olena. *Making Ukraine Soviet: Literature and Cultural Politics under Lenin and Stalin*. London: Bloomsbury, 2020.
Panasenko, Natal'ia. *Zhabotinskii v Odesse: literaturno-kraevedcheskii spravochnik*. Odesa: Astroprint, 2018.
Pasternak, Evgenii. "Vstuplenie." In *Boris Pasternak, pozhiznennaia priviazannost': Perepiska s O. M. Freidenberg*, 3–18. Moscow: Art-Fleks, 2000.
Pasternak, Leonid. *Zapisi raznykh let*. Moscow: Sovetskii khudozhnik, 1975.
Pauly, Matthew D. *Breaking the Tongue: Language, Education, and Power in Soviet Ukraine, 1923–1934*. Toronto: University of Toronto Press, 2014.
Paustovskii, Konstantin. *Sobranie sochinenii*. Vol. 5. Moskva: Khudozhestvennaia literatura, 1982.
———. *Vremia bol'shikh ozhidanii*. Moscow: Sovetskii pisatel', 1960.
Pavlyshyn, Marko. "Literary History as Provocation of National Identity, National Identity as Provocation of Literary History: The Case of Ukraine." *Thesis Eleven* 136, no. 1 (October 5, 2016): 74–89.
Pawłusz, Emilia, and Oleksandra Seliverstova. "Everyday Nation-Building in the Post-Soviet Space. Methodological Reflections." *Studies of Transition States and Societies* 8, no. 1 (2016): 69–86.
Perelman, Aron. "Vospominaniia." *Almanakh Evreiskaia Starina* 4, no 63 (2009). http://berkovich-zametki.com/2009/Starina/Nomer4/APerelman4.php.
"Pesni dlia Stalina." Jewish.ru, July 16, 2020. https://jewish.ru/ru/people/culture/187352/.
Petrone, Karen. *Life Has Become More Joyous, Comrades: Celebrations in the Time of Stalin*. Bloomington: Indiana University Press, 2000.
Petrovsky, Miron. *Kniga o Kornee Chukovskom*. Moscow: Sovetskii pisatel', 1966.
———. "Kornei Chukovskii i Vladimir Zhabotinskii." Paper presented at the "Jewish Culture, History, and Traditions" conference, Odesa, November 29–December 3, 1994.

Petrovsky-Shtern, Yohanan. *The Anti-Imperial Choice: The Making of the Ukrainian Jew*. New Haven: Yale University Press, 2009.

———. *The Golden Age Shtetl: A New History of Jewish Life in East Europe*. Princeton: Princeton University Press, 2014.

———. "Isaak Vavilonskii: Iazyk i mif 'Odesskikh rasskazov.'" *Yehupets* 13 (2003): 93–95.

Pil'skii. Petr. "Odessa." *Probuzhdenie*, June 1, 1911.

———. *Zatumanivshiisia mir*. Riga: Grāmatu draugs, 1928.

———. "O zhemanstve." In *Zatumanivshiisia mir*, 17–28. Riga: Grāmatu Draugs, 1929.

Pines, Noah, ed. *Hazamir*. Odesa: Moriah, 1903.

Pinkham, Sophie. "Making Deals in the Paradise of Thieves: Leonid Utesov, Arkadii Severnyi, and 'Blatnaia Pesnia.'" *Ulbandus Review* 16 (2014): 177–97.

Pinnolis, Judith. "Isa Kremer." Jewniverse. Last updated November 20, 2022. http://www.holoimes.jewniverse.info/isakremer/biography.htm/.

Pinsker, Shachar M. *A Rich Brew: How Cafés Created Modern Jewish Culture*. New York: New York University Press, 2018.

Pipes, Richard. *Struve: Liberal on the Left, 1870–1905*. Cambridge, MA: Harvard University Press, 1980.

Pirie, Paul S. "National Identity and Politics in Southern and Eastern Ukraine." *Europe–Asia Studies* 48, no. 7 (1996): 1079–104.

Platt, Jonathan B. *Greetings, Pushkin! Stalinist Cultural Politics and the Russian National Bard*. Pittsburgh: University of Pittsburgh Press, 2016.

———. "Pushkin Now and Then: Images of Temporal Paradox in the 1937 Pushkin Jubilee." *Russian Review* 67, no. 4 (October 2008): 638–60.

Pogorel'skaia, Elena, and Stiv Levin. *Isaak Babel: Zhizneopisanie*. Moskva: Vita-Nova, 2020.

Polese, Abel. "Between 'Official' and 'Unofficial' Temperatures: Introducing a Complication to the Hot and Cold Ethnicity Theory from Odessa." *Journal of Multilingual and Multicultural Development* 35, no. 1 (2014): 59–75.

———. "Can Nation Building Be 'Spontaneous'? A (Belated) Ethnography of the Orange Revolution." In *Identity and Nation Building in Everyday Post-Socialist Life*, edited by Abel Polese et al., 161–75. London: Routledge, 2019.

———. "The Formal and the Informal: Exploring 'Ukrainian' Education in Ukraine, Scenes from Odessa." *Comparative Education* 46 (2010): 47–62.

———. "Too Much Corruption or Simply too Much Talk of . . . Corruption . . . ?" *Transitions*, November 11, 2018. https://tol.org/client/article/26474-too-much-corruption-or-simply-too-much-talk-of-corruption.html?print.

———. "Une Version Alternative de la 'révolution Orange': Transformations identitaires et 'nation building spontané.'" *Socio-Logos: Revue de l'Association Française de Sociologie* 4 (2009). https://journals.openedition.org/socio-logos/2315.

———. "Where Marx Meets Ekaterina (the Great): The Dichotomy between National and Plural Identities in Odessa." Paper Presented at the Annual Convention of the Association for the Study of Nationalities, New York, 2007.

Polese and Anna Wylegala. "Odessa and Lvov or Odesa and Lviv: How Important is a Letter? Reflections on the 'Other' in Two Ukrainian Cities." *Nationalities Papers* 36, no. 5: (2008): 787–814.

Polese and Wylegala. "Sprache und Identität: Reflexionen aus Odessa und Lwiw." *Ukraine-Analysen*, no. 3 (2008): 13–17.

Polese, Abel, et al. *Identity and Nation Building in Everyday Post-Socialist Life* London and New York: Routledge, 2019.

Polese, Abel, Oleksandra Seliverstova, Emilia Pawłusz, and Jeremy Morris. "Conclusion: When Post-Socialism Meets the Everyday." In *Informal Nationalism after Communism: The Everyday Construction of Post-Socialist Identities*, edited by Polese, et al., 183–87. London: Tauris, 2018.

Polese, Abel, R. Ribeye, T. Kerikmae, and S. Murru. "Negotiating Spaces and the Public-Private Boundary: Language Policies Versus Language Use Practices in Odessa." *Space and Culture* 22, no. 3 (2019): 263–79.

Polishchuk, Mikhail. *Evrei Odessy i Novorossii: Sotsial'no -politicheskaia istoriia evreev Odessy i drugikh v gorodov Novorossii 1881–1904*. Moscow: Mosty Kultury, 2002.

Poovey, Mary. *Genres of the Credit Economy*. Chicago: University of Chicago Press, 2008.

Popson, Nancy. "The Ukrainian History Textbook: Introducing Children to the 'Ukrainian Nation.'" *Nationalities Papers* 29, no. 2 (2001): 325–50.

Pushkin, Alexander. *Eugene Onegin*. Translated by Vladimir Nabokov. Rev. ed. Princeton: Princeton University Press, 1965.

Quijano, Anibal. "Coloniality of Power, Eurocentrism, and Latin America." *Nepantla: Views from the South* 1, no. 3 (2000): 533–80.

Ramer, Samuel C., and Blair A. Ruble, eds. *Place, Identity, and Urban Culture: Odesa and New Orleans*. Washington, DC: Kennan Institute, 2008.

"Rav tsa'ir" (Chaim Tczernowitz). *Mesekhet zikhronot: Partsufim veh'arakhot* [Memoirs: Portraits and Appraisals]. New York: Va'ad hayovel, 1945.

Redepenning, Dorothea. "Die Russische Romanze." In *Geschichte der russischen und sowjetischen Musik 1: Das 19. Jahrhundert*, 38–67. Laaber: Laaber-Verlag, 1994.

Regev, Motti, and Edwin Seroussi. *Popular Music and National Culture in Israel*. Berkeley: University of California Press, 2004.

Rezanov, Dmitrii. "Odesskii ledokol." Jvanetsky.ru [Zhvanetsky's official website]. Accessed September 29, 2020. http://www.jvanetsky.ru/data/text/pf/odessky_ledokol/?print=1.

Riabkov, Aleksandr. "Pamiatnik Babel'iu, Est' gorod, kotoryi ia vizhu vo sne . . . Istoriia Odessy i odesskie istorii," July 9, 2018. https://histodessa.ru/pamyatnik-babelyu/.

Richardson, Tanya. *Kaleidoscopic Odessa: History and Place in Contemporary Ukraine*. Toronto: University of Toronto Press, 2008.

Rodgers, Peter W. "'Compliance or Contradiction'? Teaching 'History' in the 'New' Ukraine. A View from Ukraine's Eastern Borderlands." *Europe–Asia Studies* 59, no. 3 (2007): 503–19.

Rogger, Hans. "The Beilis Case. Anti-Semitism and Politics in the Reign of Nicholas II." In *Hostages of Modernization: Studies on Modern Antisemitism 1870–1933/39*. Vol. 2, *Austria, Hungary, Poland, Russia*, edited by Herbert A. Strauss, 1257–73. Berlin: De Gruyter, 1993.

Rossiiskii Gosudarstvennyi Istoricheskii Arkhiv. fond 1284.

Rothman, Howard B., Jose A. Diaz, and Kristen E. Vincent. "Comparing Historical and Contemporary Opera Singers with Historical and Contemporary Jewish Cantors." *Journal of Voice* 14, no. 2 (2000): 205–214.

Rothstein, Robert A. "How It Was Sung in Odessa: At the Intersection of Russian and Yiddish Folk Culture." *Slavic Review* 60 no. 4 (2001): 781–801.

Rozenthal, Judah Leon. *Toldot khevrat marbei haskalah beyisrael beeretz rusyah meshnat 1863 'ad shnat 1885* [History of the OPE in the land of Russia from 1863 to 1885]. St. Petersburg: n.p., 1885.

Rubin, Emanuel. "The Music of David Nowakowsky (1848–1921): A New Voice from Old Odessa." *Musica Judaica* 16 (2001): 20–52.

Rubinstein, Anat. "The Cantor of the Haskalah: Life, Work and Thought by Cantor Pinkhas Minkowsky (1859–1924)." [Hebrew]. PhD diss., The Hebrew University of Jerusalem, 2013.

Sandler, Stephanie. *Commemorating Pushkin: Russia's Myth of a National Poet.* Stanford: Stanford University Press, 2004.

Saposnik, Arieh. *Becoming Hebrew: The Creation of a Jewish National Culture in Ottoman Palestine.* New York: Oxford University Press, 2008.

Sapritsky, Marina. "Negotiating Cosmopolitanism: Migration, Religious Education and Shifting Jewish Orientations in Post-Soviet Odessa." In *Post-Cosmopolitan Cities: Explorations of Urban Coexistence,* edited by Caroline Humphrey and Vera Skvirskaja, 65–93. New York, Oxford: Berghahn Books, 2012.

Sartor, Wolfgang. "Khlebnye eksportery Chernomorsko-Azovskogo regiona." In *Gretske pridpriemnyctvo i torhivlia u pivnychnomu prychornomorii XVIII-XIX st.,* edited by G. V. Boriak. Kyiv: Institut Istorii Ukrainy, 2012.

Savchenko, Boris. *Estrada retro.* Moskva: Iskusstvo, 1996.

Savchenko, Viktor A. *Neofitsial'naia Odessa epokhi NEPa, mart 1921-sentiabr' 1929.* Moscow: ROSPEN, 2012.

Savigliano, Marta. *Tango and the Political Economy of Passion.* New York: Routledge, 2018.

Schlögel, Karl. *Petersburg: Das Laboratorium der Moderne, 1909–1921,* Munich: Hanser, 2002.

Schlör, Joachim. "'On the third hand . . .': News from a Rediscovered Civilisation in Memories of Odessa." *Jewish Studies at the Central European University* 3 (2002–3): 159–74.

———. "Odessity: In Search of Transnational Odessa." *Quest. Issues in Contemporary Jewish History* 2 (October 2011): 1–25.

Schonberg, Harold C. *Great Pianists.* New York: Simon and Schuster, 1987.

Scollins, Kathleen. *Acts of Logos in Pushkin and Gogol: Petersburg Texts and Subtexts.* Boston: Academic Studies Press, 2017.

Scott, James C. *Domination and the Arts of Resistance: Hidden Transcripts.* New Haven: Yale University Press, 1990.

———. *Seeing like a State: How Certain Schemes to Improve the Human Condition Have Failed.* New Haven: Yale University Press, 1998.

———. *Two Cheers for Anarchism: Six Easy Pieces on Autonomy, Dignity, and Meaningful Work and Play.* Princeton: Princeton University Press, 2012.

———. *Weapons of the Weak: Everyday Forms of Peasant Resistance.* New Haven: Yale University Press, 1985.

Sériot, Patrick. "Diglossie, Bilinguisme ou Mélange de Langues: Le Cas du Suržyk en Ukraine." *Linguistique* 41, no. 2 (2005): 37–52.

Shevchenko, V. V. "Organizatsia funktsiiuvannia bankyrs'kykh ustanov pivdennoi Urkainy (XIX – pochatok XX st.)." *Problemy istorii Ukrainy XIX-pochatku XX st.* 16 (2008): 189–194.

Shevel, Oxana. "Nationality in Ukraine: Some Rules of Engagement." *East European Politics and Societies: and Cultures* 16, no. 2 (2002): 386–413.

Shindler, Colin. "Jabotinsky and Ukrainian Nationalism: A Reinterpretation." *East European Jewish Affairs* 31, no. 2 (2001): 122–31.

Shishova, Zinaida. "O nashei molodosti." In *Sil'nee liubvi i smerti: Stikhotvorenia, vospominania, pis'ma*, edited by Dmitrii A. Losev and Alena Iavorskaia, 91–101. Feodosiia and Moscow: Koktebel', 2011.

Shkandrij, Myroslav. "The Ukrainian Reading Public in the 1920s: Real, Implied, and Ideal." *Canadian Slavonic Papers* 58, no. 2 (2016): 160–83.

Shklovskii, Viktor. "Pis'mo v redaktsiiu." *Literaturnaia gazeta*, April 29, 1933.

———. "Yugo-Zapad." *Literaturnaia gazeta*, January 5, 1933.

Sholem Aleichem [S. N. Rabinowitz]. *The Adventures of Menahem Mendl*. Translated from Yiddish by Tamara Kahana. New York: G. P. Putnam's Sons, 1969.

———. *Menachem Mendl*. Warsaw: Progress, 1909.

Shtern, Sergei. "Gde intelligentsiia (pis'mo v redaktsiiu)." *Odesskii listok*, March 4, 1912.

Shtypel, Arkadii. "Predislovie." In *Semeinyi arkhiv*, by Boris Khersonsky, 5–8. Moscow: Novoe literaturnoe obozrenie, 2006.

Shulman, Stephen. "Ukrainian Nation-Building under Kuchma." *Problems of Post-Communism* 52, no. 5 (2005): 32–47.

Shumsky, Dmitry. *Beyond the Nation-State: The Zionist Political Imagination from Pinsker to Ben-Gurion*. New Haven: Yale University Press, 2018.

———. "An Odessan Nationality? Local Patriotism and Jewish Nationalism in the Case of Vladimir Jabotinsky." *Russian Review* 79, no. 1 (2020): 65–80.

Shvyd'ko, G. *Mykhailo Komarov i Katerynoslavshchyna*. Dnipropetrovsk: Natsional'nyi hirnychyi universytet, 2011.

Sicher, Efraim. *Babel in Context: A Study in Cultural Identity*. Boston: Academic Studies Press, 2012.

———. "Odessa Time, Odessa Space: Rethinking Cultural Space in a Cosmopolitan City." *Journal of Jewish Culture and History* 16, no. 3 (December 2015): 1–21.

Sifneos, Evrydiki. *Imperial Odessa: Peoples, Spaces, Identities*. Leiden and Boston: Brill, 2018.

Skey, Michael. "The National in Everyday Life: A Critical Engagement with Michael Billig's Thesis of Banal Nationalism." *Sociological Review* 57, no. 2 (2009): 331–46.

Skuratovskii, Vadim. "Vernost' sebe." *Toronto Slavic Quarterly* 40 (2012): 227–31.

Skvirskaja, Vera. "At the City's Social Margins: Selective Cosmopolitanism in Odessa." In *Post-Cosmopolitan Cities: Explorations of Urban Coexistence*, edited by Caroline Humphrey and Vera Skvirskaja, 94–112. New York: Berghahn Books, 2012.

Slavin, Lev. *Ardenskie strasti*. Moscow: Sovetskii pisatel', 1987.

Slezkine, Yuri. *The Jewish Century*. Princeton: Princeton University Press, 2004.

Slobin, Mark, ed. *American Klezmer: Its Roots and Offshoots*. Berkeley: University of California Press, 2002.

———. *Chosen Voices: The Story of the American Cantorate*. Urbana: University of Illinois Press, 2002.

Smirin, I. "Na puti k *Konarmii*: Literaturnye iskaniia Babelia." *Literaturnoe nasledstvo* 74 (1965): 467–82.

Smith, Anthony D. *Nationalism and Modernism: A Critical Survey of Recent Theories of Nations and Nationalism*. London: Routledge, 2013.

Sokolova, Nataliia. "Lidiia Ginzburg, rodnia, znakomye: Materialy k biografii. Vospominaniia." Russian State Archive of Literature and Arts (RGALI). F3270 inv. 1 doc. 27.

Soroka, Oleksandr. "Na Donbas." In *Ukraiins'ka avanhardna poeziia: Antolohiia, 1910–1930*, edited by Oleh Kotsarev and Iuliia Stakhivs'ka, 521–22. Kyiv: Smoloskyp, 2014.

Sosiura, Volodymyr. "*Vybrani tvory v dvokh tomakh*. 2 vols. Kyiv: Naukova dumka, 2000.

———. *Vybrani poezii*. Kyiv: Radyans'kyi pys'mennyk, 1975.

Spisok torgovykh domov i kupechestva Odessy, 1892–1894. Odesa: Odesskii Birzhevoi Komitet, 1892.

Spravochnaia kniga po voprosam obrazovaniia evreev: posobie dlia uchitelei i uchitel'nits evreiskikh shkol i deiatelei po narodnomu obrazovaniiu. St. Petersburg: n.p., 1901.

Stadelmann, Matthias. "Von Jüdischen Ganoven zu sowjetischen Helden: Odessas Wandlungen in den Liedern Leonid Utesovs." *Jahrbuch des Simon-Dubnow-Instituts* 2 (2003): 333–58.

Stanislawski, Michael. *For Whom Do I Toil? Judah Leib Gordon and the Crisis of Russian Jewry*. New York: Oxford University Press, 1988.

———. *Tsar Nicholas I and the Jews: The Transformation of Jewish Society in Russia, 1825–1855*. Philadelphia: Jewish Publication Society of America, 1983.

———. *Zionism and the Fin de Siècle: Cosmopolitanism and Nationalism from Nordau to Jabotinsky*. Berkeley: University of California Press, 2001.

Stanton, Rebecca J. *Isaac Babel and the Self-Invention of Odessan Modernism*. Evanston: Northwestern University Press, 2012.

———. "A Monstrous Staircase." In *Rites of Place: Public Commemoration in Russia and Eastern Europe*, edited by Julie Buckler and Emily Johnson, 59–80. Evanston: Northwestern University Press, 2013.

Starr, S. Frederick. *Red and Hot: The Fate of Jazz in the Soviet Union, 1917–1991*. New York: Limelight, 1994.

Stebelsky, Ihor. "Ethnic Self-Identification in Ukraine, 1989–2001: Why More Ukrainians and Fewer Russians?" *Canadian Slavonic Papers* 51, no. 1 (2009): 77–100.

Stepanov, Yevhen. *Rosiis'ke movlennia Odesy*. Odesa: Astroprynt, 2004.

Stokes, Martin. "On Musical Cosmopolitanism." *Macalester International* 21, no. 1 (2008): 3–26.

Strom, Yale. *The Book of Klezmer: The History, the Music, the Folklore*. Chicago: Chicago Review Press, 2011.

Struve, P. B. "Obshcherusskaia kul'tura i ukrainskii partikuliarizm. Otvet Ukraintsu." *Russkaia mysl'* 1 (1912): 65–86.

Suny, Ronald G. *The Revenge of the Past: Nationalism, Revolution, and the Collapse of the Soviet Union*. Stanford: Stanford University Press, 1993.

Surh, Gerald. "Ekaterinoslav City in 1905: Workers, Jews, and Violence." *International and Labor Working-Class History*, no. 64 (2003): 139–66.

———. "Russia's 1905 Era Pogroms Reexamined." *Canadian-American Slavic Studies*, no. 44 (2010): 253–295.

———. "The Jews of Ekaterinoslav in 1905 as Seen from Town Hall: Ethnic Relations on an Imperial Frontier." *Ab Imperio*, no. 4 (2003): 217–38.

———. "The Role of Civil and Military Commanders during the 1905 Pogroms in Odessa and Kiev." *Jewish Social Studies* 15, no. 3 (2009): 39–55.

Sverbilova, Tetiana, Natalia Maliutina, and Liudmyla Skoryna. *Vid modernu do avanhardu: Zhanrovo-styliova paradygma Ukraiins'koii dramaturhii pershoii tretyny XX st*. Cherkasy: Yu. A. Chabanenko, 2009.

"Svidetel'stva o prinadlezhnosti k kupecheskomu sosloviu." In "Bankirs'ka Kontora Barbasha Samuila Matusovycha (1880–1919 rr.)." Derzhavnyi arkhiv Odess'koi Oblasti, f. 175, opys 1, sprava 3.

Sylvester, Roshanna P. *Tales of Old Odessa: Crime and Civility in a City of Thieves*. DeKalb, IL: North Illinois University Press 2005.
Szporluk, Roman. *Russia, Ukraine, and the Breakup of the Soviet Union*. Stanford: Hoover Institution Press, 2000.
Tabachnikova, Olga. *Russian Irrationalism from Pushkin to Brodsky: Seven Essays in Literature*. London: Bloomsbury, 2015.
Tanny, Jarrod. *City of Rogues and Schnorrers: Russia's Jews and the Myth of Old Odessa*. Bloomington: Indiana University Press, 2011.
Tarnawsky, Maxim. *The All-Encompassing Eye of Ukraine: Ivan Nechui-Levyts'kyi's Realist Prose*. Toronto: University of Toronto Press, 2015.
Taruskin, Richard. *Defining Russia Musically: Historical and Hermeneutical Essays*. Princeton: Princeton University Press, 1997.
Thompson, John, and Howard Mehlinger. *Count Witte and the Tsarist Government in the 1905 Revolution*. Bloomington: Indiana University Press, 1972.
Timasheff, Nicholas S. *The Great Retreat: The Growth and Decline of Communist Russia*. New York: Dutton, 1946.
Tiupa, Valerii. "Mytho-Tectonics of the Petersburgian Hypertext of Russian Literature." *Russian Literature* 62 (2007): 99–112.
Topik, Steven C., and Allen Wells. "Warenketten in einer globalen Wirtschaft." In *1870–1945. Weltmärkte und Weltkriege*, edited by Emily S. Rosenberg, 687–728. Munich: C. H. Beck, 2012.
Toporov, Vladimir. *Mif, ritual, simvol, obraz: issledovaniia v oblasti poeticheskogo*. Moscow: Progress, 1995.
Trivellato, Francesca. *The Familiarity of Strangers: The Sephardic Diaspora, Livorno, and Cross-Cultural Trade in the Early Modern Period*. New Haven: Yale University Press, 2009.
Troinitskii, N. A., ed. *Pervaia Vseobshchaia perepis' naseleniia Rossiiskoi imperii 1897 g.* 89 vols. Odesa: Izdanie Tsentral'nogo statisticheskogo komiteta ministerstva vnutrennikh del, 1904.
Tsirkin-Sadan, Rafael. "Imperiya, leumiyut, vayakhasei mizrakh uma'arav baroman 'Shimshon' meet Vladimir (zeev) Zhabotinsky" [Empire, nationalism, and East-West relations in Vladimir (Zeev) Jabotinsky's novel *Samson*]. *Teoriya uvikoret: bamah yisraelit* 48 (2017): 81–104.
Uffelman, Dirk. "Is There Any Such Thing as Russophone Russophobia?: When Russian Speakers Speak Out against Russia(n) in the Ukrainian Internet." In *Global Russian Cultures*, edited by Kevin F. M. Platt, 207–229. Madison, WI: University of Wisconsin Press, 2019.
Ustav Odesskago literaturno-artisticheskago kluba. Odesa: n.p., 1909.
Ustav Odesskago literaturno-khudozhestvennogo obshchestva. Odesa: n.p., 1897.
Ustav ukrainskago kluba. Statut Odesskago ukrainskago kluba. Odesa: n.p., 1910.
Van Assche, Kristof, and Petruța Teampău. *Local Cosmopolitanism Imagining and (Re)-Making Privileged Places*. Cham: Springer, 2015.
Vasil'ieva, Elina. "Prostranstvo v romane Zhabotinskogo 'Samson Nazorei.'" *Filologicheskie chteniia* (2002): 59–68.
"Vecher o Kh. N. Bialike (lit.-art. Klub)." *Odesskie novosti*, February 2, 1913, 3.
"Vera Inber: Ia vspominaiu . . . (chitaet avtor)." *Odnoklassniki*. December 29, 2018. Video 14:48. https://ok.ru/video/872942209627/.
Vernikova, Bella. *Iz pervykh ust: odesskii tekst, istoriko-literaturnye aspekty i sovremennost'*. Moscow: Vodolei, 2015.
Vital, David. *Zionism: The Formative Years*. Oxford: Clarendon Press, 1982.

Volkov, Solomon. *Shostakovich and Stalin: The Extraordinary Relationship between the Great Composer and the Brutal Dictator.* Translated by Antonina W. Bouis. New York: Knopf, 2004.
Vorobiov, Ievgen. "Why Ukrainians Are Speaking More Ukrainian." *Foreign Policy*, June 26, 2015. https://foreignpolicy.com/2015/06/26/why-ukrainians-are-speaking-more-ukrainian/.
Walkowitz, Rebecca. *Cosmopolitan Style: Modernism Beyond the Nation.* New York: Columbia University Press, 2006.
Wanner, Adrian. "'There Is No Such City': The Myth of Odessa in Post-Soviet Immigrant Literature." *Twentieth Century Literature* 65, no. 1–2 (2019): 121–44.
Wawra, Ernst. "Verharren im Unentschieden: Babel's 'Helden' in *Benja Krik*." In *Glücksuchende?: Conditio Judaica im sowjetischen Film*, edited by Lilia Antipow, Matthias Dornhuber, and Jörn Petrick, 85–102. Würzburg: Königshausen & Neumann, 2011.
Weinberg, Robert. "The Pogrom of 1905 in Odessa: A Case Study." In *Pogroms: Anti-Jewish Violence in Modern Russian History*, edited by John D. Klier and Shlomo Lambroza, 248–290. Cambridge: Cambridge University Press, 1992.
———. *The Revolution of 1905 in Odessa: Blood on the Steps.* Bloomington, IN: Indiana University Press, 1993.
Whitmarsh, Galila. *Eliezer Ben Yehuda and the Revival of Modern Hebrew: Language and Identity.* Saarbrücken: Lambert Academic Publishing, 2009.
Wilson, Andrew. "Elements of a Theory of Ukrainian Ethno-National Identities." *Nations and Nationalism* 8, no. 1 (2002): 31–54.
Wolczuk, Katerzyna. "History, Europe and the 'National Idea': The 'Official' Narrative of National Identity in Ukraine." *Nationalities Papers* 28, no. 4 (2000): 671–94.
Zagrebel'nyi, Mikhail. *Eduard Bagritskii.* Kharkiv: Folio, 2012.
Zakharkin, Stepan, and Andrei Puchkov, eds. *Miron Petrovsky. Biobibliografiia.* Compiled by Yulia Veretennikova. Kyiv: Izdatel'skii dom A+C, 2007.
Zaltsberg, Ernst. "In the Shadows: Rosalia Pasternak, 1867–1939." *East European Jewish Affairs* 28 (1998): 29–36.
Zarubenko, T. "Pereklad 'Odissei' v interpretatsii Petra Baidy." *Mova i kultura* 17, no. 5 (2014): 11–19.
Zeepvat, Charlotte. *The Camera and the Tsars: The Romanov Family in Photographs.* Stroud: Sutton, 2004.
Zelenaia, Rina. "Razroznennye stranitsy." *Deribasovskaia-Rishel'evskaia* 34 (2008): 230–36.
Zhadan, Serhii. *Anarchy in the UKR.* Kharkiv: Folio, 2005.
Zhvanetsky, Mikhail. "Priezzhii v Odesse." Zhvanetsky's official website. http://www.jvanetsky.ru/data/text/t5/5tom_Priezzhij_v_Odesse/.
Zinberg, Israel. *A History of Jewish Literature.* Vol. 11. Translated by Bernard Martin. New York: Ktav Publishing, 1978.
Zipperstein, Steven J. "Jewish Enlightenment in Odessa: Cultural Characteristics, 1794–1871." *Jewish Social Studies* 44, no. 1 (1982): 19–36.
———. *Elusive Prophet: Ahad Ha'am and the Origins of Zionism.* Berkeley: University of California Press, 1993.
———. *Imagining Russian Jewry.* Seattle: University of Washington Press, 1999.
———. *The Jews of Odessa: A Cultural History, 1794–1881.* Stanford: Stanford University Press, 1985.
Zubacheva, Ksenia, and Anastasiya Karagodina. "How Photography Became a Hobby of the Romanovs." *Russia Beyond*, July 4, 2017. https://www.rbth.com/arts/history/2017/07/04/how-photography-became-the-hobby-of-the-romanovs_795295/.

Index

Abramovich, Sholem Yankev. *See* Mendele
Abrams, Jessie, 189–90
Adalis, Adelina, 174
Ades. *See* Odesa
Ahad Ha'am (Asher Ginsberg), 78, 81, 88, 94, 96, 102, 105–7, 112–14
Akhmatova, Anna, 203, 292–93, 296, 298
Akkerman (Tyras), 225
Aksenfeld, Yisroel, 76
Aleichem, Sholem (Sholem Rabinowitz), 3, 41, 78, 147–48, 186, 203
Alexander II, tsar, 23, 41, 120
Altalena. *See* Jabotinsky, Vladimir
anarchism, 191, 209, 242, 280
Andrukhovych, Iurii, 238
antisemitism, 3, 9, 29, 30, 118–138, 155, 177, 182, 189, 191, 199, 200, 210, 227, 279, 280, 285, 297–98
Argentina, 25, 86
Armenians, 13, 38, 119, 140, 252, 254, 258
Asch, Sholem, 41
Ascher, Abraham, 121
Ascherson, Neal, 12
Ashkenazi, Luisa, 75, 84, 87
Ashkenazi family 84
Asia, 143, 248
Auer, Leopold, 151–52
Australia, 25
Austria, 11, 31, 154
Austro-Hungarian Empire. *See* Habsburg Empire
Averchenko, Arkadii, 196
Azov Sea, 13

Babel, Isaak, 18–19, 151, 153, 156, 168, 174, 179–80, 184–85, 193–95, 197–98, 200–2, 204–6, 208–213, 215–16, 218–20, 243–44, 273–78, 281–82, 286, 290–91, 293–96, 298–99, 302–3
Bagritsky, Eduard, 4–5, 168, 174, 176, 194, 201, 203–5, 240–41, 276–77, 291
Bagrov, M. F., 182
Baida, Petro. *See* Nishchyns'kyi, Petro
Bakhtin, Mikhail, 213, 283
Bălți. *See* Beltz
Banbaji, Amir, 98
Bandera, Stepan, 285
Barbash, Samuel, 82, 87–88, 95–96
Bazhan, Nik, 245
Beatles, 299
Beethoven, Ludwig van, 145–46
Beilis trial, 199
Belinskii, Vissarion, 28
Belli, Giuseppe, 49, 54
Belousova, Lilia, 85
Beltz (Beltsy), 88, 181
Ben-Ami (Mark Mordechai Rabinovich) 78, 102, 112
Ben-David (Y. L. Dovidovitz), 9
Ben-Yehuda, Eliezer (Eliezer Yitzkhak Perlman), 52
Berdichev, 203, 297
Berkowitz, Yitskhak Dov, 77–78, 81
Berlin, 34, 87, 92–93
Berman, Jessica, 168
Bernsand, Niklas, 238n28
Bernstein-Cohen, Ya'akov, 113

Bertenson, Aleksei 82
Besredka, Alexandre, 81
Bessarabia, 159, 181
Bialik, Haim Nahman, 2, 4, 34, 78, 88, 94–95, 107, 112–13, 153, 162, 186, 220
BiBaBo, theater, 175
Bible, 62, 176, 207, 281, 304
Bilhorod-Dnistrovs'kyi. *See* Akkerman
Bisk, Aleksandr, 173
Black Sea, 1, 12, 25, 93, 95, 121, 141, 144, 179, 181, 199, 217, 224, 226, 228–30, 233–34, 239, 249–50, 273, 279, 294
Blakytnyi, Vasyl, 241
Bliumenfeld, Nadezhda, 176
Bliumenfeld family, 176
Blok, Alexander, 203, 276, 294
Blumenfeld, German 82
Blumenthal, Nissan, 148
Bluntschli, Johann Caspar, 54, 57
Bnei Moshe, 107, 112
Bobovich, Boris, 194
Bobrinets, 169
Boffo, Francesco, 278
Bohemia, 154
Bolsheviks, 2, 130, 197, 201, 203, 208–9, 215, 218, 239–40
Bondarin, Sergei, 173, 204
Borishpolets, Elena, 291–92, 294
Bosphorus, 12
Boulanger, Georges Ernest 93
Bourdieu, Pierre, 72, 271
Boym, Svetlana, 279
Breslau. *See* Wrocław
Brezhnev, Leonid, 298
Brodsky, Abraham, 52, 75, 87, 146, 276, 294
Brodsky family, 102
Brubaker, Rogers, 43
Brugger, Friedrich, 278
Budnitskii, Oleg, 209
Bund, 130
Bunin, Ivan, 5
Burliuk, David, 201
Burns, Robert, 49
Bykov, Dmitry, 292–93

Canada, 25
Casanova, Pascale, 293
Castro, Fidel, 298
Castro, Raul, 298
Catherine II, tsarina, 1, 6, 141, 162, 279
Caucasus, 203
Chaplin, Charlie, 203
Cheka, Soviet Secret Police, 4, 204, 215
Chekhovich, Pavel, 26–28
Chernetsky, Vitaly, 285
Chernivtsi (Czernowitz), 2, 276
Cherny, Sasha, 196
China, 258
Chișinău. *See* Kishinev
Chukovsky, Kornei (Nikolai Korneichukov), 9, 17, 41–50, 56, 67–68, 185, 201n27
Churchill, Winston, 302
Chykalenko, Yevhen, 42, 58
Cicero, 7
Civil War, 1, 4, 120, 140, 167, 170, 194, 197, 205, 208–212, 214, 218, 239, 242, 244, 272, 275
Clover, Joshua, 92
Constantinople. *See* Istanbul
Corday, Charlotte, 64
Corinth, 54
cosmopolitanism, 1, 4, 5, 7–16, 17, 18, 19, 21–22, 36, 38, 44, 56, 65, 68, 71, 89, 100–102, 105, 114–17, 118-23, 125, 136–38, 139–40, 160, 163, 167–68, 180, 182, 190–92, 200, 203, 218, 225, 226, 229–31, 253–55, 257–59, 274, 276, 278, 280, 282–84, 289, 304. *See also* post-cosmopolitanism
Cossacks, 178, 213, 295
Crimea, 6, 252, 254, 272, 290

Crimean War, 85, 87–90
Czernowitz. *See* Chernivtsi

Dalila, Elinoar, 63–64
Danylko, Andriy (Verka Serdiuchka), 261
Dardanelles Strait, 25
Denikin, Anton, 209
Derrida, Jacques, 43, 225
Dharwadker, Vinay, 289
Dizengoff, Meir, 2, 102, 112
Dmitrenko, Yuri, 278
Dmitrievich, Konstantin, 169
Dniester, 231
Donbas, 6, 237, 240, 277, 281, 284, 302
Donets, 242
Doroshevich, Vlas, 28, 30, 202
Dostoevsky, Fedor, 43, 299
Dovidovitz, Y. L. *See* Ben-David
Dovzhenko, Oleksandr, 245, 250
Drahomanov, Mikhailo, 42
Dreyfus affair, 29–30, 32, 34–35
Dubnow, Simon, 78, 81–82, 88, 94–96, 102, 106, 112, 116
Dunaevskii, Isaac, 162

Ecclesiastes, 207
Edwards, Boris, 28
Egypt, 63
Ehrenburg, Ilya, 296–97
Eisenstein, Sergei, 1, 121, 216, 220, 301
Elman, Mischa, 151, 158
Ems Edict, 39, 230
Entente blockade, 203, 212
Ephrussi family, 73–75, 84, 87–88
Ephrussi, Hayim, 84, 87
Estonia, 270
Euromaidan, 277, 281, 284–85, 294, 301, 302
Europe, 8, 11, 25, 28, 30–31, 36, 50, 55, 80, 88, 107–8, 111, 115, 119, 143, 147, 158, 161, 188–90, 219, 230, 250, 277, 302

Fascism, 192, 277, 286
Fasini, Sandro (Srul Arnol'dovich Fainzilberg), 185
Fastov, 88
February Revolution, 208, 209
Fichmann, Ya'akov, 77
Finkelstein, Doctor 82
Fioletov, Anatoly, 194
Fisherovich, Moisei, 82
Ford, Henry, 189
France, 29–31, 34, 215
Frangulian, Georgy, 274, 278
Franko, Ivan, 39
Freidenberg, Mikhail, 79–80
Freidenberg, Olga, 79
Freidin, Gregory, 218, 221n79, 273n1, 275
Frug, Semyon, 34
Futurism 173, 201, 220, 245
Fyodorov, Nikolai, 201

Gabrilowitsch, Osip, 151
Galicia, 33, 39, 57, 64
Gaysin (Haisyn), 88
Gekht, Semyon, 196–97, 203–4
Georgians, 56
Gerasimov, Ilya, 16, 122, 138
Germans, 1, 15, 54, 119
Germany, 11, 147–48, 150, 154
Gessen, Iosif, 79
Gessen, Vladimir, 79
Gessen, Yulii, 79
Gessen family, 79–80
Gilman, Sander L., 9
Ginsberg, Asher. *See* Ahad Ha'am
Gintsburg, Evzel, 103
Ginzburg, Lidiia, 176
Gitelman, Zvi, 282n20, 284n28
Glicksberg, Haim, 162
Gogol, Nikolai, 217
Gold, Doctor 82, 85
Goldberg family, 90

Goldoni, Carlo, 54
Golubovsky, Evgeny, 292
Gordin, Yakov, 41
Gordon, Leib, 114–15
Gorky, Maxim, 59, 181, 201, 215, 217
Granov, Vladimir 82
Grasso, Giovanni, 54, 217, 219–21
Greece, 140
Greeks, 1, 7–8, 12–13, 15–16, 54, 119, 125, 140, 143, 265, 283
Grieg, Edvard, 162
Griffith, David, 248
Grin, Aleksandr, 248
Grinberg, Abraham, 82
Gruzenberg, Saul, 109
Guenzburg family, 90
Guenzburg, Vladimir, 52
Guimera, Angel, 221n79
Gulag, 250
Gurfinkel, 176
Gurovich, Berman, 82
Gypsies. *See* Roma

Habsburg Empire, 2, 11, 39, 182
Hadzhibey (Hacıbey), 9, 258. *See also* Odesa
Haifa, 95
Halpern family, 84
Hapardes, 112
Hashiloakh, 112
Hasidism, 82.100, 159, 212
Haskalah, 2, 11, 100, 102, 110, 114, 116, 141, 150, 153, 222
Hauptmann, Gerhard, 28
Hegel, Georg Friedrich, 55
Heifetz, Israel, 28, 167, 173, 186
Heifetz, Jasha, 151
Heine, Heinrich, 43
Herder, Johann Gottfried, 55–57, 68, 188
Herlihy, Patricia, 11, 21, 86, 92, 122, 136, 141, 258

Herzl, Theodor, 112–13
Hever, Hanan, 98
Hibbat Tsion, 70, 85, 89, 94–96, 112–13
Himmelfarb, Grigorii, 82
Hitler, Adolf, 302
Holocaust, 5, 197, 279
Holovaty, Antin, 279
Homer, 42
Hrushevs'kyi, Mykhailo, 40, 68
Humphrey, Caroline, 10, 14, 118, 122, 138, 257
Hungarians, 55

Ianovs'kyi, Iurii, 3, 245–48, 250
Idelson, Avram, 113
Ilf, Ilia (Yehiel-Leyb Arnol'dovich Fainzilberg), 5, 168, 185, 197, 204–5, 277, 279, 291
Iljine, Nicolas, 141
Inber, Vera, 18, 166–82, 190–92, 194, 204, 277, 291, 296–97
India, 182
internationalism, 18, 19, 192, 216, 219, 248, 274, 283–84, 286, 287, 293, 297
Iohansen, Maik, 245, 249
Israel, Land of, 36, 52, 61, 62, 67, 69, 70, 82, 90, 94, 95, 96–97, 112, 114, 117, 153, 173. *See also* Palestine, Ottoman ruled/British Mandate; Zionism
Istanbul, 13, 88, 167, 217.
Italians, 1, 54–55, 140, 143
Italy, 54, 58, 140, 143, 145, 154, 182, 215, 219
Ithaca, 54
Ivanova, Evgeniia, 45
Izgoev, Aleksandr (Aron Lande), 27–28, 30–31

Jabotinsky, Vladimir (Zeev), 17, 29, 37–45, 47–69, 93, 101, 160, 199, 203, 228, 277, 286

Jaffa, 95
Japan, 124, 126, 137
Jeremiah, 288
Jerusalem, 212, 219
Jesus, 207
Jews 1, 2, 5, 8, 9, 10, 11, 13, 14, 15, 16, 17, 24, 25, 29, 30, 31, 34, 35, 36, 38, 42, 43, 44, 50, 51, 52, 55, 56, 57, 58, 62, 64, 65, 67, 68, 70–138, 140, 141, 145, 146, 148, 150, 151, 153, 158, 159, 163, 164, 176, 182, 186, 188, 190, 194, 199, 200, 201, 207–8, 210, 213, 216, 218–19, 227–28, 244, 263, 280, 285, 286–88, 297
Joyce, James, 219

Kakhovka, 155–56
Kalman, Imre, 182
Kamenskii, Vasilii, 201
Kant, Immanuel, 7–8, 225
Karasin, Hirsh, 84
Kataev, Valentin, 168, 172–73, 176–77, 194, 201, 204, 219, 248, 277, 291, 293
Kaufmann, Rozalia, 79
Kaulbars, Aleksandr, 131, 133–34
Kaunas, 110
Kel'man, F. (Mikhail Ferkel'man), 282n19
Kernerenko, Hryts'ko (Grigorii Kerner), 41
Kesselman, Semyon, 194
KGB, 299
Khait, Valery, 275
Kharkiv, 3, 38, 235–38, 251, 282
Khenkin, Vladimir, 175
Kherson, 25, 40, 66, 88
Khersonskaia, Ludmila, 298
Khersonsky, Boris, 19, 273–87, 289–90, 294–95, 298–304
Khmelnytsky (Proskuriv), 239
Khvyl'ovyi, Mykola, 234
Kiev. *See* Kyiv

Kiliia, 265
Kishinev, 29, 87, 127, 228, 232
Kiva, Iya, 281, 290
Klausner, Yosef, 34, 113
Kleiman, Moisei, 82
Kogan family, 75, 84
Kohl, Johann Georg, 258
Komar, Vitaly, 302
Komarov, Mykhailo, 41–42, 226
Komashko, Viktor, 226, 228–29, 231–33
Komsomol, 217, 237–38
Königsberg (Kaliningrad, Królewiec), 88
Korenman, Lazar (Karmen), 198
Koriak, Volodymyr, 241
Kornbluh, Anna, 91
Korneichukov, Nikolai. *See* Chukovsky, Kornei
Korneichukova, Katerina, 40, 56
Korostelina, Karyna, 284–85
Kotkin, Stephen, 255
Kotliarevs'kyi, Ivan, 28, 45
Kotovskii, Grigorii, 209
Kozlenko, Ivan, 250
Kremer, Isa, 18, 166–67, 173, 181–86, 188–92, 201, 203
Kremlin, 5–6, 254, 286
Kriuchkov, Pavel, 287
KROT, theater, 175–77
Ku Klux Klan, 248
Kulish, Panteleimon, 45
Kulyk, Volodymyr, 284
Kuprin, Alexander, 159, 196, 201
Kurbas, Les', 245, 249
Kyiv, 3, 38, 43, 52, 58, 87, 137, 199, 217, 230, 237, 251–52, 264, 266–67, 270, 277, 281–82, 286, 289, 291, 300

Lapervansh, Madlen, 63
Latvia, 270
Lebedev, Aaron, 157
Lefebvre, Henri, 8
Lemberg. *See* Lviv

Lenin, Vladimir, 167, 178, 181, 205
Leningrad. *See* St. Petersburg
Lerner, Joseph Judah, 78–79, 81
Levant, 198, 217
Levashov, Sergei, 34
Levin, Vladimir, 148
Lewinsky, Elhanan Leib, 78
Lilienblum, Moshe Leib, 74, 77, 94–95, 102, 111
Lilith, demon, 177
Lincoln, Abraham, 93
Linetskii, Yitskhok Yoel, 78, 81
Liszt, Franz, 143
Lithuania, 110–111
Lithuanians, 50, 56
Livshits, Isaak, 204
Lods, Jean, 216, 273n1
Lokhvitskaia, Mirra, 174
London, 92–93, 219
Lopatyns'kyi, Favst, 245
Lotman, Yurii, 198
Lviv, 39, 41–42, 51, 54, 298
Lyon, Janet, 9

Makarov, Aleksandr, 168
Makhno, 242, 244
Makolkin, Anna, 219
Maliszewski, Witold, 154
Malovichko, Ivan, 236
Mandelshtam, Osip, 217–18
Marazli, Grigorii, 28
Markevych, Oleksii (Markevich, Aleksei), 29–30
Marx, Karl, 201, 279
Marxism, 28, 192, 205, 207, 216
Mascagni, Pietro, 144
Maupassant, Guy de, 199–200, 217, 219
Mayakovsky, Vladimir, 201, 212, 220, 294
Melamid, Alexander, 302
Melnikov, Avram, 278
Mendele Moykher-Sforim (Sholem Yankev Abramovich), 3, 70–71, 81–82, 88, 96–98, 160–63, 186, 188, 286–87, 289
Mensheviks, 130
Meyerhold, Vsevolod, 220
Michelson, Doctor 82
Mignolo, Walter, 278
Mikhoels (Vovsi), Solomon, 203
Milan, 144, 181, 186, 191
Minkowsky, Pinkhas, 1, 144–46, 148, 150, 153, 160, 210
Minsk, 114
MkhAT, 208
Moldova, 181
Moldovans, 10
Morgulis, Mikhail, 78, 102–5, 107, 111, 115–16
Moscow, 1, 5–6, 18, 28, 108, 119, 137, 154, 167–68, 170, 177, 191, 194, 196, 204, 208, 212, 215, 218, 237, 275, 277, 279, 281, 283–84, 289, 291–92, 297
Mykolaiv, 25, 87–88.
Mykytenko, Ivan, 234, 236–39

Nagasaki, 172
Naidenko, Taisia, 292–94
Naples, 16, 54
nationalism, 7, 9, 11, 17–18, 19, 28, 36, 37–38, 40, 43–44, 49, 54, 67, 68, 72, 94, 96, 101–3, 112, 116, 150, 175, 190–92, 195, 217, 226, 229, 230, 232, 233, 239, 250, 282, 284, 285. *See also* internationalism
Nazism, 285
Nechui-Levyts'kyi, Ivan, 9, 226–30, 232–33, 251
Neidgart, Dmitrii, 127, 130–31, 133–34
Nekrasov, Nikolai, 28
Neophytes, Kateryna, 45
Neumann, Julius, 54
New Orleans, 159

Nikolaev. *See* Mykolaiv
Nikolai II, tsar, 24, 120, 122–24, 134
Nilus, Petr, 28
Nishchyns'kyi, Petro, 42
Novorossiia. *See* Ukraine
Nowakowsky, David, 148, 150, 153
Nussbaum, Martha, 7n16, 304

Oceania, 248
October Revolution (Bolshevik takeover), 140, 167, 196, 204, 208, 257
Odesa (Odessa)
    Brody synagogue, 146–48, 150, 163–64, 210
    cafés chantants, 4, 202, 211
    Deribasovskaia (De Ribas) Street, 1, 15, 161, 240
    Kollektiv poetov, 4, 240
    Langeron resort, 197
    Literaturka (Odesan Literary-Artistic Society), 16–17, 29, 42–44, 167, 170, 173, 175, 186, 190–91, 203
    Moldavanka, 15, 152, 154, 156, 175, 179–80, 206, 208–9, 212–13, 259, 294
    Conservatory, 154
    Opera House, 6, 119, 140, 143–46, 163–64, 180–83, 191, 199
    Palais Royal, 199
    Peresyp', 15, 197
    Potoki oktiabria, 4
    port, 1, 6, 9, 13, 15, 23, 25, 64, 69, 81, 86–87, 94, 119, 121, 127, 129, 131, 136, 141, 144, 157, 159, 164, 171, 196, 198–200, 203, 236, 246, 248, 282–83
    Primorsky /Potemkin Stairs, 1, 121
    Richelieu Lyceum, 41–42, 47, 53
    Worldwide Club of Odes(s)ans, 292
    Zelenaia lampa, 4, 173, 203, 292

Odesa Palestinophilic Committee, 82
Odesa school of writers, 5, 6, 93, 202–5, 277
Ogonyok, magazine, 219
Oistrakh, David, 152, 158
Olesha, Yurii, 168, 172–73, 176–77, 194, 197, 204, 219, 240, 277
Orlov, Boris, 303
Orshansky, Ilya, 102
Oryol, 201
Ottoman Empire, 2, 13, 25, 52, 225, 277, 289
Ovid, 178–79

Palestine, Ottoman-ruled/British Mandate, 36, 52, 61, 67, 94, 96–97. *See also* Israel; Odesa Palestinophilic Committee; Zionism
Paris, 27, 81, 87, 93, 119, 168, 170, 182, 291
Pasternak, Leonid, 79–80
Pasternak, Boris, 79
Paustovsky, Konstantin, 174, 197, 204, 213, 248
Penzo, Ida, 245, 250
Perlman, Eliezer Yitzkhak. *See* Ben-Yehuda, Eliezer
Petliura, Symon, 40, 197, 210, 239
Petrograd. *See* St. Petersburg
Petrov, Evgeny, 5, 168, 205, 277, 279, 291
Petrovsky, Miron, 45, 50
Phoebus, 179
Picquart, Marie-Georges, 31
Pidmohyln'yi, Valer'ian, 249
Piedmont, 54
Pilskii, Petr, 172, 190, 201–2
Pines, Noah, 153
Pinsker, Leon, 96, 102
Pinsker, Simkha, 85
Po'ale-Zion, 130
Podolia, 225
Poland, 57, 101, 154, 237

Poles, 1, 15, 51, 57–58, 119, 176, 239, 259
Poliakov family, 102
post-cosmopolitanism, 10, 16, 19, 276–82
Prague, 43
Pravda, newspaper, 219
Prigov, Dmitry, 303
Proskuriv. *See* Khmelnytsky
Prosvita, 33, 41–43
Proust, Marcel, 219
Pryhara, Mariia, 244
Puccini, Giacomo, 144
Puritz, Solomon, 82
Pushkin, Alexander, 3, 18, 24, 28, 143, 196, 203, 217–21, 223, 279, 286, 299–300, 303
Putin, Vladimir, 252

Quijano, Anibal, 277

Rabelais, François, 213
Rabinenko, Leizor, 227
Rabinovich, Osip, 102, 198
Rabinovitch, Mark, 102
Rabinowitz, S. N. *See* Sholem Aleichem
Rafalovich family, 73, 75, 84, 87–88
Rasputin, Grigorii, 217
Rawnitzki, Yehoshua, 78, 102, 112
Reizen, Avrum, 41
Renan, Ernest, 54–55.
Renner, Karl (Springer), 54
Reva, Mikhail, 274, 279
Ribas, Joseph de, 1, 23, 239
Richardson, Tanya, 283, 289
Richelieu, Duc de (Armand-Emmanuel du Plessis), 196, 278, 300
Riga, 88, 201
Rimsky-Korsakov, Nikolai, 143, 146, 154, 188
Robbins, Bruce, 284
Roitburd, Aleksandr, 276, 281, 298–302
Roma, 140, 158, 158–59, 160, 182, 280

Romanov dynasty, 128, 138, 171
Roosevelt, Franklin, 302
Rossini, Gioachino, 143–44
Rostov-on-Don, 25, 151
Rothstein, Robert A., 157
Rubinstein, Anton, 146
Russian Empire, 6, 8, 9, 11, 22, 24, 29, 38, 39, 48, 50, 52, 57, 58, 60, 61, 68, 76, 81, 83, 84, 85, 86, 92, 101, 119, 140, 147, 153, 154, 166, 168, 188, 226, 230, 233
Russians 1, 4, 5, 8, 13, 16, 25, 51, 54, 56, 119, 122, 124n15, 125, 126, 127, 128, 130, 131, 132, 136–37, 176, 194, 258, 262–64
Russo-Turkish War, 87
Rybnitsa (Ribnița), 88

Sabbath, 150, 160, 207, 212
Sacher, Jacob 107
Sages of Odesa, 2, 77–78, 81, 93–96, 98, 153, 196
Saker, Yakov, 82, 103
Saloniki (Thessaloniki), 2
Saratov, 154
Satyricon, magazine, 196
Savchenko, Boris, 182–83
Savigny, Friedrich Carl von, 57
Schwabacher, Simeon Leon Arie, 74
Schwartz, Abe, 159
Schwebecher, David, 148
Selabros, Arystyd, 229, 232
Semenko, Mikhail, 245, 249
Sevastopol, 93
Shelukhyn, Serhii, 28
Shevchenko, Taras, 28, 39, 41, 45–50, 56, 68, 231, 299
Shishova, Zinaida, 174–76, 194
Shklovsky, Viktor, 5, 205, 247
Shkurupii, Geo, 245, 250
Shoizdat, 281–82, 290
Shostakovich, Dmitri, 219

Shpentser, Fanni, 169
Shpentser, Moisei, 169
Shpentser family, 176
Shtern, Sergei, 33
Shtypel, Arkadii, 287
Shumsky, Dmitry, 37
Sicily, 54
Sifneos, Evrydiki, 12–14, 16, 76, 84, 122
Sigarevich, Vladimir, 42
Skobelev, Mikhail 93
Skvirskaja, Vera, 10, 257, 280
Slavin, Lev, 197, 204
Slavs, 33, 54, 287
Slavyns'kyi, Maksym, 40, 43–44
Slezkine, Yuri, 153, 218, 286
Sliozberg, Genrich, 34
Smolens'kyi, Leonid, 41
Socialism, 89, 208, 283
Society for the Promotion of Enlightenment among the Jews in Russia (OPE), 24, 74, 76, 81, 82, 85, 89, 101–117
Sokolova, Natalia, 176
Sophocles, 42
Soroka, Oleksandr, 237
Sorokin, Vladimir, 303
SOSEP, theater, 176
Sosiura, Volodymyr (Smurnyi), 239–44, 251
SotsArt movement, 303
Sparta, 54
St. Petersburg, 1, 3, 6, 12, 27–29, 34, 40, 48, 52, 67, 76, 80, 88, 90, 103, 119, 123, 137, 151–52, 154, 158, 165, 167, 168, 178, 191, 196, 198–99, 201–3, 204, 214, 217–19, 222–23, 237, 283, 297
Stalin, Joseph, 5, 9, 18, 167, 194, 205, 214, 219–20, 274–75, 280, 282, 287, 302
Stalinism, 197, 304
Stanislawski, Michael, 115
Stanton, Rebecca, 194, 200, 219, 282
Stolyarsky, Pyotr, 152

Storitsyn, Petr, 172
Struve, Petr, 28, 53–54, 56, 58
Switzerland, 60, 170
Syria, 3, 82

Talmud, 156
Tanny, Jarrod, 2
Taruskin, Richard, 144
Taurida, 40
Tbilisi, 88
Tchaikovsky, Pyotr, 143, 146, 188
Tchernikhovsky, Saul (Shaul), 34, 153
Tczernowitz, Chaim (RavTsa'ir), 102
Teheran, 167
Tel Aviv, 2, 34
Thaw, 5, 195, 197, 205, 275
Tiflis. See Tbilisi
Timnata (Timna), 62–64
Timofeev, Boris, 282n19
Tokarev, Aleksander, 279
Tolstoy, Lev, 28, 30, 43, 201, 220
Tomi (Constanța), 179
Tovbin, Getsl, 82
Trieste, 2, 11
Trotsky, Lev, 170
Tsederbaum, Alexander, 85
Tsereteli, Zurab, 279
Tsiganoff, Misha, 158
Tulchyn, 87
Turks, 1, 10, 13
Tyre (Tsor) 62, 64

Uffelman, Dirk, 285
Ukraiinka, Lesia, 3, 19, 43, 225–26, 250
Ukraine, 6, 16, 37, 39, 41, 46, 49, 51, 53, 58–59, 65, 68, 140, 170, 174–75, 177, 210, 217, 222, 224–25, 227, 229–30, 234, 236–37, 239, 248, 250–51, 253–54, 257, 260–62, 264, 271, 276–78, 280–86, 289–92, 300, 302
Ukrainians, 1, 3, 8, 16, 33, 36, 38, 40, 41, 49, 50–60, 61, 64, 65, 68, 69, 122,

124, 126, 143, 170, 226, 228, 229, 252–72, 278, 281, 286, 297,
UNESCO, 279
United States of America, 31, 117, 158–59, 183
Ushinskii, Konstantin, 169
Ussishkin, Menachem, 102
USSR, 1, 255, 289
Utiosov, Leonid (Lazar Vaysbeyn), 2, 155, 157, 159, 162, 175, 211, 237, 279, 281n19, 296
Utochkin, Sergei, 184, 201, 279

Vainshtein S., 103
Valuev decree, 39
Venice, 54
Verdi, Giuseppe, 144
Vernikova, Bella, 198
Vertinskii, Alexander, 172
Vienna, 57, 87
Vilnius (Vilna), 11, 90, 110
Vinnitskii, Misha (Yaponchik), 1, 209, 210, 276, 279, 295
Vinnytsia (Vinnitsa), 87
Vladimirsky, Boris, 273n1
Volhynia, 110, 225
Vorobiov, Ievgen, 281n18
Vorontsov, Mikhail, 74, 278
Voskresenskaia, Nina. See Bagritsky, Eduard
Voznesensk, 210
VUFKU (All-Ukrainian Photo and Cinema Administration), 245–46, 250
Vysotskii, Vladimir, 172

Wagner, Richard, 146
Walkowitz, Rebecca, 278
Warsaw, 11, 34, 101

Warshavsky, Mark, 186
Wedekind, Frank, 183
Wegelin, Daniel, 252
Weinberg, Robert, 14, 18
Weinstein, Grigorii, 82, 85, 88
Weksler, Elimelekh, 78–79, 81
Wissotsky family, 90
World War I, 1, 4, 21, 36, 138, 146, 167, 199, 201, 292
World War II, 5, 120, 155, 277, 279, 281, 284–85, 291–92, 295, 302
Wrocław, 107

Yalta, 302
Yanukovych, Vladimir, 277
Yaponchik, Misha (Vinnitskii), 1, 209–210, 276, 279, 295
Yushkevich, Semyon, 5, 165, 198–99, 201, 213
Yuval-Davis, Nira, 71

Zabila, Natalia, 244
Zabuzhko, Oksana, 238
Zagrebel'nyi, Mikhail, 241
Zamiatin, Evgenii, 181
Zamoshchin, Paltiel, 78, 81
Zanzibar, 182
Zelenaia, Rina, 4, 176–77
Zhelyabov, Andrei, 93
Zhvanetsky, Mikhail, 5, 275, 289–90
Zimbalist, Efrem, 151
Zionism, 4, 30–31, 34, 36, 37, 39, 49, 50, 52, 57, 58, 59, 62, 65, 67, 70, 72, 76, 98, 101–2, 112–14, 189, 228, 306. See also Hibbat Tsion
Zipperstein, Steven, 11, 72–73, 112, 141, 145
Zola, Emile, 28, 30–31

Printed in the USA
CPSIA information can be obtained
at www.ICGtesting.com
JSHW051750040324
58547JS00004B/105